W9-AHA-360

Encountering Enchantment

A Guide to Speculative Fiction for Teens

Susan Fichtelberg

Genreflecting Advisory Series

Diana Tixier Herald, Series Editor

LIBRARIES
UNLIMITED
A Member of the Greenwood Publishing Group

Westport, Connecticut • London

Library of Congress Cataloging-in-Publication Data

Fichtelberg, Susan.
    Encountering enchantment : a guide to speculative fiction for teens / Susan Fichtelberg.
        p. cm. — (Genreflecting advisory series)
    Includes bibliographical references and index.
    ISBN 1-59158-316-0 (alk. paper)
    1. Fantasy fiction—Bibliography. 2. Science fiction—Bibliography.
    3. Young adult fiction—Bibliography. I. Title.
    Z5917.F3F53   2007
    [PN3435]
    016.8093'876—dc22   2006033739

British Library Cataloguing in Publication Data is available.

Library of Congress Catalog Card Number: 2006033739
ISBN: 1-59158-316-0

First published in 2007

Libraries Unlimited, 88 Post Road West, Westport, CT 06881
A Member of the Greenwood Publishing Group, Inc.
www.lu.com

Printed in the United States of America

(∞)™

The paper used in this book complies with the
Permanent Paper Standard issued by the National
Information Standards Organization (Z39.48–1984).

10 9 8 7 6 5 4 3 2 1

To my father, the poet, who nurtured in me a love of words.
And to my mother, the reader, who gave me the key to the secret garden.

Contents

Acknowledgments

I would like to thank my editor Barbara Ittner and series editor Di Herald for their guidance and support throughout all the phases of this project. I also owe huge debt of gratitude to all of the authors who graciously shared their time and talent to provide thoughtful answers to the interview questions: Lloyd Alexander, Holly Black, David Clement-Davies, Nancy Farmer, Patricia A. McKillip, Kenneth Oppel, Elizabeth Wein, and Scott Westerfeld. Of course, my thanks go to my friends at the Woodbridge Public Library of Woodbridge, New Jersey, especially to the interlibrary loan department staff who brought me boatloads of books and the children's staff who offered unfailing encouragement. I'm grateful to my friends Kathleen Nicastro and Mary Pritting who read the manuscript, even though fantasy is not their favorite genre, and offered valuable insights and to my friend Lynn Hand who helped me with the initial proposal and served as my living *Chicago Manual of Style* throughout the writing process. And special thanks go to my friends: Sharon Rawlins, the youth services librarian for the New Jersey Library for the Blind and Handicapped, who checked every title for large print and Braille editions; Bonnie Kunzel, the Youth Services Consultant for the New Jersey State Library, who went through the entire manuscript even though she was recovering from emergency gallbladder surgery; and especially to my fellow writer, Sharon Hausman, who diligently combed through the manuscript, spotting misplaced commas and unclear antecedents when I missed them. I never could have done this without all of you.

Introduction

Dealing with the impossible, fantasy can show us what may be really possible. If there is grief, there is the possibility of consolation; if hurt, the possibility of healing; and above all, the curative power of hope. If fantasy speaks to us as we are, it also speaks to us as we might be.

—Lloyd Alexander, *Children's Book Council Archives* (1996–2002)

Fantasy is a literature of ideals and passion.

—Tamora Pierce, *The Cat's Meow* (December 2005)

Tales of wizards and mages, dragons and unicorns, swords and sorcery have soared to the height of popularity with readers of all ages, especially young adults, since the advent of the boy wizard Harry Potter and the story of his education at Hogwarts School of Witchcraft and Wizardry. Although fantasy has enjoyed golden ages before, notably in the mid-1960s with the paperback publication of Tolkien's The Lord of the Rings and followed a decade later with the works of Lloyd Alexander, Susan Cooper, Ursula Le Guin, and then later Robin McKinley, no works of fantasy have been as widely read by young and old as the Harry Potter books.

This phenomenon caused the publishing industry to unleash a veritable tidal wave of fantasy titles for those eager to read about more worlds imbued with magic. Older titles long out of print are resurfacing as well. They are being reissued, sometimes in both hardcover and paperback, in colorful new garb to lure today's teens. According to *Locus* in "Locus Looks at Young Adult Fiction: By the Numbers," the number of speculative fiction titles published for young adults has more than doubled. Because of this increase, fantasy titles have gone from 33 percent to 57 percent of the speculative fiction published for teens. Science fiction titles also increased, although the percentage dropped from 19 percent to 12 percent. Horror has fluctuated over the last ten years, peaking in popularity with R. L. Stine's Fear Street books and then dropping from 34 percent of the total at its height in the late 1990s to 17 percent of releases in 2005 (*Locus*, May 2006). For those who work with teen readers and build collections for them, the sheer number of speculative fiction titles can be overwhelming.

This guide seeks to lead readers and librarians through the many remarkable realms of imagination revealed in works of fantasy. Also included are fantasy's sister genres, science fiction and horror, which encompass the fantastic in different ways. Collectively, all are referred to as speculative fiction. The crucial element is their speculative nature. They all ponder the question, "What if …" but use different imaginative elements to create their answers. In *How to Write Science Fiction and Fantasy,* Orson Scott Card (1990) contends that any story taking place in a setting contrary to known reality is speculative fiction. Whereas fantasy essentially relies on magic to develop its contrary realities, science fiction relies on scientific extrapolation. Horror can draw on either, combining the components to distill the ambiance of fear. Although the approach of each genre is distinct, they share certain similarities: Because these kinds of imaginative literature stretch so far beyond the boundaries of what is known, they require a willing suspension of disbelief exceeding that required for realistic fiction; they feature stories with strong plots; and they speculate on myriad possibilities, unrestricted by reality. The variety each provides within these parameters, however, may seem infinite. This guide aims to help you navigate these genres and ultimately to put books into the hands of young adults—books that will usher them into worlds of wonder.

Purpose and Audience

The purpose of this book is twofold: first to assist with reader's advisory service; second to aid in collection development. It is intended to help librarians wend their way through the forest of books flourishing in the marketplace today. It can aid reader's advisors in locating titles for readers who want something that is just like the book they just read, who are assigned a work of genre fiction for school, and who are looking for something new. It can also assist you in deciding what to purchase by providing organized information on works in genres that appeal to teens. Since this is a collection development tool as well as a genre guide, few out-of-print titles are listed.

While this is a guide through the multiple subgenres of speculative fiction, it is a selective guide, and not intended to be comprehensive or academic in nature. There are many works that accomplish that task admirably, and they are listed in the Resources section. The primary audience for this book includes public and school librarians, educators, booksellers, fans, and anyone who enjoys recommending books.

Defining "Young Adult"

For the purposes of this book, "young adult" is defined as individuals in the age group of grades six through twelve (ages twelve through eighteen). As Michael Cart said in *Booklist* (Jan. 2005), we have reached a time when perhaps we need a new name for the categories of literature for children and young adults. What twelve year olds enjoy reading can be significantly different from what sixteen year olds enjoy reading. In some libraries, the children's department purchases books for readers through grades seven; in others, it's through grade five. The blurring of the lines between what is children's literature and what is young adult can be clearly seen in the age groups referred to by the American Library Association's Children's Section (ALSC), which awards the Newbery Medal, and its Young Adult Section (YALSA), which gives the Printz Award. In its criteria for considering books for the Newbery Medal, ALSC states on its Web site, "Children are defined as persons of ages up to and including fourteen and books for this entire age range are to be considered." In its statement of eligibility for the Printz Award, YALSA states on its Web site, "To be eligible, a title must have been designated by its publisher as being either a young adult book or one published for the age range that YALSA defines as 'young adult,' i.e., 12 through 18." Since the reading interests clearly overlap, a broad range of materials has been considered: books reviewed for grades five through eight, books designated for grades six through twelve, and adult titles that appeal to young adults.

The Speculative Fiction Reader and the Value of Imaginative Literature

There is no such thing as "the reader" of any kind of literature. Every person approaches reading as an individual. Nonetheless some common traits can be observed. Generally, fantasy readers aren't concerned with the age of the protagonist, as long as the story whisks them away into the world of the book. Science fiction readers usually want the science to be solid, and this often demands a complex story. Horror readers want to feel the thrill of fear. For all, a strong, fast-paced plot is usually essential. While well-developed characters are important, there are few, if any, novels in young adult speculative fiction that are simply character studies.

Critics often dismiss speculative fiction as merely escapist reading, and some may feel the need to steer young adult readers to more beneficial literary experiences. However, the quality of the literature is not dependent on the genre but on the writers, on how well the writers weave their words to create the tapestry of the tale. Any book that draws the reader into the story merits consideration, and because the object of reader's advisory service is to provide the reader with a book that will capture their interest, no work should be dismissed simply because it's genre fiction.

Scope, Selection Criteria, and Methodology

This book casts a net over the many types of speculative fiction and sifts the titles into categories that will help teens find the kind of books that interest them. The aim is to include as many different subgenres of speculative fiction written for readers grades six through twelve as possible. Because readers are interested in a variety of types of material, a limited number of children's and adult titles are included. Many titles written for adults feature teen protagonists. The books written for adults and for senior high students may encompass the full range of human experience. No attempt has been made to censor sexually explicit or violent material. Fantasy receives the most attention and coverage in this guide because there is more fantasy published for these grades than science fiction or horror. The focus of the book is on titles published in the last fifteen years that are still in print, although reissued books and those that are standards in the field and are still being read and enjoyed by young adults are included as well. Since short story collections often include stories that encompass a variety of subgenres, only those collections that are connected to a specific series of novels are included. Selections are based on professional reviews, best books lists, award winners, popularity with young adults, and the author's personal reading and judgment. Approximately 1,400 titles are included.

Organization

Titles are presented within subgenres deemed likely to coincide with the interests and query patterns of teen readers. Thus, the first chapter focuses on wizard fantasy. The enormous popularity of Harry Potter makes it beneficial to have other wizard stories on hand to recommend to fans. Sometimes the subgenres are subdivided into narrower categories, if the number of books published in that area demands it, as in the chapters on mythic fantasy and alternate and parallel world fantasy. Many titles can fit into more than one category. Professional resources and author judgment were used in deciding where to place the titles. Cross-referencing indicates titles that fit into a multiplicity of categories. An extensive subject index provides additional access points that readers can utilize to locate appropriate books.

Books are listed alphabetically by author. When more than one author wrote the book, it is listed under the primary author's name. The books written for grades six through twelve are accompanied by series and title annotations. The books written for adults have annotations for single titles but only a series annotation for books in a series. The books are listed in publication order unless otherwise noted. This is because, especially in extensive fantasy series, prequels presume the reader has read the books published first even though those books take place later in the chronological history of the imaginary world. Although the prequel may come first chronologically, it will contain spoilers for the original volumes. (In particular, this is the case with *The Chronicles of Narnia*. It is the subject of a fairly rigorous debate as to whether these books should be read in publication order or chronological order, especially because the publishers have renumbered the books. This author strongly recommends publication order.) Where the series is fully annotated, some plot details are divulged. The annotations are descriptive in nature to provide information about the main characters, the plot, and, when significant, the setting.

Since assisting in collection development is one of the aims of this volume, author, title, place of publication, publisher, copyright date, and ISBNs for hardcover and paperback for in-print editions are provided. For books that were originally published in other countries, the publication information provided refers to the first American edition. Many books have several paperback editions. Where there was a choice, the mass market paperback was selected, because this is the size that most appeals to teens. The author also selected the newest paperback edition available, since, generally, the newest paperbacks have the most appealing covers. Be advised, however, that books go out of print with rapidity, especially paperbacks, and all ISBN information should be verified with your book supplier.

As in *Teen Genreflecting* by Diana Tixier Herald, reading levels are indicated as follows:

M = middle school, grades 6–8

J = junior high, grades 7–9

S = senior high, grades 10–12

These are simply general guidelines, based on professional reviews and author judgment, because one review source can give an age range of grades five to eight and another says ages twelve and up. Teens should be free to select their own reading material and read what they are most interested in, regardless of assigned reading levels.

Books originally written for adults will be marked thus: [**Adult**]. If media versions of the material are available, they are labeled with symbols as follows:

AUD Audio version

VID Video version

LP Large Print

BRAILLE Braille

The Braille editions have been checked with the National Library Service for the Blind and Physically Handicapped that supplies materials for each state's library for the blind and handicapped.

Award winners are marked with 🎗, and the award is noted at the conclusion of the annotation. The Resources section lists each award and the body responsible for giving the award. The award abbreviations are as follows:

ALAN: American Library Association Notable Children's Book

BBYA: Best Books for Young Adults

TBYA: Top Ten Best Books for Young Adults

The best Web sites to check for award winners are the following:

- The Database of Award-Winning Children's Literature for children's and young adult awards: http://www.dawcl.com/search.asp

- Fantastic Fiction for the speculative fiction awards: http://www.fantasticfiction. co.uk.

Books that work well for discussion in book clubs are indicated with 📖.

Each chapter concludes with a list of the author's personal favorites of the subgenre.

Young Adult Paperback Series

Sometimes teen readers crave paperback series books. It's fun to relax with familiar friends in reliable settings and situations. Although quality can vary from series to series and even within a series, most series are ephemeral in nature. Some of the most popular, ongoing series are included at the end of the appropriate subgenre chapter. Since series books are often released several times a year, an effective way to keep up-to-date is to contact your library book jobber and put the series on standing order. Begin with number 1, because many teens will want to start at the beginning and read the books in numerical order, even if the books are episodic and not continuous.

Keeping Current with Speculative Fiction

So much fantasy is being published today that it's hard to stay current, especially with so many trilogies, quartets, and series. The professional review journal, *The Voice of Youth Advocates,* reviews the most speculative fiction for teens. Every year in April, it publishes the "Best Science Fiction, Fantasy, and Horror" compilation. *Library Journal* also publishes a periodical column reviewing science fiction and fantasy written for adults. *Locus* is a periodical dedicated to science fiction, fantasy, and horror and publishes a large number of reviews as well as notices of what new books are under contract, what manuscripts have been turned in, and what books are about to be released. Its Web site, www.locusmag.com, also provides a directory link to a listing of the newest young adult works of speculative fiction.

Author Interviews

Eight author interviews are interspersed throughout the bibliography to give readers another way to connect to the stories and their creators and gain insight into the genres. Some of the authors have written many books; some are relatively new to writing books for young adults. All were gracious in the giving of their time to this project and the sharing of their ideas. For each interview the author of this book asked some of the same questions and some questions unique to each author.

How to Use This Book

You can use this book to help spot areas of sparseness in your library's collection and provide suggestions on what materials can best increase the amount of material available in that area. It can assist you with reader's advisory by providing extensive lists of books that appeal to readers with specific interests, accessing needed titles either via the table of contents or the subject index. It can also be used by young adult readers if they want to peruse the annotations and select books for themselves.

In addition, an appendix with ideas for programming with speculative fiction will help you create programs relating to fantasy, science fiction, or horror for a library, school, or bookstore. Many of the title-specific ideas presented can be adapted to other titles that are currently popular.

The book can also prove useful for becoming familiar with a wide variety of genre literature. Each subgenre is defined to help make clear where it fits in the spectrum of speculative fiction.

I hope this volume will both help readers discover fascinating titles on their own and provide librarians with the tools to build fine speculative fiction collections, so that, in the end, readers really do "encounter enchantment."

References

Alexander, Lloyd. "On Fantasy." *The CBC Magazine Archives 1996–2002*, March 2006. http://www.cbcbooks.org/cbcmagazine/meet/lloydalexander.html (accessed March 15, 2006).

American Library Association. "Newbery Medal Home Page," 2006. http://www.ala.org/ala/alsc/awardsscholarships/literaryawds/newberymedal/newberymedal.htm (March 15, 2006).

"The Michael L. Printz Award for Excellence in Young Adult Literature," 2006. http://www.ala.org/ala/yalsa/booklistsawards/printzaward/Printz,_Michael_L__Award.htm (accessed March 15, 2006).

Card, Orson Scott. *How to Write Science Fiction and Fantasy.* Writer's Digest, 1990.

Cart, Michael. "New Things under the Sun." *Booklist* (January 1 & 15, 2005), 838.

Herald, Diana Tixier. *Teen Genreflecting: A Guide to Reading Interests.* 2nd ed. Westport, CT: Libraries Unlimited, 2003.

"Locus Looks at Young Adult Fiction: By the Numbers." *Locus*, May 2006, 32.

Pierce, Tamora. "Interview." *The Cats Meow*, December, 2005. http:www.btol.com/images/email/html/casmeow.htm (accessed December 10, 2005).

Chapter 1

Wizardry Fantasy

Since Merlin first appeared in tales of King Arthur, wizards have cast a spell over audiences. None have done so more than the wizard-in-training, Harry Potter. Readers all over the world are fascinated with the young wizard learning his craft at Hogwarts School of Witchcraft and Wizardry. The demand for and publication of other books featuring wielders of magic has multiplied exponentially. In this guide, the subgenre of wizardry embraces titles where the protagonist practices magic. Before the advent of Harry Potter, many of these titles would have been included in an "alternate worlds" category because the stories create a setting where magic is used either in a completely imaginary world or in a known reality. The popularity of Harry Potter makes it prudent to sift these titles out of their former categories and arrange them in a way that they will be easily accessible to fans.

While wizards from Merlin to Gandolf to Dumbledore have held a prominent place in fantasy, until recently, they were less frequently the primary characters. The initial volumes of The Chrestomanci Chronicles by Diana Wynne Jones and The Young Wizard Series by Diane Duane, focus on young wielders of magic and do predate the Harry Potter books, but they never achieved the same world renown, and both Jones and Duane have continued their series after each had a long hiatus. Often the primary characters in wizardry fantasy are young people who are just discovering and exploring their powers. As they experiment and make mistakes, they confront evil and grow as individuals as well as people of power. Character development and adventure are intertwined, but their stories don't reach the grand scale that they do in epic fantasy.

So whether they feature wizards, magicians, sorceresses, or enchanters, titles in which the main character works magic are listed here.

Alexander, Lloyd

The Wizard in the Tree. **New York: Dutton, 1975. 137p. Reissued by Puffin in 1997. ISBN: 014038801Xpa.** *MJ* 📖
When Mallory's favorite oak tree is chopped down, she finds a wizard trapped inside. Abrican, stuck in the tree for hundreds of years, now only wants to join his fellow wizards in their new land, but he's lost his powers. Mallory aids the gruff old man, hoping his magic will return in time to save her village from the greedy Squire Scrupner.

Avi

Bright Shadow. **New York: Bradbury, 1985. 167p. Reissued by Aladdin in 1988. ISBN: 0689717830pa.** *MJ* **AUD**
An assistant to the king's chambermaid, Morwenna knows nothing about being a wizard. She learns quickly, though, for without warning, the dying court wizard passes control of the kingdom's last five wishes to her.

Bell, Hilari

The Wizard Test. **New York: Eos, 2005. 166p. ISBN: 0060599405; 0060599421pa.** *MJ* 📖
Dayven, a Watcherlad, trains hard so that he can become a warrior Guardian, but when he turns fourteen, he must take the wizard test. When his ability to work magic reveals itself, he is horrified, for the wizards of his world are reported to be cowardly and without honor. He decides to refuse to become an apprentice until Lord Enar asks him to accept in order to spy on the wizards. Reluctantly, Dayven agrees, only to be plunged into a world where the answers are not as clear as he once thought.

Bujold, Lois McMaster

The Spirit Ring. **Riverdale, New York: Baen, 1992. 369p. Reissued in 2000. ISBN: 0671578707pa. [Adult]** *JS*
In a land reminiscent of Renaissance Italy, where the Church controls the use of magic, Fiametta Beneforte is a fifteen-year-old with budding gifts of magic that she longs to use to create enchanted works of art. Her father, a magician-goldsmith, refuses to teach her the uses of magic beyond immediate necessity because it is considered a waste of time to teach a girl any magic, other than the most basic spells. When he dies suddenly, Fiametta and her friend Thur must use their skills to stop a mercenary from stealing her father's powers with black magic.

Charnas, Suzy

The Sorcery Hall Trilogy. *JS*
Valentine thinks living in an apartment in New York City with her divorced mom couldn't be more ordinary, until she discovers that the wizards of Sorcery Hall need her help.

The Bronze King. **Boston: Houghton Mifflin, 1985. 196p. Reissued by Wildside Press in 2001. ISBN: 1587154781pa. BRAILLE**
Valentine lives a humdrum life in New York City until she notices that a bronze statue from Central Park has disappeared and becomes unwittingly involved with an aged magician who is trying to stop a thief from taking over the city.

***The Silver Glove*. New York: Bantam, 1988. 162p. Reissued by Wildside Press in 2001. ISBN: 158715479Xpa.**
Much to her surprise, Valentine discovers her grandmother has magical powers. They don't have a long time to compare experiences because her grandmother runs away from the nursing home to escape the wizard who hunts her. It's the same rogue wizard who shows up as the new psychologist at Valentine's school. When he begins to date her mother, Valentine knows she must find a way to stop him and save her mother.

***The Golden Thread*. New York: Bantam, 1989. 209p. Reissued by Wildside Press in 2001. ISBN: 1587154803pa.**
Now an apprentice-wizard, Valentine meets an exchange student at school who turns out to be a magical ruler from another world in search of her people. She wants sorcerous assistance, but a wary Val doesn't know whom to trust.

Chima, Cinda Williams

The Warrior Heir*. New York: Hyperion, 2006. 423p. ISBN: 0786839163. *MJS
Jack thinks he is a typical sixteen-year-old living in a small town in Ohio. He goes to high school because he has to and is an average soccer player. Then comes the day when he skips his medicine and discovers that he is faster and stronger than he was—but that's not all. He is part of a magical community with two factions vying for control, and his actions might determine the winner.

Clarke, Susanna

🏵 ***Jonathan Strange and Mr. Norrell*. New York: Bloomsbury, 2004. 782p. (1st American Edition.) ISBN: 1582344167; 1582346038pa. [Adult] *JS* AUD** 📖

For hundreds of years the tide of English magic had receded so far that all were convinced there was no magic left in England. Magic dwelt everywhere in England in the Middle Ages, even in the rocks and trees, especially in the North in the Kingdom of the Raven King. Now, only theoretical magicians study the theory of magic—until the bookish and reclusive Mr. Norrell proves that it is possible to work practical magic. He is the sole magician in England until Jonathan Strange also demonstrates mystical skills. The two join forces in London, but they move from master and apprentice to bitter rivals as England battles Napoleon, and the world feels the impact of the rift between them. (Hugo Award; Locus Award for Best First Novel; Adult Mythopoeic Award)

Constable, Kate

<u>The Chanters of Tremaris Trilogy</u>. New York: Arthur A. Levine Books. (1st American Editions.) *MJ* AUD
In Tremaris, a world with three moons, those with magical abilities wield their Powers through music, a process they call Chantment, of which there are nine

types. One person rarely works more than one kind of Chantment, for his or her Power would then be too great and the temptation to do harm could be overwhelming.

The Singer of All Songs. **2004. 297p. ISBN: 0439554780; 0439554799pa.**
Calwyn is studying to be an Icecall priestess when the injured Darrow breaks into her isolated world and convinces her that he needs her help to fight against the evil sorcerer Samis, who seeks to do the forbidden: combine all the nine Powers.

The Waterless Sea. **2005. 314p. ISBN: 0439554802; 0439554810pa.**
While Darrow stays behind, Calwyn and her companions journey to the Merithuros in the Waterless Sea to rescue five children whose gifts of Chantment are strong.

The Tenth Power. **2006. 306p. ISBN: 0439554829.**
A bereft Calwyn returns home hoping for comfort and instead finds the High Priestess dying and darkness brooding over the land of Antaris. Armed with the secrets of dark magic, Calwyn embarks on a journey to locate the Wheel of the Tenth Power, the only thing that can save her world.

Croggon, Alison

The Pellinor Quartet. *See* Chapter 2: "Epic Fantasy."

Duane, Diane

The Young Wizard Series. *MJ* **AUD**
Nita and Kit learn from a library book how to become wizards and battle the Lone Power each time it tries to take over the world.

So You Want to Be a Wizard. **New York: Delacorte, 1983. 226p. Reissued by Harcourt in hardcover in 2003. ISBN: 0152047387; 0152049401pa.**
Running from a gang of bullies at school, Nita finds sanctuary in the library. She also finds a book on wizardry that not only convinces her that magic is real, but also shows her how to use it. As she is learning, she meets Kit, a boy from her school that she hadn't known before. He's discovered the same book, and they decide to work together. They prepare for their Wizard Ordeal and are shifted to an alternate Manhattan, where they come into their powers and attempt to fight the forces of darkness.

Deep Wizardry. **New York: Delacorte, 1985. 272p. Reissued by Magic Carpet in 2001. ISBN: 0152162577pa. BRAILLE**
Kit and Nita are summoned to assist a wounded whale who is actually S'ree, a whale wizard. After rescuing S'ree, they become enmeshed in the battle of deep wizardry—which is the kind practiced by the creatures of the sea—against the Lone Power.

High Wizardry. **New York: Delacorte, 1990. 269p. Reissued by Magic Carpet in 2001. ISBN: 0152162445pa.**
When Nita's little sister, computer genius Darine, finds Nita's wizardry book, she wants to be a wizard, too. Her way to magic is through her computer's new software program. She is drawn into a universe-wide, magical conflict with the Lone Power, and Nita and Kit follow to lend their aid.

A Wizard Abroad. Orlando, FL: Harcourt, 1997. 352p. Reissued by Magic Carpet in 2005. ISBN: 0152055037pa.
Thinking she needs a vacation from wizardry, Nita's parents send her to Ireland to visit her aunt for a month. What they don't realize is that there is even more magic on the Emerald Isle, where Nita is thrust into a raging conflict with monsters from myth and legend.

The Wizard's Dilemma. San Diego: Harcourt, 2001. 403p. ISBN: 0152025510; 015205491Xpa.
After a bitter argument, Nita and Kit, partners in wizardry, decide to go their separate ways. Nita's mother has a brain tumor, and Nita is determined to find a cure, no matter what the price.

A Wizard Alone. San Diego: Harcourt, 2002. 319p. ISBN: 0152045627; 0152055096pa.
Grieving over her mother's death, Nita shuts Kit out both emotionally and telepathically. Meanwhile, Kit must discover why a new wizard is taking so long to complete his ordeal. As Kit investigates, he finds Darryl, an eleven-year-old autistic boy who can create worlds that contain the Lone Power. The boy becomes trapped, as does Kit. By the time Nita realizes they need her help, it may be too late.

A Wizard's Holiday. Orlando, FL: Harcourt, 2003. 415p. ISBN: 0152047719; 0152052070pa.
Dairine, Nita's little sister, seeks to enroll them both in a wizarding exchange program. Although it is discovered that she acted without permission, she still is allowed to host three alien wizards, while Nita and Kit go to the idyllic world of Alaalu where the Lone Power has been defeated. All is not as ideal as it appears, however, and the young wizards once again must thwart their perpetual adversary.

Wizards at War. Orlando, FL: Harcourt, 2005. 560p. ISBN: 0152047727.
When Nita and Kit return to Earth, they and Dairine realize that their fellow wizards seem to have disappeared, while a series of strange happenings continue to occur on the planet. Quickly they learn that their magical colleagues are fighting an invading force of dark wizards who serve the Lone Power.

Feist, Raymond E.

The Chronicles of Midkemia. [Adult] *S*
Pug, an orphan, arrives in Midkemia and becomes an apprentice magician, never dreaming that his actions could determine the fate of two worlds—and this is only the beginning of the ongoing saga.

The Riftwar Saga

Magician. Garden City, NY: Doubleday, 1982. 545p. Reissued by Spectra in paperback in two volumes: *Magician: Apprentice* in 1989. ISBN: 0553564943pa. *Magician: Master* in 1994. ISBN: 0553564935pa.

Silverthorn. Garden City, NY: Doubleday, 1985. 325p. Reissued by Bantam in 1996. ISBN: 0553270540pa.

A Darkness at Sethanon. Garden City, NY: Doubleday, 1986. 425p. Reissued by Bantam in 1987. ISBN: 0553263285pa.

The Serpent War Duet

Prince of the Blood. New York: Doubleday, 1989. 353p. Revised and reissued by Bantam in hardcover in 2004. ISBN: 0553803808; 0553588117pa.

The King's Buccaneer. New York: Doubleday, 1992. 465p. Reissued by Bantam in 1996. ISBN: 0553563734pa.

The Empire Sequence written with Janny Wurtz

Daughter of the Empire. Garden City, NY: Doubleday, 1987. 394p. Reissued by Bantam in 1991. ISBN: 055327211Xpa.

Servant of the Empire. New York: Doubleday, 1990. 580p. Reissued by Spectra in 1996. ISBN: 0553292455pa.

Mistress of the Empire. New York: Doubleday, 1992. 613p. Reissued by Bantam in 1993. ISBN: 0553561189pa.

The Serpentwar Saga

Shadow of a Dark Queen. New York: William Morrow, 1994. 382p. Reissued by Avon in 1995. ISBN: 0380720868pa.

Rise of a Merchant Prince. New York: William Morrow, 1995. 406p. Reissued by Avon in 1996. ISBN: 0380720876pa.

Rage of a Demon King. New York: Avon Books, 1997. 436p. Reissued in 1998. ISBN: 0380720884ps.

Shards of a Broken Crown. New York: Avon Eos, 1998. 417p. Reissued by Avon in 1998. ISBN: 0380789833pa.

The Riftwar Legacy

Krondor: The Betrayal. New York: Avon, 1998. 376p. Reissued by Eos in 1999. ISBN: 0380795272pa.

Krondor: The Assassins. New York: Avon Eos, 1999. 374p. Reissued by HarperCollins 1999. ISBN: 0380803232pa.

Krondor: Tear of the Gods. New York: Eos, 2000. 372p. Reissued by HarperCollins in 2002. ISBN: 0380795280pa.

The Conclave of Shadows

Talon of the Silver Hawk. New York: Eos, 2003. 380p. Reissued by Harper Torch in 2004. ISBN: 0380803240pa.

King of Foxes. New York: Eos, 2004. 381p. ISBN: 0380977095; 0380803267pa.

Exile's Return. New York: Eos, 2005. 345p. ISBN: 0380977109; 0380803275pa.

Legends of the Riftwar

Honored Enemy with William Fortschen. New York: Eos, 2006. 384p. ISBN: 0060792833pa.

Jones, Diana Wynne

The Chrestomanci Chronicles. New York: Greenwillow. (1st American Editions.) *MJ* AUD

The Chrestomanci is revered as the most powerful enchanter in multiple worlds and is responsible for guiding young workers of magic along their way.

Charmed Life. 1977. 218p. Reissued by Trophy in 2001. ISBN: 006447268Xpa.

Cat doesn't mind living in his sister Gwendolen's shadow. After all, his sister is the most talented witch ever seen on Coven Street, and she has been taking care of him since they became orphans. When they receive an invitation to move to Chrestomanci Castle, unusual events lead Cat to question Gwen's ulterior motives.

The Magicians of Caprona. 1980. 223p. Reissued by Trophy in 2001. ISBN: 0064472698pa.

When an evil enchantress tries to destroy Caprona by dividing its two families of magicians, only the children of the feuding families, Tonino and Angelica—with some help from Chrestomanci—can save them.

Witch Week. 1982. 213p. Reissued by HarperCollins in 2001. ISBN: 0064472698pa.

Someone in 6B is a witch, and witchcraft, in this alternate-world English boarding school, is punishable by burning at the stake. Magical things begin to happen, and an inquisitor is summoned.

❦ *The Lives of Christopher Chant*. 1988. 230p. Reissued by Trophy in 2002. ISBN: 006447268Xpa.

In this prequel to *Charmed Life,* when Christopher realizes that his dreams are so real that he can visit and bring things back from other worlds and that he actually has nine lives, he begins training to become the next Chrestomanci. (ALAN)

Mixed Magics: Four Tales of Chrestomanci. **2001. 134p. Reissued by HarperCollins in 2003. ISBN: 0064410188pa.**
Chrestomanci, the powerful guardian of magic in a plethora of realms, is featured in each of these tales of magic.

Conrad's Fate. **New York: Greenwillow, 2005. 375p. ISBN: 0060747439; 0060747455pa.**
In this novel that is a companion to *The Lives of Christopher Chant,* Conrad's magician uncle convinces him that a doom shadows his life. To escape his dark fate, Conrad takes a job at Stallery Manor, where a charming young lad named Christopher also works. Together they discover that the Manor is the focal point of magic for multiple universes. Someone is misusing this power, and Conrad and Christopher must uncover the perpetrator before the collision of parallel universes is inevitable.

The Pinhoe Egg. **2006. 515p. ISBN: 0061131245.**
Cat, a young nine-lived enchanter first encountered in *Charmed Life,* is settling in to life at Chrestomanci castle where he is learning to be the next Chrestomanci. In addition to his studies, he spends time discovering the powers of his new horse, Syracuse. Meanwhile, in the magical village of Ulverscote, a young witch named Marianne Pinhoe is having a terrible summer. She is training to be the next Gammer, head of her witch family, because her grandmother is increasingly unstable. She must care for Gammer's cat Nutcase, mind the concoctions with which her family creates their illegal spells, and run errands for her entire family. But everything changes when she meets Cat.

Deep Secret. **New York: Tor, 1999. 383p. Reissued in 2002. ISBN: 0765342472pa.** *JS*
Rupert is a junior magid, one of the many mages who oversee the workings of the Multiverse. He is searching for a replacement for his dead mentor while simultaneously looking for the unknown heir of the Empire of Korfyros.

The Dark Lord of Derkholm. **New York: Greenwillow, 1998. 345p. Reissued by Trophy in 2001. ISBN: 0064473368pa.** *JS*
Derk, an unconventional wizard who likes to breed unusual animals (griffins, flying pigs, winged horses, etc.) and his magical family become involved in a plan to stop the devastating tours to their world arranged by the tyrannical Mr. Chesney.

Year of the Griffin. **New York: Greenwillow, 2000. 267p. Reissued by Trophy in 2001. ISBN: 006447335Xpa.** *JS*
In this sequel to *The Dark Lord of Derkholm,* Wizard Corkoran is in charge of the Wizard University and is obsessed with being the first man on the moon. He decides to teach the first-year students himself in hopes of finding new funding sources. One of his new pupils is Wizard Derk's own daughter, Elda.

🏵 ***The Merlin Conspiracy.*** **New York: Greenwillow, 2003. 468p. ISBN: 0060523182; 0060523204pa.** *JS*
In this companion to *Deep Secret,* Arianrhod travels with the court on the King's Progress throughout an alternate Britain, while Nichothodes yearns to walk between

worlds. When Nichothodes is pushed into Arianrhod's England, they are caught up in myriad plots and counterplots. (ALAN)

Le Guin, Ursula K.

The Earthsea Cycle. *See* Chapter 2, "Epic Fantasy."

Lubar, David

> *Wizards of the Game.* **New York: Philomel, 2003. 166p. ISBN: 0399237062; 014240215Xpa.** <u>*M*</u>
> Eighth-grader Mercer loves nothing better than playing Wizards of the Warrior World and suggests a gaming day at school as a way to raise money for the local homeless shelter. When he meets four men from the shelter, they call him Magus and implore him to help them find a way back to their own world, where they are indeed wizards.

Profile of Patricia A. McKillip

Born February 29, 1948, in Salem, Oregon, Patricia McKillip, began writing when she was fourteen. She sold her first novel, *The House on Parchment Street,* by the time she finished college. Although she is most well known for her works of fantasy, she has written science fiction and realistic fiction as well. In 1975, she won the World Fantasy Award for best novel for *The Forgotten Beasts of Eld,* a feat she repeated in 2003 with *Ombria in Shadow* (*Contemporary Authors Online*, Infotrac Galegroup Database).

Interview with Patricia A. McKillip

Conducted via e-mail January 27–February 2, 2006

> **SF:** Your books often feature strong female protagonists. Why do you feel that it's important for fantasy to have such protagonists?

> **PM:** When I started reading and writing, in the '50s and early '60s, there were very few female protagonists in any genre. The men and boys got all the adventures. They got to sail pirate ships, go on quests, become warriors, fight evil, rule a kingdom, study sorcery, fly a spaceship, or explore the world; they got all the good lines. Nancy Drew was a notable exception, but even in novels for older readers and adults, there were extremely few adventurers who were not young men. In college back then, when I majored in English literature, nearly every book that was required reading for my degree had a male protagonist as a hero. As a female reader, I only got to look on; I wasn't allowed to identify with the action in the plot. Somewhere between college and my first published novel I realized what an amazing gold mine of unwritten stories there were about women. This began to change in the late '70s and '80s; now no one thinks twice about writing or reading about a female protagonist. But once

they were very few and far between. And I have a great deal of fun with my women characters: being so relatively new on the literary stage, they can still surprise the reader in ways that male protagonists don't.

SF: Your early books were published as young adult novels and your books are popular with young adults, however they are marketed. How do you decide who your audience is?

PM: Unless I'm specifically writing a YA novel, I don't think about readers when writing fantasy. In my rare forays into science fiction, I was very much aware of the fact that my readers might know a great deal more about the genre and science in general than I do; I was very careful to try to avoid stupid mistakes. Usually, when I think about readers at all, I just assume they are people who have read all the books I've read—which is very many, and in every kind of genre— and I try to keep them happy.

SF: You won the World Fantasy (WF) Award in 1975 for *The Forgotten Beasts of Eld* and 2003 for *Ombria in Shadow*. How did it feel to win the award each time?

PM: When I won the award the first time, it was the very first WF award given, and I had no idea what it was, or that it would become so important. All I knew was that some group had given me a weird pewter bust of H. P. Lovecraft, which came in the mail with its neck broken (my father, who was very proud of it, soldered it back together). I didn't even know who H. P. Lovecraft was, at that time. When I won the award in 2003, I was far more appreciative. It's not an easy award to win; I certainly learned that over the years!

SF: What would you say your method of writing is (i.e., working from an outline, going where the story takes you, etc.)?

PM: I don't like working from an outline; I'd rather let all the details of the story come out as I go along. It gets boring if I know too much, and I don't feel any incentive to continue. I like to be surprised by the plot, too. But usually I know where the story begins and where it will end. The rest I let come out of the pen. (I write my first drafts by hand.)

SF: Of your books, which are your favorite books and/or characters and why?

PM: I usually like the ambiguous characters. The ones who aren't exactly what they seem. Like Luna in *Song for the Basilisk,* Deth in *The Riddle-Master,* Faey in *Ombria in Shadow,* and Brume in *In the Forests of Serre.* I don't have favorite books. They all have favorite parts; they all have flaws.

SF: What were your favorite books growing up and/or who were your favorite authors?

PM: I read Nancy Drew, Grimm's Fairytales, Sue Barton when I was pretty young. Later I liked adventure stories—R. L. Stevenson, Alexandre Dumas,

Kipling. I discovered André Norton and Fritz Leiber around that time, too. I remember being intrigued by *The Hobbit* when I found it in the high school library; I also read T. H. White's *Once and Future King* quite a number of times then. I found <u>The Lord of the Rings</u> when I was seventeen, just about the time the rest of my generation was discovering it. Nothing in fantasy with that scope and incredible detail had ever been published before. It stunned me, and it inspired me—along with quite a few other writers of my generation—to write fantasy.

SF: What do you think is the merit or importance of reading fantasy?

PM: I have a rather Jungian view of fantasy, myth, and fairytale. I think the symbols and quests in fantasy are stepping stones for emotional growth; at their best and strongest they lead the hero and heroines beyond themselves and into society, to which they bring their hard-won knowledge, strengths and gifts. That's why evil in fantasy is never stronger than the hero or heroine; the evil that is fought—Darth Vader, Sauron, the wicked witch—is actually another face of the questing protagonist. The journey made, the challenges encountered, are all aspects of the protagonist; they are the story which that particular protagonist must tell in order to grow beyond the inherited impulses, fears and childhood experiences. It's possible to read fantasy at many levels, according to how much a reader might need to emotionally invest in a certain aspect of the story. Sometimes you learn something about yourself from reading fantasy. Sometimes you just have fun with it.

Reference

"Patricia McKillip," *Contemporary Authors Online*, Infotrac Galegroup Database (accessed March 10, 2006).

McKillip, Patricia A.

The Forgotten Beasts of Eld. New York: Atheneum, 1974. Reissued by Magic Carpet Books in 2006. ISBN: 0152055363pa. *JS*
Sybel, daughter of a wizard and granddaughter of a wizard, has spent her life in her crystal hall caring for the legendary beasts of Eld. Then she is asked to raise Tam, an abandoned baby. She grows to love him and learns too late that he is the son of an enemy. (World Fantasy Award)

Od Magic. **New York: Ace. 2005. 315p. ISBN: 0441012485; 0441013341pa.**
Generations past, the mysterious wizard Od stopped the city of Numis from being destroyed so that she could locate her school of magic there. Now the working of magic has come more and more under the control of the king, and Od summons Brenden Vetch, a gardener with untapped power, to her school to cultivate more than flowers.

Nimmo, Jenny

The Children of the Red King. New York: Orchard. (1st American Editions.) *M*
AUD

The magically gifted Red King had ten children, but when his wife died suddenly, despair overcame him. He left his heirs alone, trusting them to use their "endowments" (magical gifts) to rule the kingdom wisely in his stead, but not all followed their father's wishes. Now his descendants have special powers, but some use them for good and some for evil.

Midnight for Charlie Bone. 2003. 401p. ISBN: 0439474299.
Ten-year-old Charlie lives an ordinary life until he starts hearing the people in photographs speaking. His nasty Grandma Bone then insists he attend Bloor's Academy, where the Endowed (magically gifted) descendants of the Red King all go to school with the rich and talented. Once there, Charlie must decide whose side he will join.

Charlie Bone and the Time Twister. 2003. 402p. ISBN: 043949687X.
In January 1916, Henry Yewbeam and his brother James are sent to stay at Bloor's Academy, but a strange marble whisks Henry from his own time to Charlie's, where he is in greater danger than ever.

Charlie Bone and the Invisible Boy. 2004. 432p. ISBN: 0439545269.
As Charlie begins his next semester at Bloor's Academy, a new art teacher has joined the staff. Charlie and his friends learn that he is searching for his brother, Ollie Sparks, who disappeared, and they are determined to help him.

Charlie Bone and the Castle of Mirrors. 2005. 410p. ISBN: 0439545285.
When Charlie's friend Billy Raven is adopted by a couple who actually hates children, Billy Raven is bribed into signing an obedience oath and then locked up behind a force field. Ever ready for a challenge, Charlie and his companions set about finding a way to free him.

Charlie Bone and the Hidden King. 2006. 464p. ISBN: 0439545307lb.
Mysterious occurrences continue to plague the students at Bloor's Academy, and Charlie Bone discovers that the shadow of the Red King has escaped from his portrait. The Flame Cats send Charlie a warning, and he knows he must do whatever he can to protect his family.

Nix, Garth

The Abhorsen Sequence
See Chapter 2, "Epic Fantasy."

Pierce, Tamora

The Magic Circle Chronicles. New York: Scholastic. *MJS*
The mage Niko brings four young people to the Temple of the Winding Circle, where they discover their magical abilities and how to use them.

The Magic Circle Quartet. All reissued by Point. AUD

***Sandry's Book*. 1997. 252p. Reissued in 1999. ISBN: 0590554085pa.**
Four young misfits find themselves living in a strictly disciplined temple community, where they become friends while learning to do crafts and use their magical powers.

***Tris's Book*. 1998. 251p. Reissued in 1999. ISBN: 0590554093pa.**
With the defenses of Winding Circle Temple seriously weakened by an earthquake, Tris and her fellow mages-in-training try to join their different magic powers to protect the Winding Circle community from a pirate attack.

***Daja's Book*. 1998. 234p. Reissued in 2000. ISBN: 0590554107pa.**
While at Gold Ridge castle to the north of Winding Circle, Daja and her friends develop their unique magical talents as they try to prevent a devastating forest fire from consuming everything in its path.

***Briar's Book*. 1999. 258p. Reissued in 2000. ISBN: 0590554107pa.**
Briar, a young mage-in-training, and his teacher, Rosethorn, must use their magic to fight a deadly plague that is ravaging Summersea.

The Circle Opens Quartet

***Magic Steps*. 2000. 264p. Reissued by Point in 2001. ISBN: 0590396056pa.**
While perfecting her art of magic-weaving, Sandry finds a pupil of her own. They combine their talents to uncover the guilty party in a series of murders.

***Street Magic*. 2001. 300p. Reissued by Point in 2002. ISBN: 0590396439pa.**
Briar leaves Winding Circle with his mentor, Rosethorn, to share his plant magic with farmers in need. Along the way, he must deal with street gangs and an evil aristocrat, all the while convincing street-rat Evvy that she needs to find a mage who can teach her to use her stone-magic.

***Cold Fire*. 2002. 355p. ISBN: 0590396552; 0590396560pa.**
On her own in a northern city, Daja continues to study smith-magic while reluctantly taking on a pair of gifted twins to train. Meanwhile, someone is setting fires throughout the town, and Daja's magic is needed to quell the flames and reveal the culprit.

***Shatterglass*. 2003. 363p. ISBN: 0590396838; 059039696Xpa.**
Tris, a weather-mage, journeys to the city of Tharios to explore her interest in glassmaking. There she encounters Keth, a glassblower who creates living glass dragons and globes whose depths reveal visions of victims of a serial killer.

***The Will of the Empress*. 2005. 550p. ISBN: 0439441714.**
When Sandry is summoned to the court of her cousin, the Empress Namorn, her three friends from Winding Circle, Tris, Daja, and Briar, accompany her.

But the friends have grown apart in their years spent exploring their own interests. Caught up in the dazzling court life, it's almost too late before they recognize the danger they are in from the empress's secret manipulations.

Pratchett, Terry

The Tiffany Aching Adventures. *See* Chapter 5, "Alternate and Parallel Worlds."

Rowling, J. K.

The Harry Potter Series. New York: Arthur A. Levine. (1st American Editions.) *MJS* **AUD LP BRAILLE**
A magical community of witches and wizards coexists with the everyday world and for years they have fought the evil wizard Voldemort until one child arrives whom he cannot kill—Harry Potter. As "the boy who lived" discovers his magical heritage and learns to use his powers, He Who Must Not Be Named casts an ever-lengthening shadow over Harry's life.

> ✿ *Harry Potter and the Sorcerer's Stone.* **1998. 309p. ISBN: 0590353403; 059035342Xpa. VID**
> Harry Potter thinks that he is just an ordinary boy living in suburban England with his cruel aunt, uncle, and cousin when a letter inviting him to Hogwarts School of Witchcraft and Wizardry changes his life forever. (ABBY; ALAN: BBYA)

> ✿ *Harry Potter and the Chamber of Secrets.* **1999. 341p. ISBN: 0439064864; 0439064872pa. VID**
> When the mysterious Chamber of Secrets opens at Hogwarts and releases a monster that is petrifying students and creatures, friends Harry, Ron, and Hermione apply their talents to solve the mystery. (ALAN; BBYA)

> ✿ *Harry Potter and the Prisoner of Azkaban.* **1999. 435p. ISBN: 0439136350; 0439136369pa. VID**
> Sirius Black, a mass murderer, has escaped from the wizard-prison, Azkaban, and is determined to hunt down Harry, so all at Hogwarts do their best to protect him. (ALAN; BBYA; Bram Stoker Work for Young Reader Award; Children's Whitbread Award; Locus Award; Smarties Gold Award)

> ✿ *Harry Potter and the Goblet of Fire.* **2000. 734p. ISBN: 0439139597; 0439139600pa. VID**
> When Harry's name is drawn from the Goblet of Fire, although he is underage, he must participate in a magical contest with representatives from two other schools of witchcraft and wizardry. (ALAN; BBYA; Hugo Award)

> ✿ *Harry Potter and the Order of the Phoenix.* **2003. 870p. ISBN: 043935806X; 0439358078pa.**
> Harry knows that the wizard who murdered his parents and terrorized the wizarding community, Lord Voldemort, has returned, and so does Professor Dumbledore, Hogwarts' headmaster. Dumbledore has organized a group of wizards to fight the Dark Lord because the Ministry of Magic refuses to believe that He Who Must Not Be Named is back. Meanwhile, Harry must prepare for his

O. W. L. (Ordinary Wizarding Levels) exams. Things go from bad to worse at Hogwarts as the vindictive Professor Umbridge takes over the school. (ALAN; Bram Stoker Work for Young Readers Award)

***Harry Potter and the Half-Blood Prince*. 2005. 652p. ISBN: 043978454; 0439785960pa.**

As Harry turns sixteen, Dumbledore undertakes to give him private lessons. Together they journey to the past through the pensieve, a memory holder, and witness crucial moments in the life of Tom Riddle, the wizard who became Lord Voldemort. Meanwhile, Harry is convinced that Draco Malfoy is plotting something. His friends and teachers ignore his warning, which leads to disaster.

Sabin, E. Rose

The School for Sorcery Trilogy. New York: Tor. *JS*
At the Leslie Simonton School for the Magically Gifted, students must learn not only how to develop their powers, but also how to fight off attacks from the Dire Realm.

A School for Sorcery. 2002. ISBN: 0765302896; 0765342197pa.
When Tria attends magic school, she contends with an unpredictable roommate who turns into a panther when she's angry and a classmate bent on releasing forces of evil magic.

A Perilous Power. 2004. Reissued in 2004 by Starscape. ISBN: 0765347601pa.
In this prequel to *A School for Sorcery*, Trevor and his best friend Leslie are sent to the city of Port-of-Lords so that Trevor can study with two powerful teachers and learn to control his power. When they arrive, they discover the teachers are at odds with each other, and they become embroiled in the ensuing conflict.

***When the Beast Ravens*. 2005. 287p. ISBN: 0765308584; 0765347598pa.**
One year after the events in *A School for Sorcery*, Gray Becq, who had been banished to the Dire Realm, returns to school. When demons attack again, Gray and the other students fear that he brought the demons with him.

Sage, Angie

The Septimus Heap Series. New York: Katherine Tegen Books. *MJ*
In the world of ordinary wizard Silas Heap, there are many ordinary wizards and one Extraordinary Wizard, as well as myriad magical creatures and more danger for him and his family then he ever anticipated.

Magyk. 2005. ISBN: 0060577312; 0060577339pa. AUD
Silas Heap discovers an infant girl outside the walls of the village and brings her home, only to learn that the midwife claims that his newborn son, Septimus, the seventh son of a seventh son, has died. Although they

deeply morn the loss of their son, Silas and his wife adopt the baby girl. Naming her Jenna, they raise her as their own until Marcia, the Extraordinary Wizard, warns them that they are in grave danger from the Necromancer DomDaniel, for Jenna is actually a person of great importance to the realm. They flee together, along with the mysterious Boy 412.

Flyte. **2006. 544p. ISBN: 0060577347.**
One year after the end of *Magyk*, Septimus, now apprenticed to Extraordinary Wizard Marcia, studies Magykal Charms, but DomDaniel lures away his older brother, Simon. Not content to simply master Dark Magyk, Simon kidnaps Princess Jenna and embarks on a mission to destroy the Dragon Boat. Jenna must find a way to escape, and Septimus needs to stop Simon from using his new power of Flyte to destroy them all.

Shinn, Sharon

The Shape-Changer's Wife. **New York: Ace, 2003. 224p. ISBN: 044101061Xpa.** **[Adult]** <u>S</u> **LP**
Aubrey, a gifted sorcery student wishing to perfect his craft, seeks out the great Shape-Changer and discovers that the lure of the Shape-Changer's wife may be more than he can handle.

Stroud, Jonathan

The Bartimaeus Trilogy. New York: Hyperion. **MJS AUD**
In an alternate London, magicians control the government and have for centuries. The most powerful of them control the highest levels of djinni to assist them in their schemes.

🪶 *The Amulet of Samarkand*. **2003. 462p. ISBN: 078681859X; 0786852550pa.**
Nathaniel has grown up in an England where magicians run the government and magically talented children are apprenticed at a young age. He has lived with his master, Mr. Underwood, since he was five, and by the age of eleven he knows more about magic than Underwood ever will. Determined to prove himself, he summons the djinni Bartimaeus and orders him to steal the Amulet of Samarkand from his enemy, the magician Simon Lovelace. That amulet, however, is more important than Nathaniel dared to dream. (ALAN; BBYA; Boston Globe Honor; TBYA)

The Golem's Eye. **2004. 562p. ISBN: 0786818603; 0786836547pa.**
Now fourteen and apprenticed to the powerful Jessica Whitwell, Nathaniel is trying to ferret out the leaders of the Resistance (ordinary humans who do not want to be ruled by magicians) when he discovers an unknown power threatening England. He summons Bartimaeus to help him locate and defeat the evil.

Ptolemy's Gate. **2006. 501p. ISBN: 0786818611.**
Three years after the end of *Golem's Eye,* Nathaniel serves as the Minister of Information, producing propaganda that attempts to convince commoners the ruling magicians are winning their overseas war. He still summons Bartimaeus, whose essence has been sadly depleted since he's had no respite in the "Other Place." All the while Kitty, the Resistance leader that Nathaniel thinks is dead, se-

cretly studies the ways of magicians. All three must unite when demons of undreamt of might rampage through London.

Yolen, Jane

Wizard's Hall. **San Diego: Harcourt, 1991. 131p. Reissued by Magic Carpet Books in 1999. ISBN: 0152020853pa. _M_ LP**
Even though Henry seems to have no talent, his mother sends him to Wizard's Hall to study magic. There, the fate of the school rests on his shoulders because he is the 113th student.

The Finest in the Realm

Jonathan Strange and Mr. Norell by Susannah Clarke

The Chrestomanci Chronicles by Diana Wynne Jones

The Harry Potter Series by J. K. Rowling

The Septimus Heap Series by Angie Sage

The Bartimaeus Trilogy by Jonathan Stroud

Chapter 2

Epic Fantasy

Epic fantasy features a hero or heroine who embarks on a quest of grand or grave significance. Set in an imaginary world that is sometimes mythical, sometimes preindustrial with a medieval or Renaissance ambiance, and sometimes postindustrial with a slightly more modern reality, these stories conjure universes imbued with magic. This magic plays an integral part in accomplishing whatever task the hero, heroine, or group of companions strives to complete. Almost always, the quest involves the classic battle of good versus evil, with the hero or heroine overcoming a series of obstacles and challenges while the fate of the kingdom hangs in the balance. The essence of epic fantasy lies in the scope of the protagonist's effort to overcome evil. Often this protagonist is a youth who grows from innocence to mastery during the course of the quest. Generally, the protagonist is not a magician or a wizard, although he or she may have a companion who is one, but is a more ordinary mortal thrust into circumstances that require heroic action. The combination of grand adventure in an imaginary realm with the coming-of-age motif draws young adults to these tales.

Epic fantasy traces its literary roots back through the history of Western literature to the epics of Homer's *Iliad* and *Odyssey* and through the history of English literature to *Beowulf*. Many consider J. R. R. Tolkien's <u>The Lord of the Rings</u> the quintessential modern epic fantasy and refer to Tolkien as the father of modern fantasy. Tolkien himself defined the kind of fantasy he wrote in his essay "On Fairy Stories" (Tolkien, 1966), saying, "The definition of a fairy-story … does not [depend] on any definition or account of elf or fairy, but upon the nature of Faerie; the Perilous Realm itself." The nature of Faerie, he says, is "Enchantment, [which] produces a Secondary World into which both designer and spectator can enter, to the satisfaction of their senses while they are inside." While writers created epic fantasy before Tolkien (as William Morris did in *The Wood Beyond the World*, published in 1894), Tolkien's masterpiece revolutionized and popularized the form in literature for adults and for young adults, inspiring many to follow in his footsteps. Both the Peter Jackson films of Tolkien's epic and the popularity of Harry Potter, which has affected all fantasy subgenres, have reignited interest in epic fantasy, also called heroic or high fantasy, creating a plethora of teen readers eager to embark on magical adventures of their own.

Mythic Epic Fantasy

Mythic epic fantasy refers either to novels inspired by a previously established mythology or to books where the gods and goddesses of the imaginary world interact with the protagonists. In books that are inspired by mythology, the authors use that mythology as the cauldron from which to ladle out ideas. Books more closely linked to the mythology that inspired them are listed in Chapter 3, "Myth and Legend Fantasy."

Profile of Lloyd Alexander

Born in 1924 in Philadelphia, Lloyd Alexander is often called a master storyteller, especially in regard to his works of fantasy. In 1964, he published *The Book of Three,* first of The Chronicles of Prydain. The second book in the series, *The Black Cauldron,* was a Newbery Honor book. The concluding volume, *The High King,* won the Newbery Medal. He also won the National Book Award twice, in 1970 for *The Marvelous Misadventures of Sebastian* and in 1982 for *Westmark,* the first in the *Westmark* trilogy. He expressed some of his feelings about writing fantasy in an interview published in *The Pied Pipers.* "I used the imaginary kingdom not as a sentimentalized fairyland, but as an opening wedge to express what I hoped would be some very hard truths. I never saw fairy tales as an escape or a cop out. . . . On the contrary, speaking for myself, it is the way to understand reality" (Wintle, 1974; *Contemporary Authors Online*, Infotrac Galegroup Database.)

Interview with Lloyd Alexander

Conducted via mail June 21–24, 2005

SF: How did you first come to write fantasy for young people?

LA: I came to fantasy fairly late. For some ten years, I had been happily writing fiction and nonfiction for adults. But I always loved fantasy, whether for adults or young people; and at that particular point in my life, I wanted to try it, to understand it, as part of the process of learning to be a writer. The results were beyond anything I could have foreseen. As I've said often and elsewhere, it was the most creative and liberating experience of my life. Paradoxically, in fantasy for young people I was able to express my own deepest feelings and attitudes more than I had ever done in writing for adults.

SF: Why do you think people read fantasy?

LA: Ever since human beings learned to talk to each other, we've been fascinated with storytelling of every kind. Blessed (or cursed) with insatiable curiosity, we have to know what happens next. Fantasy, however, in addition to being great storytelling, moves us at some unique and profound level. It has, I think, the power of mythology, or ancient dreams we have always and forever shared. In it, we find our real world and our real selves.

SF: Of all your books, do you have a favorite book or character?

LA: I can't single out one of my books or characters as a favorite. In the same way that I don't have a favorite kidney, my books are organically all part of myself. I might even say that put all together, the books are one ongoing, developing story—which, not coincidentally, happens to be my own lifestory.

SF: What was it like to win the Newbery Medal?

LA: The only way I can describe winning the Newbery Medal is: indescribable. Elation? Astonishment? Those are very pale words. What I did realize after the jubilation calmed down a little (it never calmed down completely) is that all awards, marvelous as they are to receive, are given for something already done. The point is not to look back, but to look ahead to what you hope still to do.

SF: What were your favorite books growing up, and who were your favorite authors?

LA: Favorite books and authors while growing up—I'd need a book to list them all. For the sake of brevity: Shakespeare, Dickens, Mark Twain, Victor Hugo, world's mythology, the Arthurian legends. And the unabridged dictionary. And they're still my favorites. They get better each time I read them.

SF: What would you say your method of writing is?

LA: I need a fairly extensive outline, which takes a long time to prepare. It always changes and surprises me as the work goes on. Even so, it's at least a kind of blueprint giving me some sense of proportion—so that the garage, in effect, doesn't turn out to be bigger than the living room.

SF: What do you think is the merit or importance of reading fantasy?

LA: I'm convinced that imagination is at the heart of everything we do—in art, science, even astrophysics and higher mathematics. Imagination leads us to ask, "What if?" Fantasy is, I believe, the great nourisher of imagination. To paraphrase Einstein on how to develop intelligence in young people: Read fairy tales. Then read more fairy tales. If we nourish imagination, we nourish everything else.

Alexander, Lloyd

The Chronicles of Prydain. New York: Henry Holt. Revised editions published in hardcover in 1999. _MJS_ BRAILLE
Assistant Pig-Keeper Taran and his companions dwell in the mythical land of Prydain, a kingdom inspired by the Welsh mythology set down in a collection of tales known as _The Mabinogion_ and embark on a series of adventures that ultimately lead to a confrontation with Arawn, Death-Lord.

> _The Book of Three._ **1964. 217p. Revised edition: ISBN: 0805061320; 0805080481pa. AUD**
> Taran, who has grown up in the care of the enchanter Dallben, wants to be more than just an Assistant Pig-Keeper. He wants to do something important, something exciting. When the Horned King threatens Prydain, Taran gets more excitement than he anticipated. Although Taran enters the forest only to save his charge, Hen-Wen, the oracular pig, he encounters Gwydion, Prince of Don. Striving to assist Prince Gwydion, Taran acquires an array of companions: Princess Eilonwy, the enchantress with the red-gold hair; Gurgi, the faithful and fearful forest creature who is fond of crunchings and munchings; Fflewddur Fflam, the bard who must be truthful; and Doli, the determined dwarf.

> ✿ _The Black Cauldron._ **1965. 224p. Revised edition: ISBN: 0805061312; 080508049Xpa. AUD VID**
> Arawn, Death-Lord, is building an army to destroy Prydain, and Prince Gwydion calls a council at Caer Dallben. Taran, reunited with his companions several months after they parted company at the end of _The Book of Three,_ learns that the Death-Lord's army is made up of cauldron-born soldiers created by Arawn using bodies of the slain. Taran and company must seek out the cauldron and destroy it before the deathless warriors deliver Prydain to Arawn. (Newbery Honor)

> _The Castle of Llyr._ **1966. 201p. Revised edition: ISBN: 0805061339; 0805080503pa. AUD**
> Protesting all the while, the Princess Eilonwy leaves Caer Dallben for the Isle of Mona so that she can be trained to be a proper princess. She does not know that the evil enchantress Achren desperately wants to steal her magical powers. When something sinister happens to Eilonwy, Taran and his friends set out to rescue her, but it is Eilonwy who must save herself.

> _Taran Wanderer._ **1967. 356p. Revised edition: ISBN: 0805061347; 0805080511pa. AUD**
> Taran dreams of asking Princess Eilonwy to marry him, but first he needs to learn the secret of his true identity. Accompanied by Gurgi, Taran travels across Prydain searching for the mystical Mirror of Lunet, which may show him a truth he cannot bear to face.

❦ *The High King*. 1968. 385p. Revised edition: ISBN: 0805061355; 080508052Xpa. AUD

The sword Dyrwyn, the most powerful weapon in the land, has fallen into the hands of Arawn, Death-Lord, and he threatens all Prydain with annihilation. Taran and his companions join Prince Gwydion in raising an army to march against Arawn in a battle that may be their last. (Newbery Medal)

***The Foundling and Other Tales*. 1973. 87p. Revised edition: ISBN: 0805061304; 0140378251pa.**

This volume contains eight tales of Prydain concerning events that took place before the birth of Taran, Assistant Pig-Keeper, including the childhood of Dallben the enchanter, the history of the sword Dyrwyn, and the romance of Princess Angharad, Eilonwy's mother. The revised edition adds the two long-out-of-print picture book stories, "Coll and His White Pig" and "The Truthful Harp."

❦ *The Iron Ring*. New York: Dutton, 1997. 283p. Reissued by Puffin in 1999. ISBN: 0141303484pa. *JS* AUD 📖

Young Tamar, ruler of a small, mythical Indian kingdom, wagers with a visiting king and loses his kingdom and his freedom. To fulfill the promise of his wager, Tamar, to whom honor is everything, sets out on a journey full of magic and danger, in which he meets a courageous and lovely milkmaid, a cowardly eagle, and a crafty monkey king who used to be a man. Refusing to be deterred from his goal of finding the kingdom of the mysterious stranger whose iron ring symbolizes his promise, Tamar persists in a journey that may cost him his life. (ALAN; BBYA)

Bujold, Lois McMaster

❦ *The Curse of Chalion*. New York: Eos, 2001. 442p. Reissued in 2006. ISBN: 0380818604pa. [Adult] *S* AUD BRAILLE 📖

A former courtier and soldier, Lord dy Cazaril was betrayed by his general and tortured by his captors. He returns to the castle where he served as a page, hoping for a quiet job in the stables. Instead, he is appointed tutor of the Royesse Iselle, sister of the heir to the throne of Chalion. Drawn into the dark maze of politics and magic, Cazaril must choose either to perform forbidden death-magic or to sacrifice all in the royal house, including Iselle. (Adult Mythopoeic Award)

❦ *Paladin of Souls*. New York: Eos, 2003. 456p. ISBN: 0380979020; 0380818612pa. [Adult] *S* AUD

This sequel to *The Curse of Chalion* takes place three years later. The Lady Ista, Royina Dowager of Chalion, having recovered from her years of god-touched madness, embarks on a pilgrimage to escape the suffocating life she leads in her mother's castle in Valenda. She has in mind a quiet journey across the country, but the gods have other plans. When her second-sight returns, she becomes embroiled in a desperate race to protect the hard-won peace of Chalion from the supernatural elements that threaten it. (Hugo Award; Nebula Award; Locus Award for Best Fantasy Novel)

***The Hallowed Hunt.* New York: Eos, 2005. 470p. ISBN: 0060574623; 0060574747. [Adult]** *S*

In this companion novel to *The Paladin of Souls* and *The Curse of Chalion,* the exiled Prince Boleso has been murdered, and Lord Ingrey is sent to escort the accused maiden Lady Ijada to Kingstown for trial. As the long journey progresses, the two grow closer each day, but their love seems doomed as they near a city rife with magical and political intrigue. Ingrey must uncover the truth to save the city and his lady.

Eddings, David

The Belgariad and The Malloreon (sequential series). New York: Ballantine. [Adult] *JS* **AUD**

Garion, an orphan, has grown up on a quiet farm in Sendaria under the care of Aunt Pol. Then Uncle Wolf, the storyteller, comes and wants to whisk away Garion and Pol. Durnik, the farmhand, insists on accompanying them. Together they journey through many kingdoms in search of the stolen Orb. As others join them, Garion discovers that he has a pivotal part to play in saving the world from the evil god Torak.

The Belgariad BRAILLE

Pawn of Prophecy. 1982. 262p. Reissued in 1990. ISBN: 0345335511pa.

The Queen of Sorcery. 1982. 327p. Reissued in 1989. ISBN: 0345335651pa.

The Magician's Gambit. 1983. 308p. Reissued in 1995. ISBN: 0345335457pa.

Castle of Wizardry. 1984. 375p. Reissued in 1991. ISBN: 0345335708pa.

Enchanter's End Game. 1984. 372p. Reissued in 1988. ISBN: 0345338715pa.

The Malloreon

Guardians of the West. 1987. 439p. Reissued in 1988. ISBN: 0345352661pa.

King of the Murgos. 1987, 454p. Reissued in 1995. ISBN: 0345358805pa.

Sorceress of Darshiva. 1989, 371p. Reissued in 1990. ISBN: 0345369351pa.

The Seeress of Kell. 1991, 399p. Reissued in 1995. ISBN: 0345377591pa.

The Belgariad Prequels (with Liegh Eddings)

Belgarath the Sorcerer. 1995. 644p. Reissued in 1996. ISBN: 0345403959pa. **BRAILLE**

Polgara the Sorceress. 1997. 643p. Reissued in 1999. ISBN: 0345422554pa.

The Rivan Codex. 1998. 404p. Reissued in 1999. ISBN: 0345435869pa.

Fisher, Catherine

The Oracle Prophecies. New York: Greenwillow. (1st American Editions.) **_MJS_**

In the realm of Two Lands, which is reminiscent of both ancient Greece and ancient Egypt, the Nine are priestesses who serve the god. Each generation, the god chooses someone to speak through, and there is no end to that one's power—if the chosen ones and their servants can resist corruption.

🦇 *The Oracle Betrayed.* 2004. 341p. ISBN: 0060571578; 0060571594pa.

Mirany is youngest of the Nine. She is suddenly thrust into a world of deceit and betrayal when the Bearer-of-the-God dies and she must find the new true Archon, despite the plots of those around her. (ALAN; BBYA)

The Sphere of the Secrets. 2005. 370p. ISBN: 0060571616.

Although the god now resides in ten-year-old Alexos, drought still plagues Two Lands. With Seth and Oblek, Alexos crosses the desert, seeking the Well of Songs, to right an ancient wrong and restore the rivers. While Alexos is gone, Mirany remains behind to uncover the perpetrators of a poisoning plot.

Day of the Scarab. 2006. 416p. ISBN: 0060571632.

When General Argelin stages a coup so that he can rule in the Two Lands, Mirany goes into hiding. Seth and the Jackal work to organize a resistance movement, since Alexos is now powerless.

Meyer, Kai

The Dark Reflections Trilogy. New York: Margaret K. McElderry Books. (1st American Editions.) **_MJ_** AUD LP

In a mythical Venice of the late nineteenth century, the Flowing Queen has always been able to keep her city safe from pharoah's armies, but now she has been captured and needs the help of two apprenticed orphans.

The Water Mirror. 2005. 256p. ISBN: 0689877870.

Thirteen-year-old Junipa and fourteen-year-old Merle are orphans apprenticed to a mirror-maker who uses a secret magic in his art. Junipa, who is blind, submits to a dangerous procedure to have her eyes replaced with magic crystal shards, and Merle overhears a plot to place the city in the hands of the invading Egyptians. Hurtling headlong into danger, Merle is determined to find a way to help her homeland stay free.

Preindustrial Epic Fantasy

Preindustrial worlds along with a reigning monarchy are constructs that characterize a great deal of epic fantasy. Often these worlds have a medieval or Renaissance atmosphere. Some are filled with historically accurate details, combined with magic and adventure, and some contain completely created societies.

Ash, Sarah

The Tears of Artamon Trilogy. New York: Bantam. [Adult] *S*

Gavrial Andar grows up sheltered by his mother, knowing nothing of his father until the day of his father's death, when Gavrial learns of a dark legacy. Like his father before him, he is a Drakhaoul, a man whose blood binds him to the warrior-dragons. As Gavrial wrestles against the blood-lust, the fate of his kingdom—and all of the five kingdoms—is at risk.

Lord of Snow and Shadows. 2003. 480p. ISBN: 0553803344; 0553586211pa.

Prisoner of the Iron Tower. 2004. 466p. ISBN: 055338211X; 055358622Xpa.

Children of the Serpent Gate. 2005. 528p. ISBN: 0553382128; 0553586238pa.

Bell, Hilari

The Farsala Trilogy
See Chapter 5, "Alternate and Parallel Worlds."

Brooks, Terry

The Shannara Series. New York: Ballantine. [Adult] *S* AUD

In the magical land of Shannara, the races of elves, dwarfs, trolls, and druids struggle to coexist while the forces of evil are ever-vigilant in their attempts to rule the world. As with the Eddings epics, these trilogies and quartets are sequential except where noted.

The Shannara Trilogy

The Sword of Shannara. 1977. 726p. Reissued in 1995. ISBN: 0345314255pa.

The Elfstones of Shannara. 1982. 469p. Reissued in 1990. ISBN: 0345285549pa.

The Wishsong of Shannara. 1985. 499p. Reissued in 1992. ISBN: 0345356365pa.

The Heritage of Shannara Quartet

The Scions of Shannara. 1990. 465p. Reissued in 1993. ISBN: 0345370740pa.

The Druid of Shannara. 1991. 423p. Reissued in 1992. ISBN: 0345375599pa.

The Elf Queen of Shannara. 1992. 403p. Reissued in 1993. ISBN: 0345375580pa.

The Talismans of Shannara. 1993. 453p. Reissued in 1994. ISBN: 0345386744pa.

First King of Shannara. Prequel to The Shannara Trilogy. 1996. 489p. Reissued in 1997. ISBN: 0345396537pa.

The Voyage of Jerle Shannara Trilogy

> *The Ilse Witch.* 2000. 454p. Reissued in 2001. ISBN: 0345396553pa.
>
> *Antrax.* 2001. 375p. Reissued in 2002. ISBN: 0345397673pa.
>
> *Morgawr.* 2002. 401p. Reissued in 2003. ISBN: 0345435753pa.

The High Druid of Shannara Trilogy

> *Jarka Ruus.* 2003. 398p. Reissued in 2004. ISBN: 0345435761pa.
>
> *Tanequil.* 2004. 357p. ISBN: 0345435745; 034543577Xpa.
>
> *Straken.* 2005. 384p. ISBN: 0345451120.

Cherryh, C. J.

Fortress Quartet. New York: HarperPrism. [Adult] *S*

Mauryl the wizard, kingmaker for a thousand years, toils in an isolated castle to work his last weave of magic—a Summoning, a Shaping—to send into the world and right the wrongs of magic gone awry. But the being he returns to his world, Tristen, is an innocent young man who cannot remember who he was or what powers he used to wield. Still, armed with a sword named Truth on one side and Illusion on the other, Tristen goes forth, the fate of the kingdoms riding uneasily on his shoulders.

> *Fortress in the Eye of Time*. 1995. 568p. Reissued in 1996. ISBN: 0061056898pa.
>
> *Fortress of Eagles*. 1998. 335p. Reissued in 1999. ISBN: 006105710Xpa.
>
> *Fortress of Owls*. 1999. 406p. Reissued in 2000. ISBN: 0061020087pa.

> *Fortress of Dragons*. 2000. 422p. Reissued in 2001. ISBN: 0061020443pa.

Croggon, Alison

The Pellinor Quartet. Cambridge, MA: Candlewick. *JS*

In Annar and the Seven Kingdoms, the powers of the Light strive to engender peace and harmony while the powers of the Dark have receded to husband their strength. The Bards are the servants of the Light. Born with the Gift of Speech that enables them to understand animals and to work magic, they seek out those that are Gifted and train them in their Schools. When the school of Pellinor is attacked, the powers of the Dark are once again on the move. The Bards must ready themselves for battle, but they forget the ancient prophecy about one who will lead them in the time of strife.

> *The Naming*. 2005. 492p. ISBN: 0763626392; 0763631620pa.
> Sixteen-year-old Maerad's life of drudgery as an orphan slave changes dramatically when she helps the Bard Cadvan. Recognizing that she has the bardic gifts, he frees her. Together they begin a harrowing journey to

the School at Norloch, where Cadvan can consult with his former mentor and Maerad can learn to use her gifts. But treachery entraps them as the powers of the Dark seek to snuff them out.

***The Riddle.* 2006. ISBN: 0763630152.**
Maerad and Cadvan have escaped from the corrupted powers of the Light at Norloch, and now embark on a peril-fraught journey so that Maerad can learn to use her power. As they battle the forces of evil, they seek the mysterious Treesong which may provide the key to overcoming the Dark.

Cook, Glen

The Black Company Chronicles. New York: Tor. [Adult] *JS*
The land of Taglios is torn asunder by the strife of sorcerers and demigods who hire mercenary troops to do their fighting for them. One such troop is the Black Company, fierce soldiers loyal only to each other. Their captain, Croak, leads them through the intricacies of magical mayhem first in the quintet of novels and then in the quartet.

The Black Company Series

> ***The Black Company.* 1984. 320p. Reissued in 1996. ISBN: 0812521390pa.**
>
> ***Shadows Linger.* 1984. 320p. Reissued in 1990. ISBN: 0812508424pa.**
>
> ***The White Rose.* 1985. 320p. Reissued in 1990. ISBN: 0812508440pa.**
>
> ***Shadow Games.* 1989. 311p. ISBN: 0812533828pa.**
>
> ***Dreams of Steel.* 1990. 346p. ISBN: 0812502108pa.**

The Glittering Stone Quartet

> ***Bleak Seasons.* 1996. 316p. ISBN: 0812555325pa.**
>
> ***She Is the Darkness.* 1997. 384p. Reissued in 1998. ISBN: 0812555333pa.**
>
> ***Water Sleeps.* 1999. 412p. Reissued in 2000. ISBN: 0812555341pa.**
>
> ***Soldiers Live.* 2000. 496p. Reissued in 2001. ISBN: 0812566556pa.**

Dickinson, John

***The Cup of the World.* New York: David Fickling Books, 2004. (1st American Edition.) 418p. ISBN: 0385750250. *S* AUD**
Sixteen-year-old Phaedra is heir to her father's lands, so even royalty considers her a marital prize. Phaedra, however, rejects all suitors in favor of the knight of her dreams. Since childhood, a knight has indeed visited her in her dreams. When he woos her in the waking world, she disobeys her father and marries him, unwittingly plunging her land into civil war. When her new husband, Ulfin, departs for the battle, Phaedra uncovers dark secrets of black magic and must choose between her husband and her child.

The Widow and the King. New York: David Fickling Books, 2005. (1st American Edition.) 624p. ISBN: 0385750846. *S* AUD
This sequel to *The Cup of the World* begins twelve years later. Ambrose, Phaedra's son, is sick and tired of the quiet life on the farm that he has been living in exile with his mother. When a strange knight enters their world, Ambrose is forced to strike out on his own, eventually finding refuge in the house of the Widow. There, he must work out a way both to avoid assassination and to halt the cycle of violence and injustice that plagues the kingdom.

Donaldson, Stephen R.

The Chronicles of Thomas Covenant. [Adult] *S*

When leper Thomas Covenant finds himself in the Land—a place with giants, dwarfs, sorcerers, and evil spirits, a place where he can feel—he doesn't believe it's real, let alone that the fate of the Land lies in his hands.

The Chronicles of Thomas Covenant the Unbeliever. New York: Ballantine. BRAILLE

> *Lord Foul's Bane*. 1977. 396p. Reissued in 1984. ISBN: 0345348656pa.

> *The Illearth War*. 1977. 407p. Reissued in 1989. ISBN: 0345348664pa.

> *The Power That Preserves*. 1977. 379p. Reissued in 1993. ISBN: 0345348672pa.

The Second Chronicles of Thomas Covenant. New York: Ballantine. BRAILLE

> *The Wounded Land*. 1980. 497p. Reissued in 1995. ISBN: 0345348680pa.

> *The One Tree*. 1982. 475p. Reissued in 1993. ISBN: 0345348699pa.

> *The White Gold Wielder*. 1983. 485p. Reissued in 1993. ISBN: 0345348702pa.

The Last Chronicles of Thomas Covenant

> *The Runes of the Earth*. New York: Putnam, 2004. 523p. Reissued by Ace in 2005. ISBN: 044101304Xpa. AUD

Duncan, Dave

Tales of the King's Blades. New York: Avon/Eos. [Adult] *S*

In Chivial, where sorcery reigns hand-in-hand with politics, rebellious boys with nowhere else to turn attend Ironhall. There, years of rigorous training in the art of swordsmanship produce an elite troop of fighters dedicated to safeguarding their king and his court, as each fighter is bound through a magic ritual to the knight he will protect with his life.

The Gilded Chain. 1998. 338p. Reissued in 1999. ISBN: 0380791269pa. BRAILLE

Lord of the Fire Lands. 1999. 352p. Reissued in 2000. ISBN: 0380791277pa. BRAILLE

Sky of Swords. 2000. 358p. Reissued in 2001. ISBN: 0380791285pa. BRAILLE

Paragon Lost. 2002. 348p. Reissued in 2003. ISBN: 0380818353pa. BRAILLE

Impossible Odds. 2003, 365p. Reissued in 2004. ISBN: 0060094451pa.

The Jaguar Knights. 2004. 386p. Reissued in 2005. ISBN: 0060555122pa.

Farland, David

Runelords Series. New York: Tor. [Adult] *S*
Runelords accrue their magical powers by draining the endowments of others. Those who have willingly, or not so willingly, made such a donation become the dependents of the recipient Runelord. Each Runelord is gifted but responsible for many lives because, if those whose powers now reside in the Runelord die, their endowments disappear with them. Prince Gaborn, a young Runelord, becomes ensnared in the woes of the realm and engages in a constant race to avert disaster.

The Runelords. 1998. 479p. Reissued in 1999. ISBN: 0812541626pa.

Brotherhood of the Wolf. 1999. 480p. ISBN: 0312867425; 0812570693pa.

Wizardborn. 2001. 428p. ISBN: 0312867417; 0812570707pa.

The Lair of Bones. 2003. 429p. ISBN: 0765301768; 0765341077pa.

Farmer, Nancy

🏵 *The Sea of Trolls*. New York: Atheneum, 2004. 480p. ISBN: 0689867441; 0689867468pa. *MJ* AUD LP 📖
Jack, a Saxon lad, is being trained by the village Bard to work magic. He can call up fire and fog and feel the flow of power connecting all living things, but his life changes abruptly when Olaf One-Brow and his band of berserkers from the North capture him and his little sister, Lucy. The berserkers carry them across the sea to their home country. Once there, Jack unwittingly makes an enemy of the half-troll queen who takes Lucy hostage. To save Lucy's life, Jack embarks on a quest to troll country, seeking the magical elixir found in Mirmir's Well and battling dragons, giant spiders, and trolls on the way. (ALAN; BBYA)

Flanagan, John

The Ranger's Apprentice Quartet. New York: Philomel Books. (1st American Editions.) *MJ*
In the kingdom of Araluen that must be ever-alert for magical threats, a small group of people known as the Rangers, work secretly to keep their homeland safe.

The Ruins of Gorlan. 2005. 249p. ISBN: 0399244549; 0142406635pa.
Fifteen-year-old Will, an orphan, trains with his friends at Castle Redmond. He hopes to enter Battleschool and become a warrior, but his build is deemed too slight. Instead, he is apprenticed to the Rangers. While Will hones his skills in archery, stealth, and woodcraft, techniques that will be Araluen's first defense against the exiled Lord Morgarath, he also faces the bullies in his life and learns to turn enemies into friends.

The Burning Bridge. 2006. ISBN: 0399244557.
As Will and his friends continue their Ranger training, they uncover a plot of Lord Morgarath's that will devastate the forces of Araluen unless the friends can find a way to thwart their enemy.

Hill, Stuart

The Cry of the Icemark. New York: Scholastic, 2005. (1st American Edition.) 472p. ISBN: 0439686261; 043968627Xpa. *MJ* AUD LP
When the Polypontian Empire sends its first wave attack against the kingdom of Icemark, they succeed in killing the king. Fourteen-year-old Princess Thirrin, who was always more interested in warfare and weaponry than her studies, becomes queen much earlier than she'd anticipated. Desperate to save Icemark from the second attack she knows is coming, she forms alliances with old friends and former foes, including werewolves and vampires—anyone who will help her in her fight for freedom.

Hobb, Robin

The Farseer and **The Tawny Man Trilogies** (sequential trilogies). **New York: Bantam. [Adult] S**
At age six, Fitz, the bastard son of Prince Chivalry, is sent to be a stable hand. As he enters adolescence, he demonstrates magical abilities that bring him to the attention of King Shrewd. He apprentices Fitz to the Royal Assassin, never realizing that ultimately the fate of the kingdom will rest in Fitz's hands.

The Farseer Trilogy

Assassin's Apprentice. 1995. 356p. Reissued in 1996. ISBN: 055357339Xpa.

Royal Assassin. 1996. 581p. Reissued in 1997. ISBN: 0553573411pa.

Assassin's Quest. 1997. 692p. Reissued in 1998. ISBN: 0553565699pa.

The Tawny Man Trilogy

Fool's Errand. 2002. 486p. ISBN: 0553582445pa.

Golden Fool. 2003. 520p. ISBN: 0553582453pa.

Fool's Fate. 2004. 631p. ISBN: 0553801546.

Jones, Diana Wynne

The Dalemark Quartet. *See* Chapter 5, "Alternate and Parallel Worlds."

Jordan, Robert

The Wheel of Time. New York: Tor. [Adult] $\underline{S}$ AUD
In the beginning, the Creator bound the Dark One, but a time came when the Aes Sedai, male and female workers of magic, unknowingly created a hole in the Dark One's prison through which he tainted the world. Now only women can safely channel the Power. Men who try go mad. So the Aes Sedai are on the lookout for men who can channel. They must stop them before they wreak havoc. In particular, they search for one man, named in prophecy, whose actions will have dire consequences. In this world of turmoil, Rand, a youth who once lived a quiet village life, and his companions venture forth, first together and then separately following the paths that destiny has laid before them.

> *The Eye of the World.* 1990. 670p. ISBN: 0312850093; 0812511816pa.
>
> *The Great Hunt.* 1990. 600p. ISBN: 0312851405; 0812509714pa.
>
> *The Dragon Reborn.* 1991. 595p. ISBN: 0312852487; 0812513711pa.
>
> *The Shadow Rising.* 1992. 701p. ISBN: 0312854315; 0812513738pa.
>
> *The Fires of Heaven.* 1993. 702p. ISBN: 0312854277; 0812550307pa.
>
> *Lord of Chaos.* 1994. 716p. ISBN: 0312854285; 0812513754pa.
>
> *A Crown of Swords.* 1996. 684p. ISBN: 0312857675; 0812550285pa.
>
> *The Path of Daggers.* 1998. 604p. ISBN: 0312857691; 0812550293pa.
>
> *Winter's Heart.* 2000. 668p. ISBN: 0312864256; 081257558Xpa.
>
> *Crossroads of Twilight.* 2003. 700p. ISBN: 0312864590; 0812571339pa.
>
> *New Spring.* 2004. 334p. ISBN: 0765306298; 0765345455pa.
>
> *Knife of Dreams.* 2005. 1000p. ISBN: 0312873077.

Kaaberbol, Lene

The Shamer Chronicles. New York: Holt. (1st American Editions.) $\underline{MJ}$
In a land where most people live in small villages, one person holds a position of utmost responsibility, the Shamer. A Shamer can gaze into people's eyes and see the deepest secrets of their souls.

> *The Shamer's Daughter.* **New York: Holt, 2004. ISBN: 0805075410.**
> Dina and her mother both possess the Shamer's Gift. While her mother holds the valued village position of Shamer, determining accused wrongdoers' guilt or innocence, Dina is new to her gift and having trouble adjusting. It's hard to make or keep friends when no one will look you in the eye. When Lord Drakan summons Dina's mother to the Castle Dunark to discern the truth of a triple murder, Dina

expects her mother will be home shortly. She does not return, and Dina searches for her, only to find her imprisoned and in desperate need of help.

The Shamer's Signet. **New York: Holt, 2005. 314p. ISBN: 0805075429.**
Dina and her mother are hiding in the Highlands, but Drakan is still trying to destroy them. When an assassination plot is foiled, the evil Valdracu kidnaps Dina and tries to force her to use her Shamer's Gift against his people. Dina's brother, Davin, sets out to rescue her, but he may be too late.

Serpent Gift. **2006. 384p. ISBN: 0805077707.**
When Dina's father enters her life, he disrupts the lives of all in her family. He bears the Serpent Gift and has mastered the art of lie and illusion. While fleeing from danger, Dina must hone her Shamer's Gift to see beyond the web of deceit spun by her father.

Kay, Guy Gavriel

🎗 *Tigana*. **New York: Viking, 1990. 687p. Reissued in paperback in 1999. ISBN: 0670833339pa. [Adult]** S
Long after warring sorcerers destroy the realm of Tigana, a small band of survivors struggles to oust the tyrants and restore the kingdom. They are led by the last prince of the royal house, Alessan, who wages psychological warfare in a desperate attempt to win freedom for his people. (Prix Aurora Award)

Lackey, Mercedes

The Tales of Valdemar. *See* Chapter 5, "Alternate and Parallel Worlds."

Le Guin, Ursula K.

The Earthsea Cycle. *MJS* **AUD BRAILLE**
Many of those who can wield magic, from hedgewitches to mages, live in the archipelago Earthsea. Ged is destined to be one of the greatest mages of all time, and his struggle with evil matches the magnitude of his gifts.

🎗 *A Wizard of Earthsea*. **Berkley, CA: Parnassus Press, 1968. Reissued by Bantam in 2004. ISBN: 0553262505pa. VID**
Young Ged, called Sparrowhawk, does not possess the patience that he should and is eager for knowledge and power—too eager. While studying the art of wizardry, he accidentally unleashes a terrifying creature that he must subdue to save Earthsea. (Boston Globe Award)

The Tombs of Atuan. **New York: Atheneum, 1971. 163p. Reissued by Simon & Schuster in hardcover in 1991. ISBN: 0689316844; 1416509623pa. VID**
Tenar, high priestess to the Nameless Ones, guards the catacombs of the Tombs of Atuan. She has given up everything—home, family, and

possessions—to become Arha, the Eaten One. When Ged, a young wizard, invades the labyrinth, searching for its dearest treasure, Tenar can follow the light of magic, helping him and escaping with him, or she can choose to stay and serve the Dark Ones.

🌳 *The Farthest Shore.* **New York: Atheneum, 1972. 223p. Revised edition published by Simon & Schuster in hardcover in 2001. ISBN: 0689316836; 141650964Xpa.**

All of the magic is draining out of Earthsea. Ged, now the Archmage of Roke, and Arren, Prince of Enlad, embark on a journey beyond the domain of death to discover the source of the evil and the way to thwart it. (National Book Award)

🌳 *Tehanu.* **New York: Atheneum, 1990. 226p. ISBN: 0689315953; 1416509631pa.**

Archmage Ged, who lost his powers when he saved the world, returns to Gont. Tenar, now a middle-aged widow, takes on the task of healing Ged and Therru, a disfigured and abused child. Gradually Ged begins to recover, but evil still lurks in the world. When it threatens Tenar, Therru unexpectedly responds. (Nebula Award; Locus Award for Best Fantasy Novel)

Tales from Earthsea. **New York: Harcourt, 2001. 296p. Reissued by Ace in 2002. ISBN: 0441011241pa.**

In these five tales (two novellas and three short stories), the doings of the denizens of Earthsea—dragons, sorcerers, and witches—are recounted chronologically according to Earthsea history. "The Finder," the first story, recreates the founding of the school of wizardry on the Isle of Roke three hundred years before Ged was born. "Dragonfly," the concluding novella, takes place just after the end of *Tehanu* and relates the tale of a girl who has the audacity to try to break the ban on female mages by attempting to enroll in school on Roke.

🌳 *The Other Wind.* **New York: Harcourt, 2001. 246p. Reissued by Ace in 2003. ISBN: 044101125Xpa.**

Alder, a simple sorcerer whose gift is mending, is troubled by dreams of his dead wife, Lily. In the dreams, she touches him. Disturbed, he seeks advice from the mages on Roke, but they send him to Ged. The former Archmage, now powerless and retired, realizes the dreams may mean a great unbalancing in the world and sends Alder to King Lebannen in Havnor. After conferring, Ged, Tenar, Tehanu, King Lebannen, and Irian journey with Alder to Roke to make their last stand. (World Fantasy Award)

Marillier, Juliet

The Sevenwaters Trilogy. *See* Chapter 3, "Myth and Legend Fantasy."

Martin, George R. R.

The Song of Ice and Fire. **New York: Bantam. [Adult]** *S* **AUD**

In the realm of Westeros, made up of seven kingdoms forcibly united by a dragon-riding tyrant generations ago, seasons last for decades, and two families, the Starks and the Lannisters, vie for control. While brutal political intrigue ensnares Lord Eddard Stark and his children, the Others prepare for war beyond the Wall in the North, and a princess who comes to command dragons plots to regain the family throne from the usurper.

🌑 *A Game of Thrones*. 1996. 694p. ISBN: 0553103547; 0553588486pa. (Locus Award for Best Fantasy Novel)

🌑 *A Clash of Kings*. 1999. 761p. ISBN: 0553108034; 0553579908pa. (Locus Award for Best Fantasy Novel)

🌑 *A Storm of Swords*. 2000. 973p. ISBN: 0553106635; 055357342Xpa. (Locus Award for Best Fantasy Novel)

A Feast for Crows. 2005. 1078p. ISBN: 0553801503.

McKillip, Patricia A.

Riddle-Master: The Complete Trilogy. New York: Ace, 1999. 578p. ISBN: 0441005969pa. *JS*

Morgan, Prince of Hed, and Raederle, the woman he is to marry, take separate paths to unravel the complex and magical riddle that is their only hope for preserving the kingdom. (Originally published as three separate books, this is now available only as an omnibus paperback.)

The Riddle-Master of Hed. New York: Atheneum, 1976. 226p. (Out of Print) BRAILLE

Wizards have vanished from the world, leaving only riddles in their wake. Prince Morgan has mastered those riddles. But when evil threatens, he must seek out the High One to solve the most compelling riddle of all.

The Heir of Sea and Fire. New York: Atheneum, 1977. 204p. (Out of Print)

Rumors abound that Morgan is dead, but Raederle, the Princess of An whom Morgan is pledged to marry, wants to know the truth. Armed with her small gift of magic, she sets out to search for Morgan, with only a friend and Morgan's sister to aid her.

🌑 *Harpist in the Wind*. New York: Atheneum, 1979. 256p. (Out of Print)

In the midst of growing strife between the shape-shifters and the land rulers, Morgan and Raederle must risk everything to solve the final riddle that will enable them to save all that is dear to them. (Locus Award for Best Fantasy Novel)

McKinley, Robin

🌑 *The Blue Sword*. New York: Greenwillow Books, 1982. 272p. ISBN: 0688009387; 014130975Xpa. *MJS* AUD BRAILLE

Harry Crewe, a young woman who is bored with a life of growing oranges in the isolated colony of Daria, is kidnapped by Corlath, King of the Damarians.

Corlath recognizes right away that Harry can wield the legendary Blue Sword, and he trains her to use the magic sword to fight a common enemy. (Newbery Honor)

🐾 *The Hero and the Crown*. **New York: Greenwillow Books, 1985. 246p. ISBN: 0688025935; 0141309814pa.** *MJS* **AUD BRAILLE** 📖
In this prequel to *The Blue Sword,* Aerin is the only child of a witch-woman from the North and the king of the mythical Damar. Determined to prove herself, Aerin researches the art of dragon slaying. She practices what she learns—first on very small dragons, then on larger ones. Eventually, she faces Maur the Black, a powerful dragon, and encounters Luthe, the wizard. Luthe reveals the truth about her mother and gives her the Blue Sword to use against the evil mage, Agsded. (Newbery Medal)

Odom, Mel

The Librarian Trilogy. New York: Tor. [Adult] *S*
Edgewick, a Level Three Librarian, enjoys his life acquiring knowledge and guarding the books in the Vault of All Knowledge. When Grandmagister Frollo entrusts him with an errand at the docks, pirates capture him. He discovers unexpected uses for his wit and vast store of knowledge, as adventure whirls him away from his quiet world.

🐾 *The Rover*. **2001. 400p. ISBN: 0312878826; 0765341948pa. (Alex)**

The Destruction of the Books. **2004. 381p. ISBN: 0765307235; 0765346494pa.**

The Lord of the Libraries. **2005. 384p. ISBN: 0765307243.**

Pattou, Edith

Hero's Song: First Song of Errin. **New York: Harcourt Brace Jovanovich, 1991. 290p. ISBN: 0152338071; 0152055428pa.** *MJ*
When Collun's sister disappears, he leaves the farm he loves to search for her, his only weapon a simple dagger with his mother's luck-stone in the hilt. Joined by his best friend, Talisen, who longs to be a bard, Brie the archer, and the elflike Silien, an ally's betrayal sets him on a path that will lead to a confrontation with the Firewurme, to save his sister and all of Errin.

Fire Arrow: Second Song of Errin. **New York: Harcourt Brace Jovanovich, 1998. Reissued in 2005. ISBN: 0152055304pa.** *MJ*
Brie, the archer maiden who accompanied Collun on his quest, sets out on a journey of her own, searching for her father's murderers. She carries with her the powerful fire-arrow to aid her and discovers that her destiny leads her not only to personal justice but also to a confrontation with the evil wizard who would win the arrow and rule the world.

Pierce, Tamora

The Song of the Lioness Quartet. *See* Chapter 5, "Alternate and Parallel Worlds."

Tolkien, J. R. R.

The Hobbit. Boston: Houghton Mifflin, 1938. Reissued in hardcover 1997, 288p. ISBN: 0395873460; 0618260307pa. *MJS* AUD BRAILLE LP VID GN

Bilbo Baggins, a hobbit who is half the size of a man, likes living comfortably in his hobbit hole. Despite Bilbo's protests, the great wizard Gandalf the Grey convinces him to taste the delights of adventure. Traveling with dwarfs, Bilbo heads for the Lonely Mountains, home of Smaug the Magnificent, the most dangerous dragon in Middle Earth.

<u>The Lord of the Rings Trilogy</u>. Boston: Houghton Mifflin. (1st American Editions.) [Adult] *MJS* AUD BRAILLE LP VID

When Bilbo's nephew Frodo inherits Bilbo's magical ring, he quickly learns that it is far from a simple toy that makes the bearer invisible. The small hobbit and his companions embark on a dangerous quest across Middle Earth with the slim hope of casting the ring into the fires of Mount Doom before the master of evil, Sauron, finds it and reclaims his lost tool of power, bringing darkness to the hobbits' beloved Shire as well as to the lands of men, elves, and dwarfs.

> *The Fellowship of the Ring*. 1954. Reissued in hardcover in 1986. 423p. ISBN: 0395082544; 0618574948pa.

> *The Two Towers*. 1954. Reissued in hardcover in 1986. 352p. ISBN: 0395489334; 0618574956pa.

> *The Return of the King*. 1955.Reissued in hardcover in 1986. 440p. ISBN: 039548930X; 0618574972pa.

❀ *The Silmarillion*. 1977. 365p. Reissued in hardcover in 2004. ISBN: 0618391118; 0618126988pa. [Adult] *JS* AUD LP

Published posthumously and edited by Tolkien's son Christopher, this collection of legends and tales relates the epic history of Middle Earth before the time of Frodo and the quest of the members of the Fellowship of the Ring. (Locus Award for Best Fantasy Novel)

Williams, Tad

<u>Memory, Sorrow and Thorn</u>. New York: DAW Books. [Adult] *S*

Simon, a lowly kitchen worker, is secretly being tutored by the magician Morgenes. When evil threatens the peaceful kingdom of Orten Ard, Simon and all who care about the realm use every tool and talent they have to stem the tide of wild magic.

> *The Dragonbone Chair*. 1988. 654p. Reissued in 1999. ISBN: 0886773849pa.

> *Stone of Farewell*. 1990. 589p. Reissued in 1991. ISBN: 0756402972pa.

To Green Angel Tower. **1993. 1083p. (Original hardcover, one volume; reissued as two volumes in paperback in 1994. ISBN: 0886775981pa., part one; 0886776066pa., part two)**

Postindustrial and Modern Epic Fantasy

Occasionally epic fantasy evolves in worlds formed after an industrial revolution, endowing the story with a contemporary component. Although many of these also can fit into the Alternate and Parallel Worlds chapter, their scope places them squarely in Epic Fantasy.

Cooper, Susan

The Dark Is Rising Sequence. *MJS* AUD LP BRAILLE
Inspired by English legends, this sequence interweaves the stories of the three Drew siblings and Will Stanton as they endeavor to aid the forces of the Light in their battle against the Dark.

Over Sea, Under Stone. **New York: Harcourt, Brace and World, 1966. 252p. Reissued in hardcover in 1977. ISBN: 015259034X; 0689840357pa.**
While on holiday in Cornwall, Simon, Jane, and Barney Drew find a manuscript that sends them on a hazardous quest for King Arthur's grail. This reignites the battle between the Light and the Dark.

🌳 *The Dark Is Rising.* **New York: Atheneum, 1973. 216p. ISBN: 0689303173; 0689829833pa.**
On his eleventh birthday, Will Stanton, the seventh son of a seventh son, discovers a special gift. He is the youngest of the Old Ones, immortals dedicated to fighting the Dark. To fulfill his destiny, Will braves the dangerous powers arrayed against him and seeks the six magical signs that will enable the Light to defeat the Dark. (Boston Globe Award; Newbery Honor)

Greenwitch. **New York: Atheneum, 1974. 147p. ISBN: 0689304269; 0689840349pa.**
After learning that the golden grail recovered in *Over Sea, Under Stone* has been stolen from the British Museum, the Drews journey to Cornwall in an attempt to recover it. When they first meet Will, they are wary of him, but eventually they all join forces in negotiating the perils that plague them while they fight for possession of King Arthur's grail.

🌳 *The Grey King.* **New York: Atheneum, 1975. 208p. ISBN: 0689500297; 0689829841pa.**
While recuperating in Wales from a severe illness, Will meets Bran, a boy with silver eyes and a white dog who can see the wind. Both are key to retrieving the legendary golden harp that is needed to awaken King Arthur's knights. (Newbery Medal)

Silver on the Tree. **New York: Atheneum, 1977. 256p. ISBN: 0689500882; 0689711522pa.**
Will, Bran, and the Drews are summoned to the Welsh Mountains, where Will and Bran search for the Crystal Sword while Simon, Jane, and Barney meet King Arthur and prepare for the final confrontation with the Dark.

Ende, Michael

The Neverending Story. Garden City, NY: Doubleday, 1983. 396p. Reissued by Penguin in hardcover in 1997. ISBN: 0525457585; 0140386335pa. [Adult] *MJS* BRAILLE VID

Bastian likes to keep to himself and stay out of other people's way. One day he discovers a mysterious book about an enchanted kingdom in need of a hero. The book is so engrossing, Bastian never wants to put it down. His connection to the book transports him into the story to fulfill an important mission.

Nix, Garth

The Abhorsen Sequence. *JS*

In the Old Kingdom, Charter Magic created an ordered world where magic could be used for the benefit of all, but the creatures of Free Magic opposed this order. The Abhorsen, the Royal Family, the Charter Stones, and the Charter Mages all are charged with the responsibility of keeping Free Magic at bay and the kingdom strong. But when the Charter Stones are broken and only the Abhorsen is left to stand against the evil, disaster looms. Meanwhile, those who live in the neighboring Ancelstierre for the most part believe in science, not magic.

🎗 *Sabriel*. New York: HarperCollins, 1995. 292p. ISBN: 0060273224; 0064471837pa. AUD

The daughter of Abhorsen, the necromancer who uses magical bells to make sure the dead stay dead, Sabriel was born in the Old Kingdom but schooled in the modern world of Ancelstierre. She doesn't know it, but in the Old Kingdom the ordered workings of Charter Magic are beset by the forces of wild Free Magic, and a wielder of those forces has lured her father into Death. Now, with only some small training as a Charter Mage, she must go back to find a way to save him and, if she can, the Old Kingdom. (ALAN; BBYA)

🎗 *Lirael: Daughter of the Clayr*. New York: HarperCollins, 2001. 487p. ISBN: 0060278234; 0060590165pa. AUD

Lirael is a Daughter of the Clayr, the people of the Old Kingdom who have the Sight. When she never develops the gift of glimpsing the future, she becomes instead a Charter Mage librarian and joins with Sabriel's son, Prince Sameth, in a race to prevent the destruction of the Old Kingdom. (BBYA; Australia Science Fiction Achievement Award)

Abhorsen. New York: HarperCollins, 2003. 385p. ISBN: 0060278250; 060594985pa. AUD

Abhorsen-in-Waiting Lirael and Prince Sameth, a Wallmaker, continue their desperate quest to confront and bind the evil Free Magic that seeks to annihilate not just the Old Kingdom, but also the entire world.

Across the Wall. New York: Eos, 2005. 305p. ISBN: 0060747137.

This collection of short stories features "Nicholas Sayre and the Creature in the Case." Nicholas has spent months in Ancelstierre recovering from his encounter with the Destroyer chronicled in *Abhorsen*. When his uncle, the Chief Minister, sends him to the secluded home of a family who could be a political allies, he finds something from the Old Kingdom that is harmless only as long as no magic comes near it.

Pullman, Philip

His Dark Materials Series. **New York: Knopf. (1st American Editions.)** *MJS* **AUD LP BRAILLE**
Many worlds coexist, some similar to commonplace reality, some as different as Earth and Middle Earth. Lyra and Will are called on to do everything in their power to keep all of the many worlds from destroying each other.

🖋 *The Golden Compass*. **1996. 399p. ISBN: 0679879242; 0440238137pa.**
Lyra lives in an alternate England. As everyone in her world does, Lyra has a daemon, a creature that is like an animal form of her spirit. She and her daemon, Pan, live at Jordan College and are being raised by Oxford professors. Lyra's far fonder of investigating things for herself than studying. Her curiosity sets her on a path of adventure, armed with a golden compass that will answer her questions, if only she can learn how to read it. On her journey, she encounters an armored bear, a flock of witches, and a diabolical plot: a group of scientists are kidnapping children and using them and their daemons in horrifying experiments. (ALAN; BBYA; Carnegie Medal)

🖋 *The Subtle Knife*. **1997. 326p. ISBN: 0679879250; 0440238145pa.**
Will Parry, a boy from contemporary Oxford, is trying to protect his fragile mother and to find his missing father. He stumbles into the haunted world of Cittagazze, which is full of soul-eaters, and meets Lyra. Together, they practice a perilous method of navigating between different worlds, while their search for Will's father continues until the fate of many worlds rests in Will's knife-wielding hands. (BBYA)

🖋 *The Amber Spyglass*. **2000. 518p. ISBN: 0679879269; 0440238153pa.**
As soon as Lyra and Will return to Lyra's world, she is kidnapped. Will is determined to rescue her, but a pair of winged companions who want to take him to Lord Asriel hinder him. Meanwhile, two factions of the Church are racing to reach Lyra first. This puts her in more danger than ever, as she is being held captive by Mrs. Culter, who has never before had Lyra's best interests at heart. Lyra must find a way to escape and venture into the land of the dead and beyond to halt the destruction of the worlds. (ALAN; BBYA; Whitbread Award)

Lyra's Oxford. **2003. 49p. ISBN: 0375828192.**
Lyra is lured into the streets of Oxford by a witch's daemon that has his heart set on murder.

The Finest in the Realm

The Chronicles of Prydain by Lloyd Alexander

The Curse of Chalion, **The Paladin of Souls**, and **The Hallowed Hunt** by Lois McMaster Bujold

The Dark Is Rising Sequence by Susan Cooper

The Earthsea Cycle by Ursula K. Le Guin

The Song of Ice and Fire by George R. R. Martin

The Riddle-Master of Hed Trilogy by Patricia A. McKillip

The Blue Sword and **The Hero and the Crown** by Robin McKinley

The Abhorsen Trilogy by Garth Nix

His Dark Materials by Philip Pullman

The Lord of the Rings by J. R. R. Tolkien

References

"Lloyd Alexander." *Contemporary Authors Online,* Infotrac Galegroup Database (accessed July 1, 2005).

Tolkien, J. R. R. *The Tolkien Reader.* New York: Ballantine Books, 1966.

Wintel, Justin, and Emma Fisher. *The Pied Pipers: Interviews with the Influential Creators of Children's Literature.* New York: Paddington Press, 1975.

Chapter 3

Myth and Legend Fantasy

When the gods and goddesses of ancient times weave their way into the lives of mortals when King Arthur or Robin Hood strides into the story, then the novel is myth or legend fantasy. The mythic fantasy listed here focuses on the novels that retell well-known myths in addition to those that are inspired by figures and events from that mythology but then take the stories in a new direction.

Mythic Fantasy

World Mythologies

Mythology from around the world has served as a muse to authors who create their own versions of these well-known tales. Some are retellings in novel form, and some are new creations featuring the mythic characters and settings.

Greek

Bradley, Marion Zimmer

> *The Firebrand*. **New York: Simon & Schuster, 1987. 608p. Reissued by Roc in 2003. ISBN: 0451459245pa. [Adult]** S
> The god Apollo bestows the gift of prophecy upon Kassandra, the daughter of King Priam. She rejects him, and he curses her so that no one will believe her prophecies, even when she warns of the fall of Troy.

Cooney, Caroline

🏺 *Goddess of Yesterday*. New York: Delacorte, 2002. 263p. ISBN: 0385729456; 0440229308pa. *JS* AUD

The capture of six-year-old Anaxandra leads to her donning the identities of two different Greek princesses to survive. Calling on her goddess, Medusa, for help, she ends up in Troy just before the war begins, facing decisions that will shape her destiny and that of those around her. (ALAN)

Gellis, Roberta

Bull God. Riverdale, NY: Baen, 2000. ISBN: 0671578685pa. [Adult] *S*

When she is thirteen, Ariadne's parents, the rulers of Crete, dedicate her to the service of the god Dionysus. But she returns home when her mother gives birth to a monster, part-child and part-bull. Dionysus warns Ariadne to kill him or disaster will befall Crete. Ariadne cannot bring herself to commit murder and helps raise the child who will grow up to be the Minotaur.

Geras, Adele

Troy. San Diego: Harcourt, 2001. 340p. Reissued in 2002. ISBN: 0152045708pa. *S* 📖

The Trojan War has raged for ten years, and the people trapped in the city under siege have grown weary of the fighting. This is especially so for the sisters Xanthe, nurse to Hector's newborn son, and Marpessa, a handmaid to Helen. Eros and Aphrodite, bored with the war, meddle in the sisters' lives, beginning a series of extraordinary events that play out against the backdrop of the doomed city.

Ithaka. Orlando, FL: Harcourt, 2006. ISBN: 0152056033. *S*

Years after the conclusion of the Trojan War, Penelope still waits in Ithaka for Odysseus. The servant girl Klymene waits with her, secretly nurturing romantic feelings for Penelope's son, Telemachus. While the gods wreak havoc through Penelope's many suitors, Klymene's heart aches as well, and chaos may be all there is to welcome Odysseus home.

Kindl, Patrice

Lost in the Labyrinth. Boston: Houghton Mifflin, 2002. 194p. ISBN: 061816684X; 0618394028pa. *MJ* 📖

Princess Xenodice, younger sister of the heir Princess Ariadne, cares for animals and for her half-brother, the Minotaur of Crete, and she yearns for the love of Icarus. Each year, Athens sends sons and daughters as a tribute to Crete, not as sacrifices to the Minotaur who lives in the Labyrinth under the palace, but as recompense for murdering the queen's oldest son. This year, Thesus arrives on Crete with plans to murder the Minotaur. Xenodice valiantly tries to protect her brother but is assailed by betrayal from unexpected sources.

Napoli, Donna Jo

The Great God Pan. New York: Random House, 2003. 194p. ISBN: 0385327773; 0440229251pa. *JS*

Pan, the nature god who is half-god and half-goat, thoroughly enjoys the physical pleasures of life without giving them much thought until he meets Ipheginia, the bastard daughter of Helen of Troy. He falls in love with her and begins his own search for truth.

🏵 *Sirena*. **New York: Scholastic, 1998. 210p. Reissued in 2000. ISBN: 0590383892pa. *JS* BRAILLE** 📖
When Sirena, a mermaid who loves to sing with her sisters, discovers that their song lures sailors to their death, she vows to live in solitude on the deserted island Lemnos. Falling in love with a marooned sailor makes keeping her vow much more difficult and puts them both in danger. (BBYA)

Riordan, Rick

Percy Jackson and the Olympians. **New York: Hyperion.** *MJ*

🏵 *The Lightning Thief*. **2005. 377p. ISBN: 0786856297lb; 0786838655pa. AUD LP**
Perseus Jackson is a troubled teen who gets kicked out of one school after another until his mother sends him to Camp Half-Blood Hill, where he learns that, like all the campers, he is half-human and half-god. As he adjusts to being the son of Poseidon, he stumbles upon a plot to start a war between the gods that he and his friends must find a way to avert. (ALAN; BBYA)

The Sea of Monsters. **2006. 288p. ISBN: 0786856866. AUD**
After helping save the world, Percy thinks seventh grade seems rather quiet until he learns that the magical borders that keep Half-Blood Hill safe have been poisoned by an unknown enemy. To keep the camp from being destroyed, Percy and his friends must find the Golden Fleece and return before the end of summer.

Spinner, Stephanie

Quiver. **New York: Knopf, 2002. 192p. ISBN: 0375814892; 0440238196pa. *JS***
Although abandoned at birth, Atalanta was saved by a she-bear and raised by hunters. She grew to be a shrewd huntress and the fastest runner in the land. Thankful to Artemis for saving her life, she vows to remain chaste to serve the goddess. When her father, Iasus, summons her to marry and produce heirs, since he has no other children, Atalanta devises a test she hopes will deter her suitors: Any man wishing to wed her must first beat her in a race.

Quicksilver. **New York: Knopf, 2005. 229. ISBN: 0375826386. *JS***
Hermes, whose winged sandals make him the ideal messenger for his father Zeus, escorts the dead to the underworld and meddles in the lives of mortals. As he runs his errands, he witnesses key moments in the lives of Persephone and Demeter, Perseus and Medusa, Paris, and Odysseus.

Tarr, Judith

***Queen of the Amazons*. New York: Tor, 2004. 320p. Reissued in 2005. ISBN: 0765303965pa. [Adult]** *S*
When Hippolyta, Queen of the Amazons, hears the seer proclaim that her infant daughter is soulless and must be destroyed, she refuses to kill her. Assigning the baby's care to Selene, both the warrior queen and the nursemaid watch the girl grow to one who could not dress or feed herself but who could ride and hunt like no other. When word of Alexander the Great reaches them, the child escapes to find him, and the queen and Selene can do nothing but follow her to his camp.

Ursu, Anne

***The Shadow Thieves*. New York: Atheneum, 2006. 384p. ISBN: 1416905871.**
Thirteen-year-old Charlotte Mielswetzski and Zee, her cousin from England, realize that something sinister is happening when the same plague that struck the children in England is now running rampant in America as well. When they learn that Philonecron, a son of the Underworld, is stealing children's shadows, they journey to Hades to stop him.

Yolen, Jane, and Robert Harris

<u>The Young Heroes Series</u>. New York: HarperCollins. *M*
Each novel relates the youthful adventures of famous characters from Greek mythology.

> ***Odysseus in the Serpent Maze*. 2001. 248p. Reissued by Trophy in 2002. ISBN: 0064408477pa.**
> Thirteen-year-old Odysseus longs for adventure and gets the chance to test his mettle when Cretans kidnap him. With his friend Mentor and his new companions, spoiled Princess Helen and her bold cousin Penelope, Odysseus escapes only to find he must negotiate a way through the labyrinth and past a multiheaded serpent.

> ***Hippolyta and the Curse of the Amazons*. 2002. 248p. (Out of Print)**
> Teenaged Hippolyta, an Amazon princess, relishes the thrill of the hunt and her battle training, but it takes all of her skill to carry out the task her mother has given her. In violation of Amazon law, her mother refuses to kill her second-born son. Secretly, she entrusts the infant to Hippolyta and bids her bear him to safety.

> ***Atalanta and the Arcadian Beast*. 2003. 245p. Reissued by Trophy in 2004. ISBN: 0064409805pa.**
> Atalanta, an infant abandoned on a hillside, has been raised by a hunter. After a mysterious beast kills her protector, the twelve-year-old Atalanta sets out in search of the beast, determined to mete out the death the beast deserves.

> ***Jason and the Gorgon's Blood*. 2004. 246p. ISBN: 0060294523.**
> Jason, future leader of the Argonauts, grows up under the tutelage of the wise centaur Chiron. When the evil centaur Nesseus steals the Gorgon's blood from Chiron, Jason and five other apprentices race against time to thwart the thief and save the kingdom of Ioclus.

Celtic

Billingsley, Franny

🎖 *The Folk Keeper*. **New York: Atheneum, 1999. 162p. ISBN: 0689828764lb; 0689844611pa.** <u>*MJS*</u> **BRAILLE LP**
Corinna is never cold, always knows exactly what time it is, and has silvery hair that grows two inches every night. An orphan, she disguises herself as a boy so that she can become the Folk-Keeper of Rhysbridge, sitting hour after hour in the dark cellar, drawing off the anger of the fierce, gremlin-like Folk. She does this until Lord Merton summons her to the vast island estate of Cliffsend, where she is to be both Folk-Keeper and, inexplicably, a member of the family. (Boston Globe Award)

Farrell, S. L.

<u>**The Cloudmages**</u>. **New York: Daw. [Adult]** <u>*S*</u>
In the realm of Innish Thuaidh, magic once thrived. Mage-lights danced in the night skies, and Cloudmages drew down the power of those lights and stored it in spell stones. When the mages grew corrupt, the mage-lights disappeared. Then came the day seventeen-year old Jenna, who led a tranquil life caring for her sheep and crops, was beckoned out into the night by the reappearing mage-lights. They led her to a special stone, one that could shift the balance of power in all the regions of the kingdom.

> *Holder of Lightning*. **2003. 494p. ISBN: 0756401305; 0756401526pa.**
>
> *Mage of Clouds*. **2004. 514p. ISBN: 0756401690; 0756402557pa.**
>
> *Heir of Stone*. **2005. 464p. ISBN: 0756402549; 0756403219pa.**

Marillier, Juliet

<u>**The Sevenwaters Trilogy**</u>. **New York: Tor. [Adult]** <u>*S*</u>
In ancient Ireland, when the Fair Folk flitted through the forest and magic could protect or harm, the children and grandchildren of Lord Colum of Sevenwaters become embroiled in the sorcerous and military threats to their homeland.

> 🎖 *Daughter of the Forest*. **2000. 400p. ISBN: 031284879X; 0765343436pa.** (Alex)
>
> *Son of the Shadows*. **2001. 462p. ISBN: 0312848803; 0765343266pa.**
>
> *Child of the Prophecy*. **2002. 528p. ISBN: 0312848811; 0765345013pa.**

<u>**Wolfskin**</u> and <u>**Foxmask**</u>. *See* Chapter Seven 7, "Fantasy Romance."

Pattou, Edith.

Hero's Song and *Fire Arrow*. *See* Chapter 2, "Epic Fantasy."

Chinese Mythology

Bass, L. G.

Outlaws of Moonshadow Marsh. New York: Hyperion. *MJ*
In a land inspired by ancient China, the forces of good gather to battle the Lord of the Dead.

Sign of the Qin. 2004. 384p. ISBN: 0786819189lb. LP
The Emperor Han serves the Lord of the Dead, but his infant son, Prince Zong, was born with the sign of the Qin, which marks him as a Starlord and an enemy of Han. To protect the prince, the Lord of Heaven intervenes and appoints the trickster Monkey and the Tattooed Monk to be his guardians. They must help him escape and grow safely to manhood while being pursued by bandits and the demon hoards of the Lord of the Dead.

Napoli, Donna Jo

Bound. New York: Atheneum, 2004. 186p. ISBN: 0689861753; 0689861788pa. *JS* LP
In this retelling of Cinderella, after the death of her father, Xing Xing lives with her stepmother and half-sister in the family cave in the northern province of Shaanxi during the Ming dynasty. When her sister's feet become infected from being bound, Xing Xing is sent to seek help from a traveling herbalist. As she experiences the world around her in new ways, she develops the courage to use the treasures passed down from her mother to create a life of her own.

Yep, Laurence

The Tiger's Apprentice Series. New York: HarperCollins. *M*
Contemporary teens from San Francisco's Chinatown are drafted to help protect a crucial magical artifact.

The Tiger's Apprentice. 2004. 184p. ISBN: 0060010134. LP
Twelve-year-old Tom lives in San Francisco and studies magic with his Chinese grandmother. She dies trying to protect a coral rose. A dragon, a golden monkey, and a flying rat join Tom as they attempt to retrieve the stolen coral.

Tiger's Blood. 2005. 226p. ISBN: 0060010169; 0060010185pa.
Tom and his friends are charged with keeping the coral, which is actually a phoenix egg, safe. They escape to the underworld realm of the dragons to guard it.

Tiger Magic. 2006. ISBN: 0060010193.
The phoenix egg that Tom was guarding has hatched prematurely, and it's up to Tom and his mythological companions to protect the baby bird.

Other Myth-Related Fantasy

Novels with a decidedly mythic tone and those that combine elements from many different traditions are grouped here.

Bruchac, Joseph

Wabi: A Hero's Tale. **New York: Dial Books, 2006. 208p. ISBN: 0803730985.** <u>*MJ*</u>

Wabi, a fledgling great-horned owl, encounters adventures very early in life, beginning when his brother knocks him out of the nest while a hungry fox prowls the area. His great-grandmother swoops in to save him, keeping him safe as he grows, and sharing with him the secret that the two of them can communicate in the language of humans, owls and all the animals of the forest. As Wabi explores his surroundings each day, he becomes fascinated with Dojihla, a beautiful girl who lives in the nearby Abenaki village. When his great-grandmother informs him that he cannot only understand human language but also transform into a human, he shape-shifts, hoping to win Dojihla's heart, unaware of the dangerous quest that awaits him.

Gaiman, Neil

🦋 *American Gods*. **New York: Morrow, 2001. 465p. ISBN: 0380973650; 0380789035pa. [Adult]** <u>*S*</u> **AUD**

Shadow, released a few days early from his three-year prison sentence because of the untimely death of his wife, agrees to be a bodyguard for the mysterious Wednesday. Wednesday, it turns out, is the Old Norse god Odin, who came to America with the Viking settlers. He and his fellow gods from around the world are being displaced by the modern American gods of television, money, and technology. He is organizing a war against the new gods, and Shadow is central to his plans, but he doesn't count on Shadow having a mind of his own. (Bram Stoker Award; Hugo Award; Locus Award; Nebula Award)

🦋 *Anansi Boys*. **New York: Morrow, 2005. 336p. ISBN: 006051518X. [Adult]** <u>*S*</u> **AUD LP**

In this companion to *American Gods,* Fat Charlie (who isn't fat) returns from England to his hometown in Florida to attend his father's funeral, only to discover that his father, Mr. Nancy, was in fact the trickster god Anansi. He also learns that he has a brother who inherited all of the family's supernatural tendencies. When Spider turns up on his doorstep in England, Fat Charlie's well-ordered life crumbles into chaos. (Alex; BBYA)

Paver, Michelle

The Chronicles of Ancient Darkness. **New York: Katherine Tegen Books. (1st American Editions.)** <u>*MJ*</u>

In ancient times, the people dwelt in clans throughout the primeval forest, drawing their sustenance with respect from the natural world around them, until the Soul Eaters, evil mages who were defeated once, menace the clans again.

Wolf Brother. **2004. 295p. ISBN: 0060728256; 0060728272pa. AUD**
Twelve-year-old Torak witnesses a bear possessed by a demon maul his father. His dying father sends him away, but Torak hears the bear murder him. Torak makes his way in the forest alone until he comes upon a wolf-pup whose mother and littermates were killed when the river flooded. They bond, and the wolf becomes Torak's Guide—for Torak is not just any boy, as he discovers when the Wolf Clan captures him. The clan believes he is the prophesied one called the Listener. Torak escapes with the help of Renn, a Wolf Clan girl. Together they brave the elements and the workings of malevolent magic to save the forest from the demon.

Spirit Walker. **2006. 368p. Katherine Tegen Books. ISBN: 0060728280.**
When an insidious sickness seeps into the lives of all the clans, Torak ventures into the Deep Woods in an attempt to find a cure. Soon his friend, shaman-in-training Renn, and his beloved Wolf join him, and they journey to the sea, searching for the Mage of the Seal Clan, who could have the knowledge that will heal those struck down.

Yolen, Jane

The Great Alta Saga. New York: Tor. [Adult] *JS*
The presentation of myths, legends, and scholarly debates intertwines to create a world where women have an uncanny power that will help them overthrow the usurper and win back their land.

Sister Light, Sister Dark. **1988. 244p. Reissued by Starscape in 2003. ISBN: 0765343576pa.**

White Jenna. **1989. 265p. Reissued by Starscape in 2004. ISBN: 0765343584pa.**

The One-Armed Queen. **1998. 332p. Reissued by Starscape in 2004. ISBN: 0765343592pa.**

Fantasy Featuring Characters from Legend

From Shahrazad to King Arthur, literature is brimming with figures from legend, magical and otherwise. Many authors either retell the legends in novel form, or create new stories featuring the legendary figures and those related to them.

Arthurian Fantasy

Barron, T. A.

The Lost Years of Merlin. New York: Philomel. *MJ* AUD
Before Merlin was the aged wizard who guided Arthur to his kingship and beyond, he was a young boy who had to learn the ways of magic.

***The Lost Years of Merlin*. 1996. 326p. ISBN: 0399230181; 0441009301pa.**
A strange boy washes up on a rocky shore of ancient Wales, with no name, no memory, no identity. He undertakes a dangerous journey to the enchanted land of Fincayra to discover his true destiny.

***The Seven Songs of Merlin*. 1997. 306p. ISBN: 039923019X; 0441009476pa.**
Now a teenager, Merlin is still on the Isle of Fincayra and wanders from place to place playing the magic harp that brings new life to the land. Before he can complete his task, however, his desire to see his mother causes him to teleport to her. When the death-shadow meant for him falls on her, Merlin embarks on a quest to cure her, striving to master the Seven Songs of Wisdom.

***The Fires of Merlin*. 1998. 261p. ISBN: 0399230203; 0441009573pa.**
Merlin is beginning to understand and control his powers when Valdearg the Dragon threatens Fincayra. Merlin is recruited to help. But when his magic is stolen, he must use his wits to try to defeat the forces moving against him.

3

***The Mirror of Merlin*. 1999. 245p. ISBN: 0399234551; 0441009654pa.**
Teleporting with two friends, Merlin enters the Haunted Marsh and battles an array of enemies on his way to look in the magic mirror and glimpse his future.

***The Wings of Merlin*. 2000. 352p. ISBN: 039923456X; 0441009883pa.**
All who dwell on the isle of Fincayra are in danger as the evil forces of the spirit world prepare their invasion. Merlin must convince the various beings who dwell on the Isle to join forces to survive.

Borchardt, Alice

The Tales of Guinevere. New York: Del Rey. [Adult] $\underline{S}$
Hunted by Merlin as he attempts to prevent a future in which Arthur and Guinevere are wed, the young princess Guinevere is sent to the shores of Scotland to be raised by dragons. But even they cannot keep her safe. As she grows to womanhood surrounded by magic, she must learn to draw on her own power to defeat Merlin.

***The Dragon Queen*. 2001. 473p. Reissued in 2003. ISBN: 0345444000pa.**

***The Raven Warrior*. 2003. 470p. Reissued in 2004. ISBN: 0345444027pa.**

Bradley, Marion Zimmer

🎗 ***The Mists of Avalon*. New York: Knopf. 1982. 876p. Reissued by Ballantine in 2000. ISBN: 0345441184; 0345350499pa. [Adult] $\underline{S}$ AUD BRAILLE VID (Locus Award)**

This novel reimagines tales of King Arthur and Camelot, following the perspectives of the women whose hearts beat in the legend. It begins with the young and pretty Igraine, who becomes Arthur's mother. She was reared on the priestess-run Isle of Avalon and sent into a loveless marriage to strengthen the bond between the nobles in Britain and the rulers of the Holy Isle. The narrative moves to her daughter Morgaine, who cared for her little brother Arthur but then was sent to Avalon to learn its secrets and train to be its high priestess. Morgause, Gwenifair, and Nymue each have a critical role to play as the retelling rides down the road to the final battle of King Arthur.

The Early Avalon Series. New York: Viking. [Adult] _S_
Before King Arthur, before Avalon faded into the mists, priestesses ruled in Avalon and kept the old ways in their worship of the Goddess and care of her land.

> **_The Forest House_. 1994. 416p. Reissued by Roc in 1995. ISBN: 0451454243pa.**

> **_Lady of Avalon_. 1997. 460p. Reissued by Roc in 1998. ISBN: 0451456521pa. AUD**

> **_Priestess of Avalon_ (with Diana L. Paxson). 2001. 394p. Reissued by Roc in 2002. ISBN: 0451456521pa. LP**

> **_Marion Zimmer Bradley's Ancestors of Avalon_ (by Diana L. Paxson). 2004. 363p. ISBN: 0670033146; 0451460286pa.**

Clement-Davies, David

> **_The Telling Pool_. New York: Harry N. Abrams, 2005. 360p. ISBN: 0810957582.** _MJ_
> Rhodri, the son of a falconer who has followed his master on King Richard's Third Crusade, comes across a mystical pool deep in the forest. It reveals episodes of Arthurian legend and the crusade, leading Rhodri to take up a quest to save his captured father.

Crossley-Holland, Kevin

The Arthur Trilogy. New York: Scholastic. _JS_ **AUD**
As the thirteenth century dawns in England, Arthur, the second son of a manor lord, longs to become a knight and take part in the crusades, little knowing how much his life parallels the legendary king whose name he shares.

> ✿ **_The Seeing Stone_. 2001. 342p. Reissued by in 2002. ISBN: 0439263271pa.**
> In the England of 1199 lives a young lad named Arthur whose life is changed completely when his friend, Merlin, gives him a magical stone in which he can see the life of the once and future king. (ALAN; Smarties Bronze Award)

> **_At the Crossing Places_. 2002. 394p. ISBN: 0439265983; 0439265991pa.**
> Young Arthur's dreams are coming true as he is sent to be a squire-in-training to Lord Stephen. While he learns to perform his duties, he seeks to discover more about his birth mother and begins a gentle courtship with the feisty Winnie. Mysteries abound as his life continues to parallel that of King Arthur.

King of the Middle March. 2004. 409p. ISBN: 0439266009; 0439266017pa.

At last Arthur's dearest desire is fulfilled, and he and Lord Stephen join a Crusade. They travel to Venice where ships for the journey have been built, but internal bickering and papal politics turn an adventure into a disaster. After two years of warfare in his life and in the Seeing Stone, Arthur returns home with a new perspective to face the challenges waiting for him in England.

Hemingway, Amanda

The Sangreal Trilogy. New York: Ballantine. (1st American Edition.) *IS*

A legendary chalice haunts the visions of young Nathan Ward, so that he must seek out the meaning of his dreams.

The Greenstone Grail. 2005. 360p. ISBN: 0345460782; 0345460790pa.

When Annie flees with her infant son, Nathan, she winds up in a small English village at the doorstep of Bartlemy Goodman, who has secrets of his own. As Nathan grows up under his care, he lives an ordinary life until the age of eleven when he starts to have visions of an emerald-encrusted chalice that lead him to people of another world in desperate need of his help.

The Sword of Straw. 2006. 336p. ISBN: 0345460804pa.

Now thirteen-years-old, Nathan has learned to control his ability to dream himself to other worlds. His task is to gather the Grail relics and the Sword of Straw which lurks cursed in a world where it threatens the lives of all involved with it. Nathan must find a way to retrieve the sword before the others who are searching for it as well.

McKenzie, Nancy

The Arthurian Trilogy. New York: Del Rey. [Adult] *S*

The tales of Guinevere, Lancelot, Galahad, Tristan, and Essyllte are reimagined as successive sagas of Camelot and Britain.

Queen of Camelot. 2002. 640p. ISBN: 0345445872pa.

Grail Prince. 2003. 510p. ISBN: 0345456483pa.

Prince of Dreams. 2004. 416p. ISBN: 0345456505pa.

Miles, Rosalind

The Guenevere Trilogy. New York: Crown. [Adult] *S*

Guenevere is queen in her own right, a warrior and a servant of the Goddess. She chooses Arthur, the unknown son of Uther Pendragon, as her consort. Together they rule Camelot.

Guenevere: Queen of the Summer Country. 1998. 424p. Reissued in 2000. ISBN: 0609806505pa.

> *Knight of the Sacred Lake*. 2000. 417p. Reissued in 2001. ISBN: 0609806505pa.

> *The Child of the Holy Grail*. 2001. 433p. Reissued by Three Rivers Press in 2002. ISBN: 0609809563pa.

The Tristan and Isolde Trilogy. New York: Crown. [Adult] S

Tristan is a knight of King Arthur's Round Table, and Isolde is the daughter of the Queen of Ireland, pledged to wed King Mark of Cornwall. When Tristan and Isolde first meet, they fall in love, but their paths are indeed star-crossed.

> *Isolde: Queen of the Western Isle*. 2002. 349p. Reissued by Three Rivers Press in 2003. ISBN: 1400047862pa.

> *Maid of the White Hands*. 2003. 320p. ISBN: 0609609610; 1400081548pa.

> *The Lady of the Sea*. 2004. 356p. ISBN: 0609609629; 0307209857pa.

Morris, Gerald

The Squire's Tales. Boston: Houghton Mifflin. *MJ*

These tales feature the adventures of a variety of knights from King Arthur's Round Table, told from a slightly different perspective than the most well-known tales.

> *The Squire's Tale*. 1998. 212p. ISBN: 0395869595; 0440228239pa. LP
> Terence, an orphan, lives a quiet life with the hermit who has taken him in, until a mischievous sprite leads him to Gawain, King Arthur's young nephew. Although Terence knows little about the tasks required to be a squire, he joins the would-be knight on his quest. Along the way, he is amazed at the manifestation of his own magical abilities.

> *The Squire, His Knight, and His Lady*. 1999. 232p. ISBN: 0395912113. LP
> During the Christmas feast at Camelot, a giant green knight bursts in and issues a life-threatening challenge. Sir Gawain answers the call, and once again he and Terence embark on a dangerous quest.

> *The Savage Damsel and the Dwarf*. 2000. 213p. ISBN: 0395971268; 0618196811pa. LP
> Sixteen-year-old Lady Lynet lives in the family castle with her older sister, the Lyonesse. Their home is under siege as the ever-watchful Red Knight battles all of the Lyonesse's suitors. Lady Lynet escapes by night to fetch help from the knights of King Arthur's court, but she is not sure he will grant her aid because of the enmity between her deceased father and the king.

> *Parsifal's Page*. 2001. 232p. ISBN: 0618055096; 061843237Xpa.
> Piers longs for the glamour of French court life and attaches himself as a page to the first knight he finds. When that does not work out well, he agrees to tutor the uncouth Parsifal in courtesy, but he discovers that he is the one with much to learn.

***The Ballad of Sir Dinadan*. 2003. 245p. ISBN: 0618190996; 0618548947pa.**
Sir Dinadan, younger brother of Sir Tristram, would rather be a troubadour than a knight. But his father forces knighthood on him, and he rides out to make his way to King Arthur's court.

***The Princess, the Crone, and the Dung Cart Knight*. 2004. 310p. ISBN: 0618378235.**
Sarah seeks revenge on the knight who murdered her mother. During the course of her quest, she witnesses the kidnapping of Queen Guinevere. She joins Sir Gawain and Squire Terrence as they search for a way to rescue the queen and learn the grim consequences of vengeance.

***The Lioness and Her Knight*. 2005. 352p. ISBN: 0618507728.**
Luneta lives in Orkney and is so bored that she would do almost anything for the chance to visit Camelot. Her parents give her permission to travel to the castle of her cousin as long as the knight Ywain is there to protect her. Along the way they encounter Rhience, a former knight who now plays the fool, a lioness, and the enchantress Morgan Le Fey, who teaches her the ways of magic.

***The Quest of the Fair Unknown*. 2006. 264p. ISBN: 0618631526.**
Seventeen-year-old Beaufils has lived his entire life with is mother in their quiet forest cottage. After her death, he ventures forth into the world as she wished him to do, heading for King Arthur's court and hoping to find the father he has never known. He arrives as the Knights of the Round Table are preparing for their Grail quests. He joins Sir Galahad and company, innocently subduing evil and helping his friends while he continues his own search.

Paxson, Diana L.

The Early Avalon Series. *See* Bradley, Marion Zimmer.

Springer, Nancy

I Am Mordred*. New York: Philomel. 1998. 1984p. Reissued by Firebird in 2002. ISBN: 0698118413pa. *MJ
From the day of his birth, Mordred, the son of King Arthur and his sister Morgan Le Fay, had a great doom shadowing his life. Merlin foretold that he would kill his father. As Mordred grows up and journeys to Camelot, he wrestles with his fate, hoping to find a way to avert his destiny. (BBYA)

***I Am Morgan Le Fay*. New York: Philomel. 2001. 227p. Reissued by Firebird in 2002. ISBN: 0698119746pa. *MJ* BRAILLE**
At age six, Morgan's father, the Duke of Cornwall, was ripped from her life when Uther Pendragon had him murdered. She lost her mother when that same king claimed Igraine to be his wife. When Pendragon died, Morgan and her sister were sheltered by their nurse until the priestesses of Avalon summoned Morgan to their Isle. There she learns to be a great sorceress and must make a choice regarding the fate of her half-brother, Arthur.

Stewart, Mary

The Arthurian Saga. New York: Morrow. All reissued by HarperCollins in 2003. [Adult] _S_ **BRAILLE**
These novels retell the Arthurian saga from Merlin's perspective.

The Crystal Cave. 1970. 521p. Reissue ISBN: 0060548258pa.

The Hollow Hills. 1973. 499p. Reissue ISBN: 0060548266pa.

The Last Enchantment. 1979. 538p. Reissue ISBN: 0060548274pa.

The Wicked Day. 1983. 453p. Reissue ISBN: 0060548282pa.

Sutcliff, Rosemary.

The Arthurian Legends. New York, Dutton. _MJ_
The author retells the most famous of the Arthurian legends, drawing on Mallory's *Le Morte d'Arthur*.

Tristan and Iseult. 1971. 150p. Reissued by Sunburst in 1991. ISBN: 0374479828pa.

The Light beyond the Forest: The Quest for the Holy Grail. 1979. 143p. Reissued by Puffin in 1994. ISBN: 0140371508pa.

The Sword and the Circle: King Arthur and the Knights of the Round Table. 1981. 260p. Reissued by Puffin in 1994. ISBN: 0140371494pa.

The Road to Camlann: The Death of King Arthur. 1982. Reissued by Puffin in 1994. ISBN: 0140371478pa.

Vande Velde, Vivian

The Book of Mordred. Boston: Houghton Mifflin, 2005. 342p. ISBN: 061850754X. _JS_
Sir Mordred of Camelot deeply affected the lives of three women who loved him: the widow Alayna, the sorceress Nimue, and the magically gifted Kiera. When Alayna seeks help in Camelot after her five-year-old daughter Kiera is kidnapped, Mordred comes to her aid and rescues Kiera. Later, as Nimue tries to live a quiet life of a healer under the shadow of Merlin's disappearance, she cannot stop her life from being entwined with Merlin's. Finally, when Kiera, who has always adored Mordred, reaches the age of fifteen, she sees the fracturing of Camelot and begins to doubt the knight who saved her.

Profile of Elizabeth Wein

Photo by Tim Gatland

Born October 2, 1964, in New York, New York, Elizabeth grew up loving books and wanting to be a writer. Although she spent her early childhood in New York City, the family moved to Jamaica when she was seven. Her grandmother sent her books monthly, and this nurtured her love of story and her desire to write. Now she lives in Scotland with her husband and two children (*Contemporary Authors Online*, Infotrac Galegroup Database; www.elizabethwein.com).

Interview with Elizabeth Wein

Conducted via e-mail January 19–March 8, 2006

SF: What originally inspired you to reimagine a portion of the Arthurian legend for *The Winter Prince*?

EW: I came to Arthurian legend when I was fourteen, via three books, all recommended about the same time by three different people: my best friend, my grandfather, and my aunt, in that order. The books were, respectively, Susan Cooper's *Over Sea, Under Stone*; Mary Stewart's *The Crystal Cave*; and T. H. White's *The Once and Future King*. I had there three very different approaches to Arthurian legend, and as I read further I found myself picking out bits and pieces of the various retellings and putting them together to form my own storyline. You could perhaps say that I took the original character of Mordred from T. H. White's *The Once and Future King*; the setting of post-Roman Britain from Mary Stewart; and the idea of Arthur and Guinevere having children of their own from Susan Cooper (Bran in *Silver on the Tree*).

About a year later, I read Alan Garner's *The Owl Service* and through it discovered *The Mabinogion*, a collection of medieval Welsh tales which include a good many Arthurian stories in their own right. I, however, became particularly enraptured with one of the four "native" tales that had nothing to do with Arthur: the "Fourth Branch" of *The Mabinogion*, the story of Lleu Llaw Gyffes. He is not a "sun god" in the story, but he is closely related to the Celtic sun god Lugh, and his story is one of death and rebirth, jealousy and betrayal. It was a simple matter for my twisted, sophomoric brain to braid the story of Lleu Llaw Gyffes into the story of King Arthur, although it took ten years to turn itself into *The Winter Prince*.

I don't think it's far-fetched to say that *The Winter Prince* is, at the bottom line, a glorified piece of fan-fiction using characters from Arthurian legend and *The Mabinogion*. I've just gone back and reread the introductory description of Mordred in *The Once and Future King,* and the prototype for Medraut is right there. Not only that, it's also SO familiar to me that I recognize it as I would recognize a painting, and I suddenly know I read it over and over again too many times to count: "so fair-haired that he was almost an albino: and his bright eyes were so blue, so palely azure in their faded depths, that you could not see into them…. He had a non-commital voice, beautifully modulated—its words might have meant the opposite of what they said" (T. H. White, *The Once and Future King,* New York, Berkley Medallion Books, 1966 [1940], p. 431). My character's Welsh name, Medraut, came to me years later, from Rosemary Sutcliff's *Sword at Sunset.*

SF: Why did you move the story to Africa in the subsequent novels, and are you planning to bring the characters back to Britain?

EW: The original African thread came to the story in the summer of 1987 when I decided it would be a nice touch for Medraut to have had a "girlfriend" during his travels, and I wanted to add a tiny bit of diversity to a story that was otherwise constricted by time and place. I asked my uncle, who had lived and worked in Ethiopia for two years, if he knew of "a north African or middle Eastern country that would have been Christian in the sixth century A.D." Ethiopia, or more specifically, Aksum, was his unhesitating answer. And that is how Turunesh came to be.

I honestly can't remember why I moved the story to Africa. I think it was partly because of my longing for "diversity." But I also suspect it was strictly due to Plot Integrity; for the short story "Fire," written in the months immediately following my completion of *The Winter Prince,* I had to "get rid" of Medraut. I didn't want to kill him off, so I conveniently sent him back to Aksum. It was only later that I sent Goewin there as well.

Once I started doing research on Aksum, I had no doubt that I wanted to write a book about it. There were a lot of nice coincidences. The most detailed pieces of history from Aksum happened to occur at almost exactly the same time as the widely accepted dates for Arthur's existence.

Yes, I am bringing the characters back to Britain. The plan is that following *The Sunbird* there will be two books, *The Lion Hunter* and *The Mark of Solomon* (they will be published separately in hardback, but in paperback as a single volume), which mostly take place in Southern Arabia (modern day Yemen). These are about Telemakos. Then I envisage one more book to bring the cycle to its natural conclusion. I think this book will be called *The Sword Dance,* and it will mostly take place back in Britain. I'm writing it now.

SF: Why do you consider your stories more historical fiction than fantasy, since originally you began with Arthurian legend?

EW: I wouldn't categorically call my novels historical fiction. *Technically* that's what they are, but I stuff them so full of foreshadowing and portent and symbolism that they feel like fantasy to me. If they were set on another planet, or in a world that didn't exist—like Ellen Kushner's novels—they would be fantasy, right? But they happen to be set in *our* world, and they follow the known rules of our world, so they're historical fiction.

The book I am working on now, *The Sword Dance,* is a straight-up large-sized slice of Grail legend; but the reader won't, and shouldn't, need to know that in order to appreciate the story. In many ways *The Winter Prince* was, too. *The Sunbird* is classic in its construction as a Quest. For some reason I have this highbrow notion that it is more difficult, and therefore more satisfying, to construct my "fantasies" within the confines of the "real world." It makes me able to harbor a special secret, mad conviction that my stories are *true*. Or might have been true. That these people really might exist.

SF: What kind of research do you do before you begin a novel, and how long does that part of the process take?

EW: It does depend on the novel. For *A Coalition of Lions,* I spent about six months in the Bodleian Library, reading absolutely everything that was ever written about Aksum. Much of this was in the form of archaeological reports; I also read quite a few ancient Ethiopian manuscripts in translation, and I got to look at some real ones, too. I spent a lot of time looking at travel guides, because they are full of wonderful pictures. I even studied an Amharic phrase book. One of the neatest things I managed to do was to get permission to look at the British Museum's collection of Aksumite coins. That was exciting for me because I had never seen anything from ancient Aksum before in real life. I did finally get to go to Aksum, but this was after the books were published; my uncle called it "retro-research."

For *The Sunbird,* I hardly had to do any research at all; I'd done it when I researched *A Coalition of Lions.* Any time I needed to check a detail, I could look it up in a book I already owned or on file cards I'd already made notes on. For the new books, which are set in Yemen, I acquired a new set of travel guides.

I am obsessed with maps. I cannot write a story without a map. I cannot *think* of a story that I wrote without referring to a map. I have got a Xeroxed copy of an Ordnance Survey map of Cheshire and Derbyshire (in England) with the whole of Lleu and Medraut's final journey from *The Winter Prince* marked on it in highlighter pen; I have got detailed U.S. aeronautical charts for all of Ethiopia and southern Yemen (ancient Aksum and Himyar), as well as just about every available tourist map on the market; my chart of northern Ethiopia has got all the known Aksumite towns and roads drawn in by me. Goewin's route from Adulis to Aksum, and Telemakos's route from Aksum to Afar, were traced on these maps in careful detail. Even my short stories are all written paying close attention to geography and landscape.

I drew the maps that are in *A Coalition of Lions* and *The Sunbird.*

SF: What would you say your method of writing is (i.e., working from an outline, going where the story takes you, etc.)?

EW: I think I generally have got an outline in my head, although I rarely put it on paper. I usually do a "chapter" outline. I work with a clear idea of the climax and ending of the story, though it's always a bit of a struggle actually getting there. I'll make notes as I go along, and refer back to them when the time comes to use them.

Here's a good example of how my brain works during this process. In *The Sunbird,* when Telemakos finally comes home from his mission in the Salt Desert, I wanted his mother to be waiting at the top of the front steps for him and to greet him with the words, "Go take a bath." I wanted to set this scene this way because it echoed an earlier scene, and because it was a prosaic welcome back to the simplicity and comfort of home life after a harrowing adventure. The problem that I faced was that I could not for the life of me work out why his mother would be waiting for him *at home.* Why wouldn't she be waiting for him in her uncle's house in the port city of Adulis, where they had parted company three months earlier? Wouldn't she be *desperate* to wait for him in the first place he'd come back to? What would have made her leave Adulis and go home without Telemakos?

So I decided that she was newly pregnant and needed to travel across the mountains before the weather changed and she got bigger. In other words, her pregnancy was manufactured entirely to facilitate her one-liner, "Go take a bath." And yet within the context of the story her pregnancy makes perfect sense. A lot of details come to me this way, by accident or by structural necessity, and later become integral parts of the story.

SF: Which are your favorite characters and why?

EW: For years and years, Lleu was the darling of my heart, my shining one, much as he is Artos's in *The Winter Prince.* Originally, in my head, he was a flawless creature; his arrogant self-assurance came later, and was crafted into his character *on purpose* to make him more realistic (a happy result of this change was that it mitigated the original Medraut's foundationless hatred of him). It did not change *my* feelings about Lleu, although I think it unfairly encourages readers to sympathize with Medraut.

But you must remember that Lleu was around for fifteen years before I ever thought of Telemakos.

There is no doubt that Telemakos is my favorite. Sometimes, when people ask me how many children I have, I accidentally answer, "Three." And although I laugh and catch myself and correct it to two, I do sometimes absently think of my children as Sara, Mark, and Telemakos.

But when I was writing *The Sunbird* I did not think of him as my child: I *was* Telemakos. The whole story came to me as though out of memory. I drew on my own experiences of climbing and running and hiding as I wrote. I have never experienced anything quite like it before or since.

SF: What were your favorite books growing up and/or who were your favorite authors?

EW: I think my all-time favorite book is James Thurber's *The Thirteen Clocks*. My father first read it aloud to me when I was three. I can recite large chunks of it from memory.

Not long after that my father also read aloud to me several of Alan Garner's books, *The Weirdstone of Brisingamen* and *The Moon of Gomrath* and *Elidor*. Alan Garner is probably still my favorite author (hard to say, though). My favorites of his books are *Elidor, The Owl Service,* and *The Stone Book Quartet*.

When I was seven and lived in Jamaica, my grandmother sent me a new book every month. She sent me all the Laura Ingalls Wilder books, and *The Long Winter* is still on my top-ten list. Another book my grandmother sent me at this time which makes the top ten is *The Horse without a Head* by Paul Berna (its original title, in French, is *Le Cheval sans tête*). This is about a group of Parisian schoolchildren who get involved in a train robbery in the years immediately following World War II.

My grandmother also sent me Lloyd Alexander's *Prydain* series. My paperback copy of *The High King* has got a note scrawled inside the back cover by my eight-year-old self: "The best book I ever read." And my grandmother is responsible for introducing me to Frances Hodgson Burnett. There are at least five copies of *A Little Princess* in my house, not including two copies of *Sara Crewe,* the original, shorter version. I used to sign myself "Elizabeth Eve Sara Wein." It is not a coincidence that my daughter is named Sara!

At about ten years old I was able to go to the library on my own, and discovered Edward Eager, Elizabeth Enright, and Joan Aiken. I devoured and adored these authors again and again, yet except for *Nightbirds on Nantucket,* I never owned a single copy of any of their books until I was an adult.

My father gave me a beautifully bound edition of J. R. R. Tolkien's <u>The Lord of the Rings</u> for my eleventh birthday. Over the next three years, I became utterly obsessed with this series, and even now I can see echoes of its influence in my own writing. The chapter "The Copper Mines" in *The Winter Prince* owes a great stylistic debt to the Moria episode in *The Fellowship of the Ring*.

As an older teen, there is no doubt that Ursula K. Le Guin was the author who exerted the most influence over me. I used her *Earthsea* books (only the first three existed then) as a kind of spiritual guide: They helped me to recognize balance in all things, to accept and appreciate the inevitability of opposites.

SF: Why do you think it's important for people to read imaginative fiction?

EW: Well, in a sense my teenage reading of Ursula Le Guin is a good example of why I think it's important. Fiction is a guide to reality. I have just finished *Reading Lolita in Tehran* by Azar Nafisi, and my most overwhelming impression of this book is that *imaginative fiction helps you cope with the real world.* What you read as fantasy you can apply to real life to impose order and meaning on events that may otherwise seem senseless and unfair. I also find that, as a writer, fiction helps me to work through my own past and my own life: to recreate and understand relationships, to learn how to face difficulties, to accept responsibility.

Throughout my childhood I strove (and failed) to be as gracious and as self-controlled as Sara Crewe; indeed, there is a lot of Sara Crewe in Telemakos, and the plot arc of *The Sunbird* is very like the plot arc of *A Little Princess* (maybe I shouldn't point this out!). In *A Wizard of Earthsea*, Ged's arrogance in his talent, and his abuse of power, were a warning to me. Luke Skywalker's lame decision to quit his training with Yoda in *The Empire Strikes Back* inspired me to focus on my high school work at a time when it seemed pointless to me.

I also think that fiction is a useful vehicle for presenting fact. I learned more about modern Afghanistan from reading *The Kite Runner* by Khaled Hosseini than I ever picked up from the news. I hope that *A Coalition of Lions* introduces people to an important ancient African civilization which they otherwise might never hear of. These books are fiction, obviously; as fiction, the *narrators* are unreliable. Everything is seen through their eyes. They are interpreting, not informing. But they are *preparing* the reader to be informed, helping the reader to open him or herself to new ideas and concepts.

I had an argument with a friend of mine while I was writing *The Winter Prince*. She objected to Medraut referring to the legends, poetry, and plays on his bookshelves as stories "that are not true." She argued, validly, I think, that these books were in fact the *truest* things among his reading material. I left the line in, because I think Medraut wouldn't agree with her, and it is his narrative. But I do believe that the paradox of fiction is that it is a lie that tells the truth.

References

"Elizabeth Wein." *Contemporary Authors Online*, Infotrac Galegroup Database (accessed March 12, 2006).

Wein, Elizabeth. "Home Page," 2004, http:www.elizabethwein.com (accessed March 12, 2006).

Wein, Elizabeth

The Aksumite Cycle. *JS*

Artos, High King of Britain, has two sons and a daughter. When disaster strikes, those who remain flee to the African country of Aksum for shelter.

The Winter Prince. New York: Atheneum, 1993. 202p. (Out of Print)

Born of incest between Artos and his sister Morgause, Medraut, the High King of Britain's oldest son, returns to Britain from Aksum to find his half-brother, Lleu, dying. While he bends all his skill toward healing him, his mother visits Camlan. She uses her sorcery to lead Medraut into betrayal, but he discovers that the choice between good and evil is his own.

A Coalition of Lions. New York: Viking, 2003. 210p. ISBN: 0670036188; 0142401293pa.

When Princess Goewin, daughter of King Arthur, loses her entire family in the Battle of Camlan, she flees to Aksum, the country in Africa where her half-brother Medraut served as an ambassador. She is guarded by Ras Priamos and seeks her cousin and betrothed, Constantine. She finds the royal family in political turmoil and discovers Medraut's son, Telemakos.

The Sunbird. New York: Viking, 2004. 184p. ISBN: 0670036919; 0142401714pa.

When a deadly plague strikes Britain, Princess Goewin, now the British ambassador, advises the emperor to close the ports to prevent the disease from entering Aksum. He follows her advice, but someone is breaking the quarantine. Telemakos is disguised and sent on a dangerous journey to ferret out the traitor.

White, T. H.

The Once and Future King. New York: Putnam, 1958. 677p. Reissued by Ace in 1976. ISBN: 0441627404pa. [Adult] *JS*

This is the classic retelling of the legend of King Arthur, his knights, his queen, and his wizard.

Yolen, Jane

🎗 *Sword of the Rightful King*. San Diego: Harcourt, 2003. 349p. ISBN: 0152025278; 0152025332pa. *MJ* AUD BRAILLE 📖

This reimagining of Arthurian legend sets the tale of the sword in the stone at the beginning of Arthur's rule. Merlinnus would like to use the sword in the stone as a device to consolidate Arthur's hold on the kingdom. While he lays his plans, Queen Morguase plots to steal Arthur's throne, and a lad named Gawen comes to court and becomes Merlinnus's assistant. (BBYA)

Zettel, Sarah

The Camelot Series. New York: Luna. [Adult] *S*

The brave (and lesser-known) women of Camelot embark on daring and romantic quests.

In Camelot's Shadow. 2004. 490p. Reissued in 2005. ISBN: 0373811128pa.

For Camelot's Honor. 2005. 506p. ISBN: 0373802188pa.

Under Camelot's Banner. 2006. 560p. ISBN: 0373802315pa.

Other Characters from Legends

Dokey, Cameron

The Storyteller's Daughter. New York: Simon & Schuster, 2002. 221p. ISBN: 0743422201pa. _MJ_
When King Shahrayar's wife betrays his trust and attempts to kill him, she does more than break his heart; she turns it to stone. He is convinced he will never love or trust again. In his agony, he declares that he will take a new wife each day who will be beheaded the next morning so that he will never be forsaken again. One woman steps forward with a bold plan to save his future wives from this dreadful fate and to restore the king's faith. Shahrazade, the blind storyteller, uses all the arts of her mother's people to help her spin the tales that will save her life and Shahrayar's.

Sunlight and Shadow. New York: Simon & Schuster, 2004. 184p. ISBN: 0689869991pa. _MJ_
Inspired by Mozart's *The Magic Flute,* this tale relates the story of sixteen-year-old Mina, who is the daughter of the Queen of the Night and the Mage of the Day. She has grown up to be comfortable in the dark, which is what her father fears most. When he steals her away to live in the day with him, her mother calls forth a prince with a magic flute to rescue her. Tern and Mina fall in love, but her father is furious and sets a deadly trial for Tern. Mina, refusing to simply wait and watch, aids Tern, determined that they will be together, no matter the cost.

Gallego Garcia, Laura

🌑 *The Legend of the Wandering King.* New York: Arthur A. Levine Books, 2005. 213p. ISBN: 0439585562; 0439585570pa. _MJ_ AUD
In pre-Islamic Arabia, Crown Prince Walid ibn Hujr longs for recognition as the greatest poet of all. At his father's insistence, he holds an annual poetry contest, sure that he will win, but each time he is defeated by an unassuming carpet weaver. Transforming from open-hearted to bitter, the prince sets the weaver a series of impossible tasks culminating with the weaving of a carpet that will show all of mankind's past present and future. With supernatural assistance the carpet is completed. When it's stolen, Walid, now full of remorse, searches for it in the desert, unaware of the beings that are observing his struggle. (ALAN)

McKinley, Robin

🌑 *The Outlaws of Sherwood.* New York: Greenwillow, 1988. 282p. Reissued by Ace in 2005. ISBN: 0441013252pa. _MJ_
Robin Hood and his Merry Men dwell in the Greenwood, and Marion attempts to straddle both the world of twelfth-century Norman nobility and life in the forest with Robin. As their relationship blossoms into romance, she becomes the best archer in the band. (ALAN)

Springer, Nancy

The Rowan Hood Series. New York: Philomel. *MJ* AUD

Unbeknownst to Robin Hood, he has a thirteen-year-old daughter living in the forest. When her mother, the healer Celandine of the forest fair folk, is murdered, Rosemary decides to search for her famous father.

Rowan Hood. 2001. 170p. ISBN: 0399233687; 069811972Xpa.

Rosemary changes her name to Rowan and disguises herself as a boy as she combs through Sherwood Forest attempting to locate her father, Robin Hood. Along the way, she encounters many dangers, including those posed by her father's old nemesis, Guy of Gisborn. She also makes some new friends, among them a wolf, a minstrel, and a runaway princess.

Lionclaw. 2002. 122p. ISBN: 039923716X; 014240053Xpa.

Lionel the minstrel would rather play the harp than draw a sword. His father disowns him as a coward, and he hides with Rowan Hood's band in the wood. When Rowan herself is kidnapped, however, Lionel must find the courage that has eluded him in order to free her.

Outlaw Princess of Sherwood. 2003. 122p. ISBN: 0399237216; 0142403040pa.

Etty, the runaway princess, has lived happily in Sherwood Forest with Rowan Hood and her band for a year. But when her father wants her back and places her beloved mother in a cage to lure her to return, she battles him with her wits and newfound skills for the right to live her own life.

Wild Boy. 2004. 115p. ISBN: 0399240152; 0142403954pa.

Rook, who joined Rowan Hood's band after the Sheriff of Nottingham ordered his father executed, has his chance for revenge when he discovers the Sheriff's son caught in a mantrap in Sherwood Forest.

Rowan Hood Returns: The Final Chapter. 2005. 169p. ISBN: 0399242066.

When Etty returns to tell Rowan the names of the four men who murdered her mother, Rowan sets out on a course of revenge. As she draws closer to her goal, the healing gift she has relied on diminishes. Facing the struggles of the forest, she realizes that the price of revenge may be her life as a healer.

The Finest in the Realm

The Folk Keeper by Franny Billingsley

The Mists of Avalon by Marion Zimmer Bradley

The Arthur Trilogy by Kevin Crossley-Holland

American Gods by Neil Gaiman

The Sevenwaters Trilogy by Juliet Marillier

The Squire's Tales by Gerald Morris

Sirena by Donna Jo Napoli

The Aksumite Cycle by Elizabeth Wein

Sword of the Rightful King by Jane Yolen

Chapter 4

Fairy Tale Fantasy

Novels in many of the fantasy subgenres draw on the oral traditions of world cultures and imaginatively combine those themes, ideas, and characters. J. R. R. Tolkien was influenced by Nordic mythology and folklore when he wrote <u>The Lord of the Rings</u>. However, he created his own complete secondary world and quest fantasy. Fairy tale fantasy stays closers to its original inspiration, focusing on a particular fairy tale (such as *Cinderella* or *Beauty and the Beast*) and reimagines the story as a novel, elaborating with details and depth.

Fairy tales are a subset of folklore, part of the body of tales told in villages and passed down from generation to generation. They feature fantastical creatures, such as elves and trolls, goblins and fairies (although fairies do not have to be present), and they often depict peasants' unaccustomed interaction with royalty. These stories can contain archetypal characters and endings in which the good are rewarded and the evil are punished. When novelists weave the threads of fairy tales into the warp and weft their creations, they may keep the general gist of the traditional tale but deepen the personalities of the main characters, enrich the setting with more details, and take the plot in unexpected directions. Fantasies that follow the format of fairy tales and fantasies that can be traced back to a particular tale are listed here. This includes novels that retell the story in a modern setting, those that follow the life of a previously minor character, and those that explain what happened after the traditional tale concluded. Novels that are not as closely tied to particular well-known fairy tales and that concentrate more on human and faerie interaction are listed in Chapter 6, "The Faerie Realm."

Butcher, Nancy

Beauty. **New York: Simon & Schuster, 2005. ISBN: 0689862350pa. _JS_**
Sixteen-year-old Princess Ana knows that the only way to attempt to win her mother's love is not to be beautiful, for her mother is ferociously jealous of any who are. So Ana overeats, doesn't bathe, and cuts her hair in ragged swathes. Nothing works, however,

and her mother sends her away to school with all the beauties in the kingdom. The sinister headmaster has fatal instructions from the queen, and only Ana can stop him.

Calhoun, Dia

The Phoenix Dance. **New York: Farrar, Straus & Giroux, 2005. 273p. ISBN: 0374359105.** *JS*
Phoenix Dance, an apprentice shoemaker, lives in the kingdom of Windward. She loves creating beautiful shoes but suffers from a serious illness. Her moods shift from the Kingdom of Brightness to the Kingdom of Darkness, and only a dulling herb can ease her trouble. She is summoned to the palace to discover why the twelve princesses wear their shoes to shreds every night. Braving magical danger and her own disease, she must find a way to save them and herself.

Card, Orson Scott

Enchantment. **New York: Ballantine, 1999. 390p. Reissued in 2000. ISBN: 0345416880pa. [Adult]** *JS* **AUD**
When Ivan is ten years old, he encounters a princess frozen in time in an ancient Russian forest. Although a deep sense of menace frightens him away, he returns ten years later. He is a track-and-field athlete and a scholar of Russian folklore. He returns to his sleeping beauty, defeats her evil guardian, and awakens her with a kiss, only to discover that he must find a way to keep her safe from Baba Yaga.

Dokey, Cameron

Beauty Sleep. **New York: Simon & Schuster, 2002. 186p. ISBN: 074342221Xpa.** *MJ*
Aurore is cursed at her christening to die in her sixteenth year, but her godmother softens the doom and changes the forthcoming death to sleep. Aurore grows up a strong-willed tomboy. When she does not die or go into an enchanted sleep when she is sixteen, one disaster after another afflicts her kingdom. Making up her mind to take her fate into her own hands, Aurore ventures into the forest to find a way to break the curse.

Golden. **New York: Simon & Schuster, 2006. ISBN: 1416905804pa.** *MJ*
When Rapunzel was born, her mother wanted nothing to do with her because she had no hair. Melisande the sorceress agrees to take the infant as compensation for a theft from her garden. She showers Rapunzel with love and tenderness. By the time she turns sixteen, Rapunzel has developed the gift of seeing into other people's hearts. In her adopted mother's heart, she sees that Melisande's own daughter, Rue, has been cursed to live alone in a tower. When Rapunzel and Melisande are forced by suspicious villagers to leave their home, they flee to the tower, where Melisande hopes that Rapunzel can devise a way to free Rue.

Ferris, Jean

🏵 *Once upon a Marigold.* **San Diego: Harcourt, 2002. 266p. ISBN: 0152167919lb; 0152050841pa.** *MJ* **BRAILLE** 📖
Chris, a child of six who is both strong-willed and clever, runs away from home. He's determined to live on his own in the forest, but he quickly attaches himself to Eldric the

troll. Eldric reluctantly provides food and shelter, and Chris grows up inventing things. He gazes at the Princess Marigold through a device of his own making, never dreaming that one day he might meet her or that his inventions could save the entire kingdom. (ALAN; BBYA)

Goldman, William

The Princess Bride. **New York: Harcourt, 1972. 308p. Reissued in by Ballantine hardcover in 1998. ISBN: 034543014X; 0345418263pa. [Adult] VID _S_**
Country lad Westley and his true love, Buttercup, encounter a Spanish swordsman, a gentle giant, and an evil prince on their way to the happily-ever-after ending.

Haddix, Margaret Peterson

❦ *Just Ella*. **New York: Simon & Schuster, 1999. 185p. ISBN: 06898218671b; 0689831285pa. _MJ_ AUD LP**
Ella learns, to her dismay, that finding Prince Charming isn't all that it's supposed to be. When she tells him that she'd rather not get married after all, he has her thrown in the dungeon. With no fairy godmother to help her out, Ella must use her wits to escape and create her own destiny. (BBYA)

Hale, Shannon

The Goose Girl. **New York: Bloomsbury, 2003. 383p. ISBN: 158234843X; 1582349908pa. _JS_ AUD** 📖
Princess Ani, a shy but magically talented seventeen-year-old, journeys to a strange kingdom to marry a prince she has never met. Along the way, she is betrayed by her lady's maid and serves as a goose girl while she searches for a way to regain her rightful place.

Enna Burning. **New York: Bloomsbury, 2004. 317p. ISBN: 1582348898. _JS_**
This companion to *The Goose Girl* is an original story that grows out of the previous novel. While Ani was a goose girl, she became close friends with Enna. Now that Ani is restored to her rightful place and is Princess Isi, Enna returns to her forest home to care for her dying mother. When her brother finds a piece of vellum that teaches him the art of firecalling, it proves to be his death. Fearful, yet drawn to the power, Enna learns the magic herself and then must find a way to use it without being destroyed by the fire.

Harrison, Mette

Mira, Mirror. **New York: Viking, 2004. 314p. ISBN: 0670059234. _MJ_**
Mira's mother negotiates with a witch and, in exchange for firewood, gives the witch her daughter Mira. Mira works for her as a second apprentice with a beautiful young woman who first embraces her as a sister and then betrays her, transforming Mira into a mirror. While her "sister" at first still returns periodically over time, one day she disappears. Mira is left in isolation for a hundred years until Ivana, a peasant girl, discovers the magic mirror. Convincing Ivana

to take her in her mirror form, Mira plots ways to steal enough power to become human again.

Profile of Patrice Kindl

Born October 16, 1951, in Alplaus, New York, Patrice burst into the world of young adult fantasy publishing with her novel *Owl in Love*, which was placed on several "best books" lists and won the Mythopoeic Fantasy Award in 1995. She has since published three more books, and all received positive reviews. In her spare time, she raises monkeys that are trained to help quadriplegics for the organization Helping Hands. (*Contemporary Authors Online*, Infotrac Galegroup Database; www.patricekindl.com)

Interview with Patrice Kindl

Conducted via e-mail March 6–8, 2006

SF: How did you first come to write fantasy for young people?

PK: I think most writers write what they would themselves like to read. I enjoy reading a number of genres, but the one that comes closest to where I live is fantasy. While still a very beginning writer, I read a how-to book that insisted I must master mainstream fiction before attempting fantasy. I found this advice so depressing that I ignored it entirely and wrote fantasy exclusively. Ever since I have regarded any rules about writing (beyond the basic one about how you must write to be a writer) with deep suspicion.

SF: For your fantasy, you have a realistic setting in *Owl in Love*, a fairy tale setting in *Goose Chase*, and Ancient Crete in *Lost in the Labyrinth*. Do you have a preference as to kind of setting? And how do you choose?

PK: The story tells you. Or, conversely (but less often), the setting comes first and dictates the story. The seed for a story may be an image—in *Owl in Love*, I imagined a woman so in love that she turned into an owl to watch over the sleep of her lover. Then it somehow came to me that he was her high school science teacher, which automatically made the story modern and the character an adolescent. In *The Woman in the Wall*, setting and character were integral to one another (Anna needed a big old house to disappear into —a two-bedroom apartment just wouldn't have worked). The genesis of *Goose Chase* was the line, "The King killed my canary today," which showed up in my mind and on my computer screen one day. I had no idea what the story was about, but there was clearly a king involved, which suggested a medieval time frame. And *Lost in the Labyrinth*'s setting was already laid out for me, of course.

I tend to mentally set my books in upstate New York, where I live. Obviously *Labyrinth* is an exception, but even *Goose* is really set here; most of the place-names come from the county where I live (Dorloo, Gilboa, Roseboom, etc.).

SF: What kind of research do you do for you novels?

PK: Quite a bit. How I love the Internet! For *Owl* I would save up lists of questions I wanted resolved and then spend hours researching at the library. It is so much easier now to just break off writing when I need to know something and turn to online sources. For *Woman in the Wall,* I read about social anxiety and its treatment, as well as drawing out a floor plan of my old childhood home (it had only fourteen rooms rather than the twenty-two I gave to Anna's house) and trying to work out exactly how she could construct her passages and secret rooms in an actual structure. Although *Goose* was a fairy tale, I wanted details of castle construction, daily life and vocabulary to be as accurate as possible (in my mind, it takes place in the fifteenth century). I have been waiting all these years for someone to challenge me about the fact that Alexandria's geese can fly (most modern domestic geese have all but lost this ability) so that I can explain that, up until the nineteenth century, it was common to breed domestic geese back to their wild cousins. Sadly, no 4H teen has written to complain. *Lost in the Labyrinth* required the most research. I used online sources (such as Brown University and Washington State University Web sites) as well as a long list of scholarly books and a two-week trip to Crete.

Fantasy requires just as much research as any realistic novel—you have to believe in the story yourself if you want to convince anybody else.

SF: What would you say your method of writing is (i.e., working from an outline, going where the story takes you, etc.)?

PK: Writers are commonly divided up into two broad categories: plotters (your first example) and plungers (your second example). I am emphatically a plunger. I once did a survey of writers on their habits and gave people the option of describing themselves as Extreme Plungers, Moderate Plungers, Moderate Plotters and Extreme Plotters. The rarest bird was the Extreme Plotter. The most common was the Moderate Plunger. I am an Extreme Plunger. I have no idea what is going on while composing the majority of the book and am kept in suspense on major points until I have completed my first draft.

SF: Of your books, who is your favorite character, and which is you favorite book?

PK: They are all my children, and I love them equally.

SF: *Owl in Love* won the Mythopoeic Fantasy Award for Children's Literature and was selected both as an ALA Notable Book for Children and an ALA Best Book for Young Adults. How did it feel to have the book recognized in this way?

PK: Oh, I was delirious, of course. My goal had been simply to get it published without having to pay anybody.

SF: What were your favorite books and authors growing up?

PK: I have always been something of an Anglophile. As a child I loved *The Borrowers* and *Mary Poppins*. I discovered *The Once and Future King* as a young teen. Jane Austen was a favorite also when I was a teen.

SF: What do you think is the merit or importance of reading fantasy?

PK: I think that all literature is fantasy anyway. Literature allows you to see through someone else's eyes. Literature allows you to say, "What if?" and follow a hundred different paths you could never travel in reality. Fantasy simply expands your options from the mundane and physically possible to the exotic and impossible. Fantasy gives us a larger world to live in and explore. Fantasy is often a metaphor, as well, and can present us with truths more real than realism can. Well written fantasy can portray the heart, rather than just the surface, of the universe.

References

"Patrice Kindl." *Contemporary Authors Online*. Infotrac Galegroup Database (accessed March 13, 2006).

Kindl, Patrice. "Home Page," http:www.patricekindl.com (accessed March 13, 2006).

Kindl, Patrice

Goose Chase*. Boston: Houghton Mifflin, 2001. 214p. ISBN: 0618033777; 0142302082pa. *MJ
Alexandra Aurora Fortunato only wants to take care of her geese. But when she brushes her hair, gold dust falls out, and when she cries, her tears become diamonds. This attracts the attention of King Claudio the Cruel and Prince Edmond of Dorloo. Locked in a tower by these suitors, she finds freedom flying away from the rooftop with the help of her geese—but winds up in more trouble than she was in, in the first place.

Lackey, Mercedes

Elemental Masters. New York: Daw. [Adult] *S*
The classic fairy tales *Snow White, Sleeping Beauty, Cinderella,* and *The Snow Queen* are recast as romantic fantasies set in different periods of English history.

> ***The Serpent's Shadow*. 2001. 343p. ISBN: 0886779154; 0756400619pa.**
>
> ***The Gates of Sleep*. 2002. 389p. ISBN: 0756400600; 0756401011pa.**
>
> ***Phoenix and Ashes*. 2004. 405p. ISBN: 0756401615; 0756402727pa.**
>
> ***The Wizard of London*. 2005. 342p. ISBN: 0756401747.**

Levine, Gail Carson

🏵 *Ella Enchanted*. New York: HarperCollins, 1997. 232p. ISBN: 0060275103; 0060558865pa. *MJ* AUD BRAILLE VID 📖
Lucinda, a foolish fairy, bestows the gift of obedience on Eleanor. Consequently, all her life Ella is compelled to do everything she is told to do. In an attempt to break the spell, Ella ventures out on her own and encounters dwarfs, giants, wicked stepsisters, and her prince charming. (ALAN; BBYA; Newbery Honor)

Fairest. New York: HarperCollins, 2006. 326p. ISBN: 0060734086.
In this companion novel to *Ella Enchanted*, Levine re-imagines the tale of "Snow White." Aza, abandoned as a baby at the Featherbed Inn in the kingdom of Ayortha, is different from everyone around her. She's larger, clumsier, and not at all pretty. In fact, although her adoptive parents love her very much, they rarely let her wait on customers. Aza does have two talents, however: an incredible singing voice (a trait greatly appreciated in Ayortha); and the ability to throw her voice, making it sound like someone else is talking (or singing). When the one customer that she has waited on, a duchess, invites her to court for the king's wedding, Aza is amazed. She never imagined that she would end up a lady in waiting for the new queen, or that she would find a magic mirror that could make her the fairest in the land.

McKillip, Patricia A.

In the Forests of Serre. New York: Ace, 2003. 295p. Reissued in 2004. ISBN: 0441011578pa. [Adult] *S*
Grieving over the death of his wife and his newborn child, Prince Ronan accidentally tramples a white hen while he is riding in the Forest of Serre. The hen belonged to Brume, the Mother of All Witches, and she curses him to wander the forest until he can capture the fabled firebird and bring it to her.

McKinley, Robin

🏵 *Beauty: A Retelling of the Story of Beauty and the Beast*. New York: Harper & Row, 1978. 247p. ISBN: 0060241497; 0060753102pa. *MJS* 📖
Contrary to her name, Beauty is not the loveliest girl in her family, but she is the cleverest, the bravest, and the most honorable. When her father makes a terrible pledge to a beast that lives in an enchanted castle, Beauty fulfills her father's promise. She enters the beast's domain, but all is not as it appears to be. (ALAN)

🏵 *Rose Daughter*. New York: Greenwillow, 1997. 306p. Reissued by Ace in 1998. ISBN: 0441005837pa. *MJS* 📖
Young Beauty is well loved by her family and has a gift with gardens. When she is compelled to join the Beast in his magical imprisonment, she concentrates on reviving his rose garden while she grows to love the mystifying Beast. (BBYA)

Spindle's End. **New York: Putnam, 2000. 422p. ISBN: 0399234667; 0441008658pa. _MJS_**

On her name day, infant princess Briar Rose receives an assortment of gifts from her fairy godmothers, until the evil fairy Pernicia curses her. To save Briar Rose, the youngest fairy whisks her away to a remote part of the magical kingdom to grow up safe from Pernicia. But she can only be protected for a short while before she must confront the evil fairy.

Deerskin. **New York: Ace, 1993. 309p. Reissued in 2005. ISBN: 0441012396pa. [Adult]** _S_

As each day passes, the Princess Lissar looks more and more like her late mother. All the kingdom remarks on her great beauty, but none know that it has inflamed the desire of her father the king. After he rapes her, she flees, seeking solace in her loyal dog and the great forest where magic lurks. (BBYA)

McNaughton, Janet

An Earthly Knight. **New York: HarperCollins, 2004. ISBN: 006008992X; 0060089946pa. _JS_**

In twelfth-century Scotland, Jenny is the sixteen-year-old daughter of a Scottish nobleman. When her older sister, Isabel, disgraces the family name by running away with one of her father's knights and then returning, it is up to Jenny to make an important marriage in her place. Her father brings her to court to betroth her to the king's brother, but she has already given her heart to Tam Lin and must find the courage to pursue her love. (BBYA)

Napoli, Donna Jo

The Magic Circle. **New York: Dutton, 1993. 118p. Reissued by Puffin in 1995. ISBN: 0140374396pa. _JS_**

A good-hearted woman, a hunchback known as "Ugly One," is a midwife who learns sorcery to become a healer. After nine years of success, she is tricked by the devil's minions, loses her gifts, and is forced to become a witch, waiting for Hansel and Gretel.

Zel. **New York: Dutton, 1996. 227p. Reissued by Puffin in 1998. ISBN: 0141301163pa. _JS_ AUD**

A woman unable to have children sells her soul to have power over all plants. She uses this power to steal a baby girl, Zel. She loves and nurtures Zel until Zel is thirteen and begins to take an interest in Konrad, a young nobleman. In her rage, the witch locks Zel in a tower and watches Zel's sanity slip away with the seasons.

Spinners **(with Richard Tchen). New York: Viking, 1999. 192p. Reissued by Puffin in 2001. ISBN: 014131110Xpa. _JS_**

A young weaver wishes to wed his beloved, who is carrying his child, but her father does not think that the weaver can earn a decent living. He wants his daughter to marry the wealthy miller. The weaver vows that he will clothe his bride in gold and becomes obsessed with learning to spin straw into gold. In the process, he turns himself into a little man with a deformed leg. In the meantime, his beloved marries the miller, but she dies in childbirth. The miller raises the girl as his daughter, and so Saskia grows up knowing nothing of her real father. She becomes famous for her beautiful yarns and thus draws the attention of the king as the miller's beautiful daughter.

Beast. New York: Atheneum, 2000. 260p. ISBN: 0689835892lb; 0689870051pa. AUD _JS_ 📖

Prince Orasmyn, the heir to the throne of Persia, is a devout Muslim who makes a grave error when it comes time to make the sacred sacrifice. Djinn curses him after he selects a scarred animal for the sacrifice. Transformed into a lion, he will remain a beast until a woman loves him. Although his body is that of the great cat, his mind remains his own. He flees the family compound immediately, for his father's favorite sport is lion hunting. As he struggles to balance his animal needs and instincts with the intellectual desires of his human mind, he makes his way across continents until he settles in a castle in France.

Pattou, Edith

❦ *East.* **Orlando, FL: Harcourt, 2003. 498p. ISBN: 0152045635; 0152052216pa. _MJS_ AUD** 📖

Rose was raised in a small Norwegian village. Her mother would like to keep her close to home, but Rose has a wandering spirit. When her sister becomes ill and a white bear offers a cure in exchange for Rose coming to live with him, she agrees to accompany him to his castle-in-a-cave. While her sister recovers, Rose finds enchantment and danger in her new home. (ALAN; BBYA; TBYA)

Stanley, Diane

Bella at Midnight. New York: HarperCollins, 2006. 288p. ISBN: 0060775734.

Growing up in the medieval village of Castle Down, Bella lives with her peasant family enjoying the kindness of her parents and the unlikely friendship of Prince Julian. But when first Julian betrays her and then Bella is called away by her real father, a knight she does not know, misery besets her. Forced to live in the kitchen by her new stepmother, homesickness plagues her until she learns from her stepsister that Julian is in danger. With the help of her godmother, an enchanted emerald, and a pair of glass slippers, Bella sets out to warn her prince.

Tepper, Sheri S.

❦ *Beauty.* **New York: Doubleday, 1991. Reissued by Spectra in 1992. ISBN: 0553295276pa. [Adult]** _S_

Born in 1347, Beauty is the daughter of a woman with faerie blood and a father who does not have time for her. As her sixteenth birthday draws near, Beauty conceives of a way to sidestep the curse she knows is coming. While the household drifts off into enchanted sleep, Beauty travels in time to the twentieth century. (Locus Award)

Thesman, Jean

Singer. **New York: Viking, 2005. 304p. ISBN: 0670059374; 0142406503pa.** *JS*
Gwenore's mother, the evil witch Rhiamon, thirsts for her daughter's magical power.
With the help of the Fair Folk, Gwenore runs away from home when she is twelve and
shelters in Blessingwood, where she learns the arts of music and healing. Her mother
never ceases hunting for her. When she draws near, Gwenore flees. Traveling the British Isles as Mary Singer, she comes to the Irish Kingdom of Lir. Taken in by the king,
she becomes a much-loved teacher for his children. When he marries Rhiamon, the
witch turns the children into swans. Gwenore must delve deep into her magical abilities to restore those she loves.

Yolen, Jane

🎗 *Briar Rose*. **New York: Tor, 1993. 190p. Reissued in 2002. ISBN: 0765342308pa.**
[Adult] *JS* **AUD**
Rebecca and her sister always loved to hear their grandmother tell the story of Sleeping
Beauty as they were growing up, although they were never sure why she insisted that
she was Briar Rose. When Becca becomes an investigative reporter, she decides to
delve into the mystery surrounding her grandmother, but she does not expect to find
the horror of the Holocaust pulsing just beneath the surface of her grandmother's tale.
(Adult Mythopoeic Award)

Young Adult Paperback Series

Mass, Wendy

<u>**Twice upon a Time**</u>. **New York: Scholastic.** *M*
Traditional fairy tales appear with a new twist.

The Finest in the Realm

Once upon a Marigold by Jean Ferris

The Goose Girl by Shannon Hale

Ella Enchanted by Gail Carson Levine

Beauty: A Retelling of the Story of Beauty and the Beast by Robin McKinley

Beast by Donna Jo Napoli

East by Edith Pattou

Chapter 5

Alternate and Parallel Worlds

All fantasy takes place, essentially, in one of three worlds: a world that is completely imaginary, with no points that touch the world we know; a world that is very much like our own but has a magical or inexplicable difference; or a world that includes the known world with one or more imaginary worlds linked to it. For some fantasies, the kind of world in which they are set most clearly defines the kind of fantasy they are; for others, the kind of plot or characters is of greater importance. The titles in this chapter are defined by the types of world they depict: "Secondary Worlds," "Reality with a Twist," "Gateway Fantasy," and "Alternate Histories." Fantasies that fit well into other subgenres have been listed in the more appropriate chapter (for example, the <u>Harry Potter series</u>, which could be in "Reality with a Twist," is in "Wizard Fantasy," and <u>The Lord of the Rings</u>, which also fits into "Secondary Worlds," is in "Epic Fantasy"). Although time travel or time slip fantasies do transport the main characters from one reality to another, they generally involve only moving from one known reality to another, and the only magic is in the time travel, not in one or both of the worlds. Therefore, time travel fantasy is listed in a separate chapter.

Secondary Worlds

"Secondary Worlds" is a phrase Tolkien defined in his essay "On Fairy Stories" (Tolkien 1966). He identified the world we know as the primary world and the world in a work of fiction, where the action occurs in a completely imaginary realm, as a Secondary World. A Secondary World is independent from the known world. There are no points where the two intersect or where beings from the known world can cross into the imaginary realm. Although creators of such fantasies often are inspired by familiar myths and legends, they take meticulous care to create an imaginary realm that is fully realized, believable, and independent. This may include providing a map and inventing languages. Often great adventures occur there. Most epic fantasies and dragon fantasies occur in secondary worlds, as do many wizard fantasies, and each of these is large enough to demand its own subgenre. The created realm does not require an element of magic to be considered a fantasy. If all of the action takes place in an imaginary realm, then it is a "Secondary World" fantasy.

Alexander, Lloyd

🌑 *The Marvelous Misadventures of Sebastian*. **New York: Dutton, 1970. 204p. Reissued by Puffin in 2000. ISBN: 0141308168pa. _MJ_ BRAILLE**
When fourth fiddler Sebastian loses his place in the baron's orchestra, he ventures forth to seek a new position and finds his troubles have just begun. He rescues a stray cat from a group of torturers, who then smash his precious violin; and he tries to help a troubled boy who turns out to be a crown princess on the run from an arranged marriage. Together, they dodge hired assassins and furious guards and discover a magic violin. (National Book Award)

The Westmark Trilogy. New York: Dutton. All reissued by Firebird in 2002. _JS_
In Westmark, the king grieves for his missing daughter and neglects his royal responsibilities. Aristocratic corruption sets the stage for rebellion and war as Theo, Mickle, and Florian find their way first to friendship and then to battle.

🌑 *Westmark*. **1981. 184p. ISBN: 0141310707pa. BRAILLE**
Theo, an orphan, flees for his life from criminal charges. He meets a roguish doctor, his dwarf attendant, and an urchin girl. Together they devise a dangerous plan to save themselves and the kingdom. (ALAN; National Book Award)

🌑 *The Kestrel*. **1982. 244p. ISBN: 0141310693pa.**
War devastates Westmark, and Theo becomes a fierce fighter as he defends his love, Mickle, who is now Queen Augusta. (ALAN)

The Beggar Queen. **1984. 237p. ISBN: 0141310707pa.**
Mickle is a benevolent queen, but whispers of war still haunt her realm. The banished Duke Conrad of Regia plots to seize the throne. The queen and Theo must find a way to stop him before all the reforms they've worked so hard for are lost.

Bell, Hilari

🌑 *The Goblin Wood*. **New York: HarperCollins, 2003. 294p. ISBN: 060513713; 006051373Xpa. _JS_**
A hedgewitch like her mother, twelve-year-old Makenna eagerly learns the skills she will need until the day her mother is brutally executed by neighbors who once appreciated her art. Makenna escapes to the wood, where she eventually joins with the goblins to stop the rulers who want to rid the land of magic. (BBYA)

The Farsala Trilogy. New York: Simon & Schuster. _MJ_
In the kingdom of Farsala, the Deghans rule their lands and preserve the peace with foreign nations through their military might. But a new enemy, the Hrum, approaches, and the Farsalans are not prepared. Three young people—Soraya, the general's daughter; Jiann, the general's bastard son; and Kavi, the thief—become embroiled in affecting the fate of the nation. (This trilogy was originally titled The Book of Sorahb, and the first book was issued as *Flame*. It has been retitled and repackaged, although the text remains the same.)

Fall of a Kingdom. **2003. 352p. ISBN: 1416905456; 0689854145pa.**
Soraya, the daughter of a wealthy general, is sent into secret exile while her father fights a war she is sure he will win. Jiaan, the general's bastard son, must first see that Soraya is safe and then fight at his father's side. Kavi, a wily peddler, is kidnapped by the enemy, and must choose between serving his oppressors or the invading army. Their destinies become entwined as each struggles to meet an unexpected future.

Rise of a Hero. **2005. 462p. ISBN: 0689854153; 068985417Xpa.**
The Hrum believe they will completely conquer Farsala before their self-imposed deadline of one year is up, but Jiann holds the city of Mazad against them. Meanwhile, Soraya plays the part of a peasant searching for work with the Hrum as she attempts to rescue her mother and her baby brother from slavery. And Kavi, who once thought the Hrum would be better than the arrogant Deghans, now crafts a counterrevolution.

Forging the Sword. **2006. 512p. ISBN: 0689854161.**
Soraya, Jiann, and Kavi continue their crusade to free Farsala from the Hrum invaders. Jiann drills peasants in the ways of warfare, at their hidden desert base, while Soraya spies on the enemy and uses her fire and weather magic against them. Meanwhile Kavi does everything in his power to aid the common people in their struggle to survive.

Browne, N. M.

The Story of Stone. **New York: Bloomsbury, 2005. 334p. (1st American Edition.) ISBN: 1582346550.** *JS*
When Nela, a Findsman's daughter, unearths an unusual black stone at her father's archeological dig, she sees a vision of the past each time she touches it. The visions portray the lives of Jaret, a warrior of Chief's Brood Trove, who seeks healing for his younger brother, and Moon-Eye, an enchantress of the forest.

Calhoun, Dia

Firegold. **Delray Beach, FL: Winslow Press, 1999. Reissued by Sunburst in 2003. ISBN: 0374423113pa.** *JS* **LP**
Blue-eyed Jonathon never fits in with the rest of the dark-eyed villagers, who tell him he will go insane. When he catches a glimpse of a blue-eyed girl, he becomes convinced that he needs to answer the call that leads him to journey to the Red Mountains.

White Midnight. **New York: Farrar, Straus, & Giroux, 2003. ISBN: 0374383898.** *JS* **LP**
This prequel to *Firegold* takes place four hundred years before Jonathan journeyed to the Red Mountains. Here, fifteen-year-old Rosie serves as a bondgirl on Greengarden Orchard. She has been told all her life that she is too ugly to marry and too timid to do more than work in the orchard. Her very fearfulness attracts the attention of the owner, Mr. Brae. He wants a compliant girl to wed his grandson, the monstrous "Thing" in the attic. He needs an heir. Offering

Rosie's family freedom, wealth, and prestige, he convinces Rosie to concede to his request.

Dickinson, Peter

🔖 *The Ropemaker*. **New York: Delacorte, 2001. 375p. ISBN: 0385729219; 0385730632pa.** *MJ* 📖
When the magic in their enchanted Valley begins to fail, teenagers Tilja and Tahl, together with their grandparents, leave the only land they've ever known and travel to the heart of the evil empire in search of the powerful magician who cast the spell of protection for the Valley in the first place. (ALAN; Mythopoeic Children's Award; Printz Honor)

Hanley, Victoria

The Seer and the Sword. **New York: Holiday House, 2000. 341p. ISBN: 0823415325; 0440229774pa.** *MJ*
Princess Torina, who sometimes can see the future in the crystal her father brings to her, and Landen, a prince from a conquered kingdom who seeks to regain a stolen sword, become friends as they grow up together. Treachery separates them, and as they live in exile, each must find a path to peace and to each other.

The Healer's Keep. **New York: Holiday House, 2002. 364p. ISBN: 0823417603; 055349435Xpa.** *MJ*
In this sequel to *The Seer and the Sword*, Princess Saravelda, Queen Torina's daughter, enters the Healer's Keep to study ways of using her magic talent. But when the Keep comes under attack, she joins forces with some unlikely allies to save the school.

The Light of the Oracle. **New York: David Fickling Books, 2005. ISBN: 0385750447.** *MJ*
In this companion novel to *The Seer and the Sword* and *Healer's Keep*, Bryn, the daughter of a poor stonecutter, enters into service at the Temple of the Oracle as a handmaiden. There, she and her fellows are to be trained as candidates for the priesthood, but first they must be chosen by a bird. Bryn's gift is so great, however, that she is chosen by the wind, signifying the magnitude of her potential prophecies. All the warnings she can give will be needed to halt the evil machinations of a hidden lord.

Hearn, Lian

The Tales of the Otori. New York: Riverhead Books. [Adult] *S* **AUD**
In a mystical land resembling long-ago Japan, sixteen-year-old Takeo was raised in a mountain village with the Hidden. When the village is destroyed, Lord Otori rescues him because he knows what Takeo does not. The boy is one of the Tribe, a family group whose hereditary gifts are traditionally used to train their people to become spies and assassins. Born with special powers, they can appear in two places at one time, put people to sleep with a glance, and become invisible. As Takeo explores his new life, he becomes enmeshed in the plots swirling around him—until he decides to make his own choices.

> *Across the Nightingale Floor*. **2002. 287p. Reissued by Firebird in 2005. ISBN: 0142403245pa.**

Grass for His Pillow. 2003. 292p. Reissued by Firebird in 2005. ISBN: 1594480036pa.

Brilliance of the Moon. 2004. 330p. Reissued by Firebird in 2006. ISBN: 1594480869pa.

Jones, Diana Wynne

<u>The Dalemark Quartet</u>. New York: Atheneum. All reissued by HarperTrophy in 2001. *MJ*

In Dalemark, deep differences divide the people, and generation after generation the nobles find reasons to go to war. The mysterious gods choose champions from Dalemark's past, present, and future to bring peace to the land.

Cart and Cwidder. 1977. 193p. ISBN: 0064473139pa.
Clennen and his family of musicians travel from village to village in Dalemark, entertaining audiences all over the country. When their father is killed, the three children inherit a lute-like cwidder that is more than it appears to be, and they become embroiled in a rebellion they knew nothing about.

Drowned Ammet. 1978. 255p. ISBN: 0064473147pa.
Mitt, the son of a Free Holander, dreams of joining the Freedom Fighters, but when the plot to overthrow the tyrannical ruler goes awry, Mitt must find a place to hide among his enemies.

Spellcoats. 1979. 249p. ISBN: 0064473155pa.
In this prequel to *Cart and Cwidder*, Tanaqui and her family never quite fit in with the villagers of Shelling. When the great flood comes, the villagers blame them and force them to leave. On their dangerous trek to a new home, they discover a destiny they never imagined.

The Crown of Dalemark. 1995. 471p. ISBN: 0064473163pa.
In this concluding novel, Mitt's mission is to kill Noreth, who wants to find the treasures that will unify the kingdom. Unbeknownst to him, Maewen is sent back in time to impersonate Noreth, which will change everything.

<u>The Castle Duology</u>. New York: Greenwillow. *MJ*
Seven-league boots, invisibility cloaks, and magic spells abound, but there is only one moving castle and one wizard who inhabits it, as first Sophie and then Abdullah come to realize.

Howl's Moving Castle. 1986. 212p. Reissued in 2001. ISBN: 06441034Xpa. AUD VID GN 📖
Sophie, the oldest of three sisters, resigns herself to life as an apprentice in a hat shop until a witch transforms her into an old woman. Searching for a cure, she moves into Wizard Howl's moving castle and decides she needs to try to tame him. (ALAN; Boston Globe Honor)

🏵 *Castle in the Air*. 2001. 304p. ISBN: 0064473457pa.
Abdullah sells his rugs in the bazaar, but he prefers daydreaming. He wishes to be a prince betrothed to a lovely princess. His life changes rapidly when he acquires a magic carpet that whisks him into an adventure with an evil jinn, a stunning princess, women turned into cats, and soldiers turned into frogs. (ALAN)

Kay, Guy Gavriel

A Song for Arbonne. New York: Crown, 1992. (1st American Edition.) 513p. Reissued by Roc in 2002. ISBN: 0451458974pa. [Adult] S
Arbonne, a land of two moons that resembles twelfth-century Provence, is home to people who admire poetry and love above all else. In their sunny land, the calling to be a troubadour ranks among the highest. When their enemies to the north attack, their fate may be in the hands of Blaise, a mercenary from the north, and a young woman just learning to be a troubadour.

The Lions of Al-Rassan. New York: Viking, 1995. (1st American Edition.) 582p. Reissued by Eos in 2005. ISBN: 0060733497pa. [Adult] S
In a world reminiscent of medieval Spain, two diametrically opposed cultures clash. Those of the Asharite Empire worship the stars, but their decadent city-states are constantly at war with one another. This enables King Almalik to easily conquer one city-state after another. Moreover, the Jaddites of the far north who worship the sun god are eager to regain the realm for their god and will do whatever it takes to make it happen.

Lackey, Mercedes

The Tales of Valdemar. New York: Daw. [Adult] S
In the medieval realm of Valdemar, Companions are horses that can communicate telepathically, and Heralds are their riders and guardians of the kingdom. (Titles here are arranged by trilogies and then listed in publication order, as they are on the author's Web site: www.mercedeslackey.com.)

Heralds of Valdemar: Trilogy 1

Arrows of the Queen. 1987. 320p. Reissued in 1996. ISBN: 0886773784pa.

Arrow's Flight. 1987. 320p. ISBN: 0886773776pa.

Arrow's Fall. 1988. 320p. Reissued in 1996. ISBN: 0886774004pa.

Vows and Honor

Oathbound. 1990. 302p. Reissued in 1996. ISBN: 0886774144pa.

Oathbreakers. 1991. 318p. Reissued in 1995. ISBN: 0886774543pa.

The Oathblood. 1998. 400p. ISBN: 0886777739pa.

The Last Herald Mage

Magic's Pawn. 1989. 349p. Reissued in 1994. ISBN: 0886773520pa.

Magic's Promise. 1990. 320p. Reissued in 1994. ISBN: 0886774012pa.

Magic's Price. 1990. 352p. Reissued in 1994. ISBN: 0886774268pa.

Kerowyn's Tale

By the Sword. 1991. 426p. ISBN: 0886774632pa.

Mage Winds

Winds of Fate. 1992. 460p. Reissued in 1997. ISBN: 0886775167pa.

Winds of Change. 1993. 475p. Reissued in 1994. ISBN: 0886775639pa.

Winds of Fury. 1994. 432p. ISBN: 0886776120pa.

Mage Storms

Storm Warning. 1994. 403p. Reissued in 1995. ISBN: 0886776619pa.

Storm Rising. 1995. 384p. Reissued in 1996. ISBN: 0886777127pa.

Storm Breaking. 1996. 435p. Reissued in 1997. ISBN: 0886777550pa.

Mage Wars (with Larry Dixon)

The Black Gryphon. 1994. Reissued in 1995. 460p. ISBN: 0886776430pa.

The White Gryphon. 1996. 400p. ISBN: 0886776821pa.

The Silver Gryphon. 1997. 400p. ISBN: 0886776856pa.

Owlflight (with Larry Dixon)

Owlflight. 1998. 352p. ISBN: 0886778042pa.

Owlsight. 1999. 450p. ISBN: 0886778034pa.

Owlknight. 2000. 464p. ISBN: 0886779162pa.

Heralds of Valdemar: Trilogy 2

Take a Thief. 2001. 351p. Reissued in 2002. ISBN: 0756400589pa.

Exile's Honor. 2002. 433p. Reissued in 2003. ISBN: 0756401135pa.

Exile's Valor. 2003. 402p. ISBN: 0756402069; 0756402212pa.

Stand-Alone Novels and Short Story Collections

Brightly Burning. 2001. 448p. ISBN: 0886779898pa.

Sword of Ice: And Other Tales of Valdemar (edited by Mercedes Lackey). 1996. 350p. ISBN: 0886777208pa.

Sun in Glory: And Other Tales of Valdemar (edited by Mercedes Lacky). 2003. 352p. ISBN: 0756401666pa.

Crossroads: And Other Tales of Valdemar (**edited by Mercedes Lackey**). **2005. 352p. ISBN: 0756403251pa.**

Le Guin, Ursula K.

Gifts. **Orlando, FL: Harcourt, 2004. 274p. ISBN: 0152051236; 0152051244pa.** *JS* **AUD**
In the Uplands, the clans possess hereditary gifts of magic: to call animals, to bring forth fire, to twist a limb, to chain a mind, or to unmake stone and bone. The gifts are wondrous and dangerous. When teenagers Orrec and Gyr, who have been best friends since childhood, decide not to use their gifts, their whole world changes.

Voices. **Orlando, FL: Harcourt, 2006. 341p. ISBN: 0152056785.** *JS*
In this companion novel to *Gifts*, seventeen-year-old Memer, a child of rape, has grown up in the trade city of Ansul which was devastated when the hated Alds invaded. The Alds destroyed the university, sacked the library, burned all the books they could find, and made reading a crime. But Memer has been taught to read by the Waylord and serves as the guardian of the hidden library of Ansul. When Orrec and Gry, now older and married to each other, arrive seeking the lost literature of Ansul, they spark a rebellion, and Memer discovers her mystical gifts.

Levine, Gail Carson

The Two Princesses of Bamarre. **New York: HarperCollins, 2001. 241p. ISBN: 0060293152.** *MJ* **AUD BRAILLE**
Meryl is the adventurous sister and Addie, the timid one. When Meryl falls ill, Addie braves specters, griffins, and dragons to try to save her sister.

McKillip, Patricia A.

Alphabet of Thorn. **New York: Ace, 2004. 314p. ISBN: 0441011306; 0441012434pa. [Adult]** *JS* 📖
Nepenthe, a sixteen-year-old orphan who has been raised by the royal librarians to be a translator, receives a book in a strange language that entwines her in an ancient history threatening the kingdom of Raine.

Ombria in Shadow. **New York: Ace, 2002. 298p. Reissued in 2003. ISBN: 0441010164pa. [Adult]** *JS*
When the prince of Ombria dies, the life of its child-heir, Kyle Greve, is placed in the hands of regent Domina Pearl, who has been plotting to seize power for years. But the city of light and shadows harbors saviors, and the castoff lover, the bastard uncle, and a sorcerer's apprentice each must slip in their piece of the puzzle to rescue their prince and their home.

Nicholson, William

The Wind on Fire Trilogy. **New York: Hyperion. (1st American Editions.)** *MJ* **AUD**
Aramanth was once a safe and protected place, but when the voice of the Wind Singer is lost, internal and external menaces threaten the lives of its citizens.

★ *The Wind Singer*. 2000. 358p. ISBN: 0786805692; 0786818263pa.
In Aramanth, everyone must constantly improve. When the Hath family fails, twins Kestrel and Bowman set out on a perilous journey to find the mysterious voice of the Wind Singer in hopes that it will restore their home. (ALAN; Smarties Gold Award)

★ *Slaves of the Mastery*. 2001. 434p. ISBN: 0786805706; 0786814187pa.
After five years of peace, Aramanth comes under attack, and its people are enslaved. Bowman and Kestrel need to combine magic and cunning to overcome the Master and free their people. (ALAN)

Firesong. 2002. 422p. ISBN: 0786805714; 0786818018pa.
Bowman and Kestrel travel with their people to their promised land, but their mother, the prophetess who leads them, grows weaker as the journey ends, and they are beset with dangers and temptation.

Pierce, Tamora

The Song of the Lioness Quartet. **New York: Atheneum. All reissued in hardcover in 2002–2003. AUD**

In the kingdom of Tortall, only boys are allowed to be trained as squires and strive to become knights. When Alanna disguises herself as a boy and begins her knightly education, she sets into motion events that will alter everything in the realm.

Alanna: The First Adventure. 1983. 241p. Reissue ISBN: 0689853238; 0689878559pa. *MJ*
Alanna longs to be a knight, but women aren't allowed to train as warriors. Ignoring her magical gifts, she trades places with her twin brother, Thom. He trains to be a sorcerer while she begins life as a page.

In the Hand of the Goddess. 1984. 232p. Reissue ISBN: 0689853246; 0689878567pa. *MJ*
Alanna has won the honor of being Prince Jonathan's squire. Now it will take all of her magic power and skill as a warrior to protect him from an evil sorcerer.

The Woman Who Rides Like a Man. 1986. 253p. Reissue ISBN: 0689854293; 0689878583pa. *JS*
Alanna, the only female knight, attempts to prove herself by aiding a desert tribe and engaging in a magical duel to the death.

The Lioness Rampant. 1988. 320p. Reissue ISBN: 0689854307; 0689878575pa. *JS*
Alanna sets out to find the Dominion Jewel, but Prince Jonathan's evil uncle, Duke Roger, returns from the dead, and only Alanna has the power to prevent Tortall's utter destruction.

The Immortals Quartet. New York: Atheneum. All reissued in hardcover in 2003 by Random House. _MJ_

The kingdom of Tortall serves as the setting for more magical adventures as Alanna helps to convince young Daine that she needs her help to defeat the mysterious evil that threatens the realm.

Wild Magic. 1992. 260p. Reissue ISBN: 0689856113; 1416903437pa. AUD

Homeless and outcast, Daine gets a job as an assistant horsemistress because she has a special knack with animals. Her talents are recognized as wild magic, and they grow stronger under the guidance of mage Numair. He shows her that she can sense the evil Immortals and help save her country from invasion.

Wolf Speaker. 1994. 192p. Reissue ISBN: 0689856121; 1416903445pa.

Daine is continuing her mage training at King Jonathan's court but gets called back to Dunlath Valley by her old friends, the wolves. Once there, she must find a way to save the valley from destruction.

🎗 *Emperor Mage*. 1995. 255p. Reissue ISBN: 068985613X; 1416903372pa.

Daine, now fifteen, has grown stronger in her ability to heal animals and is sent as part of a delegation to work out a peace treaty with the barbarian Emperor Ozorne. His captive birds are dying, and he needs her to heal them. When she does, she discovers a whole new power. (BBYA)

Realms of the Gods. 1996. 209. ISBN: 0689862091; 141690817Xpa.

Daine and Numair are swept up to the realm of the gods to help the gods win their struggle, but the two must return to the battle on Earth. They enlist the aid of dragons and other immortals in the final battle for the kingdom.

Protector of the Small Quartet. New York: Random House. LP

In Tortall, ten years have passed since the decree permitting girls to train as knights was issued. No one has come forward until now, when Keladry of Mindelan undertakes the challenge.

First Test. 1999. 216p. ISBN: 0679889140; 0679889175pa. _MJ_

When Kel applies to become a page, she has no idea that the training master, Lord Wyldon, is dead set against letting women become warriors. Kel has no disguises or magic to help her through, relying on grit and determination to withstand the training and win the admiration of her fellow pages.

Page. 2000. 257p. ISBN: 0679889159; 0679889183pa. _MJ_

As Kel continues her training on her way to knighthood, she befriends a serving maid. Helping the girl overcome her fears by teaching her self-defense, Kel faces the bullies in her own life, as well as the changes in her body and her feelings for her best friend, Neal.

🎗 *Squire*. 2001. 399. ISBN: 0679889167; 0679889191pa. _JS_

As Kel becomes a squire, she hopes desperately that Alanna will choose her. Instead Lord Raoul, commander of the King's Own, selects her. Soon she finds herself battling centaurs, aiding in flood cleanup, and nurturing a baby griffin. (BBYA)

Lady Knight. 2002. 429p. ISBN: 037591465X; 037581471Xpa. *JS*
At the age of eighteen, Kel at last achieves her dream and is dubbed a knight of Tortall. Instead of getting posted to the front to fight the Scarans, she is assigned to be the commander of a refugee camp. Kel must choose to follow orders or follow her conscience and her vision.

Daughter of the Lioness Duology. New York: Random House. *JS* AUD LP
The tales from Tortall continue with the adventures of Alanna's daughter, Alianne.

🔖 *Trickster's Choice*. 2003. 422p. ISBN: 0375814663; 0375828796pa.
Alianne, the daughter of Alanna, the first Lady Knight of Tortall, would rather be a spy than a fighter. This ambition leads to her capture by slavers who whisk her off to the Copper Isles, where she must use all of her wits to survive and escape. (BBYA)

Trickster's Queen. 2004. 467p. ISBN: 0375814671; 0375828788pa.
Alianne, now called Aly, serves as maid to the Lady Dovasary but in reality is the spymaster of the raka rebellion that is determined to put the Lady's sister on the throne of the Copper Isles.

Pratchett, Terry

Discworld. AUD *S*
Discworld, a flat, circular world, travels through space on the back of four elephants standing on a turtle. A variety of beings—including vampires, witches, wizards, werewolves, dwarfs, and trolls—lives in its largest city, Ankh-Morpork. The series originally was written for adults, but recently the author has set several young adult titles in this world. These titles are annotated, and the adult titles are listed afterward.

Young Adult Titles

🔖 *The Amazing Maurice and His Educated Rodents*. New York: HarperCollins, 2001. 241p. ISBN: 0060012331; 0060012358pa. *MJS*
Maurice the cat can talk. He can talk because he ate a rat who also could talk, although Maurice did not know this at the time. Now he knows better. He makes sure the rat cannot talk before he eats him. The rats can talk because they have been dining on the debris in the dump of the Wizard's University. Maurice becomes the leader of the pack of talking rodents, and they hatch a plot with a piper named Kevin to travel from town to town pulling a pied-piper con. All goes well until they reach Bad Bintz, where the rat catchers have a scam of their own. (BBYA; Carnegie Medal)

The Tiffany Aching Adventures. New York: HarperCollins. *MJS* AUD
Granny Aching has lived on the Chalk all her life. She knows more about sheep than anyone for miles around and has quietly been working her magic to maintain the land. Tiffany has grown up loving her and learning the ways of

the land and animals, but she knows nothing of magic until after her grandmother dies and the Wee Free Men tumble into her life.

🌶 *The Wee Free Men*. **New York: HarperCollins, 2003. 263p. ISBN: 0060012366; 0060012382pa.** *MJS* **AUD**
When the Queen of the Elves invades Tiffany's home in the Chalk country where Tiffany is a shepherd just as generations before her were, this royal denizen of Fairyland kidnaps Tiffany's younger brother. Armed only with a frying pan and the aid of her new friends, the six-inch-high blue pictsies, she enters the queen's realm to rescue her brother. (ALAN; BBYA; Locus Award)

🌶 *A Hat Full of Sky*. **New York: HarperCollins, 2004. 288p. ISBN: 0060586605; 0060586621pa.** *MJS* **AUD**
In this sequel to *Wee Free Men,* Tiffany leaves her beloved land of Chalk to study witchcraft with Miss Level. Unbeknownst to either of them, a hiver wishes to possess her for her power, and Tiffany will need all the help she can find, including that of the wee free men, to help her fend off the attack and continue her studies. (ALAN; BBYA; Locus Award)

Wintersmith. **2006. 223p. ISBN: 0060890312.**
Despite warnings from her mentor, Miss Treason, thirteen-year-old Tiffany joins the Black Morris dance in which the gods salute the coming of winter. When she bumps into the god of winter, she intrigues him. He begins to court her, showering her with mounds of Tiffany-shaped snowflakes, and setting Tiffany-shaped icebergs afloat in the sea. Her beloved Chalk country is in danger from the bitter winter, and only Tiffany, with the aid of the Wee Free Men, can set the season to rights.

Adult Titles

(Original publication information refers to the first American editions. All reissued by HarperCollins. Arranged in Discworld order.) *S* **AUD**

The Colour of Magic. **New York: St. Martin's Press, 1983. 205p. Reissued in 2005. ISBN: 0060855924pa.**

Light Fantastic. **Chester Springs, PA: Gerrads Cross, 1986. 216p. Reissued in 2005. ISBN: 0060855886pa. LP**

Equal Rites. **New York: New American Library, 1988. 245p. Reissued in 2005. ISBN: 0060855908pa.**

Mort. **New York: New American Library, 1989. 240p. Reissued in 2000. ISBN: 0061020680pa.**

Sourcery. **New York: New American Library, 1989. 253p. Reissued in 2000. ISBN: 0061020672pa.**

Wyrd Sisters. **New York: Penguin, 1989. 319p. Reissued in 2000. ISBN: 0061020664pa.**

Pyramids. New York: HarperTorch, 1989. 323p. Reissued in 2001. ISBN: 0061020656pa.

Guards! Guards! New York: HarperTorch, 1989. 355p. Reissued in 2001. ISBN: 0061020648pa.

Eric. New York: ROC, 1995. 178p. Reissued in 2002. ISBN: 0380821214pa.

Moving Pictures. New York: Corgi Books, 1998. 332p. Reissued in 2002. ISBN: 006102063Xpa.

Reaper Man. New York: Transworld Publishers, 1998. 286p. Reissued in 2002. ISBN: 0061020621pa.

Witches Abroad. New York: Penguin, 1991. 252p. Reissued in 2002. ISBN: 0061020613pa.

Small Gods. New York: HarperPrism, 1992. 344p. Reissued in 1994. ISBN: 0061092177pa.

Lords and Ladies. New York: HarperPrism, 1995. 314p. Reissued in 1996. ISBN: 0061056928pa.

Men at Arms. New York: HarperPrism, 1996. 341p. Reissued in 1997. ISBN: 0061092193pa.

Soul Music. New York: HarperPrism, 1995. 389p. Reissued in 1995. ISBN: 0061054895pa. LP

Interesting Times. New York: HarperPrism, 1997. 295p. Reissued in 1998. ISBN: 0061056901pa.

Maskerade. New York: HarperPrism, 1997. 278p. Reissued in 1998. ISBN: 006105691Xpa. LP

Feet of Clay. New York: HarperPrism, 1996. 241p. Reissued in 1997. ISBN: 0061057649pa.

Hogfather. New York: HarperPrism, 1998. 292p. Reissued in 1999. ISBN: 0061059056pa.

Jingo. New York: HarperPrism, 1998. 323p. Reissued in 1999. ISBN: 0061059064pa.

The Last Continent. New York: HarperPrism, 1999. 292p. Reissued in 2000. ISBN: 0061059072pa.

Carpe Jugulum. New York: HarperPrism, 1999. 296p. Reissued in 2000. ISBN: 0061020397pa.

The Fifth Elephant. New York: HarperCollins, 2000. 321p. Reissued in 2001. ISBN: 0061020400pa. LP

The Truth. New York: HarperCollins, 2000. 324p. Reissued in 2001. ISBN: 0380818191pa.

Thief of Time. New York: HarperCollins, 2001. 324p. Reissued in 2002. ISBN: 0061031321pa.

Last Hero. New York: HarperCollins, 2001. 158p. Reissued in 2002. ISBN: 0060507772pa.

Night Watch. New York: HarperCollins, 2002. 338p. Reissued in 2003. ISBN: 0060013125pa.

Monstrous Regiment. New York: HarperCollins, 2003. 353p. ISBN: 006001315X; 0060013168pa.

Going Postal. New York: HarperCollins, 2004. 377p. ISBN: 0060013133; 0060502932pa.

Thud! New York: HarperCollins, 2005. 384p. ISBN: 0060815221; 0060815310pa.

Randall, David

Clovermead: In the Shadow of the Bear. New York: Margaret K. McElderry Books, 2004. 288p. ISBN: 0689866399; 1416907157pa. *MJ* LP
Clovermead Wickward, the twelve-year-old daughter of a country innkeeper, dreams of daring deeds and convinces a guest at the inn to teach her swordplay. Adventure comes to her sooner than expected, for when she finds a bear's tooth and wears it around her neck, she can communicate with bears. This gift grows overwhelming as secrets are revealed about her father that cause the two to journey from their home. They must right his wrong together, but along the way they get enmeshed in the conflict between the nuns of the Lady Moon and the forces of the Lord Ursus.

Shinn, Sharon.

✿ *The Safe-Keeper's Secret*. New York: Viking, 2004. 222p. ISBN: 0670059102; 0142403571pa. *MJ*
In a land where villagers grow up not only to be smiths and gardeners, millers and bakers, but also to be Dream-Makers and Truth-Tellers, a Safe-Keeper is one who keeps secrets of all kinds so that others do not have to bear their burdens alone. On the night that Fiona, the Safe-Keeper for Tambleham, gives birth to her only child, the king's Safe-Keeper arrives in secret and gives her another child to raise. Fiona cares for both as her own, ever watchful to guard the secret as the political turmoil in the king's city begins to boil. (BBYA)

The Truth-Teller's Tale. New York: Viking, 2005. 276p. ISBN: 0670060003. *JS*
Mirror-twins Adele and Eleda grow up together in their father's inn and discover their talents. Eleda is a Truth-Teller and Adele a Secret-Keeper. As the sisters turn seventeen, a good-looking dancing master and his apprentice arrive to stay at the inn, and a series of successive events begin that leads to romantic chaos.

The Dream-Maker's Magic. New York: Viking, 2006. ISBN: 0670060704.
Kellen, a resident of Thrush Hollow, dresses like a boy because her mother believes she gave birth to a son and nothing will convince her otherwise. In school, she be-

friends Gryffin, an outcast because he is crippled. As they grow closer, the two never imagine that the paths of their lives will take them to the Queen's inner circle.

Smith, Sherwood

Crown Duel. **San Diego: Harcourt, 1997. 214p. ISBN: 0152016082; 0142301515pa.** *MJ*
Siblings Count Branaric and Countess Meliara of Tlanth are left impoverished when their father dies and they cannot afford to pay King Galdran's exorbitant taxes. This, combined with their discovery that the king intends to break the traditional oath of Remalna's rulers to guard the Hill People and their colortrees, forces the brother and sister to lead a revolution.

Court Duel. **San Diego: Harcourt, 1998. 245p. ISBN: 0152016082; 0142301515pa.** *MJ*
With the revolution won, Countess Mel returns to her country estate while her brother visits the capital city to be wed. Lured to the palace by Bran's fiancée to be part of the wedding preparations, Mel finds she prefers the blunt, country way of life that she is used to. When a plot against the new king is uncovered, Mel sets out to stop the future usurper and then return home.

Stewart, Paul, and Chris Riddell

<u>**The Edge Chronicles**</u>. **New York: David Fickling Books. (1st American Editions.)** *M*
The Edge juts out over nothingness like the stone prow of a ship. Many kinds of habitats have formed above that prow, including the following: the Deepwoods, where magical and terrifying creatures dwell; the Twilight Woods, where everything can be forgotten; the Mire, polluted by the residents of Undertown; and the Stone Gardens, where the weightless stones are formed that enable the flying city of Sanctaphrax to float and the Sky Pirate ships to fly above the Edge. Thirteen-year-old Twig grew up in the Deepwoods but discovers a destiny far beyond them.

Beyond the Deepwoods. **2004. 276p. ISBN: 0385750684. AUD BRAILLE**
Twig, who has been raised by woodtrolls, is sent away from home when the sky pirates take an interest in him. He strays from the path and encounters a series of progressively menacing beings until he meets the dreaded Gloamglozer.

Stormchaser. **2004. 384p. ISBN: 0385750706. AUD BRAILLE**
Twig, who is now sixteen and part of his father's sky pirate crew, embarks on a dangerous journey in search of stromphrax, the magic substance that will save the city of Sanctaphrax.

Midnight over Sanctaphrax. **2004. 361p. ISBN: 0385750722. AUD BRAILLE**
Now a captain of his own sky pirate ship, Twig has received instructions from his father on how to save Sanctaphrax from Mother Storm, but

Twig's memory is gone and his crew scattered. Twig must recover both before the fatal storm begins.

***The Curse of the Gloamglozer*. 2005. 370p. ISBN: 0385750765.**
This prequel to *Beyond the Deepwoods* focuses on the life of Twig's parents, Quint and Maris. Quint is studying with Linus Pallitax, Maris's father, when he realizes that his mentor is involved with something secret that puts the entire city at risk.

***The Last of the Sky Pirates*. 2005. 368p. ISBN: 0385750781.**
Rook Barkwater lives on the Edge in Undertown and dreams of becoming a Knight Librarian so that he can join their fight against the tyrannical Guardians of the Night. When he sets out on a journey to the Free Glades, he encounters adventures, revelations, and the last sky pirate.

***Vox*. 2005. 384p. ISBN: 0385750803.**
The Guardians of the Night are hoarding more and more power, and Vox is now the ruler of New Sanctaphrax. So Rook joins with rebel forces as they attempt to overthrow Vox and halt the Guardians of the Night.

***Freeglader*. 2006. 416p. ISBN: 038575082X.**
Rook and his friends lead the survivors of New Undertown through the perils of the Mire and the Deepwoods to make a new home in the Free Glades.

Turner, Megan Whalen

The Attolia Trilogy. New York: Greenwillow. *MJS*
In an imaginary land reminiscent of Classical Greece, people of three neighboring countries, Sounis, Eddis, and Attolia, are caught up in political and military intrigue. While they carry out their plans, the actions of the gods can affect anyone from a queen to a lowly thief.

🏶 ***Thief*. 1996. 216p. ISBN: 0688146279; 0060824972pa. AUD BRAILLE**
Gen, a thief in the king of Sounis's dungeon, is freed to accompany the king's magus and his apprentices on a quest for Hamiathes's Gift. This god-created stone can confer the right to the throne of nearby Eddis but has been lost for generations. While Gen plots, he does not know that the gods have plans of their own. (ALAN; BBYA; Newbery Honor)

🏶 ***The Queen of Attolia*. 2000. 279p. ISBN: 068817423X; 0060841826pa. BRAILLE**
When the dangerous Queen of Attolia catches Gen spying on her, she orders his right hand cut off. As Gen recovers, his feelings for the queen alternate between love and fear. Meanwhile the queen must concoct a way to keep the looming Mede military out of her country. (BBYA)

***The King of Attolia*. 2006. 400p. ISBN: 006083577X.**
Costis, a loyal member of the Queen of Attolia's royal guard, despises the new king, until he is forced to be his lieutenant. As the king deftly navigates the perilous political intrigues and murderous plots surrounding him, Costis begins to believe the king is not exactly what he appears to be.

Whitlock, Dean

Sky Carver. **New York: Clarion, 2005. ISBN: 0618443932. *MJ***
In a land where a name signifies an occupation, Thomas Painter is convinced that he has the wrong name. His talent cries out for him to be a woodcarver. When a branch falls from the sky and in his hands becomes a magic wand, he changes his name to Carver and sails downriver, seeking someone who can teach him to use the wand.

Yolen, Jane

The Magic Three of Solatia. **New York: Crowell, 1974. 172p. Reissued by Starscape in 2004. ISBN: 0765348071pa. *MJ***
In the fishing village of Solatia, the legend of the mermaid who loved a prince is told and sung generation after generation. She traded her tail for legs and gave the prince a coat with three magic buttons. But the self-absorbed prince ignored her, and the secret of the buttons was lost. Now Dread Mary dwells in the sea, seeking to sing sailors to their deaths. When Sianna, the button-maker's daughter, is swept out to sea, Dread Mary recognizes the magic buttons on her coat and steals one. Sianna must discover the use of the other two before the magic goes astray again.

Reality with a Twist

If a created fantasy world is not a completely imaginary realm but based in familiar reality, it is listed here. This includes fantasy in which this world is only changed a small amount as well as fantasy in which this world is changed a great deal. The changes must be either magical or inexplicable in nature. Books in which the changes have a scientific explanation are in Chapter 12, "Science Fiction."

Allende, Isabel

The Alexander Cold Trilogy. New York: HarperCollins. (1st American Editions.) *MJ* AUD
Alexander and his friend Nadia are swept up into investigations of the mysterious all over the world, encountering mystical and magical beings along the way.

City of the Beasts. **2002. 416p. ISBN: 006050918X; 0060776455pa.**
Fifteen-year-old Alexander Cold has the chance of a lifetime to take a trip down the Amazon with a team searching for the legendary Yeti. Along the way, he befriends Nadia Santos. Together they go on a shamanic journey, evade the increasing dangers of the jungle, and encounter the mystical "Mist People."

The Kingdom of the Golden Dragon. 2004. 437p. ISBN: 0060589426; 0060589442pa. LP

Alexander and Nadia travel to the Himalayas, where they, along with the heir to the Forbidden Kingdom, use everything from telepathy to technology to save the Golden Dragon.

Forest of the Pygmies. 2005. 296p. ISBN: 0060761962; 0060761989pa. LP

Alexander, now eighteen, and his friend Nadia journey to the plains of Kenya to investigate the Elephant-led safaris. Once there, they discover a mysterious disappearance that leads them to rely on their animal totems, Jaguar and Eagle, and the elusive strength they provide.

Almond, David

🎗 *Skellig.* New York: Delacorte, 1999. 182p. (1st American Edition.) ISBN: 038532653X; 0440229081pa. *JS* BRAILLE LP 📖

Michael and his family have just moved into their new home, but a pall of fear haunts them. His newborn sister is gravely ill. When he explores the house's rundown garage, Michael discovers a strange creature who seems to be part man, part owl, part angel. Michael enlists the aid of his neighbor, Mina, and together they are determined to nurse the ailing, mysterious Skellig back to health. (ALAN; Carnegie Medal; Printz Honor; Whitbread Children's Book Award)

Anderson, M. T.

The Game of Sunken Places. New York: Scholastic, 2004. 260p. ISBN: 0439416604; 0439416612pa. *M* AUD BRAILLE LP 📖

When Gregory and his friend Brian visit Gregory's eccentric Uncle Max in Vermont, they unearth a board game that whisks them out into the wilds of the woods for encounters with various supernatural creatures.

Barry, Dave, and Ridley Pearson

Peter and the Starcatchers. New York: Hyperion, 2004. 451p. ISBN: 0786854456; 078684907Xpa. *MJ* AUD

Peter, an orphan living in London, boards the rundown ship, the *Never Land,* with his fellow orphans. They have been sold into slavery and will be forced to serve King Zarboff, if the ship's captain doesn't starve them first. As Peter searches for food, he spies a mysterious chest that makes creatures around it float. When upper-class passenger Molly tries to dissuade him from investigating the chest further, she confesses that the chest is full of "starstuff," which bestows the ability to fly, have a sense of well-being, and, with overexposure, makes it so you never grow old. The precious treasure from the stars that fell to Earth has been guarded by starcatchers for generations. Now she needs Peter's help because the pirate, Black Stash, is seeking the starstuff for himself.

Peter and the Shadow Thieves. New York: Hyperion, 2006. ISBN: 078683787X.

Peter and his fellow orphans live contentedly on Mollusk Island until the dark Lord Ombra arrives, searching for the starstuff. Peter leaves his friends to contend with Captain Hook while he flies to London to warn Molly and her family.

Bode, N. E.

The Anybodies Trilogy. New York: HarperCollins. _M_
In the ordinary world dwell certain individuals who have the ability to change themselves into anything.

The Anybodies. 2004. 276p. ISBN: 0060557354; 0060557370pa.
Fern Drudger, an imaginative girl growing up in a family of extremely boring people, is convinced that they are not her real parents. She's right. When she finds her real father, she discovers that he can turn himself into anyone or anything, but he's not very good at it. He needs her assistance to locate the book _The Art of Being Anybody_ to help him improve his skills and to keep it out of reach of his sworn enemy, the Miser.

The Nobodies. 2005. 292p. ISBN: 0060557389.
In this sequel to _The Anybodies_, now that Fern has been successfully reunited with her real family, they send her to camp to learn how to use her Anybody magic. Once there, she discovers an unlikely cast of orphans that needs rescuing.

The Somebodies. 2006. 279p. ISBN: 006079111X.
Fern, a royal Anybody, lives in the world above with her father and grandmother, while her fellow Anybodies inhabit the world below Manhattan. The evil Blue Queen accompanied by her minions, the Somebodies, seeks to suck the souls out of books so that someday she will be able to do the same to humans. It's up to Fern to figure out a way to stop her.

Dahl, Roald

James and the Giant Peach. New York: Knopf, 1961. Revised edition reissued in 2002. ISBN: 0375814248; 0141304677pa. _M_ AUD BRAILLE VID

When James's parents are killed by a rampaging rhino, he goes to live with his cruel aunts until magic crystals make a giant peach grow in the back yard. Inside there are human-sized, talking insects, and James travels with them all the way across the ocean.

de Lint, Charles

Newford Tales

Newford, Ontario, is a small town that could perhaps be any place in Canada. There, the residents of the town often have strange and magical encounters. Most of these novels and short stories were written for adults, although they do appeal to young adults. _The Dreaming Place_ and _The Blue Girl_ were specifically written for young adults.

The Dreaming Place. New York: Atheneum, 1990. 138p. Reissued by Firebird in 2002. ISBN: 014230218Xpa. _JS_
In the town of Newford, cousins Nina and Ashley have been roommates since Ashley's mother died three years earlier. The teens bicker con-

stantly, but when Nina starts having strange visions, she doesn't know that Ashley, who has accidentally entered the spirit realm, may be the only one that can save her.

The Blue Girl. **New York: Viking, 2004. 368p. ISBN: 0670059242; 0142405450pa.** *S*
When Imogene and her family move to Newford, she's hoping to get a fresh start at Redding High School, but her goth attire immediately gets her labeled as an outcast. She befriends a fellow misfit, Maxine, who is smart and has always obeyed the rules but longs to taste the adventurous side of life. It's not long before Imogene starts seeing a pale, geeky ghost and learns the story of Adrian, a bullied boy who committed suicide. Adrian's friends are amoral fairies who draw soul-suckers to Imogene, endangering her life and the lives of those she loves.

Newford Novels. *S* [Adult]

Memory and Dream. **New York: Tor, 1994. 400p. Reissued by Tor in 1995. ISBN: 0812534077pa.**

Trader. **New York: Tor, 1997. 352p. Reissued by Orb Books in 2005. ISBN: 0765302969pa.**

Someplace to Be Flying. **New York: Tor, 1998. Reissued by Orb Books in 2005. ISBN: 076530757X pa.**

Forests of the Heart. **New York: Tor, 2000. 397p. Reissued in 2001. ISBN: 0312875681pa.**

The Onion Girl. **New York: Tor, 2001. 508p. Reissued by Forge in 2002. ISBN: 0765303817pa.**

Seven Wild Sisters. **Burton, MO: Subterranean Press, 2002. 160p. (Out of Print)**

Spirits in the Wires. **New York: Tor, 2003. 448p. ISBN: 0312873980; 0312869711pa.**

Short Story Collections

Dreams Underfoot. **New York: Tor, 1993. 414p. Reissued by Orb Books in 2003. ISBN: 0765306794pa.**

The Ivory and the Horn. **New York: Tor, 1995. 318p. (Out of Print)**

Moonlight and Vines. **New York: Tor, 1999. 384p. Reissued by Orb Books in 2005. ISBN: 0765309173pa.**

Tapping the Dream Tree. **New York: Tor, 2002. 540p. Reissued in 2003. ISBN: 0312868405pa.**

Hour before Dawn. **Burton, MO: Subterranean Press, 2005. 114p. ISBN: 1596060271.**

Dickinson, Peter

The Tears of the Salamander. **New York: Wendy Lamb Books, 2003. 197p. ISBN: 0385730985; 0440238234pa. _MJ_ BRAILLE**

Alfredo lives in Italy and loves music and fire. When a strange accident leaves him an orphan, he goes to live with his Uncle Giorgio. He soon discovers his guardian is a sorcerer with nefarious plans that he must find a way to stop.

Furlong, Monica

<u>The Wise Child Trilogy</u>. New York: Knopf. _JS_

In Britain during the Dark Ages, a young girl is raised to be a white witch by the village healer, Juniper.

Wise Child. **1987. 228p. Reissued by Random House in hardcover in 2004. ISBN: 0394891058; 0394825985pa.**

When Wise Child is left alone, the village decides she should become a Doran, a solitary witch skilled in the art of healing. Juniper takes her in and teaches her the arts of white magic. Her real mother returns and tries to lure Wise Child into practicing the black arts.

Juniper. **1991. 198p. Reissued by Random House in hardcover in 2004. ISBN: 0394832205; 0679833692pa.**

In this prequel to *Wise Child*, Ninnoc—Juniper as a child—grew up as a princess in a castle, but because she has magical powers, she is sent to study with Euny. She must defeat her aunt, an evil sorceress, before her father, the king, is killed and her cousin takes the throne.

Colman. **2004. 267p. ISBN: 0375815147; 0375815155pa.**
Juniper, the healer, and Wise Child, her apprentice, flee their village after being accused of witchcraft. With Coman, they return to Cornwall and the castle where Juniper was born.

Funke, Cornelia

The Thief Lord. **New York: Scholastic, 2002. 349p. (1st American Edition.) ISBN: 0439404371; 0439771323pa. _M_ AUD BRAILLE LP**

Prosper and Bo are orphans, on the run from their cruel aunt and uncle. They find shelter in Venice with the Thief Lord and his band of young followers. The brothers just want to stay together, but they encounter a mysterious magic that changes their world.

Kindl, Patrice

🌟 *Owl in Love*. **Boston: Houghton Mifflin, 1993. 204p. Reissued by Graphia in 2004. ISBN: 0618439102pa. _MJ_ AUD** 📖

Owl Tycho, a shape-shifter, transforms at will from human to owl. Her parents are witches, so they understand the ways of shape-shifters. Owl is supposed to hunt at night, but she has fallen in love with her science teacher. Instead of hunting, she haunts the woods behind his house and finds an unsuspected entity in the forest. (Children's Mythopoeic Award)

Knox, Elizabeth

The Dreamhunter Duet. New York: Farrar, Straus & Giroux. (1st American Editions.) _JS_

Life proceeds much as it did in Edwardian times except for the changes wrought by the discovery of "the Place," an island where those with the gift can gather dreams and bring them back to the ordinary world.

Dreamhunter. 2006. 384p. ISBN: 0374318530.

Fifteen-year-old Laura's father is in the business of capturing dreams in "the Place" and sharing them with audiences of sleepers. When he disappears, she sets off after him, determined even to search the Place herself.

Larbalestier, Justine

The Magic or Madness Trilogy. New York: Razorbill. _JS_

In certain families, the gift of magic can be passed from one generation to the next, but the power carries dangers of its own as Reason discovers when her mother goes mad.

Magic or Madness. 2005. 271p. ISBN: 1595140220; 1595140700pa.

Fifteen-year-old Reason roams the Australian outback in her nomadic life with her mother, listening to frightening tales concerning her grandmother's use of witchcraft. When her mother succumbs to a nervous breakdown and is confined to a mental hospital, Reason moves in with the grandmother she dreads and discovers her life is not as dark as her mother made her think it would be. As she explores her new home, she finds a key and opens the door into Manhattan.

Magic Lessons. New York: Razorbill, 2006. 288p. ISBN: 1595140549.

Reason has discovered her magical heritage, which leaves her with a dire choice: use her magic and die young or refrain and go insane, like her mother. As she strives to create her own alternative and begins to trust her grandmother in Australia, she is transported to New York. There, she needs the help of her new friends to resist the machinations of her grandfather who wants her power for himself.

Lawrence, Michael

Withern Rise Series. New York: Greenwillow. _JS_

Two teenagers find a way to travel between their nearly identical worlds.

A Crack in the Line. 2004. 323p. ISBN: 0060724773; 006072479X pa. _JS_

Alaric and his father live in Withern Rise, the dilapidated Victorian family home just outside of London. Despair has permeated their lives since the death of Alaric's mother in a train wreck two years earlier. When Alaric comes in contact with a wooden sculpture carved by his mother, he is transported to a nearly identical world. There he meets Naia, who looks just like him and lives in a clean and well-cared-for Withern Rise. Their lives are very similar, except that Naia's mother is alive.

Small Eternities. 2005. 322p. ISBN: 0060724803.

Naia and Alaric have switched realities. Now Naia lives the motherless life and Alaric seems to have his family back. The sculpture that gave them each access to the other's world has been destroyed, and it seems they will be unable to travel between their worlds until a flood in both realities leads the teens to touch a large family tree that enables them to traverse the realms again.

Levine, Gail Carson

The Wish. **New York: HarperCollins, 1999. 197p. ISBN: 0060279001; 0060759119pa. *MJ* AUD**

When Wilma gives an old woman on the subway her seat, her kindness is rewarded with the granting of one wish. Wilma wishes to be the most popular kid in Claverford School. Only after she's made the wish does it occur to her that her popularity won't last long because there are only three more weeks until graduation.

Naylor, Phyllis Reynolds

Sang Spell. **New York: Atheneum, 1998. 176p. ISBN: 0689820070lb; 0689820062pa. AUD *MJ***

As Josh hitchhikes from Boston to Dallas, he grieves for his mother, who was killed in a car accident, and worries about beginning his junior year in a new school as he lives with his aunt. Things go from bad to worse when he is beaten and robbed and left at the side of the road. A woman in a horse-drawn carriage rescues him, and he wakes up in the strange community of Canara, which seems almost like a medieval village. As he heals, he learns about the people who have taken him in and discovers he may never be able to leave.

Shusterman, Neal

The Eyes of Kid Midas. **Boston: Little, Brown, 1992. 185p. Reissued by Simon & Schuster in 2004. ISBN: 0689873492pa. *MJ***

Kevin is always being bullied by Betram, but things turn around when Kevin hikes up a mountain and finds a pair of sunglasses radiating the magic of the mountain. When Kevin puts them on, anything he wishes for materializes. When he tells Bertram to go to hell, the ground literally swallows his nemesis. But revenge is not all he hoped for, and Kevin must find away to reverse all he's done before the fabric of reality unravels.

Downsiders. **New York: Simon & Schuster, 1999. 246p. ISBN: 0689803753lb; 0689839693pa. *MJ***

Instead of coping with the cliques and quizzes of high school, Talon traverses a much more dangerous place—the sewers and subways of New York City, for he lives "Downside" in the unknown underground of the Big Apple. He and the other Downsiders never mix with "Topsiders," but when his sister gets ill, he goes Topside for medicine and meets Lindsay. He is drawn to her, as she is to him. Their tenuous relationship, however, is threatened when their worlds collide.

Steiber, Ellen

The Gemstone Series. New York: Tor. [Adult] *S*

Tucked away in the modern world, lies the magical port city of Arcato where gemstones are imbued with the powers of the gods and those who find them can cast spells.

A Rumor of Gems. 2005. 464p. ISBN: 0312858795.

Stevermer, Caroline

When the King Comes Home. New York: Tor, 2000. 236p. Reissued in 2001. ISBN: 0812589815pa. [Adult] *JS*

King Julian IV of Avaris died two hundred years ago, but his people still long for him. Legend says that when the king comes home, all wishes will be granted and all dreams will come true. When Hail Rosamer, an apprentice artist, spies an old man fishing who looks remarkably like King Julian, she embarks on an adventure that may disprove the legend.

Twelve Hawks, John

The Fourth Realm Trilogy. New York: Doubleday. [Adult] *S* AUD LP

Throughout the centuries, Travelers, people who have achieved pure enlightenment, have used their gifts to aid the human race. Their enemies are the Tabulas, who seek strict control over all aspects of life. Their guardians, the Harlequins, dedicate their lives to the sole task of protecting the Travelers at all costs.

The Traveler. 2005. 456p. ISBN: 038551428X.

Wright, John C.

Orphans of Chaos. New York: Tor, 2005. 320p. ISBN: 0765311313. [Adult] *S*

Five orphans who have lived all of their lives at a strict British boarding school develop unusual powers and must solve the riddle of their true natures if they want to find a way home. **Adult**

Gateway Fantasy

Gateway Fantasies start in one type of world and move to another, the originating world providing a gateway into another world. The story usually begins in the world that is familiar and moves to a magical world, although sometimes it's the reverse, starting in a magical world and traveling to the realistic world. The most well-known example would be C. S. Lewis's Chronicles of Narnia, in which first Peter, Susan, Lucy, and Edmund and then later others find a magical passageway from England into the land of Narnia. Lewis Carroll's *Alice in Wonderland* would also seem to fit here, except that Alice was dreaming. In dream fantasy, the alternate realm disappears when the dreamer awakens. Tolkien didn't even consider this a kind of fantasy (Tolkien 1966).

Fantasy that involves comings and goings between the realm of faerie and the mortal world could also fit here, but it is such an extensive subgenre that those titles are listed in Chapter 6. Time travel fantasies could be a kind of Gateway Fantasy except the travel is not to or from a magical or alternate world but between periods of historical reality. Time travel stories are in Chapter 10.

Anthony, Piers

The Magic of Xanth. [Adult] *S*

In the world of Xanth, magic imbues all life, puns abound, and occasionally the magical folk are forced to visit a world much like Florida, known as drear Mundania.

A Spell for Chameleon. New York: Ballantine, 1977. 344p. ISBN: 0345347536pa.

The Source of Magic. New York: Ballantine, 1978. 336p. ISBN: 0345350588pa.

Castle Roogna. New York: Ballantine, 1979. 329p. ISBN: 0345350480pa.

Centaur Aisle. New York: Ballantine, 1981. 304p. ISBN: 0345352467pa.

Ogre, Ogre. New York: Ballantine, 1982. 320p. ISBN: 0345354923pa.

Night Mare. New York: Ballantine, 1982. 307p. ISBN: 0345354931pa.

Dragon on a Pedestal. New York: Ballantine, 1983. 303p. ISBN: 0345349369pa.

Crewel Lye. New York: Ballantine, 1984. 309p. ISBN: 0345345991pa.

Golem in the Gears. New York: Ballantine, 1985. 326p. ISBN: 0345318862pa.

Vale of the Vole. New York: Avon, 1987. 304p. Reissued by Tor in 2000. ISBN: 0812574966pa.

Heaven Cent. New York: Avon, 1988. 352p. Reissued by Tor in 2000. ISBN: 0812574982pa.

Man from Mundania. New York: 1989. 352p. Reissued by Tor in 2000. ISBN: 0812574974pa.

Isle of View. New York: Morrow, 1990. 344p. Issued by Avon in 1990. ISBN: 0380759470pa.

Question Quest. New York: Morrow, 1991. 359p. Issued by Avon in 1991. ISBN: 0380759489pa.

The Color of Her Panties. New York: Morrow, 1992. Issued by Avon in 1992. ISBN: 0380759497pa.

Demons Don't Dream. New York: Tor, 1993. 304p. Reissued in 1996. ISBN: 0812534832pa.

Harpy Thyme. New York: Tor, 1994. 318p. Reissued in 1995. ISBN: 0812534840pa.

Geis of the Gargoyle. New York: Tor, 1995. 320p. Reissued later in 1995. ISBN: 0812534859pa.

Roc and a Hard Place. New York: Tor, 1995. 319p. Reissued in 1996. ISBN: 0812534867pa.

Yon Ill Wind. New York: Tor, 1996. 320p. Reissued in 1997. ISBN: 0812555104pa.

Faun & Games. New York: Tor, 1997. 320p. Reissued in 1998. ISBN: 0812555112pa.

Zombie Lover. New York: Tor, 1998. 303p. Reissued in 1999. ISBN: 0812555120pa.

Xone of Contention. New York: Tor, 1999. 304p. Reissued in 2000. ISBN: 0812555236pa.

The Dastard. New York: Tor, 2000. 303p. Reissued in 2001. ISBN: 0812574737pa.

Swell Foop. New York: Tor, 2001. 300p. Reissued in 2002. ISBN: 0812574745pa.

Up in a Heaval. New York: Tor, 2002. 348p. Reissued in 2003. ISBN: 0812574990pa.

Cube Route. New York: Tor, 2003. 333p. ISBN: 0765304066; 0765343096pa.

Currant Events. New York: Tor, 2004. 336p. ISBN: 0765304074; 076534310Xpa.

Pet Peeve. New York: Tor, 2005. 332p. ISBN: 0765304082.

Stork Naked. New York: Tor, 2006. ISBN: 0765304090.

Barker, Clive

The Books of Abarat. New York: Joanna Cotler Books. AUD *JS*
In the archipelago of Abarat, every one of the twenty-five islands is a different hour of the day (with the twenty-fifth existing Outside of Time), and each hosts a corresponding variety of magical creatures. Evil stirs, and Candy Quackenbush is called to quell it.

Abarat. 2002. 388p. ISBN: 0060280921; 0060596376pa.
Bored with her life in Chickentown, Minnesota, Candy Quackenbush skips school and rides a wave all the way to the archipelago of Abarat. As Candy investigates the mysterious islands and their inhabitants, she inadvertently becomes the focus of the two rivals for power in the realm.

Days of Magic, Nights of War. 2004. 489p. ISBN: 0060291702; 0064409325pa.

The Lord of Midnight sends his henchmen to kidnap Candy Quackenbush because he believes she's a threat. While Candy tries to avoid them, she discovers that she can cast spells she never learned and remember things she never did.

Bray, Libba

A Great and Terrible Beauty. New York: Delacorte, 2003. 403p. ISBN: 0385730284; 0385732317pa. _JS_ AUD LP

Gemma, an English girl raised in India, longs to go to school in Victorian London, but her mother forbids it. When her mother is killed, however, Gemma and her grieving father return to England, and Gemma inadvertently gets her wish. Her grandmother sends her to the fashionable finishing school for young ladies, Spence Academy. Gemma encounters not only a school world full of petty rivalries and cruelties but also "the Realm," a place of dark magic where she is a person of power.

Rebel Angels. New York: Delacorte, 2005. 548p. ISBN: 0385730292. AUD

Gemma and her friends visit London for the Christmas holiday and are swept away in a swirl of social engagements and budding romances. All the while, they are searching for the Temple in the Realms, so that the dark magic can be controlled once again.

Browne, N. M.

Warriors of Alavna. New York: Bloomsbury, 2002. 308p. (1st American Edition.) ISBN: 1582347751; 1582349169. _JS_

Teenagers Ursula and Dan are on a field trip to Hastings when a mysterious yellow fog draws them into an alternate England during the time of the Roman conquest. Dan, an athlete, finds undreamt-of skill as a berserker warrior, while Ursula slowly learns that she has the same gifts of magic as the sorceress who brought them.

Warriors of Camlann. New York: Bloomsbury, 2003. 398p. (1st American Edition.) ISBN: 1582348170. _JS_

In this sequel to *The Warriors of Alavna,* Ursula and Dan step through the Veil into a Roman Britain in the time of King Arthur. They find that their talents have changed, and they must learn how to survive anew in this alternate reality.

Chabon, Michael

Summerland. New York: Miramax, 2002. 500p. ISBN: 0786808772; 0786816155pa. _MJ_ AUD LP

After the death of his mother, Ethan Feld and his father move to Clam Island, where the children all play baseball in an always-sunny spot called "Summerland." Ethan is the worst baseball player in the world, but at his

father's urging, he agrees to keep playing. Out of the blue, the long-gone ballplayer Ringfinger Brown appears and recruits Ethan. A magical community needs him to be a hero, for Summerland is no ordinary place. It connects a series of alternate worlds and magical creatures that are in danger of being destroyed by the trickster Coyote. They need baseball and Ethan to save them.

Collins, Suzanne

The Underland Chronicles. New York: Scholastic. *M* AUD
Far below New York City, a society exists where giant cockroaches, rats, spiders, and bats live alongside strangely pale humans. The humans and their bondmates, the bats, live in the city of Regalia, but the rats want to wage war against the residents of Regalia and the Overlander of prophecy.

Gregor the Overlander. 2003. 311p. ISBN: 0439435366; 0439678137pa. LP
When Gregor follows his little sister Boots down a chute in the laundry room, he finds himself in a strange underground world, populated with giant bats, spiders, rats, and roaches. The people who live there are convinced that Gregor is the hero of prophecy who will save them from the rats, but Gregor is more concerned with finding his missing father.

Gregor and the Prophecy of Bane. 2004. 312p. ISBN: 0439650755; 0439650763pa.
Gregor has sworn that he will never return to the Underland. But when giant cockroaches kidnap his sister, he goes back to the city of Regalia to find her. There, he learns of the prophecy that says he will be the end of Bane, a white super rat—but only if the rats do not get his sister first. Joining with his old companions, Gregor sets out to find Bane and keep Boots safe.

Gregor and the Curse of the Warmbloods. 2005. 358p. ISBN: 0439656230; 0439656249pa. LP
A plague is spreading in the Underland, and Gregor and his friends journey to new areas of the Underland and brave such dangers as carnivorous plants to find the medicine that's needed.

Gregor and the Marks of Secret. 2006. 325p. ISBN: 0439791456.
Riding the bats they have bonded with, Gregor and his companions, fly to the depths of the Underland in search of a missing colony of mice and the eight-foot tall rat, Bane, who is dangerously insane.

Dunkle, Clare

The Hollow Kingdom Trilogy. New York: Henry Holt. *JS*
In nineteenth-century England, Hallow Hall, a Victorian estate, is a gateway to the realm of the goblins, who work magic and whose king seeks a human to be his wife.

The Hollow Kingdom. 2003. 230p. ISBN: 0805073906. AUD LP
Newly orphaned sisters Kate and Emily are lured into an underground goblin kingdom, where Kate agrees to marry the goblin king to save her sister.

Close Kin. **2004. 216p. ISBN: 080507497X. AUD**
Years after the end of *The Hollow Kingdom,* Kate is happily married to the goblin king, and Emily enjoys living in the goblin world and taking care of the children. When she spurns the elf Seylin, he decides to seek out the others of his kind. Once he's gone, Emily realizes how much she cares for him and follows him. Along the way, she uncovers an elvish problem that only the goblins can solve.

In the Coils of the Snake. **2005. 240p. ISBN: 0805077472.**
Marak, the goblin king, has raised the human Miranda to wed Catspaw, the heir to his throne. Marak's death leaves Kate a widow and Miranda desolate. The expected marriage does not occur. Instead, Miranda is kidnapped by an elven lord and becomes the focus of what could be the final battle between the goblins and the elves.

Ende, Michael

The Neverending Story. *See* Chapter 2, "Epic Fantasy."

Funke, Cornelia

The Inkheart Trilogy. New York: Chicken House. (1st American Editions.) _MJ_ **AUD LP**
In contemporary Europe live a few gifted people who are so powerful that when they read aloud, they can read characters right out of books—and people into them.

Inkheart. **2003. 534p. ISBN: 0439531640; 0439709105pa.**
Twelve-year-old Meggie lives a quiet life with her father until the mysterious stranger, Dustfinger, disturbs their peace. Gradually Meggie uncovers the implausible truth about her father. He is not just an ordinary bookbinder. He can read characters to life. When Meggie was three, he released several characters from the book *Inkheart* into the world while at the same time he lost his wife in the world of the novel. Now danger abounds from these characters, and Meggie must help find a way to put things right.

Inkspell. **2005. 635p. ISBN: 0439554004.**
One year after the end of *Inkheart,* Dustfinger finally returns to the book through the reading of the mysterious Orpheus. Meggie and Farid follow, transported by Meggie's own power. Dustfinger is delighted to be home at last, while Meggie enjoys exploring the book world. When her parents also enter the world, they seek only to bring their daughter home. Meggie encounters Fenoglio, the original author, and at first resists his notion of changing the course of the story that has developed in ways he did not intend. But when the evil Adderhead takes over the castle of the Laughing Prince, Meggie is eager to use her power to change life in the Ink World.

Gaiman, Neil

Neverwhere. **New York: Avon, 1997. 337p. ISBN: 0380973634; 0380789019pa. [Adult]** _S_ **AUD**
Richard Mayhew, a not-quite-successful London businessman, helps a wounded girl named Door by bringing her home. When she leaves, she alters reality so that no one, not even his fiancée, can see him anymore. Needing Door's help to shift his life back, he locates her in London Below and learns that the only way to succeed is to begin a perilous quest by negotiating the nebulous underworld filled with violence, wizards, and nobility.

Hoffman, Mary

The Stravaganza Trilogy. New York: Bloomsbury. (1st American Editions.) _JS_ **AUD**
The Stravaganti are scientists who create talismans that can send their bearers through time and space to the alternate world of Talia. Three young people find the talismans and experience unexpected adventures.

> *Stravaganza: City of Masks*. **2002. 344p. ISBN: 1582347913; 1582349177pa.**
> Fifteen-year-old Lucien lives in London and is dying of brain cancer, but his father's gift of a blank, Italian journal transports him to the magical city of Bellezza, which resembles Renaissance Venice. At home he is weakened by chemotherapy treatments. In Bellezza his health returns, and he becomes entangled in the city's political intrigues.

> *Stravaganza: City of Stars*. **2003. 452p. ISBN: 1582348391; 1582349827pa.**
> Georgia buys a winged horse figurine in an antique shop, little suspecting that it will transport her to the mysterious land of Talia and the city of Remora, which mirrors a sixteenth-century Tuscany. There, she encounters a real winged horse, as well as a healthy Lucien, with whom she went to school in London, and Falco, a disabled boy who wants to travel back to her time to partake in the benefits of modern medicine.

> *Stravaganza: City of Flowers*. **2005. 488p. ISBN: 1582348871.**
> London teen Sky Meadows does his best to take care of his invalid mother. When he touches an antique perfume bottle, he becomes the newest Stravaganti and travels to Talia. Disguised as a novice friar, he must sort through the machinations of rival families and, with his fellow Stravaganti, avert disaster.

Kay, Guy Gavriel

The Fionovar Tapestry. New York: Arbor House. (1st American Editions published by Arbor House. All reissued by Roc in 2001. [Adult] _S_
The mage Loren Silvercloak invites five young Canadians to Fionovar as guests at court, where they will celebrate the anniversary of the king's ascension to the throne. Quickly, the five students realize that their role in this land of mages, immortals, and Children of the Light is far more complex than it appeared at first.

The Summer Tree. 1985. 323p. Reissue ISBN: 0451458222pa.

 The Wandering Fire. 1986. 298p. Reissue ISBN: 0451458265pa. (Prix Aurora Award)

The Darkest Road. 1986. 420p. Reissue ISBN: 0451458338pa.

Lewis, C. S.

<u>**The Chronicles of Narnia**</u>. **New York: Macmillan. (1st American Editions published by Macmillan. All reissued in hardcover in 1994 by HarperCollins.)** <u>M</u> **AUD BRAILLE**
In Narnia, animals can talk; dragons, fauns, and unicorns are real; and children from this world can become kings and queens. (Listed in publication order.)

The Lion, the Witch and the Wardrobe. 1950. 186p. ISBN: 0060234814; 0060765445pa. VID
Edmund, Susan, Lucy, and Peter, siblings who are sent from London to the country during World War II, stumble upon a magic wardrobe. When they pass through the wardrobe, they enter the land of Narnia, where animals can talk, but the White Witch rules.

Prince Caspian. 1951. 216p. ISBN: 0060234830; 0060764929pa.
Peter, Susan, Edmund, and Lucy are summoned from a dreary train station back to Narnia, where they ruled as kings and queens. Now they must help Aslan save Prince Caspian.

The Voyage of the Dawn Treader. 1952. 216p. ISBN: 0060234865; 0060764945pa.
King Caspian has built a ship, the *Dawn Treader*. Edmund and Lucy return to Narnia with their cousin, Eustace, to sail with him in search of seven lords who were banished by his evil uncle, Miraz.

The Silver Chair. 1953. 217p. ISBN: 0060234954; 0060764937pa.
Eustace and Jill escape the school bullies through a door that leads to Aslan. He sends them to Narnia on a quest to free King Caspian's missing son, Prince Rilian, from an evil enchantment.

The Horse and His Boy. 1954. 217p. ISBN: 0060234881; 0060764872pa.
During the Golden Age of Narnia, when Peter is High King, two children and their talking horses flee to Narnia.

Magician's Nephew. 1955. 186p. ISBN: 0060234970; 0060764902pa.
In this prequel to *The Lion, the Witch, and The Wardrobe*, Digory's scheming, sorcerer-uncle sends Polly to another world with no way to get back. Digory goes after her. They end up in the Woods between the Worlds, which leads them to many different worlds, including Narnia.

The Last Battle. 1956. 211p. ISBN: 0060234938; 0060764880pa.

During the last days of Narnia, the good King Tirian tries to stop the false Aslan and the ugly Ape who guards him from leading Narnians into slavery. The real Aslan calls all who love and believe in Narnia to return for the final battle against the forces of evil.

Nix, Garth

The Keys to the Kingdom. New York: Scholastic. *MJ* AUD

The Will created seven keys and designated seven guardians, one for each day, to rule the House, gateway to many worlds. When their power corrupted them, the Will sought another way and circuitously enlisted the aid of a young man of this world, Arthur Penhaligon.

Mister Monday. 2003. 361p. Reissued in hardcover in 2005. ISBN: 0439703697; 0439551234pa.

Arthur Penhaligon is an ordinary boy with asthma until Sneezer passes him one of the seven keys that leads him to the world of the House. Here, the key could help him overthrow Mister Monday and become master of the Lower House himself—if the other denizens don't kill him first.

Grim Tuesday. 2004. 321p. Reissued in hardcover in 2005. ISBN: 0439703700; 0439436559pa.

Arthur has been home with his family for less than a day when Grim Tuesday tries to foreclose on his family's home. To save them, Arthur returns to the House, determined to find the second key.

Drowned Wednesday. 2005. 389p. ISBN: 0439700868; 0439436567pa.

Arthur is in the hospital, recovering from his last venture into the House, when he receives an invitation from Drowned Wednesday. He fears she will be as difficult to deal with as the preceding Days. When he arrives in her domain, he must navigate a host of seafaring troubles in order to save her and himself.

Sir Thursday. 2006. 344p. ISBN: 0439700876.

After his encounter with Wednesday, Arthur is ready to return home. But a Spirit-eater is impersonating him there, and Arthur must stay in the House. While his friend Leaf seeks to stop the Spirit-eater, Arthur is unwillingly drafted into Sir Thursday's army.

Park, Paul

The Tourmaline Trilogy. New York: Tor. [Adult] *JS*

Sixteen-year-old Miranda lives with her adopted family in Massachusetts but dreams that she is really a princess. When the world she knows suddenly disappears, she and her two friends are transported to an Earth where England was washed away in a tidal wave and Roumania is a great power. They all discover that she is indeed a princess and is in imminent peril.

A Princess of Roumania. 2005. ISBN: 0765310961; 0765349507pa.

The Tourmaline. 2006. ISBN: 076531441X.

Stross, Charles

The Merchant Prince Series. New York: Tor. [Adult] S

When reporter Miriam Beckstein unearths evidence of a money-laundering scheme, she thinks she has her next scoop. Instead, she loses her job and finds her life in jeopardy. A locket that belonged to her mother, who was murdered when Miriam was an infant, arrives. When she gazes into it, it takes her to Gruinmarkt, where knights ride on horseback and carry automatic weapons. There she discovers that she is a lost heiress—but her life is still in danger.

Family Trade. 2004. 303p. ISBN: 0765309297; 0765348217pa.

Hidden Family. 2005. 303p. ISBN: 0765313472; 0765352052pa.

Clan Corporate. 2006. 320p. ISBN: 0765309300pa.

Vande Velde, Vivian

Now You See It. Orlando, FL: Harcourt, 2005. ISBN: 0152053115; 0152054618pa. MJ

Nothing would have changed for Wendy if only the school bully hadn't broken her glasses. In desperate need, Wendy picked up the pair of sunglasses on the lawn and found that she could see perfectly. Well, perhaps more than perfectly. Now she sees dead people, witches, and a portal that will lead her to an elf prince who needs her help.

Wolfe, Gene

The Wizard Knight Duology. New York: Tor. [Adult] S

When an American teenager is transported to Mythgarthr, an old crone casts a spell that transforms him into a man and dubs him Able of the High Heart. As he embarks on his quest for a mystical sword, the boy who now lives in a man's body struggles to make sense of the magical world he inhabits.

The Knight. 2004. 430p. ISBN: 0765309890; 0765347016pa.

The Wizard. 2004. 477p. ISBN: 0765312018; 0765314703pa.

Alternate History

Alternate history fantasy is created when the author selects a particular place and time in world history in which to set the story and then changes something so that the known history does not occur. Following the "What if" conjecture of speculative fiction, alternate histories ask questions such as: What if the South had won the Civil War? What if European settlers had found Native Americans with magical abilities? What if Hitler had not been defeated? Magic can be a part, or cause, of this divergent history. If the change in history is inexplicable, the book is also considered fantasy. If the change is scientific (the Allies lose World War II because aliens invade), the novel is listed in Chapter 12, "Science Fiction." Alternate history always concerns an event in the past that is different from known history. There is far more alternate history written for adults than young adults.

Blackwood, Gary

The Year of the Hangman. **New York: Dutton, 2002. 261p. ISBN: 0525469214; 0142400785pa. *MJ* AUD BRAILLE**
In 1777 when George Washington is captured by the British, the American Revolution succumbs to defeat. Spoiled Creighton Brown, seventeen-year-old son of a lost British officer, arrives in the colonies as the prisoner of privateer Benedict Arnold and ends up living with rebel Benjamin Franklin in Spanish New Orleans.

Card, Orson Scott

The Tales of Alvin Maker. New York: Tor. [Adult] *JS* AUD
Born and raised in a frontier America where life is hard and magic is real, Alvin is the seventh son of a seventh son, and he has the gift of Making. With the great power comes great responsibility and risk, as the Unmaker seeks to wreak destruction on Alvin and America.

> ☙ *Seventh Son.* **1987. 241p. Reissued in 1988. ISBN: 0812533054pa. [Adult]**
> (Locus Award; Mythopoeic Award)

> ☙ *Red Prophet.* **1988. 311p. Reissued in 1996. ISBN: 0812524268pa. (Locus Award)**

> ☙ *Prentice Alvin.* **1989. 342p. Reissued in 1989. ISBN: 0812502124pa. (Locus Award)**

> *Alvin Journeyman.* **1995. 381p. Reissued in 1996. ISBN: 0812509234pa.**

> *Heartfire.* **1998. 301p. Reissued in 1999. ISBN: 0812509242pa.**

> *The Crystal City.* **2003. 384p. ISBN: 0312864833; 0812564626pa.**

Harlan, Thomas

The Oath of the Empire Series. New York, Tor. [Adult] *S*
In the year A.D. 600, the Roman Empire thrives because it relies on the strength of its armies and its Thaumaturges, who wield their magic for the Empire.

> *The Shadow of Ararat.* **1999. 510p. Reissued in 2000. ISBN: 0812590090pa.**

> *The Gate of Fire.* **2000. 477p. Reissued in 2001. ISBN: 0812590104pa.**

> *The Storm of Heaven.* **2001. 558p. Reissued in 2002. ISBN: 0812590112pa.**

> *The Dark Lord.* **2002. 538p. ISBN: 0312865600; 0812590120pa.**

Lackey, Mercedes (with Eric Flint and Dave Freer)

The Heirs of Alexandria Duology. Riverdale, NY: Baen. [Adult] *S*
In 1537, the Venetian Republic is a city rife with political intrigue and magical machinations, poised on the brink of disaster.

> *The Shadow of the Lion.* **2002. 825p. Reissued in 2003. ISBN: 0743471474pa.**

> *This Rough Magic.* **2003. 822p. ISBN: 0743471490; 0743499093pa.**

MacLeod, Ian R.

The Light Ages Duology. New York: Ace. [Adult] _S_
  In a divergent Victorian England, the course of the Industrial Revolution changed when aether, a material substance from underground, enabled guild-workers to build machines with aether and the right spell.

  The Light Ages. 2003. 456p. Reissued in 2005. ISBN: 0441012744pa.

  House of Storms. 2005. 457p. ISBN: 0441012809; 0441013422pa.

Profile of Kenneth Oppel

        Born August 31, 1967, in Port Alberni on the island of Victoria in British Columbia, Canada, Kenneth Oppel decided at age twelve that he wanted to be a writer. His first novel, *Colin's Fantastic Video Adventure,* which he wrote when he was fourteen, was published in 1985 through a friend who sent the story to Roald Dahl. Mr. Dahl sent the book to his literary agent, and the young Kenneth's career was launched. His many children's books have been widely recognized in Canada. He became more well known in the United States when his book *Airborn* was named a Printz honor book in 2005 (*Contemporary Authors Online*, Infotrac Galegroup Database; www.kennethoppel.com).

Photo: Peter Riddihough

Interview with Kenneth Oppel

Conducted via e-mail February 7–10, 2006

SF: Your <u>Silverwing</u> trilogy was animal fantasy, and now you have created a world with an alternate technology. Do you have preference between the two kinds of fantasy? What is special or unique about each kind?

KO: I had always promised myself I would never write a talking animal story. I thought they were corny, especially when the animals wore clothing. But thanks to a friend, I got interested in bats and was won over by these small, winged nocturnal creatures who saw the world with their ears as much as their eyes, who were master navigators and made heroic migrations of up to 1,200 kilometres every fall—and most importantly, who until recently had inspired fear and loathing in most of Western culture. If I was indeed going to write about animals, I wanted an unlikely one, not a cute and cuddly one; I wanted one that hadn't been done before, and I saw in bats the opportunity to create a whole new world with its own mythology and technology.

Airborn was similar in that it gave me the chance to create a whole new world, this one more like our own, perhaps, but with a number of key physical, technological, and zoological differences! In both instances, I borrowed heavily from science and natural history and embellished to suit my purposes. Being a fiction writer is a license to create the world according to your rules and desires. It can be very invigorating—and equally daunting when presented with all the infinite choices! That's why it was so important and beneficial to ground the bat books firmly in science and natural history; and the Airborn books in turn-of-the-century technology.

SF: All of your work is very detailed. What kind of research do you do?

KO: For the Silverwing books, I just got out three or four books on bats from the library and read selectively. It was very important for me to get all my basic facts right: their diet, their social organization, migrations, echolocation. I needed my readers to believe these were real bats—and then they'd believe me when elements of fantasy were introduced.

Similarly, I read quite a bit about the real airships of the '20s and '30s, particularly the *Graf Zeppelin* and the *Hindenburg,* which were the models for the *Aurora*. I wanted to know all the basics about lighter-than-air flight, down to the amount of water carried in the ballast tanks, the maximum angle of ascent, the names of all the controls in the bridge. Since the book is set in an imaginary past, circa 1910, I also researched the clothing and decor and social mores of the time. My goal is to immerse the reader in a believable world, even if some of it is pure invention.

SF: *Airborn* was a Printz Honor book. How did it feel to receive that honor?

KO: Fabulous! As a Canadian, I didn't even know I was eligible! It was the first time a book of mine had received such acclaim in the United States, so I was very grateful to have the chance to become better known. The award ceremony at ALA was also a special moment for me because I was there with my whole family, and my son ran up and gave me a hug after I'd given my acceptance speech. It was very sweet—and I hadn't even paid him to do that or anything!

SF: Your books are for children and young adults. Do you think about your audience when you are writing?

KO: I always start with the idea; and the idea will inevitably determine the audience. Often it's as simple as the age of the protagonist; other times it has more to do with the subject matter or complexity of the theme. To be honest, I don't spend much time thinking about my potential audience; I'm too busy trying to write the most enjoyable story I can. I've always hoped my books can be enjoyed by people aged eight to eighty-eight and beyond. If I've done my work well, the book will find the right audience.

SF: What would you say your method of writing is (i.e., working from an outline, going where the story takes you, etc.)?

KO: I'm a big planner, so I always like to have an outline before I begin writing chapter one. I don't need to know everything that happens, but I at least like to know the general shape of the story, and some of the major incidents—the landmarks to guide me towards my destination. Inevitably, as you write, you take all sorts of detours, and those are often the most inspired and original parts of the book. Once I'm past the research and outline stage, and am actually writing the book, I try to write 1,000 words a day. Sometimes it takes me half an hour; other times seven hours; and sometimes (and this is rare, fortunately) nothing comes at all.

SF: Of your books, which are your favorite books and/or characters and why?

KO: *Airborn* and *Skybreaker,* because I fell in love with Matt Cruse and Kate de Vries, and I felt they had a depth and vitality I hadn't achieved before with my fictional characters. I also really enjoyed creating an imaginary past and alternate technology, and can see that there are many more adventures to be had in this world.

SF: What were your favorite books growing up and/or who were your favorite authors?

KO: *The Lorax* (Dr. Seuss); *The Great Brain* books (John D. Fitzgerald); *The Mad Scientist Club* books (Bertrand R. Brinley), anything by Roald Dahl; *Emily of New Moon* (L. M. Montgomery).

SF: What do you think is the merit or importance of reading fantasy?

KO: For me it's really a matter of personal preference rather than the genre's inherent "merit" or "importance." Each book should be considered on its own merits, regardless of genre. When I read I like being taken somewhere else—or maybe "other"—where I have experiences I might not be able to have in the real world. In a fantasy, we get to experience a new world, and maybe look back at our own with a new, sharper perspective. For me, there's also a huge element of escapism and adventure in fantasy—and I've always believed that a book, whatever the genre, should give the reader a good time above all else!

References

"Kenneth Oppel," *Contemporary Authors Online*, Infotrac Galegroup Database (accessed March 14, 2006).

Oppel, Kenneth. "Home Page," http:www.kennethoppel.com (accessed March 14, 2006).

Oppel, Kenneth

🦅 *Airborn*. New York: Eos, 2004. 355p. ISBN: 0060531800; 0060531827pa. _MJS_ 📖
In an alternate Victorian civilization, fifteen-year-old Matt feels most alive when he soars high above the Earth on the airship where he serves as a cabin boy. When wealthy passenger Kate comes aboard, she is determined to find the mysterious flying creatures described by her grandfather. When sky pirates attack, the ship is grounded on a mysterious island, and Matt and Kate's explorations lead to danger and discoveries. (Printz Honor)

Skybreaker. New York: Eos, 2005. 384p. ISBN: 0060532270. _MJS_
When Matt, now a student at the Airship Academy, spots the long-lost Hyperion, he and Kate take a ship equipped with brand-new skybreaker engines to hunt for the treasured airship. But others want the ship for themselves and will stop at nothing to get it.

Roth, Philip

🦅 *The Plot against America*. Boston: Houghton Mifflin, 2004. 391p. ISBN: 0618509283; 1400079497pa. [Adult] _S_ AUD BRAILLE
When Charles Lindbergh beats Franklin D. Roosevelt in the 1940 presidential election, he leads America down the path of violent anti-Semitism. The Roth family lives in terror as Hilter's allies control the White House. (New York Times Ten Best Books of 2004)

Stevermer, Caroline

The College of Magics Series. New York: Tor. [Adult] _JS_
In an alternate Edwardian Europe, young Faris Nallaneen, the Duchess of Galazon, is shipped off to school by her scheming uncle, who wants her out of the way so that he can take over Galazon. But he doesn't suspect that the magic she learns at Greenlawn will transform their world.

A College of Magics. 1994. 380p. Reissued in 2002. ISBN: 0765342456pa.

A Scholar of Magics. 2004. 300p. ISBN: 0765303086; 0765353466pa.

Turtledove, Harry

The World War II Duology. New York: New American Library. [Adult] _S_
The Japanese attack Pearl Harbor, but this time, they succeed. One by one they take over each Hawaiian island and imprison American soldiers in POW camps.

Days of Infamy. 2004. 440p. ISBN: 0451213076; 0451460561pa.

End of the Beginning. 2005. 448p. ISBN: 0451216687; 0451460782pa.

The Worldwar Series and **The Colonization Series**. *See* Chapter 12, "Science Fiction."

Young Adult Paperback Series

MacHale, D. J.

The Pendragon Series. New York: Simon & Schuster. <u>*MJ*</u> AUD
Bobby Pendragon loves playing basketball and living his ordinary life with his family. When his Uncle Press needs his help and whisks him to another dimension, he discovers that he is a Traveler, and his fate may be to save the world. (Later volumes released in hardcover as well as paperback.)

Nix, Garth

The Seventh Tower Series. New York: Scholastic. <u>*M*</u>
In a Dark World where the Chosen hoard the only light in sunstones, used to create light and warmth and magic, Tal and Milla embark on a quest to keep evil from destroying it all.

Gaming-Related Series

Wizards of the Coast (Various authors)

Dragonlance: The New Adventures. Renton, WA: Mirror Stone. <u>*MJ*</u>
Inspired by the long-running series for adults by Tracy Hickman and Margaret Weiss, <u>Dragonlance</u>, this series was designed especially for young adults. It features the adventures of the teen heroes of Krynn.

Dragonlance. Renton, WA: Wizards of the Coast. <u>*JS*</u>
Characters in the land of Ansalon adventure with elves, dwarfs, kinder, and dragons.

Forgotten Realms. Renton, WA: Wizards of the Coast. <u>*JS*</u>
These role-playing fantasy stories feature adventures in a variety of imaginary realms.

Magic: The Gathering. Renton, WA: Wizards of the Coast. <u>*JS*</u>
Adventures imbued with magic are based on the role-playing game.

The Finest in the Realm

The Marvelous Misadventures of Sebastian by Lloyd Alexander

The Tales of Alvin Maker by Orson Scott Card

The Tales of the Otori by Lian Hearn

A Song for Arbonne by Guy Gavriel Kay

Owl in Love by Patrice Kindl

The Chronicles of Narnia by C. S. Lewis

Airborn and **Skybreaker** by Kenneth Oppel

A Princess of Roumania by Paul Park

Chapter 6

The Faerie Realm

Faerie fantasy is made up of novels that have been influenced by the stories of fairies in many cultures' canons of traditional tales. The subgenre focuses on the authors' vision: of these creatures with special powers, of the realm where they dwell, of their interactions with each other and with mortals. These stories are not necessarily tied to a particular fairy tale (which may or may not have any fairies in it) but concentrate on the lives of fairies, their homeland, and their contact with mortals. Literary works that include such fairies stretch back as far as Edmund Spencer's *The Fairy Queen* and William Shakespeare's *A Midsummer Night's Dream*. In works that led to the contemporary fantasy tradition, fairies play an important role in both William Morris's *The Wood beyond the Well* and George MacDonald's *Phantasies*. Faerie fantasy is a type of alternate world fantasy, since magic permeates the faerie realm and its denizens. It can be classified as Gateway Fantasy if the characters move from this world to the faerie realm or vice versa, or as Secondary World Fantasy if all of the action takes place in the faerie realm.

Profile of Holly Black

Photo: Theo Black

Born in 1971 in New Jersey, Holly Black grew up in a decaying Victorian house and lived on a steady diet of stories featuring ghosts and faeries. Her first book, *Tithe,* was published in 2002 and received many starred reviews. It was also a finalist for the Mythopeoic Fantasy Award. She has since coauthored the popular Spiderwick series with illustrator Tony DiTerlizzi and written a companion to *Tithe* called *Valiant* (*Contemporary Authors Online*, Infotrac Galegroup Database; www.blackholly.com).

Interview with Holly Black

Conducted via e-mail January 19–February 7, 2006

SF: Why do you write fantasy for young people?

HB: Originally, when I thought of myself as a writer, I didn't see myself writing for young people, but over time I realized that when I was in middle and high school was when books were the most important to me. The books I read then changed the way I saw the world and the way I saw myself. It means so much to me to hear that the Spiderwick books were the first books a kid read on his own or that my teen books helped someone through a tough time. I don't know if writing for adults would be as rewarding.

SF: Both your Spiderwick series and your Modern Faerie Tales are filled with unusual kinds of faeries. What inspires you to write about them?

BH: I am fascinated by faeries because they are these capricious creatures that embody both beauty and terror. I love that juxtaposition and I love the intuitive, numinous magic in the old folk tales.

SF: Why do you think that people read fantasy?

HB: I think people read fantasy because of the limitless possibilities it allows. Fantasy changes the rules and lets the reader (and the writer) play out what things might be like if everything was shifted a bit to the left. What if wings sprouted out of my back tomorrow? What if there was a secret society of vampires that lived in an abandoned farmhouse on the edge of town? What if there was a world where electricity hadn't been invented but magic had?

SF: There's a lot of darkness in your fantasies. How do your readers respond to that?

HB: I think that readers respond well to darkness in fantasy, because they know that that's part of their own lives. When material is sanitized, it reads false and young people are very savvy readers.

SF: Of your books, which is your favorite book and/or character and why?

BH: I think that *Tithe: A Modern Faerie Tale* will always be my favorite book because it was my first.

SF: What would you say your method of writing is (i.e., working from an outline, going where the story takes you, etc.)?

HB: I try and plan out where a book is going to go, but usually, when I get a couple of chapters in, I realize that something isn't quite working and I go back and start rewriting. I tend to write a few chapters, go back and edit, write a few more chapters and go back to the beginning and edit all over again—all the way to the last chapter. It is a scary method because sometimes I can make a decision near the end that means massive changes to the beginning even after I've edited scenes three and four times. It also can be really frustrating because of how slow it can be, but so far it seems to be the only way I know how to work.

SF: What were your favorite books/authors when you were growing up?

HB: I was (and still am) a huge fan of Lloyd Alexander, Susan Cooper, and J. R. R. Tolkien.

SF: What would you say is the importance or merit of reading fantasy?

HB: Fantasy allows for metaphors to become fact and the familiar to become unfamiliar. Because of that, I think that fantasy readers are trained to be adaptable and creative in their thinking.

References

Black, Holly. "Home Page," http:www.blackholly.com (accessed March 14, 2006).

"Holly Black," *Contemporary Authors Online*, Infotrac Galegroup Database (accessed March 14, 2006).

Black, Holly

Tithe. **New York: Simon & Schuster, 2002. 310p. ISBN: 0689849249lb; 0689867042pa. _S_ BRAILLE LP**
After years of moving from city to city as her mother pursued her dream of being a rock star, sixteen-year-old Kaye and her mom return home to the Jersey Shore. Kaye lives in a brutal world and has always felt that she didn't fit in. When she helps a hypnotically attractive stranger, Roiben, fairy friends from her childhood, who turn out not to be imaginary warn her that he is not to be trusted. They also reveal that she is not altogether human. Plotting, they conjure a plan that places Kaye at the center of the danger-laced Unseelie Court.

🎗 ***Valiant***. **New York: Simon & Schuster, 2005. 314p. ISBN: 0689868227. _S_ AUD**
Seventeen-year-old Valerie runs away from home when she catches her boyfriend having sex with her mother. She chooses life on the streets of New York City rather than a mother who would betray her. She joins a group of teens who live in the subway tunnels. They share with her their faerie connection in more ways than one, for they are couriers who deliver Never to the magical folk of the city who need the elixir to survive, and they take the drug themselves, for it causes humans to hallucinate. (Andre Norton Award)

Brennan, Herbie

Faerie Wars. **New York: Bloomsbury, 2003. 367p. ISBN: 1582348103; 1582349436pa. _MJ_ AUD**
Distressed by the disintegration of his family's world, Henry offers to help the elderly Mr. Fogerty around the house. He expects to discover a mess. He does

not expect to discover a Faerie Prince attempting to escape from the Faeries of the Night.

The Purple Emperor. New York: Bloomsbury, 2004. 431p. ISBN: 1582348804. *MJ* **AUD**
Henry and Mr. Fogerty are now friends with Pyrgus and his sister Holly Blue, the royal faerie siblings. Pyrgus summons each human to his court as he prepares for his coronation, but the Faerie of the Night, Lord Hairstreak, chooses this moment to set his diabolical plans in motion, plunging the friends into mortal danger.

Card, Orson Scott

Magic Street. New York: Del Rey/Ballantine Books, 2005. 397p. ISBN: 0345416899. [Adult] **AUD** *S*
Mack Street, a young African American, grew up knowing that he was adopted after being found in a park in a grocery sack. His origins didn't bother him nearly as much as his strange gift does. He can dream the dreams of others and make their wishes come true. But granting wishes never quite turns out the way it should. Learning to control his talent led him to Puck, whose backyard provided an entrance to Fairyland. There, Mack finds himself trapped in a war between Titania and Oberon, the queen and king of the fairies.

Chan, Gillian

The Turning. Tonawanda, NY: Kids Can Press, 2005. 200p. ISBN: 1553375750; 1553375769pa. *S*
After the death of his mother, sixteen-year-old Ben must move from Canada to England with a father he hardly knows. There, Ben discovers that his grandfather has passed down the special skill of communicating with the Faerie Folk. When he learns that a group of Young Fey are sucking the life from humans to enhance their own power, he knows he must do everything he can to stop them.

Colfer, Eoin

The Artemis Fowl Series. New York: Miramax. (1st American Editions.) *M* **AUD**
The People—fairies, sprites, trolls, and so on—have been forced to live below ground because of uncouth Mud People (humans) and have developed a thriving society using advanced magic and technology. They are policed by LEPrecon commandos, who make sure everything runs the way it's supposed to above and below ground, until a young man named Artemis Fowl taps into their power.

Artemis Fowl. 2001. 277p. ISBN: 0786808012; 0786817879pa.
Artemis Fowl, the twelve-year-old criminal mastermind, captures the LEPrecon fairy Holly Short and demands a ransom in gold in an attempt to restore the family fortune.

Artemis Fowl: The Arctic Incident. 2002. 277p. ISBN: 0786808551; 0786851473pa.
While at boarding school in Ireland, Artemis receives an urgent message and leaves at once for the Arctic Circle, where he must rescue his father. This time, he and the fairy police help each other.

Artemis Fowl: The Eternity Code. **2003. 309p. ISBN: 0786819146;
0786856289pa.**
After five years as a captive, Artemis's father returns home a changed
man and makes his son promise to go straight. He will—right after he
pulls off the most brilliant criminal caper of his career.

Artemis Fowl: The Opal Deception. **2005. 352p. ISBN: 0786852895;
0786852909pa.**
Artemis has had his mind wiped by the fairies, so he remembers nothing
of them or their influence for good in his life. As a result, he's back to his
greedy, scheming ways. Meanwhile, Opal Koboi, the pixie archenemy of
the officers of the LEPrecon, escapes and plots revenge.

Artemis Fowl: The Lost Colony. **2006. 385p. ISBN: 0786849568.**
When the fairies moved their civilization underground and left the surface of the Earth to the humans they call "Mud People," the demons
chose to bide their time. They cast a spell that would allow them to remove themselves from the flow of time and return when their chances of
defeating the humans were better. But something went wrong with the
spell and it trapped the demons in Limbo instead. Now the spell is deteriorating and only the brilliant Artemis Fowl (with a little help from
LEPrecon Captain Holly Short) can stop the demons from returning.

Gaiman, Neil

🎗 *Stardust*. **New York: Spike, 1999. Reissued by Perennial in 2001. ISBN:
0060934719pa. [Adult]** _S_ **GN** 📖
Tristan Thorn has grown up in England in the Victorian village of Wall, unaware of his faerie heritage. When the girl he loves promises to marry him if
he brings her back the star they've just seen fall, he crosses the forbidden wall
and journeys through the Land of Faerie in search of the star—but he is not the
only one looking for it. (Alex; Adult Mythopoeic Award)

Gardner, Sally

I, Coriander. **New York: Dial Books, 2005. 280p. (1st American Edition.)
ISBN: 0803730993.** _MJ_ **AUD**
Coriander, the daughter of a merchant and a fairy princess (although Coriander does not know this until later), lives in seventeenth-century London at the
time when Cromwell and his fellow Puritans come to power. After her mother
dies suddenly, Coriander's father marries a Puritan, in hopes of hiding his roy-
alist leanings from the Roundheads. Despite her stepmother's cruelty, Coriander finds a way to her mother's fairy kingdom, where she embarks on a quest
to defeat the evil queen and set things right in both the fairy and mortal worlds.

Kushner, Ellen

🎋 *Thomas the Rhymer*. **New York: Morrow, 1990. 247p. Reissued by Spectra in 2004. ISBN: 0553586971pa. [Adult] S** 📖

Thomas the Rhymer, a gifted minstrel, happily wandered from village to village regaling fireside listeners with tales and tunes until the day the Queen of Elfland spirited him away to serve her in the realm of the Faeries. After seven years pass in the human world and Thomas does not age, the queen at last frees him, bequeathing upon him a questionable gift: He cannot tell a lie. Determined to recreate his life, he goes in search of the woman he loved. (World Fantasy Award; Mythopoeic Award)

Melling, O. R.

The Chronicles of Faerie. New York: Amulet. _MJ_
The fairy folk still dwell in Ireland although they remain hidden from all but those who truly believe.

Hunter's Moon. **2005. 296p. ISBN: 0810958570.**
Cousins Findahair and Gwenhyvar both love all things Faerie and have long planned to backpack through Ireland, searching for remnants of that magical realm. When they spend the night in a barrow, Findahair is stolen away by the King of the Fairies, and Gwen must match wits with him and win her cousin back.

The Summer King. **2006. ISBN: 0810959690.**
Laurel and Honor were twins, close as two sisters can be. Even though a year has passed since her sister's death, Laurel has still not reconciled herself to the loss. While visiting her grandparents in Ireland, a messenger from the Faerie Realm informs her that she can save her sister, who is not dead but caught in the crack between worlds. Laurel must rescue the Summer King and make sure the Midsummer Fire is lit on time, to have a chance to bring Honor back.

Prue, Sally

🎋 *Cold Tom*. **New York: Scholastic, 2003. 192p. ISBN: 0439482682; 0439482690pa. _M_ AUD**

Tom runs from the elves that raised him when they decide to kill him because he is part human. In the human city, Anna takes him in. Although his ability to call on the stars and become invisible saves him from some danger, he eventually must learn to cope in his strange new world. (Silver Smarties Award)

Sherman, Delia

Changeling. **New York: Viking, 2006. 292p. ISBN: 0670059676.**
Twelve-year-old Neef, a human changeling, has been raised by her fairy godmother, the white rat Astris, in New York Between, a Manhattan where fairies and demons, elves and vampires, live side by side. Exchanged as a child for an identical fairy, Neef loves living in New York Between's Central Park, but she's eager to explore beyond the acceptable boundaries. When she breaks the rules to attend the Soltice Dance, the Green Lady, Genius of Central Park, withdraws her protection. The Wild Hunt wastes no time in beginning the chase for their prey, but Neef negotiates a deal: If she can accomplish three impossible tasks, the Green Lady will let her return.

Shetterly, Will

Elsewhere. San Diego: Harcourt, 1991. 248p. Reissued by Magic Carpet Books in 2004. ISBN: 0152052097pa. <u>S</u>

When Ron runs away from home, he is searching for his brother. What he finds is a job at Elsewhere, a bookstore in Bordertown, located between the world he knows and Faerie.

Nevernever. San Diego: Jane Yolen Books, 1993. 226p. Reissued by Magic Carpet Books in 2004. ISBN: 0152052100pa. <u>S</u>

Now seventeen, Ron has been cursed by the lovely elf, Leda. He has been transformed into a werewolf. Even so, his task is to protect Florida, the heir to the Elflands throne, who is hiding in Bordertown, where nothing is as it appears.

Snyder, Midori

Hannah's Garden. New York: Viking, 2002. 247p. Reissued by Firebird in 2005. ISBN: 0142401358pa. <u>JS</u>

Seventeen-year-old Cassie works hard in school and at practicing for her violin recital. She is looking forward to going to the prom with her boyfriend when a phone call informing her mother that her grandfather is in intensive care changes everything. When they rush to be with him, they find him on the brink of death and the house in a ruinous state. Even her great-grandmother's spiral garden has suffered from vandalism and neglect. As Cassie tries to restore order, she becomes entangled in the plots of two rival fairy clans that have been seeking to control the garden to keep a foothold of power in the world.

Spencer, Wen

Tinker. New York: Baen, 2004. 448p. ISBN: 0743498712pa. [Adult] <u>S</u>

In the near-future, a large part of Pittsburgh exists in the Faerie world of Elfhome, and eighteen-year-old Tinker and her cousin do their best running a junkyard. Tinker likes inventing gadgets, but her life changes when Windwolf, the elven lord, is chased by wargs into her scrap yard.

Wooding, Chris

Poison. New York: Orchard Books, 2005. 288p. ISBN: 0439755700. <u>JS</u> 📖

Poison, a rebellious teenager, lives in the Black Marshes with her father, stepmother, and little sister until the phaeries steal the child away and replace her with a changeling. Determined to find her sister, Poison braves the dangers of a gruesome phaerie realm to confront the Lord of Phaerie himself.

Yolen, Jane

Boots and the Seven Leaguers. San Diego: Harcourt, 2000. 159p. ISBN: 015202557Xlb; 0152025634pa. *MJ*
Gog, a young troll, and his Pookah friend, Pook, long to see their favorite rock and troll band, but they don't have any money. Pook casts a glamour so they will look full grown and gets them a gig as roadies, but their plans are squashed when Gog's little brother, Magog, is kidnapped. Gog and Pook face the dangers of the Kingdom of Fairy to rescue Magog.

The Rock 'N' Troll Tales. New York: Starscape. *JS*
Traditional tales receive a modern and musical retelling in this series by mother and son.

Pay the Piper (with Adam Stemple). 2005. 175p. ISBN: 0765311585.
Prince Gringas is banished from Faerie for murdering his brother and must find a way to earn money to remove the murder curse. When singing in a rock-and-roll band does not pay off, he chooses to lead children into Faerie, where their souls serve as a source of energy for the land of Ever Fair.

Trollbridge (with Adam Stemple). 2006. 231p. ISBN: 0765314266.
When sixteen-year-old Moira, a harpist, arrives at the bridge in Vanderby, MN to have her picture taken with the other eleven dairy princesses, she gets there just in time to see them being carried away by a giant troll. Following them into troll country, she discovers that the troll wants them as wives for his sons. Meanwhile, fifteen-year-old Jakob and his brothers, who together make up the band the Griffson Brothers, are captured by the troll as well. He puts them into storage for dinner. Jakob escapes and together, he and Moira, with help from fiddle-playing fox, must rescue the brothers and the princesses in this tale that mixes in elements of the "The Twelve Dancing Princesses" and "The Three Billy Goats Gruff."

The Finest in the Realm

Stardust by Neil Gaiman

I, Coriander by Sally Gardner

Thomas the Rhymer by Ellen Kushner

Hunter's Moon by O. R. Melling

Poison by Chris Wooding

Chapter 7

Fantasy Romance

A fantasy romance is any kind of fantasy in which the story of the romance is central to the plot of the novel. Magic can be an essential element of the story, or the novel can be set in a completely imaginary realm. Romantic fantasy, science fiction, and paranormal fiction form their own subgenres in the adult market. Harlequin has a line of romantic fantasy for adults published by its Luna imprint. While there is a romantic element in many speculative fiction books written for young adults, the romance tends to be more dominant in the books written for adults. These adult books usually include more descriptive passages about sexual encounters as well.

Alexander, Lloyd

The Arkadians. **New York: Dutton, 1995. 272p. ISBN: 0525454152; 0140380736pa.** *M*
Lucian, a mere bean counter in the royal palace of the Kingdom of Arkadia, discovers a discrepancy in the court accounts and makes the mistake of honestly reporting his findings. Now he must flee for his life. On his journey, he acquires the companionship of Fronto, a poet transformed into a donkey, and Joy-in-the-Morning, an oracle in the service of the Lady of Wild Things. As they journey across a land resembling Ancient Greece, they encounter a host of obstacles to be overcome, and Lucian and Joy-in-the-Morning are drawn to each other. (ALAN)

Atwater-Rhodes, Amelia

The Kiesha'ra Series. New York: Delacorte. *JS*
In a world where the inhabitants can shift from human to animal form, the war between two species has continued until none will survive, unless the only heir of each weds the other.

Hawksong. 2003. 243p. ISBN: 0385730713; 044023803Xpa. AUD
The avians, those who shift from human to bird, and the serpiente, those who shift from human to serpent, have waged war for generations. The last remaining heir to the throne on each side decides to pursue peace through a royal marriage. But enemies surround them, and the heirs are unsure of the new feelings that course between them.

Snakecharm. 2004. 167p. ISBN: 0385730721; 0440238048pa. AUD
Zane, the leader of the serpiente, and Danica, the leader of the avians, have married and are expecting their first child. But their own peoples are wary of a mixed-race heir. The ancient Falcons, who are the most powerful shape-shifters of all and have virtually ignored the lower orders of shape-shifters, now seek to disrupt the fragile alliance.

Falcondance. 2005. 183p. ISBN: 0385731949. AUD
Oliza, daughter of the rulers Zane and Danica, employs Nicias, the son of two exiled Falcons, as one of her royal guards. Nicias has never felt at ease in the serpiente and avian world in which he was raised. When his powers start to grow out of control, his parents send him to the Empress of the Falcons, who will either save or destroy him.

Wolfcry. 2006. 208p. ISBN: 0385731957.
Oliza must choose a mate, and her parents would like her to choose one that will help make permanent the uneasy peace between the avians and the serpiente. Oliza is kidnapped but manages to escape and is aided by a wolf named Betia. When she returns to the turmoil of the court, she still must decide between the serpiente, Urban, and the avian, Marus, but she fears that either choice will lead to war.

Berry, Liz

🏵 *The China Garden*. **New York: Farrar, Straus & Giroux, 1996. (1st American Edition.) 285p. Reissued by HarperCollins in 1999. ISBN: 0380732289pa. _S_ AUD** 📖
Seventeen-year-old Clare Meredith finally finishes her exams for entering the university and decides to spend the summer with her mother on the Ravensmere estate, despite her mother's vehement objections. When she arrives, she finds a village full of legends and magic. She is physically and emotionally attracted to Mark, with whom she shares a mystical bond. Unbeknownst to Clare, that bond is essential if the two are to uphold the mythical Benison and save Ravensmere. (BBYA)

Bishop, Anne

Sebastian. **New York: Roc, 2006. 437p. ISBN: 0451460731. [Adult]** _S_
Sebastian is an incubus—part human, part demon—who has grown bored with sexual games and longs for true love with Lynnea, a maid from another of the many magical lands that make up Ephemera. Each separate land is guarded by a Landscaper and connected by a Bridge, each a person of exceptional magical ability. While Sebastian tries to find a way to unite with Lynnea so that his sexual magic won't destroy her, his cous-

ins Glorianna, a Landscaper, and Lee, a Bridge, need Sebastian's help to stop the Eater of the World.

Dean, Pamela

Tam Lin. **New York: Tom Doherty Associates, 1991. 468p. Reissued by Firebird in 2006. ISBN: 014240652Xpa.** *S*
Janet Carter, an English major at Blackstock College in Minnesota in the 1970s, studies hard, makes new friends, and falls in love with Nicholas Tooley, unaware of how her life parallels the plot of the Scottish ballad *Tam Lin*.

Ferris, Jean

Once upon a Marigold. *See* Chapter 4, "Fairy Tale Fantasy."

Gabaldon, Diana

The Outlander Series. New York: Delacorte. [Adult] AUD *S*
In 1945, Clare Randall, an army nurse, and her husband, Frank, are relaxing in the Scottish Highlands for their second honeymoon. When Clare steps through a circle of ancient standing stones, she is hurled back in time two hundred years. At first, she survives with quick wits and judicious use of her medical skills, but circumstances dictate she must marry Jamie Fraiser. An unwilling bride, she weds the red-headed Highlander, who woos her and becomes much more than a husband of necessity.

> *Outlander*. **1991. 627p. ISBN: 0385302304; 0440242940pa.**
>
> *Dragonfly in Amber*. **1992. 743p. ISBN: 0385302312; 0440215625pa.**
>
> *Voyager*. **1993. 743p. ISBN: 0385302320; 0440217563pa.**
>
> *The Drums of Autumn*. **1997. 880p. ISBN: 0385311400; 044022425Xpa.**
>
> *The Fiery Cross*. **2001. 979p. ISBN: 0385315279; 0440221668pa.**
>
> *A Breath of Snow and Ashes*. **2005. 979p. ISBN: 0385324162; 0385340397pa.**

Hale, Shannon

🌸 *Princess Academy*. **New York: Bloomsbury, 2005. (1st American Edition.) 314p. ISBN: 1582349932.** *MJ*
When the royal priests divine that the prince's future bride will come from Miri's mountainside village, she and all of the twelve- to seventeen-year-old girls who live there must enter the Princess Academy for princess training. While Miri learns the art of living as a princess, she also studies the mindspeech of her people, which proves useful when her village is attacked. (ALAN; Newbery Honor)

Hoffman, Nina Kiriki

A Fistful of Sky. New York: Ace, 2002. 353p. ISBN: 0441009751; 0441011772pa. *JS*

Gyp LaZelle has grown up in a family of mages. She's watched her sisters "transition" and receive their powers, and she bides her time until her turn. She almost gives up. When she turns twenty, the power that manifests in her is worse than having no power at all: She has the cursing gift. The dark power builds until she must curse someone or something, or go mad. Gyp juggles her new ability as she struggles to cope with her family duties and the new man in her life.

Kushner, Ellen

Thomas the Rhymer. See Chapter 6, "The Faerie Realm."

Lackey, Mercedes

The Black Swan. New York: DAW, 1999. 376p. ISBN: 0886778336; 0886778905pa. [Adult] *S*

Baron von Rathbart scours the countryside for women whose faults draw his angry attention. A powerful sorcerer, he captures them and transforms them into swans. They are condemned to live as swans except for the brief hours of moonlight when they regain their human form. Princess Odette, the bravest of them all, wins from him a promise: If she can earn the love of a prince, Rathbart will free them all.

Tales of the Five Hundred Kingdoms. New York: Luna. [Adult] *S*

In the land of Five Hundred Kingdoms, fairy tale romances are reborn.

The Fairy Godmother. 2004. 417p. ISBN: 0373802021; 0373802455pa.

One Good Knight. 2006. 360p. ISBN: 037380217Xpa.

Marillier, Juliet

Wolfskin. New York: Tor, 2003. (1st American Edition.) 493p. Reissued in 2004. ISBN: 0765345900pa. [Adult] *S*

Throughout his childhood, the young Viking Eyvind dreams of serving the god Thor by becoming a Wolfskin warrior like his brother. As he trains for the mystical rite of passage, he forms an uneasy friendship with the withdrawn lad Somerled. At the same time, on the distant Light Isles, Nessa, niece of the king, studies to be a priestess. Their cultures clash when Eyvind's band of settlers arrives, and the tenuous peace quickly shatters. Although Eyvind and Nessa are on opposing sides, love sparks between them. But the war between their peoples may keep them apart forever.

Foxmask. New York: Tor, 2004. (1st American Edition.) 464p. ISBN: 0765306743; 0765345919pa. [Adult] *S*

In this sequel to *Wolfskin*, the children that have grown up on the Light Isles, in a society that is now a mix of Celtic and Norse, strike out on their own adventure. Thorvald, Margaret's son by the exiled Somerled, and his friend Sam embark on a journey to find Thorvald's father. Creidhe, the daughter of Eyvind and Nessa, stows away on their boat for love of the man she has adored since childhood.

McKillip, Patricia A.

The Changeling Sea. **New York: Atheneum, 1988. 137p. Reissued by Firebird in 2003. ISBN: 0141312629pa.** *JS*
When Perriwinkle is not scrubbing floors, she is learning magic to hex the sea that has taken her father. Kir, the king's son, wants to send a message to the sea as well. They never dream that their actions might bring a sea monster, the king's second son, a magician, and a huge chain of gold.

Winter Rose. **New York: Ace, 1996. 262p. Reissued in 2002. ISBN: 0441009344pa. [Adult]** *S* 📖
Amid the whispered rumors that his father was cursed, Corbet Lynn returns to his family's home to rebuild and wins the hearts of Rois and her sister Laurel who live nearby. Corbet disappears when winter draws near. Laurel's will to live fades, and Rois must negotiate a way to the Faerie realm to save her sister.

O'Brien, Judith

Timeless Love. **New York: Simon Pulse, 2002. 231p. ISBN: 0743419219pa.** *JS*
When Samantha dents her father's BMW, she wishes she were anywhere but in that car. She wears an antique necklace that her mother had given her for her sixteenth birthday, and it magically whisks her back in time to Tudor England. Barefoot and in the bedroom of a sickly King Edward VI, Samantha begins to make a new life for herself. Along the way, she falls in love with the dashing Sir Barnaby Fitzpatrick.

Pattou, Edith

East. *See* Chapter 4, "Fairy Tale Fantasy."

Pierce, Meredith Ann

The Woman Who Loved Reindeer. **Boston: Atlantic Monthly, 1985. 242p. Reissued by Magic Carpet Books in 2000. ISBN: 0152017992pa.** *JS*
Caribou, a young wisewoman, lives on the outskirts of her village because the people fear her gifts. Barely more than a child herself, Caribou raises the infant son of her sister-in-law, who conceived the child while her husband was away. As the child, Reindeer, grows into manhood, it becomes clear that he is a shape-shifter: part man, part stag. Caribou's love for him does not falter, but it does undergo a metamorphosis into romance. Their time of testing comes when trouble threatens Caribou's village, and she and Reindeer must find a way to avert it.

Putney, Mary Jo

The Guardians Series. New York: Ballantine. [Adult] *S*
In eighteenth-century Europe, magical Guardians move in the highest circles of society. They posses great power and abide by strict rules to use their gifts only to aid the greatest number of people, not to engage in partisan politics. When the Scottish Lord Duncan MacCrae, a weather mage, and the English

Gwyneth Owens wed, their sexual passion awakens her dormant enchantress powers, but the Rising of 1745 may destroy their new-found love.

A Kiss of Fate. 2004. 340p. ISBN: 0345449169; 0345449177pa. AUD LP

Stolen Magic. 2005. 337p. ISBN: 0345476891; 0345476905pa. LP

Shinn, Sharon

Summers at Castle Auburn. New York: Ace, 2001. 355p. Reissued in 2002. ISBN: 044100928Xpa. [Adult] S

Coriel spends every summer at Castle Auburn with her half-sister Elisandra, who is betrothed to Prince Bryan. They enjoy dressing elegantly, dancing the night away, and being waited on by fairy servants. As the years pass, Coriel comes to see that the prince, whom she once adored, has cruelty woven into his nature. While Coriel tries to avoid her uncle's political plots for her, she worries about her half-sister, as Elisandra prepares to wed the less-than-desirable prince.

The Twelve Houses Quartet. New York: Berkley Books. [Adult] S

King Baryn of Gillengaria decrees that the people of his realm must accept those who work magic. The nobles of the Twelve Houses, knowing this causes dissent, use the unrest to their advantage. Baryn sends the mystic woman Senneth to discover which nobles are plotting against him. Love is the last thing she expects to find along the way.

Mystic and Rider. 2005. 440p. ISBN: 0441012469; 0441013031pa.

The Thirteenth House. 2006. ISBN: 0441013686.

Snyder, Maria V.

The Study Series. New York: Luna. S Adult

Yelena, who has spent the last year in the dungeon as a convicted murderer, agrees to become the food-taster for the Commander of Ixia. Valek, the chief of security, ensures her loyalty by spiking her food with a poison of his own. Now, she must report to him daily or die in agony. As Yelena adjusts to her new life, she discovers the Commander is not the only object of assassination attempts, while subtle signs of romance spice her daily life.

Magic Study. 2006. 392p. ISBN: 0373802498.

Poison Study. 2005. 361p. ISBN: 0373802307.

Wrede, Patricia C., and Caroline Stevermer

Sorcery and Cecelia, or The Enchanted Chocolate Pot Being the Correspondence of Two Young Ladies of Quality Regarding Various Magical Scandals in London and the Country (first published as *Sorcery and Cecelia: An Epistolary Fantasy*). New York: Ace, 1988. 197p. Revised and reissued by Harcourt in hardcover in 2003. ISBN: 0152046151; 0152046151pa. *JS*

In a Regency England where young men with magical talent can attend the Royal College of Wizards, cousins Kate and Cecelia exchange a series of letters about love, laughter, and their magical misadventures. (BBYA)

The Grand Tour, or, The Purloined Coronation Regalia: Being a Revelation of Matters of High Confidentiality and Greatest Importance, Including Extracts from the Intimate Diary of a Noblewoman and the Sworn Testimony of a Lady of Quality. Orlando, FL: Harcourt, 2004. 469p. ISBN: 015204616X; 0152055568pa. *JS*

It's 1817, and Kate and Cecelia have married their respective beaux and are traveling throughout Europe on a honeymoon grand tour. They record their various excursions in journal entries, as they become involved in a scheme to create a magical Emperor of Europe.

The Mislaid Magician, or Ten Years After: Being the Private Correspondence between Two Prominent Families Regarding a Scandal Touching the Highest Levels of Government and the Security of the Realm. Orlando, FL: Harcourt, 2006. 328p. ISBN: 0152055487.

Ten years after cousins Cecy and Kate honeymooned with their new spouses on the continent, they have settled into their domestic lives, caring for homes and children while still learning about magic. When the wizard Wellington sends James to investigate the disappearance of a German railway engineer, he and Cecy discover that the new railway lines are interfering with England's ancient underground magic. In the mean time, Kate copes with her own children as well as a mysterious abandoned child.

The Finest in the Realm

The China Garden by Liz Berry

The Outlander Series by Diana Gabaldon

Wolfskin and **Foxmask** by Juliet Marillier

Summers at Castle Auburn by Sharon Shinn

Sorcery and Cecelia by Patricia Wrede and Caroline Stevermer

Chapter 8

Fantasy Mystery

This chapter includes any fantasy in which a crime has been committed and solving the mystery is the central element of the plot. The only exception occurs with novels in which the actions of ghosts dominate the story. Those are listed under "Ghosts" in Chapter 13, "The Dark Side: Paranormal and Horror."

Anderson, Janet S.

The Last Treasure. New York: Dutton, 2003. 257p. ISBN: 0525469192; 0142402176pa. *MJ* BRAILLE

John Matthew Smith's spirit seeks to bring his bickering descendants together and so sends dream messages to cousins Zee and Jess, who've never met before. As they get to know each other, they must puzzle out the ghostly clues to the last family treasure in order to help both sides of the family.

Bloor, Edward

Story Time. Orlando, FL: Harcourt, 2004. 424p. ISBN: 0152046704lb; 0152052224pa. *MJ* AUD

Kate and George have received invitations to attend the prestigious Whittaker Magnet School. When they arrive, they find that all is not as it appears. Instead of participating in exciting classes, they practice taking tests all day. To make matters worse, an unknown evil inhabits the school, causing murder and mayhem.

Bray, Libba

A Great and Terrible Beauty. *See* Chapter 5, "Alternate and Parallel Worlds."

Brown, Rita Mae

The Mrs. Murphy Series. New York: Bantam. [Adult] S
Mary Minor Haristeen, nicknamed "Harry," lives and works in the cozy town of Crozet, Virginia. She solves crimes with the help of her two intelligent pets, Mrs. Murphy, a gray tiger cat, and Tee Tucker, a Welsh corgi, who like to talk to each other and to nudge their clueless owner in the right direction.

Wish You Were Here. 1990. 242p. Reissued in 1994. ISBN: 0553287532pa.

Rest in Pieces. 1992. 292p. Reissued in 1993. ISBN: 0553562398pa.

Murder at Monticello or, Old Sins. 1994. 298p. Reissued in 1995. ISBN: 0553572350pa.

Pay Dirt, or, Adventures at Ash Lawn. 1995. 251p. Reissued in 1996. ISBN: 0553572369pa.

Murder, She Meowed. 1996. 285p. Reissued in 1997. ISBN: 0553572377pa. AUD

Murder on the Prowl. 1998. 320p. Reissued in 1999. ISBN: 0553575406pa. AUD

Cat on the Scent. 1999. 321p. Reissued in 2000. ISBN: 0553575414pa.

Pawing through the Past. 2000. 305p. Reissued in 2001. ISBN: 0553580256pa. AUD

Claws and Effect. 2001. 292p. Reissued in 2002. ISBN: 0553580906pa. AUD

Catch as Cat Can. 2002. 287p. Reissued in 2003. ISBN: 0553580280pa. AUD

Tail of the Tip-Off. 2003. 309p. Reissued in 2004. ISBN: 0553582852pa. AUD LP

Whisker of Evil. 2004. 297p. ISBN: 0553801619; 0553582860pa. AUD LP

Cat's Eyewitness. 2005. 287p. ISBN: 0553801643; 0553582879pa. AUD LP

Sour Puss. 2006. 272p. ISBN: 055380362X. AUD LP

Butcher, Jim

The Dresden Files. New York: Roc. [Adult] S
Harry Dresden lives in Chicago and solves crimes for a living. He also happens to be a very powerful wizard.

Storm Front. 2000. 322p. ISBN: 0451457811pa.

Fool Moon. 2001. 342p. ISBN: 0451458125pa.

Grave Peril. 2001. 378p. ISBN: 0451458443pa.

Summer Knight. 2002. 371p. ISBN: 0451458923pa.

Death Masks. 2003. 378p. ISBN: 0451459407pa.

Blood Rites. 2004. 372p. ISBN: 0451459873pa.

Dead Beat. 2005. 396p. ISBN: 0451460278; 045146091Xpa.

Cunningham, Elaine

The Changeling Series. New York: Tor. [Adult] <u>S</u>
When GiGi Gelman is blamed unjustly for a bungled police raid that ends in a bloodbath, her ten-year career with the Providence, Rhode Island, police force comes to an abrupt conclusion. On her own, she goes into business as a private investigator, making use of her psychic moments to help her solve cases. As she follows clues, she uncovers evidence of her mystical heritage.

Shadows in the Darkness. 2004. 304p. ISBN: 076530970X; 0765348519pa.

Shadows in the Starlight. 2006. 288p. ISBN: 0765309718.

Fforde, Jasper

The Thursday Next Series. New York: Viking. (1st American Editions.) [Adult] <u>JS</u> AUD
In a 1980s England where dodos have been recreated and an inventor enables people literally to enter the world of a book, literary detective Thursday Next must stop criminals from destroying the world's literature.

🏅 *The Eyre Affair*. 2002. 374p. Reissued by Penguin in 2003. ISBN: 0142001805pa. (Alex) 📖

Lost in a Good Book. 2003. 416p. ISBN: 0670031909; 0142004030pa.

The Well of Lost Plots. 2004. 375p. ISBN: 0670032891; 0143034359pa.

Something Rotten. 2004. 385p. ISBN: 0670033596; 014303541Xpa.

The Nursery Crime Series. New York: Viking. (1st American Editions.) [Adult] <u>JS</u>
In a world where nursery rhyme characters are alive and well and committing crimes, it's Inspector Jack Spratt who must solve the cases and put an end to illegal activities.

The Big Over Easy. 2005. 383p. ISBN: 0670034231; 0143037234pa. AUD <u>LP</u>

The Fourth Bear. 2006. ISBN: 0670037729.

Goobie, Beth

🏅 *Before Wings*. Custer, WA: Orca, 2001. 203p. ISBN: 1551431610; 1551431637. <u>JS</u> BRAILLE
Two years ago, Adrien almost died from a brain aneurysm, and she and her family live in constant fear that it will happen again. To escape the pervasive atmosphere of death, Adrien attends her Aunt Erin's camp. There, she sees

spirit girls dancing above the lake and becomes friends with Paul, who is convinced that he will die before his next birthday. (Canadian Library Association Young Adult Book Award)

Jones, Diana Wynne

Fire and Hemlock. **New York: Greenwillow, 1985. 341p. Reissued in 2002. ISBN: 006447352Xpa.** *MJ* **BRAILLE**

At nineteen, Polly discovers that a large part of her memory is missing. Piecing together clues, she realizes that she has two sets of memories: one revolves around everyday things like going to school and her parents' divorce; the other is entangled in heroic adventures shared with a cellist named Thomas Lynn.

Morton-Shaw, Christine

The Riddles of Epsilon. **New York: Katherine Tegen Books, 2005. 375p. ISBN: 0060728191.** *MJ*

When fourteen-year-old Jess and her parents move to the isolated English Isle of Lume, Jess begins to receive riddle messages from the mysterious Epsilon. These thrust her into an ancient battle between good and evil, with her mother's life at stake.

Murphy, Shirley Roussou

The Joe Gray Mysteries. New York: HarperPrism/HarperCollins. [Adult] *S*

When ordinary tomcat Joe Gray discovers that he can understand human speech, speak it himself, and read, he thinks his life has taken a very strange turn. But it's not nearly as strange as what happens when he witnesses a murder.

Cat on the Edge. **1996. 274p. ISBN: 0061056006pa.**

🎗 *Cat under Fire*. **1997. 244p. ISBN: 0061056014pa. (Muse Medallion)**

🎗 *Cat Raise the Dead*. **1997. 288p. ISBN: 0061056022pa. (Muse Medallion) BRAILLE**

🎗 *Cat in the Dark*. **1999. 265p. Issued in paperback. ISBN: 0061059471pa.**

Cat to the Dogs. **2000. 243p. Issued in paperback. ISBN: 0061059889pa. (Muse Medallion) LP**

Cat Spitting Mad. **New York: 2001. 228p. Issued in paperback by Avon. ISBN: 0061059897pa.**

Cat Laughing Last. **2002. 273p. Issued in paperback by Avon. ISBN: 0061015628pa. BRAILLE**

🎗 *Cat Seeing Double*. **2003. 292p. ISBN: 0066209501; 006101561Xpa. (Muse Medallion) BRAILLE LP**

Cat Fear No Evil. **2004. 323p. ISBN: 0066209498; 0061015601pa. BRAILLE LP**

Cat Cross Their Graves. **2005. 305p. ISBN: 0060578084; 0060578114pa. BRAILLE**

Cat Breaking Free. 2005. 352p. ISBN: 0060578092. LP

Pope, Elizabeth Marie

⚜ *The Perilous Gard*. **Boston: Houghton Mifflin, 1974. 280p. Reissued in hardcover 2001. ISBN: 0618177361; 0618150730pa.** _MJ_ **AUD**
In Tudor England, Katherine Sutton serves as a lady-in-waiting to Princess Elizabeth, but political maneuverings cause her to be exiled to the isolated castle known as Perilous Gard. When a series of inexplicable incidents occur, Katherine investigates and is captured by the fairies. The Queen of the Fairies admires her courage and bestows on Katherine the freedom to serve her. Only then does she locate her friend Christopher who is in great jeopardy. (Newbery Honor)

Pullman, Philip

Clockwork or All Wound Up. **New York: Arthur A. Levine Books, 1998. 172p. (1st American Edition.) Reissued in 1999. ISBN: 0590129988pa.** _MJ_ **AUD BRAILLE** 📖
Clock-making is a tradition in the German village of Glockenheim, and Karl the apprentice will become a master when he crafts a piece to add to the town's great clock. The villagers eagerly anticipate this, as they gather in the tavern in the evening before Karl's big event, not knowing that Karl has failed in his task. To pass the time, Fritz, a local novelist, reads from his latest work about Prince Florian and the mad clock-maker, Dr. Kalemenius. The characters from the story suddenly come to life, and Dr. Kalemenius offers Karl a contract with evil to achieve his greatest desire.

Spradlin, Michael

<u>**The Spy Goddess Series**</u>. **New York: HarperCollins.** _MJ_
Rachel Buchanan thinks Blackthorn Academy is an ordinary boarding school—until her penchant for probing reveals its supernatural secrets.

Live and Let Shop. **2005. 211p. ISBN: 0060594071; 0060594098pa.**
When fifteen-year-old Rachel Buchanan, a rich girl from Beverly Hills, gets arrested for grand theft auto, the judge sentences her to attend Pennsylvania's Blackthorn Academy. She thinks it's strange that students all are required to study tae kwon do and criminology. When the headmaster goes missing, Rachel cannot resist investigating.

To Hawaii, with Love. **2006. 208p. ISBN: 0060594101.**
With three of her friends, Rachel escapes from Blackthorn Academy, which is in reality a spy-training school. They fly to Hawaii to track down her arch-nemesis, Simon Blankenship, who is trying to bring back the god of the underworld, Mithras. He needs seven hidden treasures to succeed and thinks not only that Rachel knows where they are but also that she is the goddess Etherea reincarnated.

Vande Velde, Vivian

🏵 *Never Trust a Dead Man*. San Diego: Harcourt, 1999. 194p. ISBN: 0152018999lb; 044022828Xpa. *MJ* 📖

Farold has been murdered, and everyone in the village is convinced that Selwyn is guilty because he and the victim were rivals for Anora's affection. Instead of executing him, they seal Selwyn in the tomb with the dead man, where he would have stayed if not for the witch. She agrees to resurrect Farold so that he can reveal his true killer. But when he returns in the body of a bat, he cannot help, for he was stabbed from behind. The witch disguises them both so that they can uncover the truth. (BBYA; Edgar Young Adult Award)

Magic Can Be Murder. San Diego: Harcourt, 2000. 197p. ISBN: 0152026657lb; 0142302104pa. *M*

Witches Nola and her mother travel from village to village to avoid suspicion, for not everyone appreciates the practice of their craft. Nola's special talent involves the waterspell. When she places a person's hair in a dish of water, she can watch what that person is doing. Nola grows careless with the spell, and when she and her mother are blamed for a murder, she must use her magic to reveal the true culprit.

Westerfeld, Scott

Midnighters. *See* Chapter 13, "The Dark Side: Paranormal and Horror."

The Finest in the Realm

The Dresden Files by Jim Butcher

The Thursday Next Series by Jasper Fforde

The Changeling Series by Elaine Cunningham

Never Trust a Dead Man by Vivian Vande Velde

Chapter 9

Creature Fantasy: Fabulous Beasts and Talking Animals

Two distinct kinds of fantasies feature representatives from the animal kingdom: those in which the animals are imaginary or mythological, such as dragons and unicorns, and those in which the creatures are relatively realistic except that they can talk.

Fabulous Beasts

Dragons and unicorns both appear in the mythologies of many cultures and have also populated fantasy novels for young adults and adults. Fantasy of this type can be "Secondary World" fantasy or "Reality with Twist." Often the setting is an imaginary medieval-style location because many of Western mythology's tales of dragons and unicorns come from the Middle Ages. Fabulous beasts made their presence known through Eastern mythology as well, however, and some authors are inspired by those myths. Others invent their own versions of these creatures and spin a completely new tale.

Dragons

Bertin, Joanne

The Dragonlord Duology. New York: Tor. [Adult] _S_
In the Five Kingdoms, select humans are transformed so that they can evolve into dragons. Linden Rathan is in the midst of that process and so can be a man or a dragon—thus, a dragonlord. The dragonlords keep the peace in the land. When two candidates claim the regency of Cassori, Linden and two fellow dragonlords are sent to arbitrate the dispute.

The Last Dragonlord. 1998. 398p. Reissued in 1999. ISBN: 0812545419pa.

Dragon and Phoenix. 1999. 539p. Reissued in 2000. ISBN: 0812545427pa.

Fletcher, Susan

The Dragon Chronicles. New York: Atheneum. *MJ*

In Elythia and its neighboring kingdoms, dragons are feared by all and pursued by the brave. But those who have the telltale green eyes are different, for rumor whispers that they can speak to dragons.

Dragon's Milk. 1989. 242p. Reissued by Aladdin in 1996. ISBN: 0689716230pa.

Kaeldra has never spoken to a dragon, although legend says she can. When her foster sister becomes ill, however, Kaeldra ventures into the mountains to find a dragon and the cure—dragon's milk. Suddenly, the mother dragon is killed, and Kaeldra is left to care for three hungry, hunted draclings.

Flight of the Dragon Kyn. 1993. 213p. Reissued by Aladdin in 1997. ISBN: 0689815158pa.

In this prequel to *Dragon's Milk,* green-eyed Kara telepathically summons birds, and so the king thinks that he can use her to rid the land of the dragons that are plaguing it. When a dragon's death is brought about because Kara called it, her guilt and anger force her to flee into the mountains and find a way to keep the other dragons safe forever.

Sign of the Dove. 1996. 214p. Reissued by Aladdin in 1999. ISBN: 0689824491pa.

In this sequel to *Dragnon's Milk,* Lyf, Kaeldra's foster sister, unexpectedly is left alone to care for Kaeldra's young son and the last hatching of draclings. The draclings are being hunted for their hearts, and Lyf has to feed, care for, and shepherd them to safety.

Funke, Cornelia

Dragon Rider. New York: Scholastic, 2004. (1st American Edition.) 523p. ISBN: 0439456959. *M* AUD LP

When humans endanger the hidden valley of the silver dragons, Firedrake embarks on a quest to find the Rim of Heaven in hopes of discovering a place of safety for all of his fellow dragons.

Hambly, Barbara

The Winterlands Series. New York: Ballantine/Del Rey. [Adult] *S*

Jenny Waynest, the sorceress, and her lover, John Aversin, battle dragons and then demons in a desperate attempt to save the Winterlands.

Dragonsbane. 1985. 381p. ISBN: 0345349393pa.

Dragonshadow. 1999. 297p. (Out of Print)

Knight of the Demon Queen. 2000. 263p. ISBN: 0345421906pa.

Dragonstar. 2002. 292p. Reissued in 2003. ISBN: 0345441710pa.

Jordan, Sherryl

🏶 *The Hunting of the Last Dragon*. New York: HarperCollins, 2002. 186p. ISBN: 0060289023; 0064472310pa. *MJ* 📖
Jude, a lad growing up in fourteenth-century Britain, joins a traveling carnival after a dragon destroys his village. His job involves caring for the needs of the Chinese woman Jing-wei, who is treated as a sideshow. When Jude rescues her from an attempted rape, the two escape and embark on a journey to rid the world of the last dragon. (BBYA)

Kerner, Elizabeth

The Lanen Kaeler Trilogy. New York: Tor. [Adult] *JS*

Although no one in her family believes that dragons are anything more than a myth, Lanen Kaeler has dreamed of dragons all her life. Despite the ridicule surrounding her, she sets out to find the mythical beasts, changing the course of her life forever.

> *Song in the Silence*. 1997. 378p. Reissued in 2003. ISBN: 076534 2685pa.

> *The Lesser Kindred*. 2000. 368p. Reissued in 2001. ISBN: 081256 8753pa.

> *Redeeming the Lost*. 2004. 398. Reissued in 2005. ISBN: 0812568761pa.

Lackey, Mercedes

The Dragon Jouster Series. New York: Daw. [Adult] *S*

The land of Alta has been conquered by the Tians, whose dragon-riding Jousters serve their king as warriors. Vetch, a serf, seeks to free himself and raise a dragon of his own.

> *Joust*. 2003. 373p. ISBN: 0756401224; 0756401534pa.

> *Alta*. 2004. 402p. ISBN: 0756402166; 0756402573pa.

> *Sanctuary*. 2005. 432p. ISBN: 0756402468; 0756403413pa.

McCaffrey, Anne

The Chronicles of Pern. *See* Chapter Twelve12, "Science Fiction."

McKinley, Robin

The Hero and the Crown. *See* Chapter 2, "Epic Fantasy."

Paolini, Christopher

The Inheritance Trilogy. New York: Knopf. *MJ* AUD
In Alagaesia, dragons and their riders once helped wise and just rulers. When one of their own turned against them, the dragons disappeared—and so did

those who knew how to speak to and ride them. The elves guarded the lone egg, but when they were attacked, it was lost in a deep wood.

> ***Eragon*. 2003. 509p. ISBN: 0375826688; 0375826696pa. VID**
> When Eragon finds a blue stone in the forest, he hopes to be able to sell it so he can buy food for his family, but this is no ordinary stone. It is a dragon egg, and the hatching of the fledgling sets a new course for Eragon's life.

> ***Eldest*. 2005. 681p. ISBN: 037582670X.**
> Eragon and his blue-scaled dragon, Saphira, have helped win the battle of Tronjheim, but Eragon realizes that to help defeat the evil emperor permanently, he needs more training as a dragon rider. So he and Saphira set out for Ellesmera, the land of the elves, while his cousin Roran aids their fellow villagers in resisting the forces of evil.

Rawn, Melanie

> **The Dragon Prince Trilogy and The Dragon Star Trilogy. New York: Daw. All re-issued in 1994. [Adult] _JS_**
> Sunrunners draw in the light of the sun and weave its colors together to create magic spells. Those with this goddess-given power and those with royal authority often are at odds, but they now must find a way to meld their strengths to bring peace to their war-torn land.

The Dragon Prince Trilogy

> *The Dragon Prince*. 1988. 574p. Reissue ISBN: 0886774500pa.

> *The Star Scroll* 1989. 589p. Reissue ISBN: 0886773490pa.

> *Sunrunner's Fire*. 1990. 479p. Reissue ISBN: 0886774039pa.

The Dragon Star Trilogy

> *Stronghold*. 1990. 487p. Reissue ISBN: 0886774039pa.

> *The Dragon Token*. 1992. 560p. Reissue ISBN: 0886775426pa.

> *Skybowl*. 1993. 672p. Reissue ISBN: 0886775957pa.

Resnick, Laura

> **The Sileria Series. New York: Tor. [Adult] _S_**
> The land of Sileria has always been oppressed by its more powerful neighbors and will be until the Firebringer of prophecy comes to unite the peoples. He must battle not only warring factions, but also vicious dragons.

> *In Legend Born*. 1998. 461p. Reissued in 2000. ISBN: 0812555473pa.

> *The White Dragon: In Fire Forged, Part One*. 2003. 494p. ISBN: 0312890567; 0812555481pa.

> *The Destroyer Goddess: In Fire Forged, Part Two*. 2003. 478p. ISBN: 0765308754; 0765347962pa.

Vande Velde, Vivian

Dragon's Bait. San Diego: Harcourt, 1992. 131p. Reissued by Magic Carpet in 2003. ISBN: 0152166637pa. _MJ_

Falsely accused of being a witch, Alys is condemned to be the dragon's sacrifice. Instead, the dragon, Selendrile, transforms himself into a young man and agrees to help Alys take revenge on her neighbors.

Watt-Evans, Lawrence

The Obsidian Chronicles. New York: Tor. [Adult] _S_

When the merciless dragons darken the sky, they bring death and destruction. Arlain, the only survivor of his village, grows up a slave, nurturing one dream: to exact retribution and obliterate the dragons.

Dragon Weather. 1999. 480p. Reissued in 2000. ISBN: 081258 9556pa.

Dragon Society. 2001. 428p. Reissued in 2003. ISBN: 0765340542pa.

Dragon Venom. 2003. 416p. Reissued in 2004. ISBN: 0765341700pa.

Wrede, Patricia C.

The Enchanted Forest Chronicles. San Diego: Harcourt. _MJ_ AUD

Princesses must be ladylike and concentrate on their embroidery, and dragons must be fought by brave knights who rescue fair maidens—until Princess Cimerone decides that she will do things differently.

Dealing with Dragons. 1990. 212p. ISBN: 0152229000; 015204566Xpa.

Princess Cimorene is sick and tired of sitting in the castle working on her embroidery. She runs away to live with the dragons and uncovers a plot being hatched by wicked wizards.

Searching for Dragons. 1991. 242p. ISBN: 0152008985; 0152045651pa.

The band of wicked wizards returns, and this time they are trying to drain all of the magic out of the Enchanted Forest. King Mandanbar and Princess Cimorene, after many misunderstandings, work to save the dragon Kazul and foil the wizards.

Calling on Dragons. 1993. 244p. Reissued by Magic Carpet in 2003. ISBN: 0152046925pa.

The dastardly wizards have stolen King Mandanbar's sword and are using it to leech all of the magic out of the enchanted forest. Queen Cimorene and company must find the sword to save the forest.

Talking to Dragons. 1993. 255p. Reissued by Magic Carpet in 2003. ISBN: 0152046917pa.

Sixteen years have passed, and King Mandanbar still is imprisoned in the castle. Queen Cimorene lives at the Forest's edge, raising their son Daystar until he is old enough to wield the magic sword and one day free his father.

Yep, Laurence

The Dragon Quartet. New York: HarperCollins. _MJ_

A clan of dragons dwells in the sea in this quartet inspired by Chinese legends. When the dragons exile their princess, they do not know that it will be up to her to save them all.

🐉 *Dragon of the Lost Sea*. 1982. 213p. Reissued in 1988. ISBN: 0064402274pa.
Shimmer, a dragon princess, has been exiled by her clan. To redeem herself, she sets out, with her human companion, Thorn, to overcome an evil enchantress. (ALAN)

Dragon Steel. 1985. 276p. Reissued in 1993. ISBN: 0064404862pa.
Her clan has been enslaved and forced to work the underwater forges, so Shimmer and Thorn brave every obstacle to free them.

Dragon Cauldron. 1991. 312p. Reissued in 1994. ISBN: 006440398Xpa.
Shimmer and Thorn, along with their new companions, must journey to unknown lands to locate the missing dragon cauldron and restore the dragon clan to its rightful place in the kingdom of the sea.

Dragon War. 1992. 313p. Reissued in 1994. ISBN: 0064405257pa.
Dragon Princess Shimmer gathers her allies to fight the Boneless King. He has stolen the powerful dragon cauldron and trapped Thorn's soul. She will need all the help her friends can give her to save him and to keep the Boneless King from using the cauldron to boil the sea dry.

Yolen, Jane

The Dragon Pit Trilogy. *See* Chapter 12, "Science Fiction."

Zhan, Timothy

The Dragonback Adventures. *See* Chapter 12, "Science Fiction."

Unicorns

Beagle, Peter S.

The Last Unicorn. New York: Viking, 1968. 218p. Reissued in 1990. ISBN: 0451450523pa. [Adult] *JS* BRAILLE VID 📖
The immortal unicorn dwells in her enchanted forest secure in the knowledge that, although she lives alone, there are other unicorns in the world—until the day she receives the disturbing news that she is the last of her kind. Determined to discover what has happened to the others, she ventures into the world, where she appears to most to be a lovely white horse. But a bumbling magician and a true maiden, who has waited her entire life for a glimpse of a unicorn, see her for what she truly is, and they accompany her. Together they must find a way to thwart the Red Bull, or the last unicorn will disappear as well.

Coville, Bruce

The Unicorn Chronicles. New York: Scholastic. *M*

Cara and her unicorn companion, Lightfoot, are entrusted with a variety of important tasks in the magic realm of Luster.

Into the Land of the Unicorns. **1994. 159p. Reissued by Apple in 1999. ISBN: 0439108381pa.**

Cara's grandmother gives her a magic amulet that transports her to the land of Luster, where she meets a young unicorn named Lightfoot. Together they face the dangers of dragons and delvers as they seek to deliver the message from Cara's grandmother to the queen of the unicorns.

The Song of the Wanderer. **1999. 330p. ISBN: 0590459538; 0590459546pa. AUD**

The queen of the unicorns returns Cara to Earth so that she can escort her grandmother back to Luster. When Cara arrives, her grandmother is trapped, and Cara must find a way to free her.

Pierce, Meredith Ann

The Firebringer Trilogy. **All reissued by Firebird in 2003. *MJ***

Among the unicorns, there is a prophecy concerning the one who will overcome the ancient evil. Only one unicorn can, but he must find his truth path to be the one foretold.

The Birth of the Firebringer. **New York: Four Winds Press, 1985. 234p. Reissue ISBN: 0142500534pa.**

Aljan son-of-Korr, the unicorn prince, is reckless and impulsive. As he is saved from one scrape after another, he begins to wonder if he has a special destiny.

Dark Moon. **New York: Four Winds Press, 1986. 237p. Reissue ISBN: 0142500577pa.**

Aljan bears the silver crescent on his brow and the white star on his heel as symbols of his destiny. It was foretold that he would be the Firebringer, but he knows nothing of fire until he witnesses its creation in a foreign land. A captive of these strangers, he must free himself and bring home the knowledge that can save his fellow unicorns.

The Son of Summer Stars. **Boston: Little Brown, 1996. 250p. Reissue ISBN: 0142500747pa.**

At last Aljan arrives home, bringing with him the knowledge of fire, which he can use to forge an alliance with his enemies and thus lead the unicorns back to their ancestral homeland. But the secret deeds of his father may destroy all Aljan can accomplish.

Talking Animals

Unlike many other kinds of fantasy, "Talking Animal" fantasy does not have to contain overt magic. Any novel in which the animals speak is a fantasy. Children's literature is replete with these. Fewer are written for young adults and very few for adults. However, animal fantasies with complex characters and plots do appeal to many teen readers.

Adams, Richard

Watership Down. New York: Macmillan, 1972. 429p. Reissued by Scribner in hardcover in 1996. ISBN: 068483605X; 0380002930pa. [Adult] *JS* AUD BRAILLE VID
When modern development threatens their natural habitat, a band of rabbits faces a series of dangers while searching for a place of safety. (Carnegie Medal)

Tales from Watership Down. New York: Knopf, 1996. 267p. Reissued in 1998 by HarperCollins. ISBN: 0380729342pa. [Adult] *JS* AUD
The rabbits of *Watership Down* share nineteen tales of their lives and adventures.

Alexander, Lloyd

The Cat Who Wished to Be a Man. New York: Dutton, 1973. 107p. Reissued in 2000. ISBN: 0141307048pa. *M*
Lionel, a ginger tomcat, begs his master, the wizard Stephanus, to change him to a man. Reluctantly, the wizard grants his wish. Lionel ventures out on his own, but experience soon shows him that humans are much more devious than he had thought. (Boston Globe Honor)

Avi

Perloo the Bold. New York: Scholastic Press, 1998. 225p. ISBN: 0590110020lb; 0590110039pa. *M* AUD 📖
Perloo, a Montmer (a jackrabbit-like creature) who likes his life of solitude studying history, has royal responsibility thrust upon him when he is summoned to see the dying Jolaine. Jolaine, the leader of the Montmers, called a Granter, has decided that Perloo must be the next Granter instead of her self-absorbed and greedy son. When Jolaine dies, the reluctant Perloo must use all his wits and knowledge to unite the Montmers and avert war with the Felbarts.

Bruchac, Joseph

Wabi: A Hero's Tale. *See* Chapter 3, "Myth and Legend Fantasy."

Profile of David Clement-Davies

Born January 6, 1964, in London, David Clement-Davies was a freelance travel journalist before the publication of his first novel, *Fire Bringer*. He graduated from Edinburgh University and worked for some time in the theater, but the writing life called to him (*Contemporary Authors Online*, Infotrac Galegroup Database; www.davidclementdavies.com).

Interview with David Clement-Davies

Conducted via e-mail March 12–14, 2006

SF: How did you first become inspired to write books for young people?

DCD: A good question, although I don't only write books for young people. I think the answer lies inside my own psyche and what I'm most like as a person, in many ways both the adult and the child. For me my own writing maintains a bridge between the two. When I first decided to write a novel I sought around for a vision and a voice, and although I wanted to be Tolstoy, or Shakespeare (!), or write the great twentieth-century novel, what most echoed back at me were the thrilling stories that I had read when I was younger—*White Fang, The Call of The Wild, The Hobbit, The Lord of the Rings*. I realize now a lot of that is purely about great adventures and I've always wanted to go on a great adventure, while those stories were also about the isolation of the hero figure. I realise also that I love narratives, and the great narratives are still possible in fantasy fiction in a way they are perhaps not in "adult" literature. I love "the story."

SF: *Fire Bringer* and *The Sight* are both animal fantasies and your newest book, *The Telling Pool*, switches to Arthurian. What moved you to change subgenres, and which do you prefer?

DCD: I have never wanted to get stale as a writer and of course, while *Firebringer* and *The Sight* are "animal fantasies," they are essentially about people, and our relationship with nature. *The Telling Pool* is actually a domestic drama, about a family, which in part came out of a dream and then developed towards Athurian myth. It was great to move away from the animals with that, as it was with my third book, *The Alchemists of Barbal*, which is a quite difficult, experimental novel, that is again different from the other three. But it was also wonderful to return to nature with a sequel to *The Sight, Fell*, which I'm writing at the moment. I think the powerful poetic voice in me is most strongly rooted in nature, while my love of detail and painting with words comes a lot from my experience as a travel writer.

SF: What kind of research do you do for your books? And is the research different for the different subgenres?

DCD: Research can involve many things from books, films and the library, to the Internet. Because I want to root my fantasies in some kind of truth it was important to me that the animal details in *Firebringer* and *The Sight* were true to the nature of the animals, red deer and wolves. Their stories and mythologies come out of those researched facts, as perhaps ours do, while the struggle between true facts and believable fantasy, a talking animal for instance, is a wonderful source of creative tension, and allows you to explore lots of ideas about the nature of storytelling itself. The research process is much the same, but where it leads you can be different. In *The Alchemists,* for instance, I threw in lots of crazy references to modern relativity, Wittgenstein and Chaos and String theories. Those poor kids!

SF: Have there been any significant changes to your books between the British editions and the American editions?

DCD: Funnily enough there have, especially in *The Sight.* My U.S. editor asked for much more detail about the facts and history of Transylvania, while to the great vision on the mountaintop I added some particularly American elements, which I thought would resonate in American minds. Some people find this strange, namely that a book isn't just a book, or a finished work of art. But I am quite flexible as a writer and I like adapting to things.

SF: What would you say your method of writing is (i.e., working from an outline, going where the story takes you, etc.)?

DCD: Going where the story takes me, although *The Telling Pool* had a much clearer synopsis than the others. I think I'm an organic writer, if that doesn't sound too vegetarian, and I work back and forwards through the plot, trying to enrich the whole, or find surprising moments of transition or catharsis. In stories moments echo to each other and set up resonances, much like music. The image of one moment can start a book in your head, though, and it can be anything, an opening, a great conflict, the battle of important ideas, even a startling ending, although if you are trying to force your story towards a particular ending it will probably feel contrived. I started *Firebringer* two years before I actually sat down to write it, with ten pages of handwritten text, about a noble stag who is murdered just as his son is born.

SF: Of your books, which is your favorite character and/or book?

DCD: My favourite book is *Firebringer,* I think because it was my first, was a testing ground for me, was the first time I saw my books in the shops and is associated with so many good memories. I shed a tear when it first arrived in the post from the publisher, although I did have a bad hangover at the time. It's interesting to me, though, that *The Sight* seems more popular in America. Perhaps it's because it's about wolves, or perhaps because the conflicts in it are darker, in a society that has bigger demons. My favourite characters change, according to mood, and maybe because there are elements of me in all the characters, goodies and baddies. Sometimes it's Rannoch, sometimes Kar, sometimes even Sgorr. Oh yes, and Rhodri Falcon. At the moment it's Fell.

SF: What were your favorite books growing up and/or who were your favorite authors?

DCD: I think I've answered that a bit, but let me add some more. I liked a lot of "boys own" stuff, not in the Enid Blyton or Just William category, but thrilling books like Forester's <u>Hornblower</u> series or anything by Robert Louis Stevenson, the supreme storyteller. I suppose that is also about historical imagination and wanting to be in some other place, or some other time. I also loved Kipling's great animal books, from the *Just So Stories* to *The Jungle Books,* which are nothing at all to do with the Disnifications on film. I was brought up on C. S. Lewis, although I think the titles, like *Voyage of the Dawn Treader* or *Prince Caspian*, were just as inspiring to me as the stories, although for "through the doorway" fantasies do you get much more inspiring than walking through that wardrobe into Narnia? I loved Roald Dahl, too, particularly *James and The Giant Peach*—it must be that tickertape parade through New York, which I'm still dreaming of. I also read comics and was completely hooked on *Asterix* and *Tintin*. They don't make 'em like that anymore, very possibly because we are becoming so politically correct. Finally Tolkien, because <u>The Lord of the Rings</u> so gripped me that I couldn't be pried away with a monkey wrench.

SF: What do you think is the merit or importance of reading fantasy?

DCD: Lord, there's the question. I just spoke at Arizona State University about exactly that. I think that the merit or importance of reading a good book lies in the quality of the book alone. Like bad movies or TV, I don't think kids should be sanctimoniously made to read books if they are bad or boring books but should be encouraged to hurl them away and pick up a good one. Reading itself, the understanding and mastery of language, the development of ideas and insights into character, circumstance and possibility, these are all part of the "educational" aspects of reading books, whether fantasy or not. But I do think fantasy literature has a particular role to play, because I think powerful fantasy writers are creating those bridges between the young and the adult imaginations, between worlds. I also think all fantasy literature is in some ways about the loss of childhood and the loss of God too. As we grow up we are faced with the often bitter realities of life and great fantasy prepares us for that and returns us to our early idealisms as well. In a setting that is archetypal and not bound to a particular creed or political reality, it can also provide us with symbols of hope or resistance that we can carry to some of the darkest places in life—think of Frodo's journey to destroy the ring of power, or on the adult level of Bulgakov's desperate magical realism under Stalin's Russia, in *The Master and Margherita*. There are lots more things to say, especially about science fiction/fantasy because there real technologies and possibilities, always created first in the human imagination, can be explored and examined through storytelling.

References

Clement-Davies, David, "Home Page," www.davidclementdavies.com (accessed March 16, 2006).

"David Clement-Davies," *Contemporary Authors Online*, Infotrac Galegroup Database (accessed March 16, 2006).

Clement-Davies, David

Fire Bringer. **New York: Dutton Books, 2000. (1st American Edition.) 498p. Reissued in 2002. ISBN: 0142300608pa. *JS***
In Scotland, the herds of red deer refer to themselves as Herla and have a long tradition of passing on leadership at the yearly dance of antlers. But the bucks Drail and Sgorr seize control and end this practice, taking over herd after herd. When the fawn Rannoch is born with an oak-leaf-shaped mark on his forehead, the Elders know that he must be protected as the deer of prophecy, for he is the one who will challenge Sgorr for the freedom of all Herla. (BBYA)

The Sight. **New York: Dutton Children's Books, 2002. (1st American Edition.) 465p. ISBN: 0525467238; 014250047Xpa. *JS***
Sheltered in the shadow of an ancient and uninhabited castle in Transylvania, the she-wolf Palla, one of the Varg, gives birth to two pups as her sister Mogra, who is gifted with the Sight, hunts her. Mogra seeks to kidnap the cubs and use their power for her evil ends, but Palla's pack will do everything in their power to protect them.

Conly, Jane Leslie

Racso and the Rats of NIMH. **New York: Harper & Row, 1986. ISBN: 0060213620lb; 0064402452pa. *M* BRAILLE**
This sequel to *Mrs. Frisby and the Rats of NIMH* by Robert O'Brien was penned by his daughter. Racso, son of the rebel rat, Jenner, leaves the city and looks for the intelligent rats of Thorn Valley. He wants an education. As he searches for the fabled colony, he encounters Timothy Frisby, also on his way to school with the rats. Their friendship progresses as they journey together. When they arrive at last, they learn that the colony is in danger from humans who plan to flood their valley.

R-T, Margaret, and the Rats of NIMH. **New York: Harper & Row, 1990. Reissued in 1991. ISBN: 0064403874pa. *M* BRAILLE**
When siblings Margaret and Artie get lost in the forest while their family is on a camping trip, the rats of NIMH rescue them. Although the brother and sister are fascinated by the rat community, they must return home. Before they go, Racso and Isabella must find a way to help them keep the secret of Thorn Valley.

Hunter, Erin

The Warrior Series. New York: HarperCollins. *M*

Four Clans of wild cats rule in the forest, guided by the laws created by their warrior ancestors. But trouble threatens as the ShadowClan rebels against tradition and ThunderClan's noble warriors are slain.

Into the Wild. 2003. 272p. ISBN: 0060000023; 0060525509pa.

Rusty, a house-kitten, longs for adventure, so when the ThunderClan invites him to join them, he eagerly changes his name to Firepaw and trains as an apprentice warrior. The ThunderClan will need every paw and claw as the ShadowClan moves against them.

Fire and Ice. 2003. 317p. ISBN: 0060000031; 0060525592pa.

When warrior apprentice Firepaw becomes a full warrior cat, he is dubbed Fireheart and given his first mission. He must delve into the unknown and locate the WindClan, to aid them in returning to their traditional hunting ground.

Forest of Secrets. 2003. 312p. ISBN: 006000004X; 0060525614pa.

Fireheart has unearthed a terrible secret about Clan deputy Tigerclaw, but he has no proof. As he searches for it, he discovers other brutal truths of life with rival clans and must create a way to set things right without being tainted as a traitor.

Rising Storm. 2004. 315p. ISBN: 0060000058; 0060525630pa.

Now deputy of ThunderClan, Fireheart works to win the trust of his Clan, find his runaway apprentice, and keep his fellow feral cats safe when fire sweeps through the forest.

A Dangerous Path. 2004. 313p. ISBN: 0060000066; 0060525657pa.

Fireheart worries that ShadowClan's new leader, Tigerstar, will not be content to simply rule his Clan but will seek revenge. In the meantime, his own leader, Bluestar, seems to have lost faith in the StarClan, and a pack of wild dogs ranges through the forest killing animals of all kinds.

The Darkest Hour. 2004. 315p. ISBN: 0060000074; 0060525851pa.

As Fireheart feared, Tigerstar has brought those of the forest to the brink of war. To save his Clan, he must unravel the prophecy of the StarClan.

Warriors: The New Prophecy Series. New York: HarperCollins. *M*

The StarClan, warrior cat ancestors whose spirits dwell in the stars, pronounces a new prophecy of doom that will take a cat from each Clan to avert.

Midnight. 2005. 303p. ISBN: 0060744499; 0060744510pa.

Firestar's daughter, Squirrelpaw, is the cat selected to join with three other cats, one from each Clan, to set out on the mission given to them by the StarClan.

Moonrise. 2005. 287p. ISBN: 0060744529.

Squirrelpaw and her fellow cats continue to search for the key to stopping the twolegs from destroying their forest home. As they look, they encounter a strange new tribe that believes one of the four searchers is their prophesied savior.

***Starlight*. 2006. ISBN: 0060827580.**
The twoleggeds have destroyed the world and the Cat Clans have succeeded in their quest to find a new world to live in, but they must also locate a new Moonstone so that they can communicate with the StarClan.

Jacques, Brian

<u>Redwall Series</u>. New York: Philomel. (1st American Editions.) AUD *MJ*
In a land much like pastoral England, a large abbey provides a home to the peaceful forest creatures of the surrounding countryside. Although they love their quiet lives, they must be ever-vigilant against the evil creatures that would destroy them. The titles are listed here in publication order.

***Redwall*. 1986. 351p. ISBN: 0399214240; 0441005489pa. BRAILLE LP VID**
All is calm at Redwall Abbey, where the mouse inhabitants cherish peace, until the marauding rats, led by the evil Cluny, attack. Young Matthias Mouse scours the countryside for the lost Sword of Martin the Warrior, knowing that it will help him defeat Cluny.

***Mossflower*. 1988. 431p. ISBN: 0399215492; 0441005764pa. BRAILLE**
The clever, greedy cat Tsarmina has become the wicked ruler of Mossflower Woods. The brave mouse Martin the Warrior and his friend Gonff, the mouse-thief, set out to find the missing ruler of Mossflower, while the woodland creatures prepare to rebel.

***Mattimeo*. 1990. 446p. ISBN: 039921741X; 0441006108pa. BRAILLE**
Preparations for the feast of the Summer of Golden Rain are underway at Redwall Abbey. Young Mattimeo, son of Matthias, guardian of Redwall, is working with the others, completely unaware that Slagar the Fox is planning to kidnap him and the other woodland children.

***Mariel of Redwall*. 1992. 387p. ISBN: 0399221441; 0441006949pa. BRAILLE**
When the mouse-ship carrying Joseph the Bellmaker and his daughter, Mariel, is boarded by Gabool the Wild, king of the pirate searats, the mousemaid is tossed overboard. She arrives half-starved at Redwall, where the animals care for her. As she recovers, Mariel becomes determined to exact revenge.

***Salamandastron*. 1993. 391p. ISBN: 0399219927; 0441000312pa. BRAILLE**
When Salamandastron, a mountain stronghold near Redwall, is besieged by the weasel Feragho the Assassin and his corps of vermin, and Martin the Warrior's sword is stolen, the creatures of Redwall join with their neighbors to overcome the menacing creatures.

***Martin the Warrior*. 1994. 376p. ISBN: 0399226702; 0441001866pa. BRAILLE**
Badrang the Tyrant, a heartless stoat, is the chieftain of a horde of weasels, ferrets, foxes, and rats who are ruthlessly using slave labor to build a fortress. Little

does Badrang realize that the quiet, nameless mouse he is holding captive will soon become Martin the Warrior.

***The Bellmaker*. 1995. 336p. ISBN: 0399228055; 044100315Xpa. BRAILLE**

Joseph the Bellmaker is worried about his daughter Mariel. He has had no news from her in several seasons. Then Martin the Warrior warns him in a dream that disaster looms. With a small band of friends, Joseph confronts the diabolical Foxwolf Nagra, who not only conquered the Southland, but has also imprisoned Mariel.

***Outcast of Redwall*. 1996. 360p. ISBN: 0399229140; 0441004164pa. BRAILLE**

Abandoned as an infant, Veil the ferret has been lovingly raised by mousemaid Bryony of Redwall. After committing an unforgivable crime, he is cast out. His vicious father, Swartt Sinclaw, invites him to join his attack on Redwall, and Veil must choose his destiny as friend or foe.

***Pearls of Lutra*. 1997. 408p. ISBN: 0399229469; 044100508Xpa. BRAILLE**

When Emperor Ubla, a pine martin known as Mad Eyes, sends his lizard army to conquer Redwall and to demand the return of stolen pearls, the residents of Redwall must respond. Tansy the hedgehog leads a group in an attempt to find the pearls, and Martin, grandson of Matthias, takes a band of brave companions in pursuit of the enemy.

***The Long Patrol*. 1998. 358p. ISBN: 039923165X; 0441005993pa. BRAILLE**

Tammo wants more than anything to join the Long Patrol, the legendary army of fighting hares that serves the Lady Gregga Rose Eyes, Ruler of Salamandastron. He gets his chance to fight when the Rapscallions first attack Salamandastron and then Redwall.

***Marlfox*. 1999. 386p. ISBN: 0399233075; 0441006930pa. BRAILLE**

New villains are prowling through Mossflower Woods. They can disappear at any time and use their stealth to steal Redwall's precious tapestry of Martin the Warrior. Eager to prove themselves, the squirrel and shrew children of heroes set out to recover the treasure.

***The Legend of Luke*. 2000. 374p. ISBN: 039923490X; 0441007732pa. LP**

Continuing the story of Martin the Warrior, here he leaves Redwall to return to the land of his youth and to seek out the truth of his father, Luke, while battling weasels, water rats, crows, and tree vermin along the way.

***Lord Brocktree*. 2000. 370p. ISBN: 0399235906; 0441008720pa. BRAILLE**

Dotti, a feisty young haremaid, and the badger Lord Brocktree, a fierce warrior, journey to Salamandastron to take back the mountain home of the badger lords, which is being besieged by the Wildcat Ungutt Truni and his Blue Hoards.

***Taggerung*. 2001. 438p. ISBN: 0399237208; 0441009689pa. BRAILLE LP**
Denya, a baby otter of Redwall, is kidnapped by Sawney Rath, a vicious ferret, who leads a dangerous vermin clan. He raises the otter in hopes of forging a weapon, but he does not take into account the otter's own nature.

***Triss*. 2002. 389p. ISBN: 0399237232; 0441010954pa. BRAILLE LP**
Triss, a squirrelmaid, and her friends escape from slavery and head for Redwall, all the while being pursued by nasty brother and sister ferrets, Prince Bladd and Princess Kurda.

***Loamhedge*. 2003. 424p. ISBN: 0399237240; 044101190Xpa.**
Martha, a wheelchair-bound young haremaid, is convinced that a cure can be uncovered in the deserted Abbey of Loamhedge. Inspired by Martin the Warrior, two old warriors embark on the quest, unwittingly leaving Redwall vulnerable to invasion.

***Rakkety Tam*. 2004. 372p. ISBN: 0399237259; 044101318Xpa.**
Gulo the Savage, a wolverine from the northern wasteland, and his vicious followers invade Mossflower County, hunting his brother Askor, who has stolen the Walking Stick, a symbol of great power. Rakkety Tam MacBurl, a highland squirrel warrior, along with his friend Wild Doogy Plumm, agree to march with the hares of the Long Patrol Regiment to fight for the county and Redwall Abbey.

***High Rhulain*. 2005. 341p. ISBN: 0399242082.**
Tiria, the ottermaid, lives in Redwall with her family. When she begins to dream about Green Isle and Martin the Warrior, she knows she is destined to follow in the footsteps of the great otter queen, the High Rhulian.

Jarvis, Robin

The Deptford Trilogy. New York: SeaStar. (1st American Editions.) _MJ_
Two animal worlds collide in the London borough of Deptford when the peaceful mice from above encounter the evil rats from below.

***The Dark Portal*. 2000. 241p. Reissued in 2001. ISBN: 1587171120pa. AUD**
When mouse Albert Brown, who lives in a mouse community in an abandoned house, is lured into the sewers, where rats enjoy capturing mice, peeling them, and then eating them, his son and daughter, Arthur and Audrey, mount a dangerous rescue mission.

***The Crystal Prison*. 2001. 250p. ISBN: 1587171074; 1587171619pa.**
To save her friend Oswald, Starwife decrees that Audrey must accompany the rat Madame Akkikuyu to the countryside. Although Madame Akkikuyu wins approval for her helpful healing, Audrey's city ways are viewed with suspicion by the country mice, and an ancient evil uses the rat in an attempt to destroy the mice.

***The Final Reckoning*. 2002. 298p. ISBN: 1587171929; 1587172445pa.**
Jupiter, the evil leader of the London sewer rats, returns from the dead and steals the magical Starglass of the Deptford mice. He hopes to use it to capture the sun

and the moon and plunge the world into eternal winter. Although their chances of success seem slim, Audrey, with her fellow mice and their allies, must face the ravening rats.

The Deptford Histories. San Francisco: SeaStar. _MJ_
This trio of tales provides the background for the events portrayed in <u>The Deptford Mice Trilogy</u>.

The Alchemist's Cat. **San Francisco: SeaStar, 2004. 304p. ISBN: 1587172577.**
In 1664 London, young Will Godwin, unjustly accused of murder, flees for his life and stumbles into the service of the evil apothecary, Elias Theophratus Spittle. Sent in search of items for his master in a graveyard, Will finds a mother cat and her three kittens. Thinking to rescue them, he brings them back with him and begins a chain of disastrous events, which lead to the creation of the malevolent cat mage, Jupiter.

The Oaken Throne. **San Francisco: SeaStar, 2005. 382p. ISBN: 1587172771.**
A brutal war dominates the lives of the bats and the squirrels. But when Vesper the bat and Ysabelle the squirrel maiden team up to return the Silver Acorn to its rightful owners, they discover their real foe is the demon rat, Lord Hobb.

Thomas. **San Francisco: SeaStar, 2006. ISBN: 0811854124.**
Shipmouse Thomas and his best friend fieldmouse Woodget embark on a voyage across the sea to protect the jade fragment of an egg that must be kept separate from the other fragments at all costs. If the fragments are joined, the evil snake-god will return.

King, Gabriel

The Wild Road. **New York: Ballantine, 1998. 460p. Reissued in 1999. ISBN: 0345423038pa. [Adult] _JS_**
Tag, a young gray kitten, enjoys leading a pampered life indoors, but not so much that when temptation comes his way, he doesn't dash outside. When he gets distracted by a host of other animals, he loses his way. He lives as a stray on the streets of London's eastside until the one-eyed black cat, Majicou, reveals that he must find the king and queen of cats and escort them along the Wild Road to Tintagel before the spring equinox, for they are in danger from the evil Alchemist who seeks to use them in hideous experiments.

The Golden Cat. **New York: Ballantine, 1999. 287p. Reissued in paperback. ISBN: 0345423054pa. [Adult] _JS_**
When the Queen of Cats gives birth to three golden kittens, any one of them can be the cat of prophecy. When two of the three are captured, the remaining kitten, Leonora, convinces Tag to help her travel the Wild Road to find her siblings and stop the Alchemist, who is scheming again.

O'Brien, Robert

🎀 *Mrs. Frisby and the Rats of NIMH*. **New York: Atheneum, 1971. 233p. ISBN: 0689206518; 0689710682pa.** *MJ* **AUD BRAILLE VID** 📖
When the widowed mouse Mrs. Frisby learns that she must move her family early to their summer home to keep them safe, even though her youngest son Timothy is ill with pneumonia, she seeks help from a group of rats that possess extraordinary intelligence. (Boston Globe Honor; Newbery Medal)

Oppel, Kenneth

The Silverwing Trilogy. New York: Simon & Schuster. *MJ* **AUD**
Silverwing bats encounter adventures as they struggle to survive.

🎀 *Silverwing*. **1997. 217p. Reissued by Aladdin in 1999. ISBN: 0689825587pa.**
Shade, a small Silverwing bat, becomes separated from his colony during a storm while they are in the midst of their migration flight. As he struggles to catch up, he befriends Marina, a Brightwing bat, and learns that he must warn his colony about the tropical bats with cannibalistic tendencies. (CLABYC)

🎀 *Sunwing*. **2000. 266p. Reissued by Aladdin in 2001. ISBN: 0689832877pa.**
Shade and Marina are companions again as Shade hunts for his missing father. Their quest becomes perilous as danger threatens from both humans and cannibal bats. (CLABYC)

Firewing. **2003. 270p. ISBN: 0689849931lb; 0689869886pa. LP**
Shade and Marina's young son Griffin is having trouble living up to the legendary status of his parents. When he tries to impress his friends by stealing fire, he begins a chain of events that leads him to the Underworld.

Seidler, Tor

A Rat's Tale. **New York: Farrar, Straus & Giroux, 1986. 185p. Reissued by Trophy in 1999. ISBN: 0064407799pa.** *M*

Because they work with their paws, Montague Mad-Rat and his artist parents are cast out of upper-class rat society. They live in the sewers of New York City. Montague, a shy young rat, likes to paint pictures on shells. He doesn't know that he and his family are outcasts until he meets the lovely Isabel Moberly-Rat and escorts her home to the posh wharves. There, her mother makes it clear that no wharf rats would ever work with their paws. Montague departs feeling ashamed. When he learns of a plan to demolish the wharves, he is determined to help save them to prove his worth, never dreaming that his own talent might save them all.

The Revenge of Randal Reese-Rat. **New York: Farrar, Straus & Giroux, 2001. 233p. ISBN: 0374362572; 0060508671pa.** *M*
Montague and Isabel are betrothed but must wait to marry until Montague's Aunt Elizabeth brings his cousin Maggie back from Africa. When a mysterious fire destroys their honeymoon crate, Isabel's former fiancé, Randal Reese-Rat, is suspected. Randal escapes to the Bronx Zoo, disguises himself as Gregory Sad-Rat, and meets the musical Maggie, who changes his life.

Williams, Tad

Tailchaser's Song. **New York: Daw, 1985. 333p. Reissued in 2000. ISBN: 0886779537pa. [Adult]** *JS*

Fritti Tailchaser, a ginger tomcat who is still a bit young to be a hunter, is disturbed to find out that his friend Hushpaw has disappeared, as have many other cats, and so embarks on a quest to find her.

The Finest in the Realm

Perloo the Bold by Avi

The Last Unicorn by Peter Beagle

Mrs. Frisby and the Rats of NIMH by Robert O'Brien

A Rat's Tale by Tor Seidler

The Enchanted Forest Chronicles by Patricia Wrede

Chapter 10

Time Travel Fantasy

Time travel, sometimes referred to as time slip, is a popular plot device, most often used to move characters back in time and then relate historically accurate fiction. It is a conceit that is used in science fiction as well as fantasy. If the method of time travel is explained scientifically, through the use of a machine or invention, then it is a work of science fiction. If it is explained mystically, or not explained at all, it is fantasy. Often time travel is the only fanciful element of a novel, so these stories appeal more to those who like their fantasy to be more realistic than fanciful. They also appeal to fans of historical fiction.

Bennett, Cherie

Anne Frank and Me. **New York: Putnam, 2001. 291p. ISBN: 0399233296; 0698119738pa.** *JS*
Tenth-grader Nicole Burns would rather muse about boys than do her homework, reading *Anne Frank: The Diary of a Young Girl.* After doing a quick Internet search and reading some material minimizing the Holocaust, she adopts that point of view until she suffers a concussion during a school trip to the Holocaust museum. She wakes up in 1942 Paris as a member of a Jewish family and finds that she is the key to helping the others survive.

Bond, Nancy

🌢 *A String in the Harp.* **New York: Atheneum, 1976. 370p. ISBN: 068950036Xlb; 0689804458pa.** *MJ* **AUD BRAILLE**
When Peter Morgan moves with his family from New England to Wales, he finds a harp key that magically transports him to sixth-century Wales, where he encounters the famous bard, Taliesin. (ALAN; Boston Globe Honor; Newbery Honor)

Cooney, Caroline

The Time Travel Quartet. New York: Delacorte. All reissued by Laurel Leaf. BR _JS_
First Annie Lockwood and then her brother Tod move back and forth between their everyday lives in the twentieth century and Victorian living of the 1890s.

Both Sides of Time. **1995. 210p. Reissued in 1997. 0440219329.**
Fifteen-year-old Annie Lockwood longs to live in a time of romance when she can have a boyfriend that pays more attention to her than he does to his car. Her wish is granted when, as she is exploring a mansion that is about to be torn down, she tumbles through time and ends up in 1895. Through the haze of adjusting to the time shift, she witnesses a murder and subsequently meets the dashing Hiram Stratton, Jr. They fall in love, but Annie realizes she must find a way back to her own time.

Out of Time. **1996. 210p. Reissued in 1997. ISBN: 0440219337pa.**
When their parents separate, both Annie and her brother are caught in the tangle of emotions. Although it means abandoning her brother, Annie wistfully wishes to be with Stratton again and so returns to the past. This time she finds Stratton locked up in a mental institution for insisting that she was from the future. He is in desperate need of her help—both for himself and for his sister, who may end up in the hands of a man who only wants her fortune.

Prisoner of Time. **1998. 200p. Reissued in 1999. ISBN: 044022019Xpa.**
Devonny Aurelia Victoria Stratton, Hiram's sister, dreads her marriage to the impoverished British lord her father has arranged for her and, while she is walking down the aisle, wishes for someone to rescue her. Her wish draws Tod Lockwood, Annie's brother, to her. When Tod succeeds in bringing Devonny forward to the twentieth century, the Victorian lady is by turns relieved, astounded, and dismayed. Although she sees the strides that women have made, she fervently wants to return home.

For All Time. **2001. 263p. Reissued in 2003. ISBN: 0440229316pa.**
Annie and Tod's parents have reconciled, remarried, and are away on their honeymoon, leaving Annie four days to figure out a way to return to "Strat" in 1899. She visits an Egyptian exhibit at the Metropolitan Museum of Art because it is displaying artifacts found by an expedition in which Strat took part. She's transported back in time—not to Strat, but to the Egypt of four thousand years ago. Although she is rescued by an Egyptian woman, she still must face danger from unexpected sources and find a way to be reunited with Strat.

Cooper, Susan

🏵 *King of Shadows*. **New York: Margaret K. McElderry Books, 1999. 186p. ISBN: 068982817 9lb; 1416905324pa. _MJ_ LP AUD** 📖
Nat Field loves acting and spends every moment he can practicing his role as Puck in *A Midsummer Night's Dream*. He is selected with other young American actors to perform the play at a historically reconstructed Globe theater and travels to England with high hopes. But when he arrives, a mysterious illness strikes. He wakes up in Shakespeare's time and finds himself rehearsing with the Bard himself, who is playing Oberon. (BBYA; Boston Globe Honor)

Curry, Jane Louise

The Black Canary. **New York: Margaret K. McElderry Books, 2005. 279p. ISBN: 0689864787.** _MJ_ 📖

Twelve-year-old biracial James is the son of two musicians and resents the demands their musical lives place on the family. Reluctantly, he journeys with his parents to London, where his mother is performing. In the basement of their flat, he discovers a shimmer, a time portal that transports him back to the year 1600. In his new time, he becomes a member of the Children of the Royal Chapel who will sing for Queen Elizabeth. As he grows to love his new life, he must decide whether to try to return home.

Gabaldon, Diana

Outlander Series. *See* Chapter 7, "Fantasy Romance."

Hearn, Julie

Sign of the Raven. **New York: Atheneum, 2005. (1st American Edition.) 328p. ISBN: 0689857349.** _MJ_

Twelve-year-old Tom thinks he should be spending his summer at home in Dorset, relaxing with his friends. But his mother, who is fighting cancer, drags him to London to spend time with her mother. In the basement of his grandmother's house, a whirling gap turns out to be a time portal. When Tom plunges in, he winds up in the eighteenth century in a house filled with the sideshow freaks of the Bartholomew Fair, who desperately need his help.

Heneghan, James

🎗 *The Grave*. **New York: Farrar, Straus & Giroux, 2000. 356p. ISBN: 0374327653.** _JS_ **AUD**

Left in a department store as a baby in Liverpool, thirteen-year-old Tom has bounced from one foster home to another, never feeling at home or loved. When construction begins on the new school, Tom is lured to investigate the mysterious hole dug by the workers. He finds it's a mass grave. Accidentally, he tumbles in. Suddenly, he is no longer in 1974 England, but 1847 Ireland. (BBYA)

Jones, Diana Wynne

A Tale of Time City. **New York: Greenwillow Books, 1987. 278p. Reissued in 2002 by HarperCollins. ISBN: 0064473511pa.** _MJ_

In 1939, Vivian Smith boards a train with dozens of other children fleeing London during the Blitz. She thinks she is on her way to stay in the country with her cousin, but when Jonathan meets her train instead, she ends up being farther from home than she'd anticipated. He kidnaps her and takes her to Time City, thinking she is Lady Time, the only one who can save the city. Now, whether she wants to or not, she must help him find the elusive Lady Time, or she may never return home.

Lasky, Kathryn

Blood Secret. New York: HarperCollins, 2004. 249p. ISBN: 006000066X; 0060000635pa. *MJ*

When her mother disappeared from the campground in Albuquerque, Jerry was sent to Catholic Charities. Jerry moved from home to home until age fourteen, when finally her Great-Great-Aunt Constanza de Luna was located and agreed to take her in. Mute from the trauma in her life, Jerry arrives silent and unsure of herself. She finds a trunk full of family mementos in her aunt's basement, and each item carries her back in time to witness a bit of family history. As Jerry watches incidents of persecution, she realizes that her family is Jewish; and, as she experiences her aunt's love and makes new friends, she begins to find her voice again.

Niffenegger, Audrey

🐦 *The Time Traveler's Wife*. San Francisco: MacAdam/Cage, 2003. 518p. ISBN: 1931561648; 015602943Xpa. [Adult] *S* AUD

Henry and Clare De Tamble live in Chicago and seem to be an ordinary couple, but their lives are consistently disrupted by Henry's chrono-displacement disorder, which causes him to move back and forth in time. (Alex)

O'Brien, Judith.

Timeless Love. *See* Chapter 7, "Fantasy Romance."

Park, Linda Sue

Archer's Quest. New York: Clarion Books, 2006. ISBN: 0618596313. *M*

Kevin, a twelve-year-old Korean American, living in Dorchester, New York, was a math whiz but he thought social studies was the most boring subject ever. His knowledge of history is soon put to the test, but not in the usual way. While studying in his room, he is astounded by the appearance Koh Chu-mong, Skillful Archer, a legendary leader from Korea's past who was jolted forward in time when he fell off his tiger. The two must find a way to send Koh back to his rightful time before history is changed.

Peck, Dale

Drift House: The First Voyage. New York: Bloomsbury, 2005. 437p. (1st American Edition.) ISBN: 158234969X. *M* AUD

After 9/11, siblings Susan, Charles, and Murray are sent to Canada to live with their Uncle Farley. He lives in a strange house on the Bay of Eternity, and they soon discover that the house is not a house, but a ship, and they are sailing across the Sea of Time. The mermaids have conjured them to come to their aid because the Time Pirates have captured one of their number. The trio must find a way in and out of time to rescue her.

Vick, Helen Hughes

The Walker of Time Trilogy. Tucson, AZ: Harbinger House. *M*

Walker, a fifteen-year-old Hopi boy, and Tag, the twelve-year-old son of an archeologist, journey back eight hundred years and find themselves in the midst of a Sinagua Indian settlement.

***Walker of Time*. 1993. 205p. ISBN: 0943173809pa.**
When Walker makes his way to the sacred cave in Walnut Canyon, Arizona, because his dying uncle requests it, he meets Tag, the son of an archeologist, who shelters in the cave to escape the rain. A burst of blue lightning throws them back to a village of ancient Sinagua Indians in desperate need of a leader. (BBYA)

***Walker's Journey Home*. 1995. 182p. ISBN: 157140001Xpa.**
The Sinagua's water supply has been poisoned, and Walker needs all of his skill to lead the cliff-dwelling people out into the mesas, where they are destined to become the ancestors to the Hopi people.

***Tag against Time*. 1996. 189p. ISBN: 1571400079pa.**
Tag endeavors to "walk time" to return to his own time frame and his mother and father. Each time he enacts the prayer stick ritual, it brings him forward in time, but he cannot continue his journey until he fulfills his reason for being in that time.

Williams, Maiya

***The Golden Hour*. New York: Amulet Books, 2004. 259p. ISBN: 0810948230; 0810992167pa. _M_ AUD**
After their mother is killed in a car accident, their father sends siblings Rowan and Nina from their home in New York City to Owatannauk, Maine, to spend the summer with their two great-aunts. The pair quickly become friends with visiting twins Xavier and Xanthe. At the outskirts of the tiny town, they come upon an eerie abandoned hotel that is in reality a rest stop for time-traveling tourists. When Nina runs away, the three friends visit eighteenth-century France to locate her.

***The Hour of the Cobra*. 2006. ISBN: 0810959704. _M_**
The four friends travel back in time to ancient Egypt, but Xanthe forgets the cardinal rule of time travel: Don't change history. When Cleopatra prays for her help, thinking Xanthe is the goddess Isis, Xanthe passes on some advice. Cleopatra follows it. The friends must find a way to restore the course of history or be trapped forever in the new past.

Wood, Beverly, and Chris Wood

***Dogstar*. Custer, WA: Polestar, 1997. 253p. Reissued in 2004. ISBN: 1551926385pa. _MJ_**
Jeff Beacon, distraught by the death of his dog, carries Buddy's ashes with him everywhere, even on the trip to Alaska that his parents take him on to distract him from his sadness. When they arrive in Juneau, Jeff is fascinated by the statue of Patsy Ann, a bull terrier like Buddy, who waited in the harbor in the 1930s and welcomed the sailors home when they returned. Jeff expects his time in Juneau will be boring, but it is anything but when a living Patsy Ann greets him and leads him back to 1932, where Captain Harper needs his help solving a mystery.

Yolen, Jane

🏵 *The Devil's Arithmetic*. **New York: Viking, 1988. 170p. ISBN: 0670810274; 0142401099pa.** *MJS* **AUD VID** 📖
Twelve-year-old Hannah is annoyed at always having to remember the Holocaust. She knows that her grandparents lost all of their family during that time, but she doesn't want to hear about it. Then, one evening during the Passover Seder, Hannah is selected to open the door for Elijah. When she does, she is whisked to 1942 Poland, where everyone believes her to be Chaya. When the Nazis come, she is taken to the death camp with the other villagers, and only her friend Rivka can help her survive. (Sydney Taylor Award)

The Finest in the Realm

King of Shadows by Susan Cooper

The Time-Traveler's Wife by Audrey Niffenegger

The Devil's Arithmetic by Jane Yolen

Chapter 11

Science Fantasy

It can be easy to confuse fantasy with science fiction, especially when books contain elements of both. Orson Scott Card says, in *How to Write Science Fiction and Fantasy*, you can tell which is which by looking at the book covers: Science fiction has rivets; fantasy has trees (Card, 1990). This is not always the case though, for Anne McCaffrey says that her <u>Pern</u> novels are science fiction, even though they feel like fantasy and have dragons on the covers. Authors who like to combine elements of magic with scientific extrapolation place their works in the center of the speculative fiction continuum, fusing the scientific with the fanciful, forming science fantasy.

Abouzeid, Chris

Anatopsis. **New York: Dutton, 2006. 336p. ISBN: 0525475834.** <u>*MJ*</u>
On a future Earth, Princess Anatopsis is a witch like her mother, Queen Solomon, however she would greatly prefer channeling her magical abilities into becoming a knight-errant like her father. But her mother insists she study with the family tutor, Mr. Pound. He takes her on his quest for the Os Divinitas, but as she learns about her power, she also learns that Mr. Pound may not have the world's best interests at heart.

Anderson, Kevin J.

Hopscotch. **New York: Bantam Books, 2002. 354p. ISBN: 0553104748; 0553576402pa. [Adult]** <u>*S*</u>
In the future, no one needs to experience pain or suffering, because when the hard times come, people can just swap bodies. Four friends, finally old enough to be free of the orphanage, waste no time and go straight to the Club Masquerade center for body swappertunities.

Anthony, Piers

The Apprentice Adept Series. [Adult] *S*
Two worlds exist side-by-side and yet connected. One is Proton, a world governed totally by technology, and the other is Phaze, a world where magic imbues every facet of life. The serf Stile can navigate both worlds, but his life is in danger.

Split Infinity. **New York: Ballantine, 1980. 372p. Reissued in 1987. ISBN: 0345354915pa.**

Blue Adept. **New York: Ballantine, 1981. 327p. Reissued in 1991. ISBN: 0345352459pa.**

Juxtaposition. **New York: Ballantine, 1982. 358p. Reissued in 1991. ISBN: 0345349342pa.**

Out of Phaze. **New York: Putnam, 1987. 288p. Reissued by Ace in 1994. ISBN: 0441644651pa.**

Robot Adept. **New York: Putnam, 1988. 286p. Reissued by Ace in 1989. ISBN: 044173118Xpa.**

Unicorn Point. **New York: Putnam, 1989. 303p. Reissued by Ace in 1990. ISBN: 0441845630pa.**

Phaze Doubt. **New York: Putnam, 1990. 303p. Reissued by Ace in 2005. ISBN: 0441662633pa.**

Baird, Alison

The Dragon Throne Series. [Adult] *S*
On the planet Mera, the tyrant Khalazar crushes the native peoples. They look for the prophesied one who can wield the Stone of Stars to free them.

The Stone of the Stars. **New York: Aspect, 2004. 418p. Reissued by Warner in 2005. ISBN: 0446613029pa.**

The Empire of the Stars. **New York: Warner, 2004. 406p. ISBN: 0446690961pa.**

Archons of the Stars. **New York: Aspect, 2005. 327p. ISBN: 044669097Xpa.**

Barron, T. A.

Heartlight. **New York: Philomel, 1990. 272p. Reissued by Ace in 2003. ISBN: 0441010369pa.** *MJ*
When Kate and her parents move to a new house and Kate starts at a new school, she has trouble adjusting. Her closest friend is her grandfather, who lives nearby. She visits him every day after school. But he is busy working on a top-secret project creating Pure Concentrated Light, a magical illumination that can free heartlights and enable people to traverse the vast distances of space. When he discovers the sun is dying, he needs Kate's help to find a replacement star.

Ancient One*. New York: Philomel, 1992. 367p. ISBN: 0399218998; 0441010326pa. *MJ

Kate visits her Aunt Melanie in Oregon and joins the fight to save the old-growth redwoods in the lost crater. Thrust five centuries back in time, she embarks on a search for the crystal amulet that will help her protect the ancient Halami tribe and the redwoods in her own time.

The Merlin Effect*. New York: Philomel, 1994. 254p. ISBN: 0399226893; 0441012221pa. *MJ

Kate accompanies her historian father on an expedition to locate a sunken Spanish galleon. Her father believes the Horn of Merlin was lost to the watery depths when the ship went down and may still be there. They find the ship at the bottom of a whirlpool and get swept up into the centuries-old conflict between Merlin and Nimue.

Card, Orson Scott

Songmaster*. New York: Dial, 1980. 338p. Reissued by Orb in 2002. ISBN: 0312876629pa. [Adult] *JS

Ansset grew up in the Songhouse, surrounded by music, and when he sings, he has a voice like no other. Power flows through the music he makes, for he can perceive the emotions of his listeners and use those feelings to heal or to destroy. When the Emperor summons him to Old Earth, the fate of humanity rests in Ansset's song.

Engdahl, Sylvia Louise

🏵 ***Enchantress from the Stars*. New York: Atheneum, 1970. 275p. Reissued by Walker in hardcover in 2001. ISBN: 0802787649; 0142500372pa. *MJ***

Elana's father works for the Federation Anthropological Service, studying civilizations that are not yet aware of interplanetary travel. He is always careful never to reveal himself to local populations, until his daughter stows aboard his ship when they are bound for the medieval world of Andrecia. Once there, they discover the indigenous people—who believe in magic, dragons, and sorcerers—are in danger from invaders from another planet. They must find a way to help without revealing who they are to either civilization. (Newbery Honor)

The Far Side of Evil*. New York: Atheneum, 1971. 292p. Reissued by Walker in hardcover in 2003. ISBN: 0802788483; 0142402931pa. *MJ

After Elana graduates from the Federation Anthropological Service's training program, her first assignment is to observe the people of Toris. They are on the cusp of nuclear annihilation, and Elana's fellow agent, Randil, has fallen in love with a Torisian. He's desperate to intervene, although it is against the rules, and Elana must chose between joining him or doing everything in her power to stop him.

Foon, Denis

The Longlight Legacy. Toronto, New York: Annick Press. _M_
In this post-apocalyptic dystopian future, violent forces threaten to destroy society. It is up to siblings Roan and Stowe, who have undiscovered powers, to salvage what they can.

The Dirt Eaters. 2003. 313p. ISBN: 1550378074; 1550378066pa.
Several years after the Abominations spread toxins that transformed the desert into the Devastation, one city of peace remains, Longlight. Roan lives there with his father and sister, so secluded from the world that they thrive until the raiders find them and destroy the enclave. Roan survives, but the desire for revenge burns in him, contradicting his father's pacifist teaching. Finding sanctuary with the Brothers, Roan is on the brink of joining them when he learns that all is not as it appears and that the sister he thought he lost needs his help.

Freewalker. 2004. 387p. ISBN: 1550378856; 1550378848pa.
The Keeper of the City has captured Roan's sister Stowe and seeks to use her special talents to enter the Dreamfield and solidify his control of society. Meanwhile, Roan attempts to locate the forces he will need to thwart the Keeper.

Hopkinson, Nalo

🦋 **_Brown Girl in the Ring_. New York: Warner, 1998. 250p. ISBN: 0446674338pa. _JS_**
In the future, the city of Toronto slides into economic ruin and is abandoned by the wealthy and the police. The poor struggle on as gangs take over. Ti-Jeanne finds she must embrace the spirit magic passed down through her Jamaican heritage if she is to save herself and her infant son. (Locus Award for Best First Novel)

Jones, Diana Wynne

Hexwood. New York: Greenwillow, 1994. 295p. (1st American Edition.) Reissued by HarperTrophy in 2002. ISBN: 0064473554pa. _MJ_
Twelve-year-old Ann Stavely believes that she is just the greengrocer's daughter in a quiet English village, until she witnesses a variety of strangers entering Hexwood Farm. When she investigates and finds a castle in woods, as well as such characters as Arthur and Merlin, she discovers that she is the catalyst to a struggle with the Reigners, who have ruled the galaxy for one thousand years.

L'Engle, Madeleine

The Time Quartet. New York: Farrar, Straus & Giroux. _MJS_ AUD BRAILLE
The siblings in the Murry family—Meg, her little brother Charles Wallace, and twins Sandy and Dennys—embark on adventures through time and space to keep evil at bay.

🦋 **_A Wrinkle in Time_. 1962. 203p. Reissued in 1976. ISBN: 0374386137; 0440998050pa. LP VID 📖**
Meg Murry, a misfit in school, Charles Wallace, her younger brother, and their new friend Calvin are whisked away by the beings that were once stars, Mrs. Whatsit, Mrs. Who, and Mrs. Which, on a perilous journey through space and time to other worlds on a mission to rescue Mr. Murry. (Newbery Medal)

A Wind in the Door. **1973. 211p. ISBN: 0374384436; 044098761Xpa.**
When Charles Wallace becomes ill, Meg and Calvin need the dragons in the vegetable garden to battle against evil to help Charles Wallace recover.

🏵 *A Swiftly Tilting Planet*. **1978. 278p. ISBN: 0374373620; 0440901588pa.**
Charles Wallace, now fifteen, has twenty-four hours to save the universe from destruction. He must go back in time to change a might-have-been and avert disaster. (National Book Award)

Many Waters. **1986. 310p. ISBN: 0374347964; 0440227704pa.**
Meg and Charles Wallace's twin brothers, Sandy and Dennys, wish to be someplace warm and sunny just when their parents are working on a time travel experiment. They end up with Noah and his family and have no idea how they will get back home.

Lyon, Steve

The Gift Moves. **Boston: Houghton Mifflin, 2004. 230p. ISBN: 0618391282; 0553494945pa.** *MJ*
In a future United States where people have moved beyond desire for material acquisition, batteries grow on trees and cats talk. Path leaves her sheep-herding family to work with Heron, a famous weaver in the town of Banks, where she befriends, Bird, a thirteen-year-old baker. As the two become close, Path shares her dark secret with Bird.

McCaffrey, Anne

The Chronicles of Pern. AUD
On the planet of Pern, "thread" that destroys any life-form it touches, periodically falls from the sky. To fight the thread, a select group of people is trained to bond with and fly dragons to burn the thread from the sky. The Wyers of dragonriders, the Halls of craftspeople, and the lords who oversea the working of the land all must work together to keep Pern safe. (All the Pern books except the Harper Hall Trilogy were written for adults. The Harper Hall Trilogy was written for young adults.)

The Dragonriders of Pern. New York: Ballantine. [Adult] *JS* BRAILLE

Dragonflight. **1969. 309p. Reissued in 2005. ISBN: 0345484266pa.**

Dragonquest. **330p. Reissued in 1990. ISBN: 0345335082pa.**

The White Dragon. **1978. 497p. Reissued in 1990. ISBN: 0345341678pa.**

The Harper Hall Trilogy. New York: Atheneum. *MJS* BRAILLE

Dragonsong. **1976. 202p. Reissued by Aladdin in 2003. ISBN: 0689860080pa.**

Menolly loves to sing, but more than that, she loves to create music. Her strict father, however, refuses to allow her to do what she loves best, and Menolly runs away from the Hold. Escaping the dangerous thread, she discovers a cache of firelizard eggs just as they are hatching, which changes her life forever.

***Dragonsinger*. 1977. 264p. Reissued by Aladdin in 2003. ISBN: 0689860072pa.**
Menolly thinks that all her dreams have come true when Masterharper Robinton brings her to Harper Hall so that she can learn all the skills she needs to be a Harper of Pern. Quickly she finds that life with the other apprentices is a tangled web of alliances, and skill with music alone will not help her negotiate the new obstacles in her path.

***Dragondrums*. 1979. 240p. Reissued by Aladdin in 2003. ISBN: 0689860064pa.**
When Menolly's friend Piemur's voice begins to change so that he can no longer sing soprano, Masterharper Robinton recruits him to serve the Harper Hall as a spy.

Individual Pern Novels. New York, Ballantine. [Adult] _JS_

Moreta: Dragonlady of Pern. 1983. 286p. Reissued in 1991. ISBN: 034529873Xpa.

Nerilka's Story. 1986. 182p. Reissued in 1995. ISBN: 0345339495pa.

Dragonsdawn. 1988. 431p. Reissued in 1995. ISBN: 0345339495pa.

The Renegades of Pern. 1989. 384p. Reissued in 1990. ISBN: 0345369335pa.

The Chronicles of Pern: First Fall. 1993. 306p. Reissued in 1994. ISBN: 0345368991pa.

The Dolphins of Pern. 1994. 340p. Reissued in 1995. ISBN: 0345368959pa.

Dragonseye. 1997. 353p. Reissued in 1998. ISBN: 0345418794pa.

The Masterharper of Pern. 1998. 431p. Reissued in 1999. ISBN: 0345424603pa.

The Skies of Pern. 2001. 434p. Reissued in 2002. ISBN: 0345434692pa.

Dragon's Kin (with Todd McCaffrey). 2003. 292p. Reissued in 2004. ISBN: 0345462009pa.

Dragonsblood (by Todd McCaffrey). 2005. 438p. ISBN: 0345441249; 0345441257pa.

Dragon's Fire (with Todd McCaffrey). 2006, 366p. ISBN: 0345480287.

McCaffrey, Todd. *See* McCaffrey, Ann

Mosley, Walter

47. New York: Little, Brown, 2005. 232p. ISBN: 0316110353. _MJ_ AUD 📖

In 1832, a fourteen-year-old slave whose name and number is "47" meets Tall John. Tall John appears to be a runaway slave, but he reveals to 47 that he sailed to Earth from the planet Elle on a Sun Ship to find 47, who will help him in is his fight against the evil Calash. Tall John carries a bag full of magical remedies and technological devices, which he gradually shares with 47 as he teaches him to value himself and his fellow slaves and shows him how to fight for freedom.

Van Lustbader, Eric

The Pearl Saga. New York: Tor. [Adult] _S_
The Kundalans rely on their tradition of sorcery and their goddess Miina to save them from technologically advanced invaders, but to no avail, for the V'ornns have oppressed them for a century. Now the Gyrgon seek the lost Ring of Five Dragons, and more than ever the Kundalans need their prophesied hero to arise.

> *The Ring of Five Dragons*. **2001. 576p. Reissued in 2002. ISBN: 0812572335pa.**

> *The Veil of a Thousand Tears*. **2002. 672p. Reissued in 2003. ISBN: 0812572343pa.**

> *Mistress of the Pearl*. **2004. 588p. ISBN: 0312872372; 0812572351pa.**

Vande Velde, Vivian

🎗 *Heir Apparent*. **San Diego: Harcourt, 2002. 315p. ISBN: 0152045600lb; 0152051252pa. _MJ_ BRAILLE**
For her fourteenth birthday, Giannine receives a gift certificate from her father for the Rasmussem Gaming Center Virtual Reality Arcade. Although protesters who think fantasy games are harmful to children are picketing, Giannine enters the arcade and selects the total-immersion game Heir Apparent. The object of the game is to be crowned king with the help or hindrance of ghosts, witches, wizards, and magical implements. The game turns deadly when the protesters damage the equipment. Giannine must get out before she suffers permanent brain damage, but the only way to do it is to win the game. (BBYA)

Vinge, Joan D.

The Snow Queen Cycle. [Adult] _S_
On the world of Tiamat, the galactic Hegemony has allowed the Winter colonists to rule for 150 years. Soon they will close the gate, and the Summer primitives will rule in peace. The Snow Queen broods upon a dark plan to foil the transfer of power, and only the mystical Moon Summer can halt her.

🎗 *The Snow Queen*. **New York: Dial, 1980. 536p. Reissued by Aspect in 2001. ISBN: 0446676640pa. (Hugo Award; Locus Award)**

The Summer Queen. New York: Warner, 1991. 670p. Reissued in 2003 by Tor. ISBN: 0765304465pa.

Yolen, Jane

The Pit Dragon Trilogy. New York: Delacorte. Reissued by Harcourt in 2004. *MJ* **BRAILLE**

Jakkin lives as a slave on the Austar IV, originally settled as a convict planet, where the only way to freedom is with a dragon.

Dragon's Blood. 1982. 243p. Reissue ISBN: 0152051260pa.

Austar IV, once a convict planet, has become a popular place for intergalactic rest and relaxation. Travelers love to watch the native dragons fighting in the pits. Jakkin serves as a bond-boy and is determined to steal a dragon and win his freedom when the dragon wins its fights in the pits.

Heart's Blood. 1984. 238p. Reissue ISBN: 015205118Xpa.

Jakkin, now seventeen, has won his freedom and his master status through the skill of his beloved dragon, Heart's Blood, who is pregnant. All would be perfect, except that his beloved, Akki, is caught in the middle of revolutionary plots, and Jakkin must risk all to rescue her.

A Sending of Dragon's. 1987. 189p. Reissue ISBN: 0152051287pa.

Jakkin and Akki are hiding in the mountains with Heart's Blood's hatchlings, able to survive because Heart's Blood gave them the ability to communicate telepathically with the dragons and to withstand the brutal elements of the planet's environment. But the gifts are pushing them apart, and the cave dwellers who capture them may defeat them when no one else could.

The Finest in the Realm

Songmaster by Orson Scot Card

Enchantress from the Stars by Sylvia Louis Engdahl

The Time Quartet by Madeleine L'Engle

The Chronicles of Pern by Anne McCaffrey

Chapter 12

Science Fiction

Where fantasy weaves a web of magic as it spins stories in response to the speculative "What if," science fiction embraces the realistic realm of science and then projects possibilities. All science fiction has at least one type of science as a base, whether it's an anthropological or sociological extrapolation about what future societies might be like or technological projections about space ships, time machines, or alien invasions.

In the realm of speculative fiction, works fall in a continuum, with fantasy at one end and science fiction at the other. Although a large amount of science fiction is published for adults, less is published for young adults. This is perhaps because, as science fiction expert David G. Hartwell says in his book *Age of Wonders*, the golden age of science fiction is twelve (Hartwell, 1996). This is when many readers first discover the wonders of science fiction, and often they discover it by reading works written for adults. Frequently, then, they may miss science fiction written for young adults because they are immersed in adult-marketed science fiction. Also, perhaps, publishers don't believe the young adult science fiction market is as strong as the fantasy market. Therefore, this chapter includes more adult titles than previous chapters.

Adventure

While most science fiction contains an element of adventure, the titles included here emphasize adventure. The plots roar to life with fast-paced, action-packed storylines. Many of these works could also be called space opera or military adventure.

Adams, Douglas

The Hitchhiker's Guide to the Galaxy Series. New York: Harmony Books. [Adult] *JS* AUD BRAILLE
When Arthur Dent is transported to a space ship seconds before the destruction of the Earth, he needs all the help he can get from his *Hitchhiker's Guide.*

> *The Hitchhiker's Guide to the Galaxy*. 1980. (1st American Edition.) 215p. Reissued in hardcover in 2004. ISBN: 1400052939; 0345391802pa. VID
>
> *The Restaurant at the End of the Universe*. 1981. 250p. Reissued by Ballantine in 1995. ISBN: 0345391810pa.
>
> *Life, the Universe and Everything*. 227p. Reissued by Ballantine in 1995. ISBN: 0345391829pa.
>
> *So Long, and Thanks for All the Fish*. 1985. 204p. Reissued by Ballantine in 1995. ISBN: 0345391837pa.
>
> *Mostly Harmless*. 1992. 277p. Reissued by Ballantine in 2000. ISBN: 0345418778pa. LP
>
> *Salmon of Doubt: Hitchhiking the Galaxy One Last Time*. 2002. 299p. ISBN: 1400045088; 0345455290pa.

Anderson, Kevin J.

The Saga of the Seven Suns. New York: Warner. [Adult] <u>S</u> AUD
By the twenty-fifth century, human begins have begun to explore space and colonize other worlds. Their interactions with aliens are peaceful until a husband-and-wife team of archeologists accidentally activates a hidden empire, and the newly awakened Hydrogues declare war on Earth.

> *Hidden Empire*. 2002. 453p. Reissued by Aspect in 2003. ISBN: 0446610577pa.
>
> *A Forest of Stars*. 2003. 478p. Reissued by Aspect in 2004. ISBN: 0446610585pa.
>
> *Horizon Storms*. 2004. 469p. ISBN: 0446528722; 0446610593pa.
>
> *Scattered Suns*. 2005. 476p. ISBN: 0446577170; 0446615242pa.
>
> *Of Fire and Night*. 2006. ISBN: 0446577189.

Bell, Hilari

🦂 *A Matter of Profit*. New York: HarperCollins, 2001. 281p. ISBN: 0060295147lb; 0064473007pa. <u>MJ</u>
The Vivitare boys grow up to be warriors, while the girls are forbidden to fight. Eighteen-year-old Ahvren has already had enough battles, while his foster sister, Sabri, would much rather go to war than marry the Emperor's unappealing son. To save Sabri and free himself, Ahvren decides to root out those who are plotting against the Emperor and thus win the ruler's appreciation. (BBYA)

Bujold, Lois McMaster

The Vorkosigan Saga. Riverdale, NY: Baen. [Adult] <u>S</u>
War batters the world of Barrayar, and Cordelia Naismith and Lord Aral Vorkosigan are on opposite sides. When Cordelia is forced to agree to peace and become Lady

Vorkosigan, she begins a chain of events that will lead to the multiple exploits of Miles Vorkosigan.

> *Falling Free*. 1988. 307p. Reissued in 1999. ISBN: 067157812Xpa. BRAILLE

> *Cordelia's Honor*. 1996. 480p. (Originally published as *Shards of Honor* and *Barrayar*.) Reissued in 1999. ISBN: 0671578286pa.

> *Young Miles*. 1997. 584p. (Originally published as *The Warrior's Apprentice* and *The Vor Game*.) Reissued in 2003. ISBN: 0743436164pa.

> *Cetaganda*. 1996. 302p. ISBN: 0671877445pa. BRAILLE

> *Ethan of Athos*. 1989. 199p. Reissued in 2003. ISBN: 1886778396; 067165604Xpa.

> *Memory*. 1996. 462p. ISBN: 0671877437; 067187845Xpa. BRAILLE

> *Komar*. 1998. 311p. ISBN: 0671878778; 0671578081pa. BRAILLE

> *A Civil Campaign: A Comedy of Biology and Manners*. 1999. 405p. ISBN: 0671578278; 0671578855pa.

> *Diplomatic Immunity*. 2002. 311p. ISBN: 0743435338; 0743436121pa.

> *Miles Errant*. 2002. 745p. (Originally published as *Borders of Infinity*, *Brothers in Arms*, and *Mirror Dance*.) ISBN: 0743435583pa.

> *Miles, Mystery and Mayhem*. 2001. 505p. (Formerly published in parts in *Cetaganda*, *Ethan of Athos*, and "Labyrinth.") Reissued in 2003. ISBN: 0743436180pa.

Child, Lincoln

> *Utopia*. New York: Doubleday, 2002. 385p. Reissued by Ballantine in 2003. ISBN: 0345455207pa. [Adult] _S_ AUD

Sixty-five thousand people a day visit the high-tech amusement park Utopia, where ages from the past come to life. Camelot, Broadway, Victorian England, and Callisto (a vision of life in space) all provide vivid holographic experiences for guests, until things start going wrong. Computer whiz Andrew Warne returns with his teenage daughter Georgia to try to figure out what's happening and stop it before anyone gets killed.

Friedman, C. S.

> *This Alien Shore*. New York: Daw, 1998. 565p. Reissued in 1999. ISBN: 0886777992pa. [Adult] _S_

When humans first discovered FTL (faster-than-light space travel), they sent colonists into space but were appalled to find that the travel caused horrible mutations. Now, only members of the Outspace Guild can safely transport humans through space—but someone has infected their computers with a virus that may cripple their entire network. Meanwhile, teenager Jamisia must flee for her life from raiders because unbeknownst to her, she may hold the key to defeating the virus.

Heinlein, Robert A.

***Have Space Suit, Will Travel*. New York: Scribner, 1958. 276p. Reissued in 2005 by Pocket. ISBN: 1416505490pa. *MJ* AUD BRAILLE**
Kip Russell has always longed to travel to the moon. When he wins a space suit instead of a trip, he never dreams that wearing it will lead to a voyage beyond the moon and encounters with species he never imagined.

🟊 ***Starship Troopers*. New York: Putnam, 1959. 309p. Reissued by Ace in 1987. ISBN: 0441783589pa. [Adult] *S* AUD VID**
After high school, Juan Rico knows that he must serve in the military if he wants his citizenship, so he joins the Terran Mobile Infantry. While boot camp is tough, it's nothing compared to fighting the worst enemy humanity has faced yet: the "bugs." (Hugo Award)

Herbert, Frank

The Chronicles of Dune. [Adult] *S*
Revolving around the lives of the people dwelling on the desert planet of Arakis, this sweeping epic focuses on the life of Paul Atreides, who becomes the Messiah of his people, and on the future happenings on his world.

🟊 ***Dune*. Philadelphia: Chilton Books, 1965. 412p. Reissued by Ace in hardcover in 1999. ISBN: 044100590X; 0441172717pa. (Hugo Award; Nebula Award.) VID**

***Dune Messiah*. New York: Putnam, 1969. 256p. Reissued by Ace in 1994. ISBN: 0441172695pa.**

***Children of Dune*. New York: Berkley, 1976. 444p. Reissued by Ace in 1991. ISBN: 0441104029pa.**

***God Emperor of Dune*. New York: Putnam, 1981. 411p. Reissued by Ace in 1991. ISBN: 0441294677pa.**

***Heretics of Dune*. New York: Putnam, 1984. 480p. Reissued in 1996. ISBN: 0441328008pa.**

***Chapterhouse: Dune*. New York: Putnam, 1985. 464p. Reissued in 1996. ISBN: 0441102670pa.**

Herbert, Brian

Prelude to Dune and The Legends of Dune (with Kevin J. Anderson). [Adult] *S* AUD
Frank Herbert's son continues setting novels on the planet Arakis as he tells the tales of what transpired before *Dune* began.

Prelude to Dune. New York: Bantam Books.

> *Dune: House Atreides*. 1999. 644p. Reissued by in 2000. ISBN: 0553580272pa.

> *Dune: House Harkonnen*. 2000. 603p. Reissued in 2001. ISBN: 0553580302pa.

> *Dune: House Corrino*. 2001. 496p. Reissued in 2002. ISBN: 0553580337pa.

Legends of Dune. New York: Tor.

> *Dune: The Butlerian Jihad*. 2002. 621p. ISBN: 0765301571; 0765340771pa.

> *Dune: The Machine Crusade*. 2003. 701p. ISBN: 076530158X; 076534078Xpa.

> *Dune: The Battle of Corrin*. 2004. 620p. ISBN: 0765301598; 0765340798pa.

McGann, Oisin

The Gods and Their Machines. New York: Tor Books, 2004. ISBN: 0765311593.

Chamus Aranson, an Altiman fighter-pilot-in-training, has to make an emergency landing in enemy territory and relies on the Bartokhrin girl named Riadni, who dreams of being a freedom fighter although her society will not allow women to fight, to help him survive. The Bartokhrin think of the Altimans as godless conquerors while the Altimans see the enemy as superstitious terrorists. Together, Chamus and Riadni, may be the salvation of their respective peoples.

Pratchett, Terry

The Johnny Maxwell Trilogy. New York: HarperCollins. *MJ*
Johnny Maxwell had no idea he had any special abilities, until he receives a message from the aliens in his video game, when he discovers he can save the world in more ways than one.

> *Only You Can Save Mankind*. 2005. 207p. (1st American Edition.) ISBN: 0060541857; 0060541873pa. AUD

> Johnny Maxwell loves playing video games. It helps him block out his parents' fights and all the news about the war on TV. When the alien fleet in the game Only You Can Save Mankind sends him a message of surrender, Johnny begins to suspect that the aliens dying in the game are real, and he must find a way to stop the killing.

> *Johnny and the Dead*. 2006. 213p. ISBN: 0060541873.

> After saving the aliens in Only You Can Save Mankind, Johnny moves on to saving the dead. He can see and hear these "post-senior citizens," and they are upset by the imminent relocation of their cemetery to make

way for corporate expansion. At first Johnny leads the fight, but soon, the dead take over.

Robinson, Kim Stanley

The Martian Romance Trilogy. New York: Bantam. [Adult] _S_ AUD
In 2026, one hundred colonists set out to make new homes on the planet Mars.

- ✿ *Red Mars*. 1993. 519p. Reissued in 1993. ISBN: 0553560735pa. (Nebula Award)

- ✿ *Green Mars*. 1994. 535p. Reissued in 1995. ISBN: 0553572393pa. (Hugo Award)

- ✿ *Blue Mars*. 1996. 609p. Reissued in 1997. ISBN: 0553573357pa. (Hugo Award)

Simmons, Dan

The Hyperion Cantos. [Adult] _S_
In the twenty-ninth century, the Human Hegemony is besieged by the threat of war on all sides. Seven pilgrims journey to Hyperion, where they will find the Time Tombs and the Shrike who is part god and part killing machine. They hope to find answers there, but they don't know that one of them holds the destiny of all humanity in his hands.

- ✿ *Hyperion*. New York: Doubleday, 1989. 481p. Reissued by Spectra in 1990. ISBN: 0553283685pa. (Hugo Award)

- ✿ *The Fall of Hyperion*. New York: Doubleday, 1990. 517p. Reissued by Bantam in 1995. ISBN: 0553288202pa. (Locus Award)

- *Endymion*. New York: Bantam, 1996. 468p. Reissued by Spectra in 1996. ISBN: 0553572946pa.

- *The Rise of Endymion*. New York: Bantam, 1997. 579p. Reissued in 1998. ISBN: 0553572989pa.

Stross, Charles

Singularity Sky. New York: Ace Books, 2003. 313p. ISBN: 0441010725; 0441011799pa. [Adult] _S_
In the future, the fate of humanity will be determined by two things: the discovery of faster-than-light travel and the formation of the Eschaton. The Eschaton were created as beings of artificial intelligence, but they developed sentience and harbor very definite ideas on the course humanity should take. When the residents of one group of colonized planets called the New Republic come under attack, the Eschaton send a fleet of battleships. But on the planet, no one knows whether the fleet is coming to aid or destroy them.

Iron Sunrise. New York: Ace Books, 2004. 355p. ISBN: 0441011594; 0441012965pa. [Adult] _S_
In this sequel to *Singularity Sky,* the planet New Moscow has been destroyed. Just before being obliterated, the New Moscow fleet launched its own slower-than-light

counterstrike. Now only the New Moscow ambassadors have the code that can stop the attacking ship, but they are being murdered one by one. Only the teenager Wednesday Shadowmist knows who the real enemy is, but she does not know that she knows.

Weber, David

<u>**The Honor Harrington Series**</u>. Riverdale, NY: Baen. [Adult] <u>*S*</u>
Commander Honor Harrington has been sent to Basilisk Station in disgrace, but she is determined to prove her worth.

On Basilisk Station. 1993. 352p. Reissued in hardcover in 1999. ISBN: 067157793X; 1416509372pa.

The Honor of the Queen. 1993. 371p. Reissued in 2002. ISBN: 0743435729pa.

The Short Victorious War. 1994. 343p. Reissued in hardcover in 2002. ISBN: 0743435516; 0743435737pa.

Field of Dishonor. 1994. 311p. Reissued in 2002. ISBN: 0743435745pa.

Flag in Exile. 1995. 405p. Reissued in hardcover in 2001. ISBN: 0671319809; 0743435753pa.

Honor among Enemies. 1996. 538p. ISBN: 0671877232; 0671877836pa.

In Enemy Hands. 1997. 530p. ISBN: 0671877933; 0671577700pa.

Echoes of Honor. 1998. 569p. ISBN: 0671878921; 0671578332pa.

Ashes of Victory. 2000. 560p. ISBN: 0671578545; 0671319779pa.

War of Honor. 2002. 869p. ISBN: 0743435451; 0743471679pa. AUD

More than Honor (with David Drake and S. M. Stirling). 1998. 384p. ISBN: 0671878573pa.

Worlds of Honor (edited by David Weber). 1999. 343p. ISBN: 0671577867; 0671578553pa.

Changer of Worlds (with Eric Flint). 2001. 374p. ISBN: 0671319752; 0743435206pa.

The Service of the Sword (edited by David Weber). 2003. 490p. ISBN: 0743435990; 0743488369pa.

Crown of Slaves (with Eric Flint). 2003. 505p. Reissued in 2005. ISBN: 0743498992pa.

The Shadow of Saganami. 2004. 640p. ISBN: 0743488520; 1416509291pa.

At All Costs. 2005. 855p. ISBN: 1416509119.

Zahn, Timothy

The Dragonback Adventures. New York: Tor. [Adult] _JS_
When fourteen-year-old orphan Jack Morgan bonds with a symbiotic, golden-scaled, draconic K'da, Draycos, they travel from planet to planet attempting to uncover the species responsible for trying to annihilate the K'da.

🏵 *Dragon and Thief.* 2003. 254p. ISBN: 0765301245; 0765342723pa. (BBYA)

Dragon and Soldier. 2004. 299p. ISBN: 0765301253; 0765350173pa.

Dragon and Slave. 2005. 300p. ISBN: 0765301261; 0765340410pa.

Dragon and Herdsman. 2006. 304p. ISBN: 0765314177.

Time Travel

Where fantasy time travel stories rely on magic or the mystical to explain the time travel element, such as the enchanted pendant in Judith O'Brien's *Timeless Love,* or leave it completely unexplained, as in Jane Yolen's *The Devil's Arithmetic,* in science fiction the time travel is made possible through some kind of scientific extrapolation, a machine, an experiment, and so on.

Baker, Kage

The Company Series. [Adult] _S_
In the twenty-fourth century, the Company, founded by Dr. Zeus, has two very profitable technologies: time travel and immortality. Agents of the Company use time travel to go back to designated periods of history to stow away significant items, artwork, rare plants, and other objects, to be revealed in the future in the hands of the Company, who can than sell the valuable item. They can't change history, but they can make a tidy profit. The only problem is that citizens of the twenty-fourth century don't like going back in time. That's where the second technology becomes useful. They can make virtually any child immortal. So they visit various historical periods rescuing waifs and then transforming them into immortal beings—immortals who have no choice but to serve the Company, forever.

In the Garden of Iden. New York: Harcourt, 1997. 329p. Reissued by Tor in 2005. ISBN: 0765314576pa.

Sky Coyote. New York: Harcourt, 1999. 310p. (Out of Print)

Mendoza in Hollywood. New York: Harcourt, 2000. 334p. Reissued by Tor in 2006. ISBN: 0765315300pa.

Graveyard Game. New York: Harcourt, 2001. 298p. Reissued by Tor in 2005. ISBN: 0765311844pa.

Black Projects, White Knights: The Company Dossiers. Urbana, IL: Golden Gryphon Press, 2002. 288p. ISBN: 1930846118; 1930846304pa.

The Life of the World to Come. New York: Tor, 2004. 334p. ISBN: 0765311321; 0765354322pa.

Children of the Company. New York: Tor, 2005. 300p. ISBN: 076531455X; 0765353679pa.

Card, Orson Scott

Pastwatch: The Redemption of Christopher Columbus. New York: Tor, 1996. 351p. Reissued in 1997. ISBN: 0812508645pa. [Adult] *S*

On a future Earth that has been devastated by years of war, famine, and plague, less than one billion people have survived. Among those, a small group of scientists and historians have been specially trained to use the TruSiteII to view the events of history. One of those is Tagiri, who realizes that as she watches Christopher Columbus and his troops slay the Caribe tribes, one of the women can see her. With the hope that she can change the future of her Earth, Tagiri attempts to influence the unfolding events.

Crichton, Michael

Timeline. New York: Knopf, 1999. 449p. ISBN: 0679444815; 0345417623pa. [Adult] *S* AUD LP VID

When the use of quantum technology creates a wormhole to the past, a group of graduate students travel to fourteenth-century France to rescue their stranded professor. There, they get caught up in the Hundred Years' War and must race against time to return home safely.

Dick, Philip K.

Dr. Futurity. New York: Ace, 1960. 169p. Reissued in 2005 by Vintage. ISBN: 1400030099pa. [Adult] *S*

When a car accident throws Dr. Jim Parsons hundreds of years into the future, he winds up in a society where it is against the law to save lives.

Flint, Eric

<u>**The Ring of Fire Series**</u>. Riverdale, NY: Baen. [Adult] *S*

With a crash of thunder and a blinding flare of lightning, a small town in contemporary West Virginia is sent back in time to 1632 Germany, where the Thirty Years' War rages.

1632. 2000. 504p. Reissued in 2001. ISBN: 0671319728pa.

1633 (with David Weber). 2002. 598p. ISBN: 0743435427; 0743471555pa.

Ring of Fire (edited by Eric Flint). 2004. 518p. Reissued in 2005. ISBN: 1416509089pa.

1634: The Galileo Affair. 2004. 549p. ISBN: 0743488156; 0743499190pa.

Goodman, Alison

🕯 *Singing the Dogstar Blues*. **New York: Viking, 2002. (1st American Edition.) 261p. ISBN: 0670036102; 014240246Xpa.** _JS_ 📖
Seventeen-year-old Joss Aaronson studies time travel at the Centre for Neo-Historical Studies. As a freshman whose virtual-reality-star mother bought her admittance, Joss feels like she doesn't fit in until she meets Mav. Mav, an alien from the planet Choria, communicates telepathically and is eager to help Joss use time travel to solve the mystery of her paternity. (BBYA)

Heinlein, Robert A.

The Door into Summer. **Garden City, NY: Doubleday, 1957. 188p. Reissued by Ballantine in 1993. ISBN: 0345330129pa. [Adult]** _JS_ **AUD**
Dan Davis, an electronics engineer, has constructed a robot that will perform myriad household tasks. Unfortunately, it can't save him from his conniving partner and fiancée, who send him unwillingly into suspended animation for thirty years. They have no way of knowing that by the time Dan wakes up, time travel will have been invented.

Levinson, Paul

The Plot to Save Socrates. **New York: Tor, 2006. 272p. ISBN: 0765305704. [Adult]** _S_ **AUD**
In 2042, Sierra Waters, a Classics graduate student, reads a new dialogue of Socrates wherein the philosopher can be saved via time travel. As she investigates the possibilities raised in the dialogue with her boyfriend Max, she unearths a time machine that might indeed enable her to save the ancient Greek, if only he would cooperate.

Lubar, David

Flip. **New York: Tom Doherty Associates, 2003. 300p. ISBN: 0765301490; 0765340488pa.** _MJ_
Eighth-grader Ryan McKenzie discovers fifty-one disks left behind by a Nexulian spaceship. When he flips a disk in just the right way, it melts into his skin and allows him to become a famous person from history for a few hours.

Niffenegger, Audrey

The Time Traveler's Wife. *See* Chapter 10, "Time Travel Fantasy."

Norton, Andre

The Time Traders Series. **[Adult]** _JS_
Enemies of the United States have developed a way to send agents back in time to retrieve technologies that will advance the creation of powerful weapons. To thwart them, the United States has created its own time travel mechanism and dubbed it Operations Retrograde. When Ross Murdoch and Travis Fox accidentally encounter the project, they become America's newest time agents.

The Time Traders (omnibus edition, originally published by World Publishers in 1958 as *The Time Traders* and in 1959 as *Galactic Derelict*). Riverdale, NY: Baen, 2000. ISBN: 0671319523; 0671318292pa.

Time Traders II: The Defiant Agents and Key Out of Time (omnibus edition, originally published by World Publishers in 1962 and in 1963.) Riverdale, NY: Baen, 2001. 370p. ISBN: 067131968X; 0671318527pa.

Firehand (with Pauline M. Griffin). New York: Tor, 1994. 220 p. Reissued in 1995. ISBN 0812519841.

Echoes in Time: A New Time Traders Adventure (with Sherwood Smith). New York: Tor, 1999. ISBN: 031285921X; 0812552741pa.

Atlantis Endgame (with Sherwood Smith). New York: Tor, 2002. Reissued in 2004. ISBN: 0812584155pa.

Price, Susan

The Sterkarm Handshake. New York: HarperCollins, 2000. 438p. (1st American Edition.) Reissued by Eos in 2003. ISBN: 0064472361pa. *JS*
The FUP Corporation plans to use its newly developed time tube to the sixteenth century to exploit the natural resources and people of the time. To further this goal, CEO Bryce Windsor sends anthropologist Andrea Mitchell back in time to live with the Sterkarms, a powerful Scottish clan. As she lives with them and falls in love with the clan leader's son, she feels torn between her new life and her old one. As conflict between the peoples of two time periods escalates, Andrea must decide whose side she's on.

A Sterkarm Kiss. New York: Eos, 2004. 277p. (1st American Edition.) ISBN: 0060721987lb. *S*
Although Andrea has adjusted to life in the twenty-first century, she agrees to return to the sixteenth, despite her misgivings. When she arrives, she realizes that, although she is with the Sterkarms, these are not the same people she knew and loved before. She has entered a dimension that parallels the one she knew. This time Windsor plans a violent overthrow to get what he wants, and it's up to her to stop him.

Roberson, Chris

Here, There, and Everywhere. Amherst, NY: Pyr, 2005. 283p. ISBN: 1591023106; 1591023319pa. [Adult] *S*
A mysterious stranger uses the last of her dying strength to give eleven-year-old Roxanne Bonaventure a silver bracelet that she calls a Sofia. Roxanne discovers that the bracelet is actually a device that will allow her to travel back and forth in time and to other worlds and dimensions of existence. As the years pass, she explores her power and visits various points in known and unknown history, ultimately searching for a cure for her father's fatal illness.

Turtledove, Harry

The Crosstime Traffic Series. New York: Tor. [Adult] *S*
In the twenty-first century, chronophysicists have not only developed a way to travel back and forth in time but also to travel to worlds that followed alternate timelines.

🦴 *Gunpowder Empire*. 2003. 288p. Reissued in 2004. ISBN: 0765346095pa. (Hal Clement Award)

Curious Notions. 2004. 272p. ISBN: 0765306948; 0765346109pa.

In High Places. 2005. 272p. ISBN: 0765306964.

Valentine, James

The Jumpman Rule Series. New York: Simon & Schuster. *MJ*
In the fifty-second century, teens entertain themselves with the TimeMaster JumpMan, which sends them back to any era they desire. Once there, they can observe dinosaurs battling or the pyramids being built, all without disrupting the timeline because they remain invisible to the people and creatures of that time. All that changes when Theodore wins the newest JumpMan but doesn't know there's a glitch in the device.

Jumpman Rule #1: Don't Touch Anything. 2004. 268p. (1st American Edition.) ISBN: 0689868723; 0689868774pa.
Although he's known Gen all of his life, thirteen-year-old Jules needs all his courage to ask her out on a date. Just as he perches on the brink of future romance, Theo materializes between them. He's a time jumper from the fifty-second century, and suddenly Jules has far more to worry about as he tries to help Theo without changing the future.

Jumpman Rule #2: Don't Even Think about It. 2005. 268p. (1st American Edition.) ISBN: 0689873530.
Jules and Gen are getting dizzy from jumping back and forth in time so much with Theo. As they try to return to the time of Franklin, the man who invented the Jumpman, and stop his partner from using the machine for nefarious purposes, Gen gets stuck in Pompeii just as Vesuvius is about to erupt.

Wells, H. G.

The Time Machine. New York: Holt, 1895. (1st American Edition.) Reissued by Wildside Press in hardcover in 2004. 124p ISBN: 0809596431; 0451528557pa. [Adult] *JS* AUD LP VID
When a Victorian scientist invents a time machine, he recklessly sends himself far into the future, only to encounter two distinct species descended from man: the elflike Eloi and the grim Morlocks.

Willis, Connie

🦴 *Doomsday Book*. New York: Bantam Books, 1992. 445p. Reissued by Spectra in 1999. ISBN: 0553562738pa. [Adult] *JS* AUD 📖
In 2048 Oxford, students study history by going back in time. Kivrin, a student of the Middle Ages, aims to go back to 1320, but she winds up in 1349 instead, when the

technician makes a mistake. As she grows close to the family that takes her in, she realizes that she is living in the time of the Black Death and may never make it home again. (Hugo Award; Locus Award; Nebula Award)

🌱 *To Say Nothing of the Dog*. **New York: Bantam Books, 1997. 434p. Reissued in 1999. ISBN: 0553575384pa. [Adult]** *JS* **AUD**
Seven years after *Doomsday Book,* Oxford University's time travel project has virtually been taken over by the wealthy Lady Schrapnell, who is determined to reconstruct the Nazi-destroyed Old Coventry Cathedral. Although operative Ned Henry suffers from advanced time lag, he is sent back to 1888 to retrieve the bishop's bird stump from the cathedral. Along the way, he connects with fellow operative Verity Kindle. Together, they discover that they must repair an incongruity or the Nazis will win WWII. (Alex; Hugo Award; Locus Award)

Aliens among Us

The possibility that we are not the only intelligent life-form weaves its way through many works of science fiction, from discovering we are not alone to coping with alien invasion to learning to get along with aliens.

Card, Orson Scott

The Ender Wiggin Series. **New York: Tor. [Adult]** *JS* **AUD**

Years before Ender or Bean were born, the "buggers" attacked Earth. Only the desperate and heroic actions of Mazer Rackham saved humanity. Now, as the military prepares for the next invasion, its Battle School personnel do their utmost to find and train the next commander before the buggers destroy them all. (Although all of the *Ender* books were written for adults, the four that center around the experiences of Ender and Bean have particular appeal for young adults because the stories begin when each character is a child. These four titles are annotated, whereas the others in the series are simply listed.)

🌱 *Ender's Game*. **1985. 357p. ISBN: 0312932081; 0812550706pa.** 📖
In a world where population growth is strictly controlled, Ender Wiggin's parents received special permission to have a third child, Ender, because the leaders of the International Fleet (I.F.) believed their combination of genes might produce the brilliant military commander needed to defeat a second invasion of alien buggers. At age six, Ender enters Battle School, where the adults in his life will do whatever it takes to make him the commander they need. (Hugo Award; Nebula Award)

🌱 *Ender's Shadow*. **1999. 379p. ISBN: 031286860X; 0765342405pa.**
In this parallel novel to *Ender's Game,* the events in Battle School and beyond are told from Bean's point of view. Bean was under Ender's command, but he grew up on the streets of Rotterdam, fending for himself and struggling to survive. Utilizing his phenomenal intelligence, he changed the lives of children all over the city by co-opting the system and helping the children get the food and care they needed. This brings him to

the attention of Sister Carlotta, who secures him a place at Battle School, where he becomes Ender's shadow. (Alex)

***Shadow of the Hegemon*. 2001. 365p. ISBN: 0312876513; 0812565959pa.**
Ender Wiggin is not allowed to return to Earth, but Bean and the other young soldiers who were part of his team are. They become the target of Bean's old enemy, Achilles, as Bean positions himself to become an adviser to Ender's brother, Peter Wiggin, the next leader of the world.

***Shadow Puppets*. 2002. 348p. ISBN: 0765300176; 0765340054pa.**
Bean and the other Battle School graduates are now in positions of power throughout the world. They think that the dangerous psychopath, Achilles, is safely imprisoned in China. When Peter Wiggin orders him released, Peter sets in motion chaos that may destroy the order he has constructed.

***Shadow of the Giant*. 2005. 367p. ISBN: 0312857586; 0812571398pa.**
Many of the twenty-something Battle School graduates are now running their respective countries, while Bean advises the Hegemon, who is Ender's older brother Peter. Bean and his wife would like to travel to a world where they can live safely, but first Peter needs their help bringing Earth back from the brink of global warfare.

🖋 ***Speaker for the Dead*. 1986. 280p. ISBN: 0312937385; 0812550757pa. (Hugo Award; Locus Award; Nebula Award)**

***Xenocide*. 1991. 394p. Reissued in 1992. ISBN: 0812509250pa.**

***Children of the Mind*. 1996. 349p. Reissued in 1997. ISBN: 0812522397pa.**

***First Meetings: In the Enderverse*. 2003. 208p. ISBN: 0765308738; 0765347989pa.**

Emshwiller, Carol

🖋 ***The Mount*. Brooklyn, NY: Small Beer Press, 2002. 232p. Reissued by Firebird in 2005. ISBN: 0142403024pa. _JS_ 📖**
Charley longs to race well and become a decorated victor, but he is not the one in control; he serves as a mount for a creature called a Hoot. Before Charley was born, the Hoots invaded Earth and subdued humankind. Now they breed humans to carry Hoots. The strongest and best are bred to race. Charley is just such a one until his complex is attacked by Wilds, free humans from the mountains. Charley rescues his Little Master but ends up with the Wilds and his father, their leader. Now he must choose between Little Master and freedom. (Philip K. Dick Award)

Gilmore, Kate

🖋 ***The Exchange Student*. Boston: Houghton Mifflin, 1999. 216p. ISBN: 0395575117; 0618689486pa. _MJ_**
In 2094, students from Earth and Chela participate in an exchange program that sends nine students from each planet to be hosted on the other. Seven-foot tall Fen, who wears gray to hide the fact that his skin tone changes with his emotions, stays with the Wells family, where sixteen-year-old Daria cares for various animals as a licensed

zookeeper. She is part of Earth's effort to restore animals to the world after global warming caused the extinction of many species, but she doesn't know how desperately Fen would like to bring new animal life to his own beleaguered planet. (BBYA)

Jeapes, Ben

The Xenocide Mission. **New York: David Fickling Books, 2002. 387p. (1st American Edition.) ISBN: 0385750072; 0440237858pa. [Adult]** *JS*
In the 2140s, humans have joined an interstellar commonwealth with Rusties. To help keep interplanetary peace, their standard practice is to observe worlds that are not yet members. Joel Gilmore and his team are monitoring a planet at war with its neighbor when its military turns its might on the supposedly hidden space station. Joel and his quadruped colleague, Boon, escape the attack but now must find a way to keep the peace as commonwealth members send teams to investigate.

Klause, Annette Curtis

🔖 *Alien Secrets.* **New York: Delacorte, 1993. 227p. Reissued by Laurel Leaf in 1999. ISBN: 0440228514pa.** *M* **AUD BRAILLE**
Expelled from school, thirteen-year-old Puck is being sent back to the planet where her scientist parents work. As the space freighter hurries through hyperspace, Puck befriends an alien named Hush. Together they attempt to untangle the truth behind a vicious shipboard murder. (ALAN)

Kress, Nancy

The Cosmic Crossfire Series. **New York: Tor. [Adult]** *S*
In the far future, the time is coming when Earth will no longer be able to sustain life. In light of this, a diverse group of wealthy people hire a starship to take them to a new world that they call Greentrees. When they arrive, they encounter two new species, one humanoid and aggressive, the other plant-based and peaceful. The two are locked in conflict and colonists must choose sides—quickly.

Crossfire. **2003. 364p. ISBN: 0765304678; 0765343894pa.**

Crucible. **2004. 384p. ISBN: 0765306883; 0765346036pa.**

Lowachee, Karin

The Warchild Trilogy. **New York: Warner. [Adult]** *S*
In a universe where humanity is at war with the aliens striviirc-na and where space pirates, who do not hesitate to use sex as a tool to manipulate and control, roam the galaxy, three young people, Jos, Ryan, and Yuri, separately struggle to find their own humanity.

Warchild. **2002. 451p. ISBN: 0446610771pa.**

Burndive. **2003. 417p. ISBN: 0446613185pa.**

Cagebird. **2005. 448p. ISBN: 0446615080pa.**

Mackel, Kathy

Alien in a Bottle. **New York: HarperCollins, 2004. 194p. ISBN: 0060292814.** *MJ*
Eighth-grader Sean longs to be a glass artist, even though his father is totally against it.
As he searches for unusual glass to design a sculpture that he hopes will win him a
scholarship to an arts high school, he comes across an unusual glass bottle. Much to his
surprise, the bottle is in fact the spaceship of Tagg Orion, a space trader fleeing an angry customer. In exchange for Sean's help hiding him, Tagg agrees to provide galactic
materials for his sculpture.

Shusterman, Neal

🐦 *The Dark Side of Nowhere*. **Boston: Little, Brown, 1997. 185p. Reissued by
Starscape in 2002. ISBN: 076534243Xpa.** *MJ*
Jason Miller thinks he's just an ordinary teen living a dreadfully dull life in the small
town of Billington, until his best friend Ethan dies of what the doctor dubs a burst appendix. Suspicious, Jason begins to investigate, uncovering secret after secret until he
learns the startling truth about his origins. (BBYA; Hal Clement Award)

Silverberg, Robert

The Alien Years. **New York: HarperPrism, 1998. 428p. Reissued in 1999. ISBN:
006105111Xpa. [Adult]** *S*
In the near future, the Entities invade Earth. When they succeed in stopping all electri-
cal power on the planet, governments and economies collapse and the peoples of the
world are completely in their power, except for the Carmichael family. They gather in
their secluded mountain ranch compound and for generations lead the resistance
against the Entities.

Slade, Arthur G.

🐦 *Dust*. **New York: Wendy Lamb Books, 2003. (1st American Edition.) 183p. ISBN:
0385730047; 0440229766pa.** *M*
During the Great Depression, a stranger, Abram Harsich, comes to a small Saskatche-
wan town, and the children begin to disappear. No one but eleven-year-old Robert remembers the missing children. As the adults go to work to build Harsich's rainmill,
Robert endeavors to learn what's happened to the children, never suspecting Harsich
might be connected with beings from beyond the stars. (BBYA; Canada's Governor's
General Award for Children's Literature)

Sleator, William

Interstellar Pig. **New York: Dutton, 1984. 197p. Reissued by Firebird in 1995.
ISBN: 0140375953pa.** *MJ*
Sixteen-year-old Barney predicts that his two-week vacation at his parents' seaside
summer home will be even more boring than school until he meets the new neighbors,
Zena, Manny, and Joe. They seem too perfect to be truly human. As they lure Barney
into playing their addictive role-playing game, he wonders whether they are indeed ex-
traterrestrials and whetherthe game is only a game.

Parasite Pig. **New York: Dutton, 2002. 212p. ISBN: 0525469184; 0142400866pa. _MJ_**
The summer after *Interstellar Pig,* Barney thinks that it's safe to keep playing the board game Interstellar Pig because the aliens have left Earth. To relieve the tedium of working over the summer, he plays with Katie and Matt. When a new player, Julian, joins them, Barney discovers how wrong he was. Julian, an alien parasite, kidnaps him, while Matt, an alien wasp, kidnaps Katie. The two humans are whisked away to the planet J'koot, where the giant crab residents want to sauté them and serve them for supper.

Turtledove, Harry

Worldwar and Colonization (sequential series). New York: Ballantine. [Adult] _S_
In this alternate history, in the midst of World War II, Earth's most vicious enemy attacks from space as a race of lizard-like aliens with superior strength and technology first attempts to conquer and then to colonize the planet.

The Worldwar Series

Worldwar: In the Balance. **1994. 488p. Reissued in 1995. ISBN: 0345388526pa.**

Worldwar: Tilting the Balance. **1995. 478p. Reissued in 1996. ISBN: 0345389980pa.**

Worldwar: Upsetting the Balance. **1996. 481p. Reissued in 1996. ISBN: 0345402405pa.**

Worldwar: Striking the Balance. **1996. 465p. Reissued in 1997. ISBN: 0345412087pa.**

The Colonization Series

Colonization: Second Contact. **1999. 486p. Reissued in 2000. ISBN: 0345430220pa.**

Colonization: Down to Earth. **2000. 489p. Reissued in 2001. ISBN: 0345430239pa.**

Colonization: Aftershocks. **2001. 488p. Reissued in 2002. ISBN: 0345430247pa.**

Wells, H. G.

The War of the Worlds. **New York: Harper, 1898. 290p. (1st American Edition.) Reissued by Wildside Press in hardcover in 2004. ISBN: 0809596474; 0812505158pa. [Adult] _JS_ AUD LP VID**
At first they looked like falling stars, but beauty quickly turns to terror as those who live in the English countryside investigate the strange containers that fell from the sky. When the Martians emerge, they begin slaughtering people immediately, endangering the survival of the human race.

Zahn, Timothy

Night Train to Rigel. New York: Tor, 2005. 349p. ISBN: 0765307162; 0765346443pa. [Adult] *JS*
Two hundred years in the future, aliens of all kinds traverse the universes by way of the Quadrail transportation system. Frank Compton, unemployed for blowing the whistle on wasted planetary development funds, finds himself with a free Quadrail ticket. Once on board, he is engaged by alien Spiders to stop an interstellar war before it begins.

Experimental Science

Plots featuring experimental science are common to science fiction. Sometimes the settings are contemporary and sometimes futuristic. Sometimes the experiments are successful, but more often than not, something goes horribly wrong.

Clements, Andrew

🏶 *Things Not Seen*. New York: Philomel, 2002. 251p. ISBN: 0399236260; 0142407313pa. *MJ* AUD 📖
Fifteen-year-old Bobby gets up and stumbles into the shower the way he does every morning as he gets ready for school, but when he stumbles out again and looks in the mirror, he's not there. He can feel his body, but he can't see himself. When he informs his scientist parents, they are confident they can find an answer and tell him to stay home, but Bobby covers himself in clothes and heads to the library to try to work out the solution on his own. There, he literally bumps into Alicia, who is blind. He confides in her, and together they set about unraveling the mystery and finding a way to make him visible once more. (BBYA)

Craig, Joe

Jimmy Coates: Assassin? New York: HarperCollins, 2005. 218p (1st American Edition.) ISBN: 0060772638; 0060772654pa. *M*
In a near-future London, Jimmy Coates thinks he's just an ordinary eleven-year-old boy—until government agents come to his house and his mother tells him to run. Then a plethora of hidden powers that make him faster, stronger, and more durable than any other human being, reveal themselves as he needs them. That's because he's not quite human. He's the product of a government experiment to develop the perfect assassin. Jimmy doesn't respond the way the agency would wish. Instead, he defies them and goes on a mission to rescue his parents.

Dickinson, Peter

🏶 *Eva*. New York: Delacorte, 1989. 219p. (1st American Edition.) Reissued by Laurel Leaf in 1990. ISBN: 0440207665pa. *JS* AUD
After a near-fatal car crash, thirteen-year-old Eva slips into a coma. Her body is crushed. There seems to be no way to save her until the scientists decide to attempt a new procedure. They transfer her memory and brain patterns to the mind and body of chimpanzee. When she wakes up, she remembers her human life and her chimp life,

and now she must adjust to life as a captive chimpanzee. (ALAN; Boston Globe Honor)

Haddix, Margaret Peterson

Turnabout. New York: Simon & Schuster, 2000. 223p. ISBN: 0689821875lb; 0689840373pa. *MJS* LP

Melly and Anny Beth are teenagers in 2085 because in 2000 they agreed to participate in the illegal Project Turnabout program. Nursing home patients at the time of the program, they let themselves be injected with a serum that reversed the aging process, but something went wrong. Each day they live, they grow younger, and there is no way to stop. Now, they are teenagers again. While they are determined to live life to the fullest, they also know they must find someone to take care of them as they revert to youth, childhood, and infancy.

Halam, Ann

Dr. Franklin's Island. New York: Wendy Lamb Books, 2002. 245p. Reissued by Laurel-Leaf Books in 2003. ISBN: 0440237815pa. *S* AUD

When a plane carrying fifty British teenagers to Ecuador crashes, only three survive: Semi, Miranda, and Arnie. They make their way to an island and do their best to make it through each day. When Arnie disappears, Miranda and Semi investigate and end up in the laboratory of a mad scientist, Dr. Franklin. He is experimenting with genetics and forces the teens to participate, injecting them with animal DNA and observing the resulting metamorphosis.

Taylor Five. New York: Wendy Lamb Books, 2004. 197p. ISBN: 0385730942; 044023820Xpa. *MJ*

Taylor Walker has known for a long time that she is different from other teens. Her parents told her that she was a test-tube baby, but they didn't tell her until she was fourteen that, in fact, she is one of only five human clones in the world. When the story of the clones makes international news, a group of outraged rebels attacks the Walker's orangutan reserve. Taylor flees with her younger brother, and the only adult left to help them to safety is Uncle—an orangutan.

Jensen, Jane

Dante's Equation. New York: Ballantine, 2003. 484p. Reissued in 2006. ISBN: 0345430387pa. [Adult] *S*

When physicist Jill Talcott develops a revolutionary theory of wave mechanics, she encounters a Talmudic scholar, a tabloid journalist, and a military agent. Their paths converge in Poland, where they are searching for physicist and mystic Rabbi Yosef Kobinski, who vanished from Auschwitz. But none of them knows that their search will lead them to an alternate universe.

Keyes, Daniel

Flowers for Algernon. New York: Harcourt, 1966. 274p. Reissued in hardcover in 1995. ISBN: 0151001634; 0156030306pa. [Adult] *JS* AUD VID
Charlie Gordon, a retarded adult, keeps a journal recording his thoughts as he agrees to undergo radical surgery to aid his intelligence. The surgery seems to be successful, turning Charlie into a genius, but the effects are only temporary.

Le Guin, Ursula K.

🏹 *The Lathe of Heaven*. New York: Scribner, 1971. 184p. Reissued by HarperCollins in 2003. ISBN: 0060512741pa. [Adult] *S* AUD VID
George Orr is convinced that he can alter reality with his dreams, and he takes sleep repressants to try to gain some control. When he's arrested for misusing prescription drugs, he is sent to behavioral psychologist Dr. William Haber. At first, Dr. Haber believes he must help his patient work through his delusions. When he realizes Orr's power is real, he tries to use that power to improve the world. (Locus Award)

Moon, Elizabeth

🏹 *The Speed of Dark*. New York: Ballantine, 2003. 340p. Reissued in 2005. ISBN: 0345481399pa. [Adult] *JS* AUD LP
In the near future, genetic diseases will be removed at birth or during infancy, but for a few, those advances will be too late. Lou Arrendal is one of those people. He received special training as a child and now lives a fulfilling life as a computer programmer with others who, like him, are autistic. When a new drug that is supposed to cure autism is introduced, the CEO of Lou's company pressures Lou and all of his autistic employees to take the drug, but they are as wary of the drug and the CEO as they are of the idea that they need to be "normal." (Nebula Award)

Patterson, James

Maximum Ride: The Angel Experiment. New York: Little, Brown, 2005. 422p. ISBN: 031615556X; 0446617792pa. *JS* AUD LP
A group of genetically altered children and teens who have spent several years in a lab in California have escaped and are on the run from wolf-human mutants called Erasers. The kids, led by fourteen-year-old Maximum Ride, are ninety-eight percent human and two percent bird, which enables them to fly and endows them with certain talents. They must find a way to outwit the Erasers, because the predators have orders to kill them.

Maximum Ride: School's Out—Forever. New York: Little, Brown, 2006. ISBN: 0316155594. *JS* AUD
Max guides her flock of flying kids to Washington, D.C., where, although they are still being pursued by the Erasers, they attempt to find their real parents. The FBI intervenes and sends them to school in the country. But things don't stay quiet for long.

Sleator, William

The Last Universe. New York: Amulet Books, 2005. 215p. ISBN: 0810958589; 0810992132pa. *MJ*

When a mysterious illness leaves Susan's older brother Gary so weak he must use a wheelchair to get around, it's Susan who spends her summer vacation pushing him around the family home and lands. Her resentment recedes as the garden changes in marked ways each day and her brother theorizes that a quantum event is the catalyst for the changes. As their lives become more bizarre, Susan must find a way to save her brother and herself.

House of Stairs. **New York: Dutton, 1974. 166p. Reissued by Firebird in 2004. ISBN: 0140345809pa. _JS_ AUD**
Five sixteen-year-olds with no one to turn to because they are orphans become the subjects of a psychological experiment when they are placed in a house with nothing but flights of stairs and a room with the red machine.

The Duplicate. **New York: Dutton, 1988. 154p. Reissued by Puffin in 1999. ISBN: 0141304316pa. _JS_**
David's in a bind. He definitely wants to go on his date with Angela, but at the same time he is supposed to be at a party for his grandmother. When he finds an unusual machine that replicates living beings, he thinks he has the answer to all of his problems.

The Boy Who Reversed Himself. **New York: Dutton, 1986. 167p. Reissued by Puffin in 1998. ISBN: 0140389652pa. _JS_**
Laura studies hard in high school because she wants to get into medical school someday. Meanwhile she has a crush on football captain, Pete, and strange things are happening in her neighborhood ever since Omar moved in. When she discovers that Omar can travel to the fourth dimension, she begs to go with him. But when she goes again, without Omar, she can't find her way back.

Singularity. **New York: Dutton, 1985. 170p. Reissued by Puffin in 1995. ISBN: 0140375988pa. _MJ_**
When twins Barry and Harry housesit for their uncle on his farm in the Midwest, it doesn't take them long to realize that something unusual is keeping the local people far away, and that whatever it is, is probably locked in the shed.

12

Thompson, Kate

The Missing Link Trilogy. **New York: Bloomsbury. (1st American Editions.) _MJ_**
In a near future world that is running out of petroleum, there's a farm in Scotland where the line between human and animal becomes blurred.

The Fourth World. **2005. 330p. ISBN: 158234650X; 1582348979pa.**
Fifteen-year-old Danny has always been different. He acts young, moves awkwardly, and is prone to fits. When he sets out to join his birth mother, Maggie, on a farm in Scotland, his stepbrother Christie accompanies him, along with two talking animals sent by his scientist mother. Although they encounter dangers along the way, nothing can compare to what is waiting for them when they reach Scotland.

Only Human. 2006. 320p. ISBN: 1582346518.
Danny and Christie have made a life for themselves on the strange farm when Maggie's husband returns from an expedition to Africa. Bernard is convinced that he has discovered the missing-link gene between animals and humans and is determined to journey to the Himalayas to find a yeti. While Danny and Christie join him, Maggie stays behind to defend the farm.

Wells, H. G.

The Island of Dr. Moreau. New York: Holt, 1896. (1st American Edition.) Reissued by Wildside Press in hardcover in 2004. ISBN: 0809596377; 1595400281pa. [Adult] *S* AUD LP VID
When two ships collide at sea, Edward Prendick is the sole survivor. He counts himself lucky to reach a nearby island until he discovers it is the home of Dr. Moreau, a mad scientist who is determined to create a creature that is part man and part beast.

Werlin, Nancy

🎗 *Double Helix*. New York: Dial Books, 2004. 252p. ISBN: 0803726066; 014240327Xpa. *JS*
High school senior Eli Samuels has always been good at everything. He's smarter and faster than almost everyone he knows. After graduation, he takes a summer job at Wyatt Transgenics, despite his father's pleas for him to turn it down. There, he locates a concealed elevator that takes him to a hidden subbasement, where the lab's secrets lurk. (BBYA)

Future Societies

A great deal of the science fiction written for young adults features societies of the future and places teenaged protagonists there. As they cope with new technologies, life-forms, and social structures, the characters struggle with the same emotions and issues as teens do today. Many are comparable to the types labeled "utopias and dystopias," portraying bleak worlds where something has gone wrong with the ideal society; others depict a post-apocalyptic world, giving a frightening look at what life might be like after a cataclysmic disaster. Although much grimmer in nature than the fantasy in Chapter 5, "Alternate and Parallel Worlds," this type of fiction is related to "Reality with a Twist" fantasy. Both begin with the known world and then change something significant. In "Future Societies" fiction, the change always involves the future. Both can also focus on characters that are searching, and the stories may be a bit more contemplative and atmospheric, emphasizing the setting and its trappings, rather than the more action-oriented works of speculative fiction.

Adlington, L. J.

🎗 *The Diary of Pelly D*. New York: Greenwillow, 2005. 282p. (1st American Edition.) ISBN: 0060766158. *JS*
A planet far from Earth has been colonized with humans bred with gills. They originally sought a life of peace and prosperity for all, but war came nonetheless. Tony V. is

on the work crew clearing the debris so that City 5 can be rebuilt when he finds the diary of Pelly D. It's forbidden to keep anything, so he smuggles it back to his room, where he reads it at night, captivated by the life of the unknown girl. Pelly D. enjoyed the luxurious life of the wealthy until mandatory genetic testing proved she was one of the despised Galrezi. As he reads of Pelly D.'s life spiraling away from her, Tony V. realizes there are things the government has never told them. (BBYA)

Anderson, M. T.

🎗 *Feed*. **Cambridge, MA: Candlewick Press, 2002. 237p. ISBN: 0763617261lb; 0763622591pa.** *JS* **AUD** 📖

Titus and his friends are constantly connected through the feed, a computer chip implanted at birth that conducts a constant bombardment of music, chat, and commercials. All anyone has to do is think of something and the message is instantly transmitted, whether it's to set a meeting with a friend or to buy a new outfit. Everything changes on a trip to the moon when Titus meets Violet. She's different than other girls. He's just getting to know her at a party when a hacker disrupts all their feeds and they are rushed to the hospital. They're off the feed for several days, and, suddenly, nothing looks the same. (BBYA; Boston Globe Honor; Hal Clement Award; National Book Award Finalist; TBYA)

Armstrong, Jennifer, and Nancy Butcher

The Fire-Us Trilogy. **New York: HarperCollins.** *MJ*

When a fatal plague wipes out the adult population on Earth, the few children that remain must find a way to survive in their post-apocalyptic world.

Kindling. **2002. 224p. ISBN: 0060080485; 0064472736pa.**

Five years after a viral plague has destroyed the adult population, a small group of children has gathered in Florida. They think of themselves as the Family. They depend on each other for support, although each has been severely traumatized, and they depend on an ever-diminishing supply of canned goods for food. When Anchorman, who has schizophrenia and is sometimes Angerman, joins them, he convinces them to go on a perilous journey to Washington, D.C., to see the President and demand Answers.

The Keepers of the Flame. **2002. 231p. ISBN: 0060294124; 0064472701pa.**

The members of the Family are at first delighted to discover that there are some Grown-ups left in the world. They are members of a church called Keepers of the Flame who went underground before the plague struck and so escaped its devastating effects. Now they live in a shopping mall and welcome the Family. But something is not right, and Angerman knows that they must escape.

The Kiln. **2003. 283p. ISBN: 0060294132b. Reissued by Eos in ISBN: 006447271X.**

As they flee from the Keepers of the Flame, the Family winds up in The Woods, a retirement community where several older women have made a comfortable life for themselves tending goats and using solar-powered golf carts for transportation. Although they are wary, the children come to see that they have found a safe place, but the safety is only temporary, for they must journey on and find the President.

Asimov, Isaac

I, Robot. **New York: Gnome Press, 1950. 253p. Reissued by Bantam in hardcover in 2004. ISBN: 0553803700; 0553294385pa. [Adult]** *JS* **AUD VID**
In the future, scientists will develop the first positronic brains with which to create sentient robots. This series of short stories shows how these robots came to be and how they and humanity adjusted to coexistence.

The Robot Series. New York: Doubleday. All reissued by Spectra. [Adult] *JS*
In the far future, human beings colonize space and develop sentient robots. Now, New York City Detective Elijah Baley must learn to work with them, for his new partner, R. Daneel Olivaw, has a positronic brain.

> *The Caves of Steel.* **1954. 224p. Reissued in 1993. ISBN: 0553293400pa.**

> *The Naked Sun.* **1957. 187p. Reissued in 1991. ISBN: 0553293397pa.**

> *The Robots of Dawn.* **1983. 419p. Reissued in 1994. ISBN: 0553299492pa.**

Atwood, Margaret

🎋 *The Handmaid's Tale.* **Boston: Houghton Mifflin, 1986. 311p. (1st American Edition.) Reissued by Knopf in 1998. ISBN: 038549081Xpa. [Adult]** *S* **AUD VID**
The conservative, religious right has taken over the United States and renamed it the Republic of Gilead. Here all women's lives are strictly controlled. They are not allowed to read or have money or jobs of their own, and they are forced to be virtuous and childless Wives, housekeeping Marthas, or childbearing Handmaids. Although she was once happily married with a daughter of her own, Offred is now a Handmaid who hopes the Commander will make her pregnant, because if she cannot bear children, she is of no value. (Arthur C. Clarke Award)

Barry, Max

Jennifer Government. **New York: Doubleday, 2003. 321p. Reissued by Vintage in 2004. ISBN: 1400030927pa. [Adult]** *S* **AUD**
In a future where Australia and the United Kingdom are part of the United States, government has become a business where making money is the bottom line. Here, people's last names indicate where they work. Field Agent Jennifer Government is on the case, tracking down the murder scheme hatched by the corrupt executives at Nike.

Bechard, Margaret

🎋 *Spacer and Rat.* **New Milford, CT: Roaring Brook Press, 2005. 183p. ISBN: 1596430583lb.** *MJ* 📖
Jack's lived all of his life on a space station in the Asteroid Belt. He's about to be promoted to a job on the distant colony of Liberty Station when he encounters a "rat."

Usually he joins with his friends in chasing rats, Earthie children abandoned by their parents, but this time he helps the girl instead and finds himself caught up in saving Kit and her amazing sentient robot, Waldo. (BBYA)

Bondoux, Anne-Laure

The Destiny of Linus Hoppe. **New York: Delacorte Press, 2005. (1st American Edition.) 152p. ISBN: 0385732295.** *JS*
In the Paris of the near future, the world is divided into three realms: Realm One is perfect, with no crime, no pollution, no poverty; Realm Two is polluted and riddled with crime; Realm Three is the worst, where the rebels and social deviants are sent for "re-education." Linus is feeling anxious, for like all fourteen-year-olds, he has to be tested by the Great Processor so that the computer can determine where he will spend the rest of his life. But when he meets Yosh from Realm Two, he's not so sure life in Realm One is perfect after all.

The Second Life of Linus Hoppe. **New York: Delacorte Press, 2005. (1st American Edition.) 200p. ISBN: 0385732309.** *JS*
When Linus changed his test results to fool the Great Processor, he expected that he would like his chosen life in Realm Two better than the elite existence in Realm One that Yosh now enjoys instead. He doesn't. The mind-numbing factory labor leaves him exhausted each day, but he is more convinced than ever that the system of the dystopic society must change. At great risk to himself, he joins the resistance movement as it works to overthrow the ruling caste system.

Bradbury, Ray

Fahrenheit 451. **New York: Ballantine, 1953. 199p. Reissued by Simon & Schuster in hardcover in 2003. ISBN: 0743247221; 0345342968pa. [Adult]** *JS* **AUD VID**
Guy Montag is a fireman. But he doesn't put out fires, he starts them, for his job is to burn books. The totalitarian government of this dystopian future has determined that the ideas in books are too dangerous and has been systematically destroying them for years. Montag completely agrees with this philosophy until he encounters Clarisse McClellan, who motivates him to reexamine his life. He begins to read the books he has pilfered from book burnings, and this sets him on the path to revolution. (Hugo Award)

Christopher, John

The Tripods Quartet. *MJS*
When the tripods landed on Earth, they carried Masters who seized control of human society. Now all adults serve them without question, and the only time of freedom is childhood.

***The White Mountains*. New York: Macmillan, 1967. 184p. Revised and reissued by Simon & Schuster in hardcover, 35th Anniversary Edition, in 2003. ISBN: 0689855044lb; 0689856725pa. LP**
Will has lived all of his life in the shadow of the Tripods, the three-legged machines that invaded Earth long ago. As he turns thirteen, his scheduled capping ceremony approaches. If he goes through with it, he will be the willing servant of the machines. Instead, he flees to the mountains of Switzerland, hoping to find the last free people on Earth.

***The City of Gold and Lead*. New York: Macmillan, 1967. 185p. Revised and reissued by Simon & Schuster in hardcover, 35th Anniversary Edition, in 2003. ISBN: 0689855052lb; 0689856660pa.**
Will finds friends his own age in Switzerland, and they train together to overthrow the Tripods. Now they have an opportunity to gather information vital to their revolution, but they must enter the City of the Tripods to do it.

***The Pool of Fire*. New York: Macmillan, 1968. 178p. Revised and reissued by Simon & Schuster in hardcover, 35th Anniversary Edition, in 2003. ISBN: 0689855060lb; 0689856695pa. LP**
Will returns to Switzerland from the City of the Tripods with appalling news. The Masters plan to alter Earth's atmosphere to that of their home planet and thus annihilate humanity. They are only waiting for the arrival of their space ship to unleash their attack. If Will and his friends cannot find a way to stop them, the human race will be doomed to extinction.

***When the Tripods Came*. New York: Dutton, 1988. 151p. Revised and reissued by Simon & Schuster in paperback in 2003. ISBN: 0689857624pa.**
In this prequel to the original <u>Tripods Trilogy</u>, the Tripods send three ships to Earth. One lands in England, one in Russia, and one in the United States. They seem to be easily overcome by military might, but people were not expecting that the invaders could control them with hypnotism. Fourteen-year-old Laurie and his family realize that they can no longer live in England and remain free of the aliens' caps that keep humans hypnotized. They escape to Switzerland and vow to fight the Tripods.

Clarke, Arthur C.

***Childhood's End*. New York: Ballantine, 1953. 214p. Reissued by Random House in 1987. ISBN: 0345347951pa. [Adult] <u>S</u>**
Humanity is hovering on the brink of universal space travel when invading aliens stop people from traveling to the stars. Although the Overlords solve the problems of the world, they also do not let people progress, casting a grim shadow on the future of humanity.

Colfer, Eoin

🦅 ***The Supernaturalist*. New York: Hyperion, 2004. 267p. (1st American Edition.) ISBN: 0786851481lb; 078685149Xpa. <u>MJ</u> AUD LP**
In a near-future dystopia, cities are owned by corporations, and their bottom line is money. The same holds true for orphanages. At the Clarissa Frayne Institute for

Parentally Challenged Boys, the orphans are required to test dangerous prototypes and often do not survive past the age of fifteen. Fourteen-year-old Cosmo Hill executes an escape that would have killed him except for the Supernaturalists who rescue him. They are dedicated to eradicating the blue parasites that feed on the life energy of humans. Cosmo is one of the very few who can see the parasites, but as he begins on his new career, evidence comes to light that shows perhaps the parasites aren't the bad guys after all. (Eleanor Cameron Award)

Danziger, Paula

This Place Has No Atmosphere*. New York: Delacorte, 1986. 156p. Reissued by Puffin in 2006. ISBN: 0142406805pa. *MJ
In 2057, fifteen-year-old Aurora thinks her life can't get any worse than when her parents accept jobs on the moon and move the entire family to the experimental colony called Luna City. Aurora gives up the Monolith Mall, her friends, and her boyfriend and struggles to find something worthwhile in the place that literally has no atmosphere.

Davidson, Ellen Dee

***Stolen Voices*. Toronto: Lobster Press, 2005. 188p. ISBN: 189707316Xpa.**
In a dystopian future, fifteen-year-old Miri is scheduled to go through the Masking ceremony that is supposed to bond her with her age-mates but will in reality force her to carry out the will of the Masker. Miri rebels and finds her way to the Secret Valley, but she cannot escape a final confrontation with the Masker.

DuPrau, Jeanne

<u>The Books of Ember</u>. New York: Random House. *MJ* AUD
The city of Ember is the only light in a dark world. Built as an underground shelter to rescue a remnant of humanity from calamity, it is meant to last for two hundred years. But the instructions were lost, and the people forgot where they came from.

The City of Ember. 2003. 270p. ISBN: 0375822739; 0375822747pa.
Two hundred and forty-two years have passed since Ember was built. The people depend on the generator for all of their light and heat, and much of their food comes from canned goods doled out from the supply room. The generator keeps breaking down, and supplies are running out. Lina and Doon, twelve-year-olds who have begun their first jobs, stumble across the clues that will help them save their people—if the corrupt mayor does not stop them first. (ALAN)

The People of Sparks. 2004. 338p. ISBN: 0375828249; 0375828257pa.
Lina and Doon have brought the four hundred residents of Ember out of the underground city. Although at first they are fascinated by the world of open sky, sparkling sun, and verdant grass, they are not well-equipped to take care of themselves in a land with no generator or supply room. They rely on the people of the farming village of Sparks to take them in.

Conflict arises when suspicions grow between the two groups and the resources each needs prove scarce.

***The Prophet of Yonwood.* 2006. 304p. ISBN: 0375875263.**
In this prequel to *The City of Ember,* Eleven-year-old Nickie Randolph visits Yonwood, North Carolina, with her aunt hoping to be distracted from disturbing thoughts of the world on the brink of war and her father who is away on a secret government mission. Instead of relief, Nickie finds a town in thrall to the Prophet who foretells the end of the world.

Profile of Nancy Farmer

Photo: Sonya Sones

Born July 9, 1941, in Phoenix, Arizona, Nancy Farmer worked with the Peace Corps in India in the early 1960s. She lived in central Africa for seventeen years, employed as an entomologist. While living in Zimbabwe, she decided she wanted to be a writer when her son was around four years old. In *Contemporary Authors* she says, "According to the Shona, the Africans among whom we lived, I had been visited by a *shave* (pronounced 'shah-vay') or wandering spirit. Shaves come from people who haven't received proper burial rites. They drift around until they find a likely host, possess whoever it is, and teach him or her a skill. In my case I got a traditional storyteller. Now I am a full-time professional storyteller myself." Her first book, *Do You Know Me?*, received critical praise, and she has since written three Newbery Honor books: *A Girl Named Disaster; The Ear, the Eye and the Arm;* and *The House of the Scorpion,* which also won a Printz Honor and the National Book Award (*Contemporary Authors Online*, Infotrac Galegroup Database).

Interview with Nancy Farmer

Conducted via e-mail January 27–February 2, 2006

SF: You've written both fantasy and science fiction for young adults. Do you have a preference? How do you decide between the genres?

NF: Fantasy is a lot easier to write than science fiction, which is why I suspect there's more of it. It's easy to make stuff up. If an idea really rivets me, though, like cloning, I will make the effort. I have been a scientist and make every effort to be absolutely accurate about any science I use. I know my novels will be used as textbooks, and therefore things such as animal behavior, geography, flora, and fauna at certain times of the year are scrupulously researched. This is Tolkien's basic rule: No fantasy is ever convincing if it doesn't have a basis in the real world.

SF: How would you say that your years living in Africa have influenced your writing?

NF: I would never have become a writer if I hadn't gone to Africa. The pace of life there is much slower, and there's much time for telling yarns. And for discovering weird stories. I have never understood why some people have trouble doing cultural research in Africa. All you have to do is ask a question and then sit back for the next five hours to listen. I have never met people more interested in imparting knowledge. My sense of humor is African as well. If you only read earnest, gloomy people like Doris Lessing, you'd never find out about their sense of fun. McCall Smith (*The No. 1 Ladies Detective Agency*) recreates it perfectly.

SF: Why do you think people read fantasy and science fiction?

NF: For the same reason they read any novel, to escape into a better, more fulfilling world than the one they have. Reading a good novel is like reincarnation, without actually having to die to get there. That's why depressing literary novels never sell well.

SF: Do you think that there are things that science fiction does better than fantasy and that fantasy does better than science fiction? If so in what way?

NF: I like both equally well, but some people have trouble letting go of reality. They feel Science Fiction is serious, while Fantasy is frivolous. What drives science fiction is ideas, and this sometimes means the characters aren't well drawn. I hear this criticism a lot. Fantasy pays more attention to character.

SF: *The House of the Scorpion* won a Newbery Honor, a Printz Honor, and the National Book Award. How did it feel to have your book win a triple crown, so to speak?

NF: It feels great. I wish it would happen again.

SF: What would you say your method of writing is (i.e., working from an outline, going where the story takes you, etc.)?

NF: I never know where the story is going until I sit down at the computer. I never make outlines. This is the method that works best for me. Through the years I've learned to open the door to the subconscious and let the story happen. It feels like the whole novel exists on some level before I write it.

SF: Of your books, which are your favorite books and/or characters and why?

NF: I like all my books because I'm totally self-centered, I guess. My favorite characters are Uncle Zeka in *Do You Know Me,* Arm in *The Ear, the Eye and the Arm* (I also like Trashman in the same book),

Tam Lin in *The House of the Scorpion* (some readers have never forgiven me for killing him off), and El Patron was a real pleasure to write about. Thorgil in *The Sea of Trolls*. Uncle Zeka and Thorgil are fun because they're out of control and half nuts. El Patron is deliciously selfish. Arm and Tam Lin are noble. Trashman was a Holy Fool, an interesting sort of character. Reviewers in the U.S. have shied away from Trashman and Thorgil. They find it very difficult to deal with a character (Trashman) who is retarded and utterly happy. Thorgil bothers them because she's a cross-dresser.

SF: What were your favorite books growing up and/or who were your favorite authors?

NF: I grew up on the Oz books and Tarzan, also on wonderfully moral Victorian books my mother had where children got struck with lightening for going fishing on Sunday. I didn't discover Tolkien, C. S. Lewis, or Roald Dahl until I was an adult, but I reread them all the time. I also like Nabokov, Lawrence Durrell, and Henry Miller.

SF: What do you think is the merit or importance of reading fantasy and science fiction?

NF: Fantasy and science fiction teach people how to let their ideas out of pigeonholes so they can play together.

Farmer, Nancy

The House of the Scorpion. **New York: Atheneum, 2002. 380p. ISBN: 0689852223; 0689852223pa.** *MJS* **AUD LP**
In a land called Opium, located between the United States and Mexico, the 142-year-old drug lord El Patron plans to live many more lifetimes. He does that using clones. Matt Alacrán is the latest of these clones, although he does not know it. He is raised in seclusion by Celia until outsiders discover him at the age of six. Then he experiences the cruelty of the Alacrán estate, where the majority of the clones who farm the opium have implants that make them "eejits." The family of El Patron despises Matt for being only a clone. But El Patron wants Matt treated well, until the day El Patron will need to have Matt's organs harvested to continue his own life. Matt's only hope for survival lies in the daring plan of the cook and bodyguard who have been plotting to save him. (ALAN; BBYA; National Book Award; Newbery Honor; Printz Honor; TBYA)

★ *The Ear, the Eye and the Arm*. **New York: Orchard Books, 1994. 311p. Reissued by Firebird in 2002. ISBN: 0141311096pa. *JS* LP**
In Zimbabwe in 2194, the three children of the country's chief of security chafe at their restricted, if technologically advanced, lives. Led by thirteen-year-old Tendai, they escape the confines of their home and embark on an adventure across the city, not realizing until it is too late that their father's enemies view the siblings' freedom as an opportunity too good to ignore. (ALAN; BBYA; Hal Clement Award; Newbery Honor)

Fox, Helen

Eager. **New York: Wendy Lamb Books, 2004. 280p. ISBN: 0385746725; 0553487957pa. *M***
In a future where starvation and homelessness have been eliminated but class distinctions abound, everyone has a house robot, even those in the middle class. Brother and sister Gavin and Fleur are embarrassed by their older-model robot, Grumps, but their parents can't afford the new BDC4. Instead they replace Grumps with the prototype robot Eager, who has been programmed to think, learn, and make mistakes. While Eager is learning about life, he and the siblings discover something very disturbing about the BDC4s.

Eager's Nephew. **New York: Wendy Lamb Books, 2006. 295p. ISBN: 0385746733.**
Twenty years after the conclusion of *Eager*, sentient robots have been outlawed, so Eager has been living in hiding. But he emerges once a year to visit the Bell family. On this visit, his nephew comes along as a stowaway and causes all manner of difficulties.

Haddix, Margaret Peterson

The Shadow Children. **New York: Simon & Schuster. *MJ***
In a far-from-perfect future, the government closely regulates how many children each family is allowed to have. Only two are permissible. If a forbidden third child is discovered, the Population Police are authorized to use any means necessary to handle the situation.

★ *Among the Hidden*. **1998. 153p. ISBN: 0689817002lb; 1416905294pa. AUD**

Twelve-year-old Luke does not know what it's like to go to school, to have a birthday party, or even to have a friend. He is an illegal third child, a shadow child. His parents violated the population laws to have him, and now they must keep him hidden. As if that isn't bad enough, a new housing development is being built around his family's farm, and Luke is no longer allowed even to go outside. Bored, he studies the patterns of life in the new house and spies another third child. Risking his life, he crosses the yard to meet her and discovers the world is more wonderful—and more dangerous—than he'd imagined. (BBYA)

Among the Impostors. 2001. 172p. ISBN: 0689839049lb; 0689839081pa.
It's too risky for Luke to remain at home, so his parents secure for him the stolen identity of a recently deceased teen, Lee Grant, and send him to Hendricks School for Boys. Where once he always had to hide and stay away from everyone, he now feels exposed and vulnerable in the open with his classmates. The harsh school is more like a prison than an institution of learning, and his roommate hazes him unmercifully. When he finds a door to the outside, he can temporarily escape. One day, he discovers a group of students in the woods forming a plan for freedom, but he isn't sure he can trust them.

Among the Betrayed. 2002. 156p. ISBN: 0689839057lb; 068983909Xpa. LP
Nina Idi has been arrested by the Population Police for being an illegal third child, but they offer to let her go free if she will get the other three children imprisoned with her to confess that they are third children as well.

Among the Barons. 2003. 182p. ISBN: 0689839065lb; 0689839103pa.
Luke is finally settling into his identity as Lee Grant and to life at the Hendricks School for Boys when Smits Grant, Lee's real younger brother, shows up to attend Hendricks as well. Afraid that Smits will expose him as a fraud, Luke is even more bewildered when the wealthy Grant family calls both of their "sons" home. As Luke meets his "family," he learns they have plans for him that may prove fatal.

Among the Brave. 2004. 229p. ISBN: 0689857942lb; 0689857950pa. LP
Luke's friend Trey, another third child, finds himself at the center of a whirlwind of political change as he witnesses an assassination attempt. He and his friend turn to Mr. Talbot, a resistance sympathizer, for help, only to watch him get arrested. Desperate to help, Trey convinces Luke's older brother, Mark, to join with him in a plan that becomes even more hazardous when the head of the Population Police seizes governmental control.

Among the Enemy. 2005. 214p. ISBN: 0689857969.
When Nina's friend Matthias tries to help the injured Alia and Percy, he acts on impulse and also rescues an officer of the Population Police. Now he must pose as a new recruit and walk the tightrope between creating a convincing life at police headquarters and finding a way to help the resistance movement.

Among the Free. 2006. ISBN: 0689857985.
In the concluding novel of the series, Luke, who has been working undercover for the Populaiton Police, is sent out with his fellow workers to distribute new identification cards. One woman's resistance sparks a revolution in which Luke has a crucial role to play.

Halam, Ann

🌿 *Siberia*. New York: Wendy Lamb Books, 2005. 262p. ISBN: 0385746504. *JS*
In this dystopian future, four-year-old Rosita and her mother are exiled to the snowy north, where they live in a camp as political prisoners. Her mother is guilty of teaching science. Under the watchful eyes of the guards, she makes nails, but at night she uses a Lindquist kit to create animals. To little Rosita, this is magic; but in actuality, it's science. When Rosita is old enough, she's sent to prison school, where cruelty dominates

her life. Tricked into betraying her mother, she changes her name to Sloe and becomes determined to find the city of safety her mother told her of, no matter what the cost. (BBYA)

Hautman, Pete

Hole in the Sky. **New York: Simon & Schuster, 2001. 179p. ISBN: 0689831188lb; 068984428Xpa.** *JS*

In 2028, the Flu decimated the population of Earth, leaving only a few survivors to live in small enclaves with the fortunate ones who never got sick. Each Survivor has been impaired in some way. In 2038, a third wave of the Flu begins threatening to claim the remaining population. In addition, a band of Survivors calling themselves Kinka terrorize the remaining inhabitants. When sixteen-year-old Ceej Kane, who lives in the Grand Canyon, suspects that the Kinka have kidnapped his Survivor sister, Harryette, he goes in search of her, along with his best friend, Tim, and a Hopi girl, Bella, who believes that a magic door can lead them to a disease-free world.

Hughes, Monica

🏵 *Invitation to the Game*. **New York: Simon & Schuster, 1990. 183p. Reissued in 1993. ISBN: 0671866923pa.** *MJ* **LP**

In 2154, many people are unemployed because robots can do the jobs that humans once did. The government controls who gets the few available jobs, and the Thought Police monitor everything. When Lissee and seven of her friends are sent to the Designated Area for the unemployed, they think they will be bored, but instead begin to play the Game. After they have played together several times, they realize that it's not a game; it's reality, and they have been transported to an entirely new world they must make their own. (Hal Clement Award)

Huxley, Aldous

Brave New World. **Garden City, NY: The Sun Dial Press, 1936. 311p. Reissued by Buccaneer Books in hardcover in 1997. ISBN: 0899664237; 0060929871pa. [Adult]** *JS* **AUD**

In the dystopian future, the World State controls every aspect of life, beginning with the generation of nearly identical human embryos that are treated so that they will fit easily into the one of five castes: Alpha, Beta, Gamma, Delta, or Epsilon, where the Alphas are the thinkers and the Epsilons carry out menial labor. In this world, babies are hatched, sex is purely for pleasure, the state educates the children for their appointed tasks, and *soma* is the happiness drug that makes everyone feel fine. When Lenina and Bernard visit the Reservation where the last group of uncontrolled people live, they find John, the son of a World State citizen who was left behind twenty years ago. He longs to see the "brave, new world" his mother speaks of, and so returns with the visitors. What he finds appalls him, and he becomes determined to overturn the system.

Kress, Nancy

The Sleepless Trilogy. [Adult] *S*

Genetic manipulation has been refined to the point where a new race of children is created. Not only are they more intelligent than other children, but they also do not need sleep and so far outshine "Sleepers." Resentment simmers between the Sleepless and the Sleepers, but the genetic enhancement continues.

> *Beggars in Spain*. **New York: William Morrow, 1993. 438p. Reissued by HarperCollins in 2004. ISBN: 0060733489pa. AUD**

> *Beggars and Choosers*. **New York: Tor, 1994. 315p. (Out of Print.)**

> *Beggars Ride*. **New York: Tor, 1996. 304p. Reissued in 1997. ISBN: 0812544749pa.**

Levitin, Sonia

The Cure. **San Diego: Harcourt, 1999. 181p. ISBN: 0152018271lb; 038073298Xpa.** *JS* **AUD**

Sixteen-year-old Gemm 16884 lives in 2407 in a dystopian society that believes that "diversity begets hostility." Unlike those around him, Gemm has a passion for music and doesn't want to let it go with a few sips of a serotonin shake. The authorities view Gemm as dangerous and offer him a choice. Either he can be "recycled" or submit to the "cure." He chooses the cure and is sent back in time to 1348, where he lives as a Jew in Strasbourg just as the Black Death is sweeping across Europe and the Jews are being blamed for it.

The Goodness Gene. **New York: Dutton, 2005. 272p. ISBN: 0525473971.** *JS*

In post-apocalyptic 2207, the Director of the Dominion of the Americas rules a world where the privileged live in atmospherically controlled domes. They trade in their pleasure rations for anything from travel to sex, but the sex doesn't lead to conception. Babies are created in labs. They are raised to be perfect participants in their society, like the twins Will and Berk, sons of the Director. But when the brothers begin to question their perfect life, their investigation leads them to shocking secrets.

Lowry, Lois

🏵 *The Giver*. **Boston: Houghton Mifflin, 1993. 180p. ISBN: 0395645662; 0440237688pa.** *MJ* **AUD LP** 📖

In an apparently utopian world where there is no war, no poverty, no turmoil, and no terror, husbands and wives are chosen for their compatibility and each couple has two children, one boy and one girl. At the age of twelve, each child is assigned a job by the Committee of Elders. Jonas is twelve, content in his world and looking forward to learning what his assignment will be. He is puzzled when he gets it, though, for he is to be a Receiver of Memory, and Jonas is not quite sure what that entails. What the Giver reveals enables Jonas to view his community in a new light and forces him to choose between accepting their Sameness or embracing a daring upheaval. (ALAN; BBYA; Boston Globe Honor; Hal Clement Award; Newbery Medal)

***Gathering Blue*. Boston: Houghton Mifflin, 2000. 215p. ISBN: 0618055819; 0553494783pa. _MJ_ AUD LP**

In the same future world as *The Giver* but with a society that has developed into hunter-gatherers after the Ruin, young Kira mourns the death of her mother and wonders how she will survive with a twisted leg. She seeks aid from the Council of Guardians, who take her in because of her amazing talent for weaving. They move her to the Council Edifice and put her in charge of completing the weaving of the ceremonial robe worn by the Singer at the annual gathering. The Singer and the robe together depict the history of the people. There she meets Thomas, the woodcarver, and Jo, the six-year-old who will be the next Singer. Although they have all they need to live, the children soon feel the restrictive hand of the Council. When they discover the Council's secrets, they must choose between serving the Council or fighting for freedom.

***Messenger*. Boston: Houghton Mifflin, 2004. 169p. ISBN: 0618404414; 0440239125pa. _MJ_ AUD LP**

In this companion to *The Giver* and *Gathering Blue,* Matty lives in the Village with Seer and is looking forward to receiving his true name from Leader, who came to the Village as a child on a red sled. Before he can be given his true name, though, an evil creeps into the Village. Once, all were welcomed. Now there are those who want to build a wall to keep out newcomers. Before the wall can be completed, Matty must brave the ominous Forest and fetch Kira, the seer's daughter, before it is too late.

McNaughton, Janet

***The Secret under My Skin*. New York: Eos, 2005. (1st American Edition.) 264pa. ISBN: 006008989X; 0060089911pa. _MJ_**

In the dystopian future of 2368, the world is recovering from a series of ecological disasters that were blamed on the scientists. All of the scientists were imprisoned in concentration camps, an event now referred to as the "technocaust." Blay lives in a work camp for homeless orphans, spending her days searching through dumps for anything useful. Because she loves to read, she is selected to be an assistant to Marrella a bio-indicator (a living being who can gauge the health of the environment). As the two work together, Blay uncovers secrets concerning the ruling Commission and her own hidden past.

Nix, Garth

***Shade's Children*. New York: HarperCollins, 1997. 310p. ISBN: 0060273240; 0064471969pa. _JS_**

Alien Overlords eliminate everyone on Earth over age fourteen and then confine all the children in Dormitories. There, the children await the time when their brains will be harvested for the Overlords' half-human, half-mechanical creatures. Only those with psychic abilities can escape. One such boy is Gold-Eye. When he is finally free, he encounters Ella, Drum, and Ninde, who convince him to join one of the teams fighting the Overlords. These are groups organized by Shade, a holographic projection of a scientist produced by a computer programmed with artificial intelligence. As the teens carry out their missions, they realize that Shade's goals are not their own and that they are the best and perhaps last hope for humanity.

O'Brien, Robert C.

🎖 *Z for Zachariah*. **New York: Atheneum, 1975. 249p. Reissued by Simon & Schuster in 1986. ISBN: 0020446500pa. *JS* AUD**
After the nuclear holocaust, sixteen-year-old Ann Burden keeps a diary recording the details of her life in the post-apocalyptic world. She believes she is the only one to survive the disaster, living in her idyllic hidden valley where she grows her own food and tends the remaining animals. When Mr. Loomis enters her farm, she is at first fearful and then tentatively hopeful, but Loomis quickly shows her she must still struggle to survive. (Edgar Juvenile Award)

Orwell, George

Nineteen Eighty-Four. **New York: Harcourt, 1949. 314p. Reissued in hardcover by Buccaneer Books in 1982. ISBN: 0899663680; 0451524934pa. [Adult] *S* AUD VID**
London is part of Oceania, and the Party controls everything from history to language, from thoughts to sex. Winston Smith is a low-level Party official who keeps a diary chronicling his hatred of the Party. Smith is sure that Big Brother is always watching, but when an attractive woman sends him a love note, he willingly begins an affair, knowing that this freedom of expression will not go unpunished.

Philbrick, Rodman

🎖 *The Last Book in the Universe*. **New York: Blue Sky Press, 2000. 223p. ISBN: 0439087589; 0439771331pa. *MJ***
When the Big Shake destroys most of civilization, a small group withdraws to a sealed enclave called Eden. They learn to make the genetic enhancements necessary to stay alive, but they abandon everyone else on the outside. The rest of the survivors live in the toxic environment that's left and are subject to the rule of thugs and bullies. Under orders, Spaz sets out to rob an old man, Ryter. Ryter will gladly give up all he has except for the book that he is writing. When Spaz sets out to find his dying foster-sister Bean, Ryter insists on joining him. As they make their way through their grim world, post-apocalyptic reality leaves livid wounds on their lives. (BBYA)

Reed, Kit

🎖 *Thinner than Thou*. **New York: Tor, 2004. 334p. ISBN: 0765307626; 076531195Xpa. [Adult] *S***
In a near-future dystopia, pursuit of the perfect body becomes a religious obsession. When Annie starves herself so that she is no more than a skeleton, her parents send her to the Dedicated Sisters. But there is a hidden connection between the Sisters and the tyrannical Reverend Earl, and twins Danny and Betz are determined to rescue Annie. (Alex)

Reeve, Philip

<u>The Hungry City Chronicles</u>. New York: HarperCollins/Eos. (1st American Editions.) *JS*

In the distant, post-apocalyptic future, cities are no longer landlocked but mobile. After the Sixty Minute War, cities were constructed to be Traction Cities that move from place to place on caterpillar tracks. As they do, they consume smaller towns, absorbing both their human and material resources.

❀ *Mortal Engines*. **2003. 310p. ISBN: 0060082070; 0060082097pa.**
Apprentice Historian Tom Natsworthy is a fifteen-year-old orphan who greatly admires Thaddeus Valentine, Head Historian of the London Museum. All that changes when Tom saves Valentine's life from the disfigured girl. Instead of being grateful, Valentine shoves Tom and Hester Shaw, the girl who would have killed him, down a waste chute. As the city rumbles away, Tom and Hester join forces, attempting to catch up to the fast-disappearing London. Meanwhile, in the traveling city, Valentine's daughter Katherine discovers her father's nefarious plans and is determined to stop him. (ALAN; BBYA; Smarties Gold Award)

Predator's Gold. **2004. 325p. ISBN: 0060721936; 0060721960pa.**
Tom and Hester, who are now lovers, have been safe for two years, traveling in the airship the *Jenny Haniver*. When their ship is damaged, they are forced to land in the declining traction city of Anchorage. Few inhabitants remain after the plague. The Margravine of Anchorage, sixteen-year-old Freya, attracts Tom's romantic attention. She wants to take her city to the dead continent—America, where rumors whisper of green lands. As they embark on their dangerous journey, they are pursued by those who want the *Jenny Haniver*.

Infernal Devices. **2006. ISBN: 0060826355.**

Sixteen years after the end of *Predator's Gold,* Tom and Hester have settled in the stationary city of Anchorage, which was grounded on the shores of North America. Their daughter Wren is fifteen. She fights with her mother and thinks her dad is dull. When the Lost Boys from her parents' past reappear, they lure her into their schemes, which lead to her capture and her parents' racing to rescue her.

Resnick, Mike

Kirinyaga: A Fable of Utopia. **New York: Ballantine, 1998. 293p. Reissued in 1999. ISBN: 034541702Xpa. [Adult]** *S*

In twenty-second-century Kenya, Koriba is disgusted by the urban sprawl taking over his country. Vowing to create a utopia, he leads a group of colonists to a terraformed planetoid, which he names Kirinyaga. There he becomes the witch doctor and recreates the strict society of his ancestors. He now decides the fate of his people, but he forgets that even a perfect society must grow and change.

Rosoff, Meg

🏵 *how i live now*. **New York: Wendy Lamb Books, 2004. 194p. ISBN: 0385746776; 0553376055pa. _S_ AUD**
In the near-future, fifteen-year-old Daisy lives in New York City with her father, who's more interested in his new wife and their soon-to-be child than he is in his anorexic daughter. Supposedly to give Daisy a change of scene, he sends her to England to visit with the family of her deceased mother's sister. At first, Daisy feels uncomfortable, but she quickly grows close to her Aunt Penn and cousins Osbert, Isaac, Edmond, and Piper. When Aunt Penn travels to Oslo for a peace conference, the cousins enjoy their independence, and Edmond and Daisy become lovers. Their world is transformed when an unnamed enemy invades England. The war separates the cousins and leaves Daisy and nine-year-old Piper to struggle across the dangerous countryside in search of home and safety. (BBYA; Printz Award)

Shinn, Sharon

Jenna Starborn. **New York: Ace Books, 2002. 381p. ISBN: 044100900Xpa.**
In a future where humanity has colonized all the planets in the universe, babies can be born or grown to order in gen-tanks. On the planet Baldus, Jenna lives the first ten years of her life with the abusive woman who commissioned her. When social workers remove her, they send her to a boarding school where she learns how to be an engineer. Accepting a job on a bleak mining planet, Jenna journeys to Thorrastone Park where she meets Mr. Everett Ravenback and changes both their lives in a manner parallel to the way Jane Erye changed the life of Mr. Rochester and Mr. Rochester changed hers.

Skurzynski, Gloria

The Virtual War Chronologs. _MJ_
In 2080, the few remaining people on Earth live in domed cities because plagues have devastated much of the Earth's surface; soldiers are genetically engineered; and wars are fought through virtual reality technology.

Virtual War. **New York: Simon & Schuster. 1997. 162p. Reissued in 2004. ISBN: 0689867859pa.**
Only one place on Earth has been reclaimed so that humans can live there, and it's up to genetically engineered Corgan and his team to win the virtual war for the Western Hemisphere Federation.

The Clones. **New York: Atheneum, 2002. 181p. ISBN: 0689842635.**
As a reward for his success in the virtual war, Corgan lives a life of luxury on the only undomed island. When his former partner Sharla smuggles a child cloned from their deceased partner, Corgan welcomes them both. But the cloned child has a twin and his deeds can lead the former teammates to disaster.

The Revolt. **New York: Atheneum, 2005. 247p. ISBN: 0689842651.**
The clones, Cyborg and Brigand, are growing at an alarming rate, and Brigand wants to spread rebellion throughout all the domed cities. Corgan and Cybory escape to Florida, but it isn't long until Brigand tracks them down and they must escape in an aging spaceship if they hope to survive.

***The Choice*. New York: Atheneum, 2006. ISBN: 0689842678.**
In this concluding novel, Corgan and his companions have escaped but must return to Earth with The Locker, a device that can halt a person's age forever. Brigand desperately wants the device and Corgan must do anything to keep him from getting it, even if he has to engage in virtual combat once again.

Stahler, David

***Truesight*. New York: Eos, 2004. 168p. ISBN: 0060522852; 0060522879pa.**
Like everyone in his colony of Harmony, Jacob was born blind. The original settlers of the planet ensured that each generation would be blind through genetic engineering to be sure that they would avoid the violence and corruption of the Seers. But as his thirteenth birthday nears, Jacob realizes that he can see and is struck by the revelation that his society is not the utopia it pretends it is.

Stevermer, Caroline

🦃 ***River Rats*. San Diego: Harcourt, 1992. 214p. ISBN: 0152008950; 0152055541pa. _JS_**
After the Flash turns the Mississippi into a polluted river, destroys a number of cities, and reduces the amount of food, water, and technology the people have access to, six orphans refit an old riverboat and survive by traveling up and down the Mississippi. Although their rule is never to take on passengers, they break it to save an old man named King. But he brings trouble with him, and the River Rats live to regret their kindness. (Hal Clement Award)

Tepper, Sheri S.

***The Gate to Women's Country*. New York: Foundation Books, 1988. 278p. Reissued by Spectra in 1997. ISBN: 0553280643pa. [Adult] _S_**
In this post-holocaust world, society has been divided into two distinct groups: the men who live in self-contained military garrisons and the women who live in gated towns in Women's Country and control agriculture, trade, medicine, and the arts. Only a few men who reject the military life live in Women's Country. If trade breaks down, the men go to war with another garrison, but that war is contained. In times of peace, they play war games to keep up their skills. The women maintain everything else and raise the children. At age five, all male children are sent to live with the men for ten years. Then they must choose either to stay in the garrison or go through the gate to Women's Country. Ten year-old Stavia grows up in this society and moves from idealistic child to angst-ridden teen to a mature doctor who learns the secrets held by the Council.

Vizzini, Ned

Be More Chill. **New York: Miramax Books/Hyperion, 2004. 287p. ISBN: 0786809957lb; 0786809965pa.** *S* **AUD**
Jeremy Heere, the class nerd in his suburban New Jersey high school, lusts after the sexy girls in his class, especially for Christine Caniglia. He watches her all day in school and at night surfs the net for porn. When they are cast opposite each other in the school play, Jeremy decides desperate measures are called for. He procures an illegal, oral "squip," a tiny computer in pill form that lodges in his brain and offers advice on how to be cool. All appears to be going well, until the squip malfunctions.

Westerfeld, Scott

The Uglies Trilogy. New York: Simon Pulse. *MJS*
In Tally's dystopic society, everyone is considered ugly until the operation—then all are beautiful and can party day and night.

🏵 *Uglies*. **2005. 425p. ISBN: 0689865384pa.** *MJS*
Tally can't wait until she turns sixteen and can undergo the operation that will transform her from an ugly into a pretty. When she meets Shay, she encounters someone who disdains being pretty. Shay plans to run away and join Smoke, a community of Uglies. Tally refuses to join her. But when Shay disappears, the authorities offer Tally a choice. Either Tally must locate and betray her friend or she will remain ugly forever. (BBYA)

Pretties. **2005. 370p. ISBN: 0689865392pa.**
In this sequel to *Uglies,* Tally has submitted to the procedure and become a pretty. Now all she can think about is how beautiful she is, what she should wear to the next party, and how hot her boyfriend Zane is. Life floats by on an ephemeral high of "prettiness" until she receives a message that reminds her why she had the operation in the first place. As a result, she must find a way to escape New Pretty Town with Zane, or both of their lives may be in jeopardy.

Specials. **2006. 384p. ISBN: 0689865406.**
In this conclusion to the Uglies Trilogy, Tally has been surgically altered to become a Special. As she joins an elite team of beautiful and dangerous military agents, Tally's only mission is to eliminate the rebels of New Smoke. And she will succeed—if the remnant of her conscience cannot catch her attention.

Media-Related Science Fiction Series

Smallville. Various authors. New York: Little, Brown. *JS*

Star Trek. Various authors. New York: Simon & Schuster. With a variety of subseries: *Star Trek: The Original Series, Star Trek: The Next Generation, Star Trek: Deep Space Nine, Star Trek: Voyager,* and *Star Trek: Enterprise.* *JS*

Star Wars. Various authors. New York: Ballantine. *JS*

Out of This World Science Fiction

The Company Series by Kage Baker

Spacer and Rat by Margaret Bechard

Fahrenheit 451 by Ray Bradbury

Ender's Game by Orson Scott Card

Things Not Seen by Andrew Clements

The House of the Scorpion by Nancy Farmer

Singing the Dogstar Blues by Alison Goodman

The Giver by Lois Lowry

Doomsday Book and **To Say Nothing of the Dog** by Connie Willis

References

Card, Orson Scott. *How to Write Science Fiction and Fantasy*. Cincinnati, OH: Writer's Digest Books, 1990.

Hartwell, David G. *Age of Wonder: Exploring the World of Science Fiction*. New York: Tor, 1996.

"Nancy Farmer," *Contemporary Authors Online*, Infotrac Galegroup Database (accessed March 15, 2006.)

Chapter 13

The Dark Side: Paranormal and Horror

Sometimes what teen readers want most are books that send shivers down their spines. In the broadest sense, horror includes any works designed to provoke fear. Horror can involve the mundane or the fantastic. The central characteristic is the atmosphere of dread. "Horror fiction upsets apple carts, burns old buildings, and stampedes the horses; it questions and yearns for answers, and it takes nothing for granted," Robert McCammon, one of the founders of the Horror Writers Association, said in *Twilight Zone Magazine,* as quoted on the association's Web site. "It's not safe, and it probably rots your teeth, too. Horror fiction can be a guide through a nightmare world, entered freely and by the reader's own will. And since horror can be many, many things and go in many, many directions, that guided nightmare ride can shock, educate, illuminate, threaten, shriek, and whisper before it lets the readers loose" (October 1986). It is this questioning and link to nightmare that carves horror a place in the speculative fiction continuum, for it asks "What if" and often relies on ghosts, ghouls, and things that go bump in the night for answers. The following titles feature works in which the fantastic, whether it's magical, ghostly, or paranormal, is central to the novel. Few straight horror novels are published for young adult readers. Subgenres such as slasher horror and psychological thrillers are not included because they lack the supernatural element present in the included subgenres. Only newest works of established adult speculative horror writers are included as a representative of their work.

Paranormal fiction can overlap with horror, sharing the dark ambience, the buildup of fear, and the presence of evil. It also includes novels that center around supernatural and inexplicable events or abilities. Ghost stories can be called paranormal or horror or both. Characters that have ESP can also be in frightening situations. The only paranormal fiction separated from the rest of horror is "Paranormal Powers."

Ghosts

Cultures throughout the world have passed down tales of noncorporeal spirits of the dead. Some of these beings haunt, some attempt to help, some seek release, some revenge. A recent fiction trend features stories related from the spirit's point of view.

Beagle, Peter S.

Tamsin. **New York: Roc, 1999. 275p. Reissued by Firebird in 2004. ISBN: 0142401544pa. [Adult]** *S* **AUD**

Thirteen-year-old Jenny Gluckstein resents it when her mother remarries and moves them from New York to Dorset, England. Jenny's life takes an interesting turn when she discovers that her new home is haunted. First she comes across a boggart, then a ghost cat, and finally Tamsin, a three-hundred-year-old ghost who can reveal dreadful secrets.

Bunting, Eve

The Presence. **New York: Clarion, 2003. 195p. ISBN: 0618269193.** *MJ* **AUD BRAILLE**

Noah, the Presence, is the ghost of a seventeen-year-old, searching for his soul mate. Catherine, also seventeen, encounters him in the churchyard while she is in California visiting her grandmother. To her, Noah appears substantial and offers to help put her in contact with her best friend, who has died in a car accident. Catherine longs to ask her friend's forgiveness, for she feels responsible for the accident, and Noah longs for Catherine. But if she doesn't love him enough, he will have to kill her.

Card, Orson Scott

Homebody. **New York: HarperCollins, 1998. 291p. Reissued in 1999. ISBN: 0061093998pa. [Adult]** *S*

When lonely widower Dan Lark buys the Bellamy house, he plans to restore the Southern mansion to its former glory. The elderly neighbor women beg him to leave the house be, but he carries on. In the midst of renovations, he meets Sylvia. At first he thinks she has just been living in the house illegally. But soon he realizes she doesn't live at the house, she haunts it—and that's not the only strange thing. The house itself takes on a life of its own and lures Dan into a battle that could cost him his life.

Colfer, Eoin

The Wish List. **New York: Miramax Books/Hyperion, 2003. 252p. (1st American Edition.) ISBN: 0786818638; 0439443369pa.** *MJ* **AUD BRAILLE LP** 📖

When Meg makes the mistake of befriending Belch and assisting him in robbing elderly neighbor Lowrie McCall, she dies when a gas tank explodes. She's hurtling toward the afterlife, but her soul is perfectly balanced between good and evil. Saint Peter and Beelzebub strike a deal to send her back to Earth as a spirit so she can tip the balance one way or another. She returns to help Lowrie, who has a wish list of things he'd like to make right before he dies. If Meg can help him, she might just swing the balance the right way.

Collier, James Lincoln

The Empty Mirror. New York: Bloomsbury, 2004. 192p. (1st American Edition.) ISBN: 1582349495; 1582349045pa. *MJ*

Thirteen-year-old orphan Nick Hodges lives with his Uncle Jack in a small coastal New England village in 1931. He has a reputation as a troublemaker, which only gets worse as destructive incidents occur around town. Nick insists on his innocence. Desperate to prove himself, he begins his own investigation, which leads him to the grave of Jared Solters.

Crutcher, Chris

Sledding Hill. New York: Greenwillow Books, 2005. 230p. ISBN: 0060502436. *JS* LP

Even though Billy has died, he still watches over his best friend, Eddie. Eddie, who has also lost his father, is so traumatized that he can't speak and seeks refuge in conservative religion. However, when his minister, who is also his English teacher, begins a campaign to ban a novel in school, Eddie begins a campaign of his own.

Cusick, Richie

The House Next Door. New York: Simon Pulse, 2002. 272p. ISBN: 0743418387pa. *JS*

Emma wants her twin brother, Charlie, to ask her friend, Val, to the winter dance, so she makes a bet with him: If she spends the night in the haunted house next door, he'll go out with Val. At first, she does not believe the house is haunted. All too soon, she becomes entangled in the affairs of a restless spirit, and Charlie and Val must intervene before the fatal finish is reenacted in Emma's life.

Hahn, Mary Downing

The Old Willis Place: A Ghost Story. New York: Clarion, 2004. 199p. ISBN: 0618430180. *M*

Miss Willis died alone in her parlor ten years ago, and no one has lived in the old Willis place since. Caretakers live on the estate, but they don't stay for long. Siblings Diana and George live on the grounds as well, but they are careful never to let anyone see them. Then a new caretaker moves in with his daughter Lissa, and Diana breaks the rules by befriending the lonely girl. When Lissa disregards Diana's warning and ventures into the house, she unwittingly frees a spiteful spirit and reveals that there is more than one ghost on the property.

Ibbotson, Eva

Dial-a-Ghost. New York: Dutton, 2001. 195p. (1st American Edition.) ISBN: 0525466932; 0142500186pa. *M* LP

When Oliver, a young orphan, inherits Helton Hall, his scheming cousins hatch a plot to oust him. They call Dial-A-Ghost and hire two terrifying spirits to scare Oliver to death, but there's been a mix-up at the agency. The terrifying spirits are sent to haunt a convent, and a friendly family of five moves in to Helton Hall.

Jackson, Shirley

The Haunting of Hill House. **New York: Viking, 1959. 246p. Reissued by Lightyear Press in hardcover in 1994. ISBN: 0899684300; 0140071083pa. [Adult]** *S*

While Dr. Montague is investigating the psychic disturbances at Hill House, he invites three people to assist him: Eleanor, who has encountered a poltergeist previously; Theodora, who is psychic; and Luke, the owner's nephew. As bizarre events escalate, the four gain access to the spirit world.

Jenkins, A. M.

Beating Heart: A Ghost Story. **New York: HarperCollins, 2006. 256p. ISBN: 0060546077.** *S*

After their parents divorce, seventeen-year-old Eric and his younger sister Libby move with their mom into a Victorian house that needs a lot of work. Deteriorating rooms are not the only century-old problems in this house, though, for it is haunted by the spirit of a young woman who lures Evan with erotic dreams.

MacPhail, Catherine

Dark Waters. **New York: Bloomsbury, 2003. 175p. (1st American Edition.) ISBN: 1582348464; 158234986Xpa.** *MJS*

Col McCann lives in Scotland with his mother and his older brother. Their father was killed years ago driving a getaway car, and the family still has a shady reputation in town. Col likes to visit the local loch, and two incidents there change his life. First, he saves the life of ten-year-old Dominique. Second, he meets Klaus, who is not as substantial as he seems.

McAllister, Margaret

Ghost at the Window. **New York: Dutton, 2002. 119p. ISBN: 0525468528.** *M*

When twelve-year-old Ewen Dart and his parents move into Ninian House in the Scottish village of Loch Treen, they experience a house like no other. The house has a habit of shifting in time, and each time it does, Ewen can see the ghosts of that time. None of them make contact until Elspeth. Her spirit is trapped, and she needs Ewen's help to set her free.

Naylor, Phyllis Reynolds

Jade Green: A Ghost Story. **New York: Atheneum, 2000. 168p ISBN: 0689820054lb; 068982002Xpa.** *JS* LP

When her mother dies in an insane asylum, fifteen-year-old Judith Sparrow is left an orphan. Her Uncle Geoffrey invites her to live with him and his grown son, Charlie, on the condition that she brings nothing green into the house. Judith agrees but surreptitiously slips in the photograph of her mother in its green, silk frame. This awakens the ghost of Jade Green, who committed suicide with a meat cleaver.

Nixon, Joan Lowery

The Haunting. **New York: Delacorte, 1998. 184p. Reissued by Laurel Leaf in 2000. ISBN: 0440220084pa.** *JS* **BRAILLE LP**

The family estate Graymoss Plantation is haunted, but Lia's mother refuses to believe it. Even though no one has lived there for decades, Lia's mom is determined to move in and adopt a group of orphans who have had no luck finding homes. Fifteen-year-old Lia decides that she will prove to her mother the ghosts are real and face the "terrible, fearful evil" her great-grandmother spoke of.

O'Nan, Stewart

The Night Country. **New York: Farrar, Straus & Giroux, 2003. 229p. ISBN: 0374222150; 0312424078pa. [Adult]** *S* **AUD BRAILLE LP**
One year after three teens, Marco, Toe, and Danielle, died in a car accident on a Halloween night in a Connecticut suburb, their ghosts are drawn back to those remembering the tragedy. Survivor Tim Morgan's guilt sets him on a deadly path, while the spirits of his friends watch.

Reiche, Dietlof

Ghost Ship. **New York: Scholastic Press, 2005. 313p. (1st American Edition.) ISBN: 0439597048.** *M* **AUD**
Twelve-year-old Vicki is working at her father's seaside restaurant in a small New England town when the removal of a ship's figurehead for restoration serves as a catalyst for a series of strange events. First, the sea withdraws from the bay and then the ship itself, the *Storm Goddess,* appears where water once lapped, complete with spirits of the long-dead crew. Vicki teams up with Peter, a tourist her own age, to decipher the clues, which puts them in danger from the curse that haunts the *Storm Goddess.*

Ruby, Laura

Lily's Ghosts. **New York: HarperCollins, 2003. 258p. ISBN: 0060518294; 0060518316pa.** *M* **BRAILLE**
When her mother breaks up with her most recent boyfriend, thirteen-year-old Lily Crabtree resents having to move again, especially to her uncle's eerie summerhouse in Cape May, New Jersey. First of all, there's nothing to do in the wintertime. Second, creepy things keep happening in the house. Her mother thinks Lily is making things up so they won't have to stay, so Lily allies herself with her new friend Vaz to discover who is haunting the house and why.

Soto, Gary

The Afterlife. **Orlando, FL: Harcourt, 2003. 161p. ISBN: 0152047743; 0152052208pa.** *JS* **AUD BRAILLE**
Seventeen-year-old Mexican American Chuy lived in California until he was brutally murdered in the bathroom of a nightclub. Now, in a ghostlike state, he

explores existence in the "afterlife." He longs to reassure his mother, to stop his cousin from seeking revenge, and to live the life that was stolen from him. Soon he meets the spirit of Crystal, a girl who took her own life. Together they must find their way through this new phase of existence.

Stahler, David

A Gathering of Shades. **New York: HarperTempest, 2005. 289p. ISBN: 0060522941.** *JS*
Distraught by his father's sudden death in a car accident, sixteen-year-old Aidan has trouble adjusting to his new life on a farm in Vermont with his grandmother. He follows her for her nightly ritual in the orchard and learns that she can summon ghosts by mixing her blood with water from the nearby spring. Aidan can see the spirits as well as she can and becomes obsessed with the spirit of a boy who runs away every time he spies Aidan.

Straub, Peter

🏵 ***lost boy, lost girl***. **New York: Random House, 2003. 281p. ISBN: 1400060923; 0449149919pa. [Adult]** *S* **AUD LP**
When writer Tim Underhill returns to his hometown for his sister-in-law's funeral, he discovers that his fifteen-year-old nephew, Mark, who had found his mother in the bathtub with her wrists slit, is becoming obsessed with a haunted house. When Mark disappears and rumors circulate about a pedophilic murderer, Tim braves the evil of the house in search of his missing nephew. (Bram Stoker Award)

🏵 ***in the night room***. **New York: Random House, 2004. 330p. ISBN: 1400062527; 0345491327pa. [Adult]** *S* **AUD**
In this sequel to *lost boy, lost girl,* writer Tim Underhill encounters a character from one of his own novels, and the two are pursued by a serial killer.

Wallace, Rich

Restless: A Ghost's Story. **New York: Viking, 2003. 167p. ISBN: 0670036056; 0142403091pa.** *S*
Seventeen-year-old Herbie wants to make varsity in both football and cross-country, and so he runs every night. When he changes his route to include a cemetery, he senses a presence following him. He wishes that it were the spirit of his brother, Frank, who died ten years ago. Frank also would like to contact his brother from the other side. As Herbie trains both his body and his psychic sensitivity, the ghost and teen struggle to find a way to reach each other.

Whitcomb, Laura

🏵 ***A Certain Slant of Light***. **Boston: Graphia, 2005. 282p. ISBN: 061858532Xpa.** *JS* **AUD**
For more than a hundred years, Helen's spirit has latched onto one person after another, until she meets James in Mr. Brown's English class. James, the spirit of a soldier, dwells in the body of Billy, a student whose body lives but whose spirit has died. Love flares between the two ghosts, and James teaches Helen how to inhabit the body

of Jenny, a girl whose fundamentalist Christian parents have beaten the soul out of their daughter. The two spirits explore their newfound sexuality as they learn the skills they need to live in the contemporary world.

Zevin, Gabrielle

🔖 *Elsewhere*. **New York: Farrar, Straus & Giroux, 2005. 275p. ISBN: 0374320918.** *JS* **AUD** 📖
Killed in a car accident on the way to the mall, fifteen-year-old Lizzie ends up in Elsewhere. Although she longs to move forward, get her license, go to the prom, and fall in love, she now lives backward, growing younger year by year until she will be reborn on Earth. She meets the grandmother she never knew, who is now in her thirties, and gradually adjusts to her new existence and the surprises it holds for her. (BBYA)

Vampires

As with ghost stories, many cultures have tales of bloodsucking creatures of different varieties, from spirits to spiders. The richest traditions can be found in the stories of Eastern Europeans, many of which inspired Bram Stoker when he wrote *Dracula*. The most familiar vampires are undead beings that need living human blood to survive, are animated only at night, and who require a stake through the heart to be set to rest. The modern permutations of vampire fiction embrace not only the traditional but also the humorous and the romantic as well. Teens can identify with creatures that live on the fringes of society and are intrigued by the dark and different world they represent.

Anderson, M. T.

Thirsty. **Cambridge, MA: Candlewick Press, 1997. 249p. Reissued in 2005. ISBN: 076362750Xpa.** *JS* 📖
As if dealing with his bickering parents and bullying older brother aren't enough, Chad is afraid that he is turning into a vampire. These supernatural beings have always been a part of life in his small Massachusetts hometown. When the local police encounter a vampire, they ordinarily drive a stake through its heart. At the annual picnic, the townspeople perform a ritual blood sacrifice to keep the Vampire Lord, Tch'muchgar, trapped in a different plane of existence. While Chad fights his transformation, he is approached by Chet, who claims to be from the Forces of Light. Chet wants Chad to disrupt the ritual, but Chad, desperate to hold onto his humanity, is not sure whom he can trust.

Atwater-Rhodes, Amelia

In the Forests of the Night. **New York: Delacorte, 1999. Reissued by Laurel Leaf in 2000. ISBN: 0440228166pa.** *JS* **LP**
Risika, a vampire, remembers her life three hundred years ago, when she was Rachel Weatere, fighting to keep her psychic twin brother safe from evil.

Now, although powerful and damned, she still struggles with what she has become and seeks to destroy the vampires who transformed her and murdered her brother.

Demon in My View*. New York: Delacorte, 2000. 176p. Reissued by Laurel Leaf in 2001. ISBN: 0440228840pa. *JS
High school senior Jessica has just published her first novel. She thinks that her story of witches and vampires springs up through her imaginative subconscious, but those creatures are quite real. While the witches strive to protect her, the vampires try to stop her any way they can.

Shattered Mirror*. New York: Delacorte, 2001. 227p. ISBN: 0385327935; 0440229405pa. *JS
Sarah, a vampire hunter, begins her senior year of high school on the lookout for infamous twin vampires Nikolas and Kaleo. When Christopher begins to woo her at school, she suspects that he is a vampire, but she is so charmed by him that she does not want to destroy him. Fearing Sarah will let her emotions lead her to the wrong decision, her mother binds her powers, placing her in grave danger.

Midnight Predator*. New York: Delacorte, 2002. 248p. ISBN: 0385327943; 0440237971pa. *JS
Once Turquoise Draka escaped from vampire slavery, she became a vampire hunter. Now she has been hired to kill Jeshickah, who vies for control of Midnight, a supernatural domain for rest and relaxation. Joined by Ravyn, another vampire hunter, the two go undercover as slaves, risking their lives in the process.

Conrad, Liza

The Lucy Chronicles. New York: New American Library. *JS*
Lucy thinks she's an average high school sophomore in Seattle until her father gives her an extraordinary diary on her sixteenth birthday.

> ***High School Bites*. 2006. 228p. ISBN: 0451217527pa.**
> Lucy worries about ordinary things like prying teachers and getting a boyfriends until she discovers, through the diary from her father, that she is descended from the Lucy in Bram Stoker's *Dracula,* and it is her destiny to do battle with vampires.

Davidson, Mary Janice

The Betsy Taylor Series. New York: Berkley Sensation. [Adult] *S* LP
Things look grim for Betsy Taylor when she loses her job and then dies in a car accident, but they become grimmer yet, for she can't stay dead. Instead, she's transformed into a vampire, and, while one group of vampires wants to destroy her, another is convinced that she is the prophesied Queen of the Vampires.

> ***Undead and Unwed*. 2004. 277p. ISBN: 042519485Xpa. AUD**

> ***Undead and Unemployed*. 2004. 294p. ISBN: 0425197484pa.**

> ***Undead and Unappreciated*. 2005. 217p. ISBN: 0425204332; 0425207226pa. AUD**

> ***Undead and Unreturnable*. 2005. 250p. ISBN: 0425208168; 0425210812pa. AUD**

Undead and Unpopular. 2006. ISBN: 0425210294.

De la Cruz, Melissa

Blue Bloods. **New York: Hyperion, 2006. 320p. ISBN: 0786838922.**
Four teens, Schuyler, Mimi, Bliss, and Jack, attend an exclusive private school in Manhattan. While enjoying the lives of young jet-setters, they also come to discover that they are "Blue Bloods"—vampires who came to America on the *Mayflower*. They are old souls that return to new bodies when their previous ones no longer function, only they don't recall being vampires until adolescence. Usually, they consider themselves immortal, but someone is killing them, and it's up to Schuyler to uncover the murderer.

Hahn, Mary Downing

Look for Me by Moonlight. **New York: Clarion, 1995. ISBN: 039569843X.**
M,J
Sixteen-year-old Cynda adamantly refuses to accompany her mother and stepfather to Italy and winds up moving into the Maine inn that her father has just purchased. Unsure of where she fits in with her father's new family, Cynda is quickly captivated by their charming guest, Vincent. But Vincent is not what he seems to be. When he endangers the life of Cynda's half-brother, she must find a way to defeat him.

Harris, Charlaine

The Sookie Stackhouse Series. New York: Ace. [Adult] *S*
Sookie Stackhouse serves cocktails in a bar in small-town Louisiana, but her life changes dramatically when her new boyfriend turns out to be a vampire.

Dead until Dark. 2001. 260p. ISBN: 0441008534pa.

Living Dead in Dallas. 2002. 262p. ISBN: 0441009239pa. LP

Club Dead. 2003. 258p. ISBN: 0441010512pa. LP

Dead to the World. 2004. 291p. ISBN: 0441011675; 0441012183pa.

Dead as a Doornail. 2005. 295p. ISBN: 0441012795; 0441013333pa. AUD LP

Hendee, Barb, and J. C. Hendee

The Noble Dead Saga. New York: Roc. [Adult] *S*
Magiere earns a living slaying vampires—or that's what she tells the simple villagers who believe in superstitions. When she and her half-elven partner decide to opt for the peaceful life, they discover that the forces of evil have heard of their reputation as well.

Dhampir. 2003. 375p. ISBN: 0451459067pa.

Thief of Lives. 2004. 410p. ISBN: 0451459539pa.

Sister of the Dead. 2005. 405p. ISBN: 045146009Xpa.

Traitor to the Blood. 2006. 355p. ISBN: 0451460669.

Huff, Tanya

The Victoria Nelson Series. New York: Daw. [Adult] _S_
Vicki Nelson once served as a homicide detective for the Toronto police department, but now she's a private investigator solving crimes with Henry Fitzroy, a 450-year-old vampire who's learned to meet his need for blood without killing.

Blood Price. 1991. 272p. ISBN: 0886774713pa.

Blood Trail. 1992. 304p. ISBN: 0886775027pa.

Blood Lines. 1993. 271p. ISBN: 0886775302pa.

Blood Pact. 1993. 332p. ISBN: 0886775825pa.

Blood Debt. 1997. 336p. ISBN: 0886777399pa.

Klause, Annette Curtis

🕴 *Silver Kiss.* **New York: Delacorte, 1990. 198p. Reissued by Laurel Leaf in 1992. ISBN: 0440213460pa.** _JS_ **BRAILLE** 📖
Seventeen-year-old Zoe is doing everything she can to cope with her overwhelming problems: Her mother is in the hospital with cancer, her father doesn't believe Zoe's strong enough to handle her mother's illness, and her best friend is moving away. Amid this turmoil emerges Simon, a strikingly handsome young man who reaches out to Zoe before revealing his true identity. (BBYA)

Kostova, Elizabeth

The Historian. **New York: Little, Brown, 2005. 642p. ISBN: 0316011770. [Adult]** _S_ **AUD LP**
When Paul's sixteen-year-old daughter finds the papers from his student days at Oxford and insists that he explain, he's loath to reveal that they trace the true history of Vlad Dracul because he fears for her safety. Then Paul disappears, and his daughter sets out to find him and unravel the mystery of Vlad the Impaler.

McKinley, Robin

Sunshine. **New York: Berkley Books, 2003. 389p. ISBN: 0425191788; 0515138819pa. [Adult]** _S_
In a world where it's not uncommon to encounter werewolves, sprites, demons, and fallen angels, Sunshine, the daughter of a sorcerer, works in her stepfather's coffee shop making cinnamon buns until she is kidnapped by a troop of vampires who leave her as a sacrifice for Constantine. Instead of draining her blood, Constantine spends the night conversing with her. As they talk, she becomes determined to find a way to save them both.

Meyer, Stephenie

Twilight. **New York: Little, Brown, 2005. 498p. ISBN: 0316160172.** *S* **AUD**

At seventeen, Isabella Swan exchanges life with her mom in sunny Phoenix for time with her dad in rainy Forks, Washington. She's expecting small-town life to be on the dull side, but she doesn't expect to fall head over heels in love with her lab partner, Edward Cullen, whose dark secret draws them ever closer together and puts Bella's life in danger.

New Moon. **New York: Little, Brown. 2006. 576p. ISBN: 0316160199.**

On her eighteenth birthday Bella's boyfriend, the dashing vampire Edward Cullen brings her to his family home for a celebration. Things go awry, however, when Bella gets cut and her blood drives the family wild. To keep her safe, they leave town, which propels Bella into a deep depression. Only her friend Jacob helps take her mind off her troubles, but it turns out that he has hidden supernatural tendencies of his own.

Rees, Douglas

Vampire High. **New York: Delacorte, 2003. 226p. ISBN: 0385731175; 044023834Xpa.** *MJ* **BRAILLE** 📖

Cody is so annoyed with his parents for moving the family from California to New Sodom, Massachusetts, that he blows off his high school courses. When his father sees his grades, he gives Cody two choices: Our Lady of Perpetual Homework or Vlad Dracul Magnate School. Cody opts for the latter, but it doesn't take him long to realize this is like no school he's ever been to before. The students are almost all vampires, or "jenti." He is considered a "gadje," whom they tolerate because the school must have a water polo team to meet the state curriculum requirements—and vampires can't swim. When Cody defends a jenti who is being bullied, the two gradually become friends, and Cody decides to leave his own mark on the vampire world.

Rice, Anne

<u>The Vampire Chronicles</u>. New York: Knopf. [Adult] *S*

The famed vampire Lestat makes an impact throughout the ages. He is seen by his enemies in the vampire world as the epitome of wickedness and by others as a figure of romance.

Interview with the Vampire. **1976. 371p. ISBN: 0394498216; 0345337662pa. AUD VID**

The Vampire Lestat. **1985. 480p. ISBN: 0394534433; 0345419642pa. AUD GN**

The Queen of the Damned. **1988. 448p. ISBN: 0394558235; 0345351525pa. AUD**

The Tale of the Body Thief. **1992. 430p. ISBN: 0679405283; 034538475Xpa. AUD**

Memnoch the Devil. 1995. 353p. ISBN: 0679441018; 0345409671pa.

The Vampire Armand. 1998. 457p. ISBN: 0679454470; 0345434803pa. **AUD LP**

Merrick. 2000. 307p. ISBN: 0679454489; 0345422406pa. **AUD LP**

Blood and Gold, or, The Story of Marius. 2001. 471p. ISBN: 0679454497; 0345409329pa. **AUD LP**

Blackwood Farm. 2002. 527p. ISBN: 0375411992; 0345443683pa. **AUD**

Blood Canticle. 2003. 305p. ISBN: 037541200X; 0345443691pa. **AUD LP**

Shan, Darren

<u>**Cirque du Freak.**</u> **Boston: Little, Brown. (1st American Editions.)** <u>**MJ**</u>
Darren Shan's invitation to a freak show plunges him into the gruesome world of vampires.

A Living Nightmare. 2001. 266p. ISBN: 0316603406; 0316905712pa. **LP**
Darren and his best friend, Steve, attend an illicit freak show, where Darren is fascinated by vampire Mr. Crepsley and his deadly spider, Madam Octa. When the poisonous spider bites Steve, Darren does the only thing he can think of to save him: He volunteers to become the vampire's assistant.

The Vampire's Assistant. 2001. 247p. ISBN: 0316606103; 0316905720pa. **LP**
Transformed into a half-vampire by Mr. Crepsley, Darren now lives at the Cirque du Freak in perpetual servitude to his vampire master. Although he needs blood to survive, he steadfastly refuses to drink human blood. He makes new friends as he struggles to hold onto his humanity, but death lurks just around the corner.

Tunnels of Blood. 2002. 229p. ISBN: 0316607630; 0316905739pa.
When Darren, his mentor, and Evra the snake-boy leave the Cirque du Freak and journey to the city, the two boys at first enjoy their time away. But when six bodies are discovered drained of blood, Darren is afraid Mr. Crepsley is the guilty vampire.

Vampire Mountain. 2002. 199p. ISBN: 0316608068; 0316605425pa.
Darren and Mr. Crepsley embark on a dangerous journey to the heart of the vampire realm, so that Darren can be presented to the vampire council in the Hall of the Vampires, where a dire prophesy awaits him.

Trials of Death. 2003. 207p. ISBN: 0316603678; 0316603953pa.
Darren agrees to undergo the Trials of Death to bond with his vampire clan, but the penalty for failure is death. When Darren is on the brink of just such a failure, his friends whisk him away. Instead of finding safety, they run into an invading army.

The Vampire Prince. 2003. 197p. ISBN: 0316607096; 0316000973pa.
Although he almost drowned, Darren recovers enough to race back to Vampire Mountain and warn the vampire clan of the coming invasion. His timely notice gives his vampire friends a chance in the coming battle.

Hunters of the Dusk. 2004. 213p. ISBN: 0316605964; 0316602116pa.
Darren, now a vampire prince, leads his people in their fight against the Vampaneze, who want to destroy all vampires. When Darren, Larten Crepsley, and Vampire Prince Vancha March embark on a search for a way to kill the Lord of the Vampaneze, it leads them back to the Cirque du Freak, where the Lady Evanna shares a dark prophesy about Darren.

Allies of the Night. 2004. 215p. ISBN: 0316155705; 0316114375pa.
Vampire Prince Darren spends all his time hunting Vampaneze until someone inexplicably registers him for school, and he is forced to attend. Although he is an adult, he looks like he's fifteen. He agrees so that he can investigate the being behind the educational reinstatement and finds his lost love, Debbie. Things do not go well for either, as all around them people turn up dead.

Killers of the Dawn. 2005. 208p. ISBN: 0316156264; 0316106542pa.
The Vampaneze relentlessly batter the vampires in their ongoing war for dominance in the bloodsucking world, as Darren and his cadre of warrior-vampires battle back to keep them at bay.

The Lake of Souls. 2005. 292p. ISBN: 0316156272.
To help his vampire clan, Darren embarks on a journey to the Lake of Souls, where the bodies of the dead await.

Lord of the Shadows. 2006. 240p. ISBN: 0316156280.
Darren returns to his home town but cannot escape the manipulations of Vampaneze Lord, Steve Leopard. Steve stages a fight between the two of them and the outcome will decide the fate of the vampire world.

Simmons, Dan

🎗 *Children of the Night*. Northridge, CA: Lord John Press, 1992. 320p. Reissued in 1993 by Warner. ISBN: 0446364754pa. [Adult] *S*
In Romania, during the dictatorship of Ceausescu, the orphanages filled up with children so that Vlad Dracula and his fellow vampires always had a blood supply. Now Dracula wants to pass his title to the infant Joshua. But Joshua has been adopted by hematologist Kate Newman, who has been studying him in the United States. She believes his blood holds the key to curing AIDS, cancer, and who knows what else. Before she can figure out how, Joshua is kidnapped and returned to Romania. Without regard for her own safety, Kate does everything she can to rescue him. (Locus Award)

Stoker, Bram

Dracula. New York: Doubleday, 1899. (1st American Edition.) Reissued by Bed Book Classics in hardcover in 2005. ISBN: 1933652357; 0743477367pa. [Adult] *S* AUD BRAILLE LP VID
Englishman Jonathan Harker travels to Transylvania to engage in a real estate deal with nobleman Count Dracula. Although the villagers warn him about the count, he takes no notice and initially is charmed by his host. When the count's three vampire females seductively attack, Harker realizes he's in trou-

ble. Although a virtual prisoner in the castle, he escapes by climbing over the outer wall. He reunites with his fiancée Mina, and they wed. When they return to England, they find that Count Dracula has made his presence known there, and they are determined to stop him.

Vande Velde, Vivian

🏅 *Companions of the Night.* **San Diego: Harcourt Brace, 1995. 212p. ISBN: 0152002219; 0152166696pa.** *JS*

Sixteen-year-old Kerry is taken by surprise when townspeople of Brockport, New York, accuse handsome Ethan of being a vampire. When she defends him, they accuse her of being a vampire as well. On the run, the two young people turn to each other for support. But when Kerry's father and brother are kidnapped, Kerry knows she must do whatever she can to save them. (BBYA)

Profile of Scott Westerfeld

Married to fellow author Justine Larbalestier, Scott Westerfeld divides his time between living in New York City and Sydney, Australia. Although he started his career writing science fiction for adults, he has become quite popular with his books for young adults, most notably the unrelated trilogies *Uglies* and *Midnighters* (*Contemporary Authors Online*, Infotrac Galegroup Database; www.scottwesterfeld.com).

Photo: Samantha Jones

Interview with Scott Westerfeld

Conducted via e-mail February 7–22, 2006

SF: Your first books were science fiction novels for adults. What made you start writing for young adults? Do you have a preference?

SW: I got the idea for *Midnighters,* and it was so obviously a YA idea—staying up late is inherently cool if you're young—that I had to do it in that context.

Writing YA is much better:

1. There are more "champions" for kids' books (school librarians, teachers, reading specialists, etc.), which means that a good book is more likely to stay on the shelves and has more time to find its audience.

2. You don't get stuck in one genre. Kids who read voraciously consume sf, fantasy, contemporary realism, autobiographies, books about sharks.. . . Adults are more likely to demand that a writer's books be

all pretty much the same. YA, though, already has its own shelf, so your fantasy and sf is all there together.

3.   Kids' librarians are the coolest people in the world. I don't know why this is; it just is.

4.   More fan mail with more exclamation points!!!

SF: You've written both science fiction and dark fantasy. Do you have a preference as to which genre you write in and why?

SW: I think I'm more of a natural at sf. Even *Midnighters* has sf-nal [science fiction-supernatural] elements, like the careful working out of times zones and such. Both genres employ rule-governed world-building, but I like building outward from the rules of sf (i.e., those of science) better, I suppose.

The whole narrative of *Peeps* comes out of the nooks and crannies of parasitology, which is a field that's changing every day and is fascinating, mind-bending, and really, really, gross. And yet utterly relevant to who we are as a species (believe it or not). Having that explosion of knowledge going on while I'm writing is really inspiring.

SF: In the world of young adult literature, there are many more works of fantasy published than works of science fiction, especially since the popularity of Harry Potter, but it was so even before Harry Potter. Why do you think that is the case?

SW: I think in young readers' literature, fantasy is less marked as a genre. That is, like magical realism with adults, it's not as ghettoized. People have realized that "fantasy" can be anything: aimed at boys, at girls, dark, funny, adventure, thoughtful and literary, more or less realistic, whatever—most of the classics are fantasy, after all. But many readers' experience with sf is only the blockbuster Hollywood version, which gives the impression that sf is a boys' action genre of limited scope.

That's why I'm glad that *Uglies* has become a big crossover hit with girls. I get so many fan mails saying, "I thought sf was just *Star Trek* novelizations, but your books actually MEAN something." So I write them back with other good sf books to read.

SF: Do you think that there are things that science fiction does better than fantasy and that fantasy does better than science fiction? If so, in what way?

SW: I think the main difference is that sf is a bit more "democratic." What I mean by that is, if you invent a new technology in a book, everyone in that world can use it. A light switch doesn't care if you're the seventh daughter of the seventh daughter, or pure of heart, or the son of Uther Pendragon. You don't have to be "the one"; you can be anyone.

As a result sf is generally better for looking at the effects of change on society at large, which is what a book like UGLIES is trying to do. Fantasy tends to focus more on how [things] in one character's life (or a small group's dynamics) are transformed by some totally uncanny event. Obviously, that's a gross simplification, but it's not entirely untrue.

SF: *Peeps* and *Uglies* are both on YALSA's 2006 list of Best Books for Young Adults. How does it feel to have the quality of your work recognized in this way?

SW: Well, obviously it's a wonderful honor. I'm particularly glad to see them both recognized because they're such different books: *Uglies* is younger, more straightforwardly allegorical and topical. Whereas *Peeps* is older, weirder, and completely invested in science. It shows that the teachers and librarians of the committee (like teens themselves) are excited by a wide variety of ideas and style. (Which you can tell from the rest of the list as well.)

SF: What kind of research do you do for your books?

SW: Usually, 90 percent of the research is done before I start. That is, I read a lot of scientific journals and random weird news and wait for it to clump together into something useable in my brain. I guess the exception to that would be *Peeps,* where I was researching parasites simultaneously with writing, and the plot kept turning to take in another scientific discovery.

SF: What would you say your method of writing is (i.e., working from an outline, going where the story takes you, etc.)?

SW: It depends on the book. *Uglies* was sold with a very long and specific outline, which I stuck very close to. That's the kind of series it is: lots of betrayals, reversals, and complications, which need an outline to work. With the Midnighters series, I've found that the five characters bounce off each other a lot, generating their own heat, so I don't have to worry about the plotting as much. I hardly outline them at all, just set up one big conflict, then throw the characters in and let their battling egos keep the ball rolling. *Peeps* was written alongside Carl Zimmer's wonderful book *Parasite Rex,* which is nonfiction but served as a sort of weird meta-outline.

SF: Of your books, which are your favorite books and/or characters and why?

SW: Argh. Right now my current book *The Last Days,* a companion novel to *Peeps,* is my favorite. But that's always the way: the youngest child is favored. But overall I think *So Yesterday* was the easiest and most fulfilling novel to write, because I was channeling my own seventeen-year-old self. Plus I love Dess from *Midnighters* and Tally from *Uglies,* although she drives me insane.

SF: What were your favorite books/authors when you were growing up?

SW: I read lots of short stories in sf magazines, and Roger Zelazny (especially the Amber books). When very young, I was addicted to the *Freddy the Pig* series, which I think has faded into oblivion. It was *Animal Farm* with no politics.

SF: What do you think is the merit or importance of reading science fiction and fantasy?

SW: Any time a book transports you into a truly different world, you look up from it realizing that the world around you could be different. I think that kids who understand that simple fact are more likely to deal with the rapid-fire changes happening around them every day and make positive changes to the world themselves.

As a kid, SF novels were the first places I really comprehended environmental concerns, racial and gender issues, and a whole raft of other stuff. (Mind you, fantasy can do this as well.)

Westerfeld, Scott

🔖 *Peeps*. New York: Razorbill, 2005. 312p. ISBN: 159514031X. *S* 📖
Nineteen-year-old Cal moves from Texas to New York City where he not only loses his virginity but also becomes a vampire by contracting "peeps," which is what they call people who are "parasite positive." The parasite enables him to see in the dark and have superhuman strength; it also gives him a constant hunger for protein. Most infected people become bloodthirsty cannibals, so Cal joins the secret government agency Night Watch to hunt down the more dangerous of his kind. (BBYA)

Werewolves

Werewolves are creatures that spring from mythic origins and are beings that can shift from human to wolf. In some traditions, this is under the influence of the full moon; in others it is caused by a curse and can be permanent. While werewolf characters can be one of an ensemble of mythic creatures such as Remus Lupin in the <u>Harry Potter</u> novels, the titles listed here are works that feature these particular shape-shifters.

Borchardt, Alice

<u>**The Wolf Trilogy**</u>. **New York: Ballantine. [Adult]** *S*
In the days of Charlemagne, a distant cousin to the emperor, Regeane, has more than royal blood flowing in her veins, for her murdered father was a

werewolf. In Rome, as Caesar nears the fateful Ides of March, another werewolf, Maeniel, lurks. When Regeane and Maeniel's paths cross, they change history.

The Silver Wolf. 1998. 451p. Reissued in 1999. ISBN: 0345423615pa.

Night of the Wolf. 2000. 512p. Issued in paperback in 2000. ISBN: 0345423631pa.

The Wolf King. 2001. 375p. Issued in paperback in 2001. ISBN: 0345423658pa.

De Lint, Charles

Wolf Moon. New York: Signet, 1988. Reissued by Firebird in 2004. 245p. ISBN: 0142400777pa. *MJS*
Kern can shape-shift from man to wolf, but when his ability manifests itself, his parents chase him away with silver daggers. Although he does not kill except in self-defense, he is constantly on the run, afraid to reveal his secret. At the Inn of the Yellow Tinker, he meets both the love of his life and his most dangerous enemy.

Dunkle, Clare B.

By These Ten Bones. New York: Henry Holt, 2005. 229p. ISBN: 0805074961. *MJ*
Maddie, who lives in a quiet Scottish village, is fascinated by the mute woodcarver, Paul, who comes to town with his friend, Ned. When Paul is wounded, the villagers believe he fought off a vicious attack. Maddie suspects a dark curse hangs over him and learns that only a human sacrifice can save him.

Jennings, Patrick

The Wolving Time. New York: Scholastic, 2003. 197p. ISBN: 0439395550; 0439395569pa. *MJ*
Laszlo herds sheep with his parents outside a small village in the French Pyrenees near the end of the 1600s. He and his family are not ordinary shepherds, however; they're werewolves, or at least his parents are. Laszlo will be as soon as he comes of age. When Muno, a village girl whose parents were killed as witches, witnesses his mother shape-shifting, he and his family must flee for their lives.

Klause, Annette Curtis

🌸 *Blood and Chocolate*. New York: Delacorte, 1997. 246p. Reissued by Laurel Leaf in 1999. ISBN: 0440226686pa. *JS* AUD BRAILLE 📖
Vivian, a young werewolf who is also a high school student, is grieving for her father, who was her pack leader as well. He died in a fire, and now the pack must move. Vivian begins at a new school and is quickly drawn to Aiden, even though her mother warns her about being involved with humans. Vivian is sure that Aiden will love her for herself and plans to reveal her true nature to him. At the same time, the pack must choose a new leader. The foremost candidate is drawn by Vivian's maturing sexuality and wants her to be his queen. (BBYA)

Myriad Creatures of Darkness

While vampires dominate teen fiction and werewolves occasionally claim some of the territory, other creatures of darkness have infiltrated novels favored by young adult readers. These creatures range from beings of legend to complete constructs of the darker hemisphere of imagination.

Bruchac, Joseph

The Dark Pond. **New York: HarperCollins, 2004. 142p. ISBN: 0060529954; 0060529989pa. *M* AUD BRAILLE**
Armin Katchatorian, part Shawnee, part Armenian, lives at a prep school in the Adirondacks. Shy with people, Armin feels a special closeness to animals and loves to hike in the mountains, until something perilous in the dark pond draws him to it. Investigating Native American myths at the library, he finds that both Iroquois and Abenakis had legends of underwater monsters, and he fears that he and a fellow Native American, Mitch Sabattis, may have to confront whatever lurks in the water.

Whisper in the Dark. **New York: HarperCollins, 2005. 174p. ISBN: 0060580879. *MJ***
After the sudden death of her parents in a car accident, thirteen-year-old Maddy, who is half Narragansett Indian, moves to Providence, Rhode Island, to live with her Aunt Lyssa. She'd always loved spooky stories, but now she fears that a creature from those tales, a demon-possessed lunatic with knives for fingers, is after her. First there are the mysterious hang-ups on the phone. Then her dog is attacked, and her aunt is missing. With her best friend, Roger, Maddy decides to stop running and face the creature of nightmare.

Gaiman, Neil

🏅 *Coraline*. **New York: HarperCollins, 2002. 162p. ISBN: 0380977788; 0380807343pa. *MJ* AUD BRAILLE LP** 📖
When Coraline moves to a new house with her parents, who don't pay very much attention to her, she discovers a locked door that supposedly connects to a part of the house her family does not own. She finds the key and opens the door, but its hallway leads to another world, where her "other mother" and her "other father" greet her warmly. They are just like her real parents, only nicer, except that they have black button eyes. Wanting Coraline to stay with them, they attempt to persuade her to let them replace her eyes with black buttons as well. When Coraline refuses and returns home, her parents are missing, and Coraline knows she must go back to the other world to rescue them. (ALAN; BBYA; Bram Stoker Award for Work for Young Readers; Hugo Award for Best Novella; Locus Award; Nebula Award)

Horowitz, Anthony

The Gatekeepers Series. *JS*
The prophecy foretells that there will be five needed to fight against the evil Old Ones and keep them from entering the world through the mysterious gates.

Raven's Gate. New York: Scholastic, 2005. 254p. ISBN: 0439679958. AUD LP
Matt Freeman's part in a robbery during which a man was stabbed leaves him with only two choices: juvenile detention or probation on Hive Hill farm. He opts for Hive Hill, but when he arrives at the farm, shrouded in the English country-side just outside of York, his life is anything but peaceful. First he gets sick. Then his guardian sets him to work mucking out the pig pen and chopping wood. He decides to return to London, but when he tries, every road leads back to Hive Hall. When someone tries to help him, Matt finds him murdered, but his body has disappeared by the time he brings the police. As strange occurrences continue, Matt realizes he must try to escape the evil that has the town in its grip, but each adult he turns to ends up dead.

Evil Star. New York: Scholastic, 2006. 320p. ISBN: 0439679966.
Matt, thrilled with his victory in *Raven's Gate*, and Richard, the reporter with whom he's been staying, are sent by the Nexus to Peru with dire warnings about the opening of a second gate. They team up with, Pedro, and the race to the Nazcan desert to prevent the Old Ones from attempting to open another gate.

King, Stephen

Cell. New York: Scribner, 2006. 384p. ISBN: 0743292332. [Adult] *S* AUD LP
When a strange pulse zaps everyone who is talking on a cell phone, it turns them all into zombies. Although those who were not on the phone escape that evil fate, they now must find a way to defeat the blood-thirsty monsters out to destroy the world of the living.

Martinez, A. Lee

🔖 *Gil's All Fright Diner*. New York: Tor, 2005. 268p. Issued in paperback in 2005. ISBN: 0765314711pa. [Adult] *S*
When Duke and Earl stop for a quick snack at Gil's All Night Diner, they discover that zombies regularly attack the eatery. They agree to help Loretta, the diner's cook, repel the undead invaders. Since Duke is the Duke of the Werewolves and Earl is the Earl of the Vampires, they have little difficulty dispatching the zombies, but they decide to stick around and unearth the source of the monster attacks. (Alex; BBYA)

Pullman, Philip

Count Karlstein. New York: Knopf, 1998. 243p. (1st American Edition.) ISBN: 0679892559; 0375803483pa. *MJ* AUD
In 1816, in a mountain village in Switzerland, Count Karlstein plots to fulfill his oath to Zamiel, the Demon Huntsman, by sacrificing his two nieces, Charlotte and Lucy, who have come to stay with him. Only the fourteen-year-old maidservant, Hildi, and

their English tutor, Miss August Davenport, have any hope of thwarting his nefarious scheme.

Shusterman, Neal

Full Tilt. New York: Simon & Schuster, 2003. 201p. ISBN: 068980374511b; 0689873255pa. *JS* LP

Sixteen-year-old Blake is responsible and cautious, while his thirteen-year-old brother is wild and self-destructive. When they are lured to a phantom carnival by the demonic Cassandra, they discover they must survive seven supernatural rides before they can win their freedom.

The Dark Fusion Series. New York, Dutton. *MJ*

This series twists together myths, monsters, and contemporary horrors to create contemporary tales.

Dread Locks. 2005. 164p. ISBN: 0525475540; 014240599Xpa.

Rich and bored, fourteen-year-old Parker Baer's life changes when his new neighbor, Tara, arrives. Tara always wears mirror sunglasses and has blond hair filled with unusual spirals. Parker first is drawn to her and then repelled as he realizes that the people in her life develop odd cravings, turn grey as they are petrified like wood, and then die. When his brother and sister become her latest victims, Parker knows he must do whatever it takes to stop her.

Red Rider's Hood. 2005. 182p. ISBN: 0525475621; 0142406783pa.

Red drives his red Mustang to Grandma's, only to find she's been thrown in the basement by the gang members of the Wolves, who are there to rob her. To learn their weaknesses, Red joins the gang and feels the same powerful pull they do during the full moon.

Duckling Ugly. 2006. 224p. ISBN: 0525475850.

Cara De Fido, who lives in the town of Flock's Rest, is so horrifying to look at that her face shatters mirrors and camera lens alike. Her snide classmates call her the "Flock's Rest Monster," and she has been miserable her entire life. When a message lures her into the hills during a storm, she makes her way to a beautiful valley, where she is allowed to drink from the Fountain of Youth. Transformed into a beauty, she longs to go back to Flock's Rest, but she is not prepared for the sacrifice her beauty demands.

Simmons, Dan

🌱 *Summer of Night*. New York: Putnam, 1991. 555p. Reissued by Warner in 1992. ISBN: 0446362662pa. [Adult] *S*

In the summer of 1960, in the Old Central School of Elm Haven, Illinois, a centuries-old evil is devouring students, while the adults of the community ignore its presence. So sixth-graders Mike, Duane, Dale, Harlen, and Kevin face the menace alone. (Locus Award)

A Winter Haunting. **New York: Morrow, 2002. 303p. Reissued by Harper Torch in 2003. ISBN: 0380817160pa. [Adult]** *S*
Forty-one years after Dale Stewart survived the frightening events of the summer of 1960, he returns to his hometown for his winter sabbatical to stay in the house of his friend Duane, who died that summer. His life is a wreck, his marriage is in shambles, and he is taking drugs for suicidal depression. His return to the scene of the trauma doesn't help, as whispers of the old evil begin to haunt him once again.

Sleator, William

The Boy Who Couldn't Die. **New York: Amulet Books, 2004. 162p. ISBN: 0810948249; 0810987902pa.** *JS*
When his best friend Roger dies in a plane crash, sixteen-year-old Ken is devastated and becomes obsessed with avoiding death himself. To that end, he pays Cheri Buttercup for a voodoo spell that will give him immortality by storing his soul in a safe place away from his body. First he proves to himself that he is indeed safe by surviving various dangerous activities. Then the nightmares of murdered people show him that his soul is being misused, and he must get it back to stop the slaughter.

Stahler, David

Doppelganger. **New York: HarperCollins, 2006. 272p. ISBN: 0060872322.** *JS*
A doppelganger by nature is a creature that kills and then inhabits its victim. When this doppelganger kills his first human, Chris, he takes over his life and finds himself a high school football hero with dark secrets.

Westerfeld, Scott

<u>**The Midnighters Trilogy**</u>. **New York: Eos.** *JS*
In Bixby, Oklahoma, anyone born exactly at the stroke of midnight lives through the Blue Time, the twenty-fifth hour of the day, when time is frozen and the "darklings" roam free. For friends Melissa, Rex, and Dess, it's the only time they can be themselves and use their powers. But when Jessica arrives, the darklings grow more dangerous, and the midnight hour will never be the same.

The Secret Hour. **2004. 297p. ISBN: 0060519517; 0060519533pa.**
When Jessica Day moves with her family to Bixby, Oklahoma, she's worried about starting in a new high school, making friends, and missing the people she left back home. What she should worry about is how to fight the "darklings," for she discovers she is a Midnighter, who can live through the secret twenty-fifth hour of the day. While it's a time of freedom for Bixby natives Melissa, Rex, and Dess, it's a time of peril for Jessica, as more and more darklings and "slithers" attack her. If Midnighters don't join together to fight the creatures, none of them may survive.

Touching Darkness. **2005. 330p. ISBN: 0060519541; 0060519568pa.**
As Jess learns to navigate her new power, she and Jonathan have a romantic rendezvous in the Blue Hour. Meanwhile, Rex learns that there have been Midnighters in Bixby in other times. When he is taken over by a darkling, the other four must use their special skills to save him.

***Blue Noon*. 2006. 378p. ISBN: 0060519576.**
Although the dangers of the Blue Hour have increased since Jess came to town, when the Blue Hour occurs has always been predictable—until now. Now it can happen in the middle of the day. Worse than that, it's fracturing. The Midnighters must find a way to stop it, or the darklings and the slithers will be free to devour any in their path.

Wooding, Chris

🔥 ***The Haunting of Alaizabel Cray*. New York: Scholastic Press, 2004. (1st American Edition.) 338p. ISBN: 0439546567; 0439598516pa. _JS_** 📖
Like his father before him, teenager Thaniel is a "wych-hunter," using a combination of magic and science to kill the creatures of darkness that threaten the folk of London. In the course of hunting a Cradlejack, he comes across the beautiful but possessed Alaizabel Cray and brings her to the home he shares with his mentor, Catherine. Together they discover whose spirit is holding her captive and why, and determine that they must use all their skill and art to save Alaizabel and the entire city. (BBYA; Smarties Silver Award)

Witches

Unlike the witches who attend Hogwarts School of Witchcraft and Wizardry, many of the witches who appear in the following novels travel a decidedly dark path. Others live in a realistic society and yet possess powers that separate them from the ordinary.

Dahl, Roald

🔥 ***The Witches*. New York: Farrar, Straus & Giroux, 1983. 201p. (1st American Edition.) ISBN: 0374384576; 0141301104pa. _M_ AUD VID**
Grandmamma always says that real witches are the most dangerous of all living creatures. They dress in ordinary clothes, but they are not ordinary. They despise children with a red-hot hatred and spend all of their time casting spells to rid the world of them. Her grandson listens closely to her stories, but nothing prepares him for the day he comes face-to-face with the Grand High Witch herself. (ALAN)

Delaney, Joseph

<u>**The Last Apprentice Series**</u>**. New York: Greenwillow. (1st American Editions.) _MJ_**
Tom, the seventh son of a seventh son, doesn't know it, but his mother has a special purpose for him. She wants to apprentice him to a Spook so that he will be able to subdue ghosts and ghouls and witches and all manner of creatures of which nightmares are made.

Revenge of the Witch. 2005. 344p. ISBN: 0060766182; 0060766204pa. AUD
The first thing that twelve-year-old Tom Ward has to do for his new master, the Spook, is spend the night in a haunted house. And that's just the beginning. It's not long before Tom tangles with the wicked witch, Madam Malkin, and the not-completely-evil witch-in-training, Alice.

Curse of the Bane. 2006. 480p. ISBN: 0060766212.
Six months of training as a Spook and Tom has gained considerable confidence. He deals handily with a boggart, but when the Bane, a blood-sucking monster who kills his victims by flattening them, begins exerting malevolent influence over the townspeople even though he is trapped in the maze beneath the Cathedral, Tom, his master, and Alice, the witch-in-training, must find a way to defeat it.

Ibbotson, Eva

Which Witch? New York: Dutton, 1999. 231p. ISBN: 0525461647; 0141304278pa. *M* LP
When Arriman the Awful, the Wizard of the North, decides he needs to have a child to carry on the dark-magic tradition of Loathing Light and Blighting the Beautiful, he holds a contest for the assorted witches of Toadcaster. Whoever works the most wicked spell of all will be his wife.

Myracle, Lauren

Rhymes with Witches. New York: Amulet Books, 2005. 209p. ISBN: 0810958597; 0810992159pa. *S*
Jane, a geeky freshman at Crestview High, longs to be one of the cool kids and join the group known as "the Bitches." She can't believe it when she receives an invitation to join the group. Ignoring rumors that report the Bitches' popularity springs from dabbling in black magic, Jane willingly goes through the initiation, brushing off the hurt of her best friend. But when the innocent Camilla is targeted for supernatural hazing, Jane begins to see the price she's paid for her popularity.

Naylor, Phyllis Reynolds

The Witch Series. **All Reissued by Aladdin.** *M*
Lynn's next-door neighbor, Mrs. Tuggle, is a witch, and her wicked ways can have a devastating effect on anyone.

Witch's Sister. New York: Atheneum, 1975. 150p. Reissued in 2002. ISBN: 0689853157pa.
Lynn's parents don't believe her when she insists that their neighbor, Mrs. Tuggle, is a witch who is forcing Lynn's sister Judith to join her coven. Lynn and her best friend Mouse become determined to prove what they say is true, but before they can, Lynn's parents go away for the weekend and leave Mrs. Tuggle and Judith in charge.

***Witch Water*. New York: Atheneum, 1977. 179p. Reissued in 2002. ISBN: 0689853165pa. BRAILLE**

Although they escaped Mrs. Tuggle once, Lynn and Mouse don't feel safe. When a threatening flock of crows follows Mouse everywhere she goes, the friends know they must pit their wits against the witch again.

***The Witch Herself*. New York: Atheneum, 1978. 164p. Reissued in 2002. ISBN: 0689853173pa. BRAILLE**

Lynn's mother still thinks of Mrs. Tuggle as their friendly neighbor and is planning to move her writing studio into Mrs. Tuggle's house for the winter. Lynn and Mouse become desperate to stop her before it's too late.

***The Witch's Eye*. New York: Delacorte, 1990. 179p. Reissued in 2003. ISBN: 0689853807pa.**

Mrs. Tuggle died in the fire that incinerated her home, so Lynn should feel safe, but she doesn't. She thinks Mrs. Tuggle's malevolent spirit is reaching out from beyond the grave, or, worse yet, she hasn't died at all.

***Witch Weed*. New York: Delacorte, 1991. 181p. Reissued in 2004. ISBN: 0689853815pa.**

When Mrs. Tuggle died, she left behind a glass eye that Lynn's little brother found. The eye works evil on anyone who holds it, so Lynn and Mouse throw it in the creek. When mysterious purple plants grow where the eye landed, Lynn worries that they are influencing the girls in school to form a coven. Worst of all, Mouse is being lured to join them.

***The Witch Returns*. New York: Delacorte, 1992. 178p. Reissued in 2005. ISBN: 0689853823pa.**

When Mrs. Tuggle's house is rebuilt and a woman claiming to be her sister moves in, Lynn knows that the old witch has returned and that it's up to her to stop the witch from destroying her friends and family.

Nix, Garth

***The Ragwitch*. New York: Eos, 2004. 391p. (1st American Edition.) ISBN: 0060508078pa. _JS_**

When Australian siblings Julia and Paul find a rag doll, Julia takes it home, although Paul knows she shouldn't. By the time night darkens the sky, the Ragwitch, a supernatural spirit from another world, has taken possession of Julia. The Ragwitch leads Julia back to the world she once ruled and longs to rule again. Paul tries to follow but ends up a prisoner of the May Dancers. Meanwhile, Julia can perceive and think, but the Ragwitch controls her body. Julia can do nothing to stop her from reigniting a war for the world she's lost. Adrift in the morass of the Ragwitch's massacres, Julia must find a way to regain control or be forever doomed.

Thesman, Jean

🔹 *The Other Ones*. **New York: Viking, 1999. 181p. Reissued by Puffin in 2001. ISBN: 0141312467pa.** *JS*
High school sophomore Brigit, who lives in a small town near Seattle, is a witch. She can read minds, move objects with her thoughts, and see spirits, but she would rather just be an ordinary teenager. She puts her misgivings about her abilities aside when her friend Jordan and a new girl at school who is a trapped shape-shifter need her help. (BBYA)

Vande Velde, Vivian

Witch Dreams. **Tarrytown, NY: Marshall Cavendish, 2005. 120p. ISBN: 0761452354.** *MJ*
Living in a medieval village, sixteen-year-old Nyssa is a witch with the ability to listen in on the dreams of others and know what they truly think, fear, and desire. Her parents were murdered six years ago, and her prime suspect is returning. Nyssa sets out to prove his guilt, but she must be careful, for the villagers will execute her if they suspect she is a witch.

Paranormal Powers

Psychic abilities, such as extrasensory perception, telekinesis, and the ability to predict the future are powers that have long fascinated teen readers. Beings with such abilities appear in many of the speculative fiction genres and are gathered here because that characteristic is essential to the story.

Bradley, Marion Zimmer

Darkover. [Adult] *S*
At the end of the twenty-first century, a spaceship carried a colony seeking to settle a new world. When trouble with the ship forced them to make an emergency landing on Cottman IV, they had no choice but to settle on this unknown world instead. They named the planet Darkover and created a new life with local inhabitants, the Chieris, who possessed powerful psychic abilities. As the generations passed, the humans found two things on Darkover that increased their own psychic powers: the kireseth flower and the Matrix crystals. (Many of the earliest novels are out of print and have been reissued in omnibus editions. They are listed as close to the original publication order as possible, given the way they have been reprinted.)

> *To Save a World*. **(Originally published as *The Planet Savers* in 1958 and *The World Wreckers* in 1971 by Ace.) New York: Daw, 2004. 416p. ISBN: 0756402506pa.**

> *The Sword of Aldones*. **New York: Ace, 1962. (Out of Print.)**

> *A World Divided*. **(Originally published as *The Bloody Sun* in 1964, *Star of Danger* in 1965, and *The Winds of Darkover* in 1970, all by Ace.) New York: Daw, 2003. 686p. ISBN: 0756401674pa.**

Darkover: First Contact. (Originally published as *Darkover Landfall* in 1972 and *Two to Conquer* in 1980.) New York: Daw, 2004. 512p. ISBN: 0756402247pa.

The Forbidden Circle. (Originally published as *The Spell Sword* in 1974 and *The Forbidden Tower* in 1977 by Daw.) New York: Daw, 2002. 570p. ISBN: 0756400945pa.

Heritage and Exile. (Originally published *The Heritage of Hastur* in 1975 and *Sharra's Exile* in 1981 by Daw.) New York: Daw, 2002. 784p. ISBN: 0756400651pa.

The Saga of the Renunciates. (Originally published as *The Shattered Chain* in 1976, *Thendara House* in 1983, and *City of Sorcery* in 1984.) New York: Daw, 2002. 1120p. ISBN: 0756400929pa.

The Age of Chaos. (Originally published as *Stormqueen* in 1978 and *Hawkmistress* in 1982.) New York: Daw, 2002. 768p. ISBN: 0756400724pa.

The Heirs of Hammerfell. New York: Daw, 1989. (Out of Print.)

Rediscovery. New York: Daw, 1993. (Out of Print.)

Exile's Song. New York: Daw, 1996. 435p. Reissued in 1997. ISBN: 0886777348pa.

The Shadow Matrix. New York: Daw, 1997. 512p. Reissued in 1998. ISBN: 0886777348pa.

Traitor's Sun. New York: Daw, 1999. 483p. Reissued in 2000. ISBN: 0886778115pa.

Cabot, Meg

The Mediator Series. [Adult] *JS* AUD

Suze, a high school student, moves to California hoping for some fun in the sun, but her supernatural ability to communicate with the dead keeps getting in the way. (Originally published under the penname Jenny Carroll.)

Shadowland. New York: Pocket Pulse, 2000. 245p. Reissued by HarperCollins in 2005. ISBN: 0060725117pa.

Ninth Key. New York: Pocket Pulse, 2001. 230p. Reissued by HarperCollins in 2005. ISBN: 0060725125pa.

Reunion. New York: Pocket Pulse, 2001. 228p. Reissued by HarperCollins in 2005. ISBN: 0060725133pa.

Darkest Hour. New York: Pocket Pulse, 2001. 243p. Reissued by HarperCollins in 2004. ISBN: 0060725141pa.

Haunted. New York: HarperCollins, 2003. 146p. ISBN: 006029471X; 0060751649pa.

Twilight. New York: HarperCollins, 2005. 245p. ISBN: 0060724676; 0060724692pa.

Dickinson, Peter

The Gift. Boston: Little, Brown, 1974. 188p. (1st American Edition.) Reissued by Delacorte in 2001. ISBN: 0375895019pa. *JS*
Davy Price, a Welsh lad, has inherited the family gift for extrasensory perception. He knows what other people think and feel, but his grandmother warns him that bad things happen when the gift is used. Nonetheless, when Davy senses that his family is in danger, he takes the risk and uses his power.

Drvenkar, Zoran

Tell Me What You See. New York: Chicken House, 2005. 304p. (1st American Edition.) ISBN: 043972452X. *S*
Alyssa visits her father's grave every year at Christmastime. But this year Berlin is blanketed in snow, and she has trouble making her way through the cemetery. Tumbling into a crypt occupied by a child's coffin, with a strange plant growing from it, Alyssa is influenced by the plant to take it home. Once there, she eats the plant and suddenly can see strange spirits that no one else can and has the ability to call back the dead.

Ewing, Lynne

Daughters of the Moon. New York: Hyperion. *JS*
Four teens who live in Los Angeles, Vanessa, Catty, Serena, and Jimena, each possess a different supernatural ability and discover that they are destined to battle the evil Atrox and his minions.

Goddess of the Night. 2000. 294p. ISBN: 0786806532.
Vanessa, a sophomore in high school, wishes she did not have the ability to become invisible at will, but her best friend Catty enjoys her power to shift time. When the friends meet Serena, who can read minds, and Jimena, who can see the future, they discover together that they are Daughters of the Moon and must use their supernatural powers to fend off the forces of the nefarious Atrox.

Into the Cold Fire. 2000. 264p. ISBN: 0786806540.
When Jimena has a premonition that Serena will enter the cold fire that will turn her to the dark side, the four best friends must unite to prevent disaster.

Night Shade. 2001. 275p. ISBN: 0786807083.
Jimena, once a gang member, has never been so terrified as when she sees Veto, her old boyfriend, for Veto died a year ago in a gang fight. Now Jimena and her friends, must find a way out of the trap unleashed by Cassandra or the friends and those they love will be doomed.

The Secret Scroll. 2001. 268p. ISBN: 0786807091.
Catty has always longed to know who her birth mother was and now makes use of her ability to travel back and forth in time to discover the truth.

***The Sacrifice*. 2001. 269p. ISBN: 0786807067.**
Stanton, an Immortal, in the unwilling service of Atrox, lures victims to the dark side. He is supposed to capture Serena, whom he has battled before for his master, but there is one problem: He's in love with her.

***The Lost One*. 2001. 274p. ISBN: 0786807075.**
When one of the Daughters of the Moon develops amnesia, she does not know that she has the power of telekinesis and is involved in an ongoing war with Atrox.

***Moon Demon*. 2002. 289p. ISBN: 0786808497.**
As Vanessa's sixteenth birthday draws near, a sense of dread fills her. She knows that in one year she will have to decide whether to "transition"—to keep her powers or to relinquish them and remain mortal. She also longs not always to be "the good girl." And that's when the handsome and mysterious Hector strolls into her life.

***Possession*. 2002. 275p. ISBN: 0786808500.**
When Serena encounters an elderly woman, her life changes. Suddenly, she acts like a person she doesn't like very much, she forgets things, and she is convinced that someone is following her.

***The Choice*. 2003. 275p. ISBN: 0786808519.**
As each of the Daughters of the Moon must wrestle with the fast-approaching decision of whether to transition, Catty takes Jimena to the past where she must make peace with an old enemy to defeat a shape-shifter.

***The Talisman*. 2003. 278p. ISBN: 0786818786.**
Maggie, who has mentored the young Daughters of the Moon, knows she must soon leave her charges and shares with them stories of her life in ancient Greece.

***Prophecy*. 2004p. 273p. ISBN: 0786818913.**
The Daughters of the Moon must locate the magic scroll so that their identities will not be disclosed to the wrong people. During the course of the search, Catty enters a parallel world and finds her real father, a follower of the dark, who tries to lure her into partnership with him.

***The Becoming*. 2004. 273p. ISBN: 0786818921.**
Tianna seems to have settled into her life in a foster home, accepting her telekinetic ability, and enjoying a secure relationship with her boyfriend. But when she learns she is linked to Atrox, her world begins to crumble.

<u>Sons of the Dark</u>. New York: Hyperion. _JS_
In this companion series to *Daughters of the Moon,* four teens, who were enslaved by evil in the parallel world of Nefandus, have escaped to live as high school guys in Los Angeles. They've retained their supernatural abilities and must fend off the forces of darkness.

Barbarian. 2004. 264p. ISBN: 0786818115.
Obie, who is secretly an immortal Visigoth warrior, adjusts to life in Los Angeles after slavery in a parallel world.

Escape. 2004. 252p. ISBN: 0786818123.
When Samuel, who is originally from 1768, arrives in Los Angeles after hard labor in Nefandus, he believes the beautiful Ashley will lead him back to his own time, despite the warnings of three former Nefandus slaves.

Outcast. 2005. 257p. ISBN: 0786818131.
Kyle, who rooms with the other immortal escapees from Nefandus, is having blackouts more and more frequently. His roommates learn that the only way to help him is to join him with the nefarious power of his past and hope that he is strong enough to overcome it.

Night Sun. 2005. 259p. ISBN: 078681814X.
A demon from Nefandus is kidnapping students from Turney High School, desperately seeking the stone that will grant wishes, and only the legendary Sons of the Dark can stop him.

Gould, Steven

🔖 *Jumper*. New York: Tor, 1992. 344p. Reissued in 2002. ISBN: 0765342286pa. *JS* BRAILLE
Teenager Davey Rice wants desperately to get away from his alcoholic and abusive father, but there seems to be no escape until the day Davey discovers his new ability. As his father lifts the belt to beat him, Davey concentrates on avoiding the blow and suddenly transports himself to the Stanville Public Library. Finally free, he teleports to New York City, uses his new power to slip into a bank vault so that he can steal the cash he needs to support himself, and decides to try to find the mother who left when he was a child. (BBYA)

Reflex. New York: Tor, 2004. 380p. ISBN: 0312864213; 0812578546pa. *JS* BRAILLE
Davey Rice, now an undercover operative for the National Security Agency and married to psychologist Millie Harrison-Rice, is in the middle of a meeting in Washington, D.C., when he is snatched by members of an organization that wants to force him to use his talents for them. They keep him chained and implant a device that makes it impossible for him to teleport. Meanwhile, Millie has discovered that she has the same supernatural ability as Davey and joins with the NSA to find her husband.

Hoffman, Alice

Probable Future. New York: Doubleday, 2003. 322p. ISBN: 0385507607; 0345455916pa. [Adult] *S* AUD BRAILLE LP
Thirteen-year-old Stella, who attends an exclusive school in Boston, comes from a family brimming with paranormal powers. Her grandmother can perceive when people are lying; her mother can view the dreams of others; and Stella can foresee death. As she struggles with her power, her plea for help lands her father in jail and brings the whole family back to a small town in Massachusetts to sort things through.

Hooper, Kay

The "Bishop" Special Crime Unit Series. [Adult] AUD _S_
FBI profiler Noah Bishop puts together a team of psychics to help solve cases all over the country.

> *Stealing Shadows.* New York: Bantam, 2000. 356p. ISBN: 0553575538pa. LP
>
> *Hiding in the Shadows.* New York: Bantam, 2000. 339p. ISBN: 0553576925pa. LP
>
> *Out of the Shadows.* New York: Bantam, 2000. 341p. ISBN: 055357695Xpa. LP
>
> *Touching Evil.* 2001. 358p. ISBN: 0553583441pa.
>
> *Whisper of Evil.* 2002. 416p. ISBN: 0553583468pa.
>
> *Sense of Evil.* 2003. 343p. Reissued in 2004. ISBN: 0553583476pa. LP
>
> *Hunting Fear.* 2004. 388p. Reissued in 2005. ISBN: 0553585983pa. LP
>
> *Chill of Fear.* 2005. 336p. ISBN: 0553803174. LP
>
> *Sleeping with Fear.* 2006. ISBN: 0553803182. LP

Koontz, Dean

> *Odd Thomas.* New York: Bantam, 2004. 416p. ISBN: 0553802496; 0553584499pa. [Adult] _S_ AUD LP
> Odd Thomas, a twenty-year-old short-order cook at the Pico Mundo Grill in California, not only sees dead people, he talks to them as well, although they don't talk back. Sometimes he helps them avenge their deaths; sometimes he passes on tips that help the local chief of police. Odd likes to keep a low profile, so only the chief and the love of his life, Stormy Llewellyn, know of his ability. It serves as a harbinger of disaster when a stranger comes to town, surrounded by the evil spirits Odd calls "bodachs." Odd investigates in an ever-intensifying attempt to ward off impending doom.

> *Forever Odd.* New York: Bantam, 2005. 351p. ISBN: 0553804162. _S_ [Adult] AUD LP

> Odd Thomas, now twenty-one, still lives in Pico Mundo, California, and can still see and talk to the dead. Dr. Wilbur Jessup's ghost leads Odd to his home, where Odd discovers that Dr. Jessup's been murdered and that Jessup's son, Danny, is missing. Following the invisible mental trail, Odd locates Danny, but it's a trap, for the evil Datura wants to capture Odd and use his powers.

McCaffrey, Anne

The Saga of the Talents. New York: Ballantine. [Adult] _S_ AUD
Molly, Charity, Barbara, baby Dorotea, and Amalda all have special Talents: mind reading, healing, and foretelling future disasters. Although they are rejected at first, eventually society sees the value of people of Talent.

> *To Ride Pegasus.* 1973. Reissued in 1991. 243p. ISBN: 0345336038pa.

> *Pegasus in Flight.* 1990. 290p. Reissued in 1991. ISBN: 0345368975pa.

> *Pegasus in Space.* 2000. 373p. Reissued in 2001. ISBN: 0345434676pa.

The Tower and the Hive. New York: Ace/Putnam. [Adult] _S_ AUD
People with Talent have become the elite and are crucial in humanity's efforts to colonize the universe.

> *The Rowan.* 1990. 335p. Reissued in 1991. ISBN: 0441735762pa.

> *Damia.* 1992. 336p. Reissued in 1993. ISBN: 0441135560pa.

> *Damia's Children.* 1993. 272p. Reissued in 1996. ISBN: 044100007Xpa.

> *Lyon's Pride.* 1994. 272p. Reissued in 1995. ISBN: 0441001416pa.

> *The Tower and the Hive.* 1999. 302p. Reissued in 2000. ISBN: 0441007201pa.

McDonald, Joyce

🌟 *Shades of Simon Gray.* New York: Delacorte, 2001. 245p. ISBN: 0385326599; 0440228042pa. _JS_
While high school junior Simon Grey lies in a coma, his spirit escapes and encounters the ghost of Jessup Wildemere, who shows him evil events from the past. Meanwhile, Simon's friends worry that he will reveal their secret if he wakes up. (BBYA)

Michael, Livi

The Whispering Road. New York: Putnam, 2005. 336p. (1st American Edition.) ISBN: 0399243577. _MJ_
In 1930s England, siblings Joe and Annie are left by their mother at the poor house. Joe always tries to look after his sister, who can see the dead and make prophecies about the future. When they end up working for an abusive farmer, the two run away, determined to find their mother.

Woodworth, Stephen

The Violet Eyes Series. New York: Bantam. [Adult] _S_
The Justice Department has help solving murder cases and convicting murderers because those born with violet eyes can become conduits for the dead. Victims can identify their own killers. This may reduce the crime rate, but it doesn't mean those with violet eyes are safe.

> *Through Violet Eyes.* 2004. 333p. ISBN: 0553803379pa.

> *With Red Hands.* 2005. 307p. ISBN: 0553586459pa.

> *In Golden Blood.* 2005. 303p. ISBN: 0440242525pa.

Young Adult Paperback Series

Cabot, Meg (Originally published under the name Jenny Carroll.)

1-800-Where-R-U. New York: Simon & Schuster. _JS_
Sixteen-year-old Jessica Mastriani has been psychic ever since she was struck by lightning. Her abilities make her especially good at finding missing persons, which is perhaps why the FBI is interested in her. But Jessica would rather be a normal high school kid.

Cole, Stephen

The Wereling Series. New York: Razorbill. _S_
All the members of Kate Folan's family are werewolves, something she desperately wants to avoid. As long as she refuses to mate with a werewolf, she has a chance. But when she falls in love with werewolf Tom Anderson, she realizes her fate soon will be sealed, unless they can find a cure.

Cusick, Richie Tankersley

The Unseen Series. New York: Speak. _S_
When Lucy, fearful of a stalker, stumbles across the body of a dying girl, she becomes the next vehicle for the girl's psychic powers. Tortured by visions of a killer, Lucy must find a way to cope with her new abilities and stay alive.

Stine, R. L.

Fear Street. New York: Simon Pulse. _JS_
The teens that live on and around Fear Street learn that the evil there never dies. This series began in 1989 and is being reissued. It also has spawned several spin-off series: *Fear Street Super Chillers, Ghosts of Fear Street, Fear Street Sagas, Fear Street Seniors,* and the most recent, *Fear Street Nights.*

Thomson, Celia

The Nine Lives of Chloe King. New York: Simon & Schuster. _S_
Usually Chloe is a good student, but on the day before her sixteenth birthday, she ditches school to hang out with her two best friends. When she falls from the top of San Francisco's Coit Tower, she dies and comes back to life with unusual powers.

Tiernan, Cate

The Sweep Series. New York: Puffin. _JS_
When Morgan, a high school junior living in upstate New York, gets invited to a Wiccan coven meeting, she feels the ritual call to something deep within her and is drawn into a world of magic.

Balefire Series. New York: Razorbill. *S*

Thais Allard lives with her father in Connecticut, completely unaware that her identical twin sister lives with their grandmother in New Orleans practicing Bonne Magie. When Thais's father dies in a tragic car accident, her new guardian, Axelle Gauvin, moves them both to New Orleans. The twins meet their first day of high school and begin to unravel the mystery that threads through their lives.

Watson, Jude

Premonitions. New York: Scholastic. *JS*

Frightening visions of the future have haunted fifteen-year-old Gracie since she almost drowned five years ago. Now, after the death of her mother, she goes to live with her Aunt Shay and finds her premonitions still plague her.

Media-Related Series

Angel. Various authors. New York: Simon & Schuster. *JS*

Buffy the Vampire Slayer. Various authors. New York: Simon & Schuster. *JS*

Charmed. Various authors. New York: Simon & Schuster. *JS*

Don't Read These Late at Night

Coraline by Neil Gaiman

The Midnighters Trilogy by Scott Westerfeld

The Haunting of Alaizabel Cray by Chris Wooding

The Violet Eyes Series by Stephen Woodworth

References

"Scott Westerfeld," *Contemporary Authors Online*, Infotrac Galegroup Database (accessed March 2006).

Westerfeld, Scott. "Home Page." http://www.scottwesterfeld.com/ (accessed March 2006).

"What Is Horror Fiction." http://www.horror.org/horror-is.htm (accessed May 2006).

Chapter 14

Graphic Novels

The graphic novel format provides a pallet of infinite artistic variety. Within the various subgenres of speculative fiction, artists imagine all manner of fantastical creatures, worlds, and adventures, without being tethered to reality. Two types of graphic novels dominate the current market: the American style, which grew out of the comic-book format, and the manga style, which originated in Japan.

Comic books generally tell one story in several episodes and then begin a new story arc and repeat the pattern, telling another story with the same characters over several episodes. A graphic novel, on the other hand, generally contains one complete story arc in each volume. Many volumes may feature the same characters, but each particular story is finished in one volume. A graphic novel can be one volume or many, with issues appearing several times a year. Graphic novels can originate as comic books and later be collected and placed in the graphic novel format, or they can be created as graphic novels. The best way to purchase graphic novel series for a library is to contact your book jobber and put them on standing order from the first volume. For that reason, complete bibliographic information is only listed for stand-alone novels or series with a limited number of volumes. Graphic novels provide an opportunity for visual literacy, develop the ability to follow a nonlinear plot, and provide an excellent opportunity to convince reluctant readers of the wonder of story.

Fantasy

Many of the genres of narrative fantasy are represented pictorially in graphic novels, from "Epic Fantasy" to "Reality with a Twist." Elves and fairies can populate their pages as easily as humans with magical talents and gods with cryptic senses of humor.

Carlton, Bronwyn

The Books of Faerie: Auberon's Tale. **New York: Vertigo, 1998. 138p. ISBN: 1563895021pa.** *JS*
By a strange twist of fate, a young boy becomes the king of Faerie.

CLAMP (a four-woman graphic novel team known collectively as CLAMP).

Tsubasa: Reservoir Chronicle. New York: Ballantine. *S*

Using crossover characters from *XXXHolic,* this series features Princess Sakura and the teenager Syaoran. When Princess Sakura visits her friend Syaoran at an archaeological dig, a recovered rune unlocks her power and scatters her memory across parallel worlds. Syaoran vows to restore it for her with the help of a wizard and a ninja. (Manga series translated from the Japanese, first released in the United States in 2004.)

Fujishima, Kosuke

Oh My Goddess. Milwaukie, OR: Dark Horse Comics. *JS*

College student Keiichi lives with three goddesses. They are sisters, and one, Belldandy, is his love. They all try to balance everyday life with the goddesses' supernatural powers. (Manga series translated from the Japanese, first released in the United States in 2001.)

Gaiman, Neil

The Sandman. New York: Vertigo. *S*

Seven Endless Beings existed before the gods. One of them is Dream, also called Morpheus. He escapes captivity in 1988, and the adventures begin. (Originally published as a series of seventy-five comic books beginning in 1991, they have been reissued as graphic novels.)

The Books of Magic. New York: Vertigo. *S*

A quartet of mystics explores a variety of magical realms.

Hyun, You

Faeries' Landing. Los Angeles: Tokyopop. *JS*

Goodfellow leads Ryang to Faeries' Landing, a magical realm where faeries dwell. There he embarks on myriad adventures. (Manga series translated from the Japanese first released in the United States in 2004.).

Martin, George, R. R.

The Hedge Knight. Acworth, GA: Dabel Brothers, 2005. ISBN: 097640110Xpa. 164p. *S*

Set in the world of the epic fantasy *Song of Ice and Fire,* Dunk, a young squire, heads off on his own to a jousting tournament after his master dies. Along the way he acquires a squire who calls himself Egg.

Matoh, Sanami

By the Sword. Houston, TX: ADV Manga. *JS*

Asagi, a demon-hunter, searches for the powerful enchanted blade that was forged long ago and will help him in his tasks. (Manga series, translated from the Japanese.)

Volume 1. 2005. 184p. ISBN: 1413902138pa.

Volume 2. 2005. ISBN: 1413902146pa.

Medley, Linda

Castle Waiting. Seattle: Fantagraphics. 2006. 456p. ISBN: 1560977477. *M*
Characters from fairy tales and nursery rhymes bring a castle to life in their own inimitable fashion. (Originally published as a comic book series beginning in 1996, it is only available in this omnibus edition.)

Moore, Alan

Promethea. La Jolla, CA: America's Best Comics. *S*
While researching a mythical warrior named Promethea, college student Sophia Bangs must master her new powers before they master her.

Pini, Wendy

Elfquest. New York: DC Comics. *JS*
In the world of Two Moons, humans and elves are mortal enemies, and the Wolfriders are a clan of forest dwellers who are intimately connected with the wolves. They must be ever-vigilant, for the humans would hunt them down if they could. At the same time, they cannot let that deter them from their quests. (*Elfquest* began as a comic book series in 1978, published by Warp Graphics. DC Comics now publishes all the reissues. They are being reissued in trim-size with black-and-white illustrations and in full-size hardcovers with color illustrations.)

Takahashi, Rumiko

Inu-Yasha. San Francisco: VIZ Media. *JS*
In ancient Japan, the priestess Kikyo defeated the half-demon Inu-Yasha. Now Kikyo has been reincarnated as a schoolgirl named Kagome. When Kagome's grandfather gives her the Shikon Jewel that Inu-Yasha had been searching for, she is transported into the past, but the jewel shatters. She must find all of the pieces and convince Inu-Yasha to help her in order to save the world. (Manga originally translated from Japanese, first released in the United States in 1998.)

Ranma ½. San Francisco: VIZ Media. *S*
Ranma Saotome, an exemplary student of martial arts, has been cursed so that whenever he touches cold water, he turns into a girl; only hot water can change him back. (Manga series translated from the Japanese, released in trim-size in the United States beginning in 2003.)

Watase, Yuu

Fushigi Yugi. Seattle: VIZ Media. *S*
Miaka Yuki, a junior in high school, is whisked into the world of the book *The Universe of the Four Gods*. Together with her mystical companions, she must find a way to survive. (Manga series translated from the Japanese, first published in the United States beginning in 2000.)

Willingham, Bill

Fables. New York: Vertigo. _S_
When the Adversary invaded the land of fables and fairy tales, its magical denizens were exiled to the real world. Now the more human characters live in a secret area of New York City called Fabletown, and the animal characters live on a farm outside the city.

Yuy, Beop-Ryong

Chronicles of the Cursed Sword. Los Angeles: Tokyopop. _JS_
Rey Yan is called to come to the aid of King Jaryoon of Hahyun with his PaSa sword, but the sword, forged with demon blood, is cursed and may cause war between gods, demons, and mankind. (Manga originally translated from Korean, first released in the United States in 2003.)

Science Fiction

Apart from the media-related and superhero graphic novels, sequential art science fiction often focuses on divergent scientific possibilities in the here and now or the near future, rather than the heavy emphasis on dystopian or post-apocalyptic fiction frequently published in straight texts for young adults. Scientific experiments and life among aliens are also represented.

Brennan, Michael

Electric Girl. San Francisco: Mighty Gremlin. _MJ_
Virginia seems like an average teenager until the shocking truth is revealed: She has the power to deliver electric discharges, which, along with the invisible gremlin, Oogleeoog, makes her life quite interesting. (Originally released as a comic book series.)

Volume 1. 2000. 160p. ISBN: 0970355505pa.

Volume 2. 2002. 159p. ISBN: 0970355513pa.

Volume 3. 2005. 159p. ISBN: 1932051384pa.

Ikumi, Mia

Tokyo Mew-Mew. Los Angeles: Tokyopop. _M_
The Mew-Mew gang, a team of girls who have been injected with animal genes to give them supernatural animal powers, fight alien invaders who wish to use animals to conquer Earth. (Manga originally translated from Japanese, first released in the United States in 2003.)

Morrison, Grant

We3. **New York: Vertigo. 2005. 104p. ISBN: 1401204953pa. _S_**
Bander, Tinker, and Pirate, once house pets (a dog, a cat, and a rabbit), are altered by government scientists to become weapons for the military. Now, when they are about to be decommissioned, a kindhearted keeper lets them go. They just want to get home,

but the government desperately wants them back. (Originally released as a comic book series.)

Naifeh, Ted, and Elmer Damaso

Unearthly. Los Angeles: Seven Seas Entertainment. *S*

In this American manga series, Ann is the shiest girl in high school until she falls for Rae. The only trouble is, he just may be an identity-stealing alien.

Volume 1. 2005. 192p. ISBN: 1933164093pa.

Volume 2. 2006. 192p. (Forthcoming)

Paranormal and Horror

As with fantasy, paranormal and horror seem aptly suited for graphic novels and can include the full range of supernatural experiences, from vampires to witches, from ghosts to psychics.

CLAMP. (A four-woman graphic novel team, known collectively as CLAMP.)

XXXHolic. New York: Ballantine. *S*

Watanuki Kimiharo can see spirits, but he can't stop them from following him around or causing trouble. When he ends up at the shop of Yuko, a lovely witch, she agrees to help him, but in exchange he must become her servant. (Manga originally translated from Japanese, released in the United States beginning in 2004.)

Gaiman, Neil

Creatures of the Night. Milwaukie, OR: Dark Horse Comics. 48p. ISBN: 1569719365. *S*

These two stories were originally published in the short story collection *Smoke and Mirrors* and have been adapted by the author. In the first story, "The Price," a small black cat makes a country house his new home but is suddenly covered with vicious and mysterious wounds. In the second story, "The Daughter of Owls," a baby girl is left, along with an owl pellet, on the steps of Dymton Church. By the time she's fourteen, she's grown to be a great beauty—but those who wish her ill, beware.

Hirano, Kohta

Hellsing. Milwaukie, OR: Dark Horse Comics. *S*

Hellsing is a secret organization, based in England, dedicated to hunting vampires. Hellsing's best vampire hunter is Alucard, but he has dark secrets of his own. (Manga originally translated from Japanese, released in the United States beginning in 2003.)

Kirkman, Robert

Walking Dead. Berkeley, CA: Image Comics. *S*
Flesh-devouring zombies have invaded the world. Officer Rick Grimes must try to avoid the monsters that remain while he searches for his missing family.

Kudo, Kazuya

Mai, the Psychic Girl. San Francisco: VIZ Media. *JS*
Mai Kuju is a fourteen-year-old girl with the power to move objects with her mind. This makes her wanted by the Wisdom Alliance, a group scheming to control the world. Mai and her father are on the run, but her friends and family remain in jeopardy. (Manga translated from Japanese, first released in the United States in 1990.)

Volume 1. 1990. 368p. ISBN: 092927928Xpa.

Volume 2. 1995. 359p. ISBN: 092927928Xpa.

Volume 3. 1996. 357p. ISBN: 1569310599pa.

Lee, Na Hyeon

Traveler of the Moon. Richmond, CA: Infinity Studios. *MJ*
When Yuh-ur asks her parents for a pet, they don't give her a cat or a dog; they give her a bat. She names it Dori and then discovers that Dori is not an ordinary bat—Dori is a vampire bat. (Manga translated from Korean.)

Volume 1. 2005. 172p. ISBN: 1596970618pa.

Volume 2. 2005. ISBN: 1596970626pa.

Volume 3. 2006. ISBN: 1596970634pa.

Naifeh, Ted

Courtney Crumrin. Portland, OR: Oni. *MJ*
Courtney is not at all happy when her parents decide to move the family into the home of Uncle Aloysius. She has to trade her friends for the spoiled brats in her new school, but, worse than that, there are creatures living in her new home, creatures her uncle calls "the night things." (Originally published as a comic book series.)

Courtney Crumrin and the Night Things. 2003. ISBN: 1929998600pa.

Courtney Crumrin and the Coven of Mystics. 2003. ISBN: 1929998597pa.

Courtney Crumrin in the Twilight Kingdom. 2004. ISBN: 1932664017pa.

Thompson, Jill

Scary Godmother. San Antonio, TX: Sirius. *MJ*
Hannah Marie lives in Fright Side, where spooky and funny things happen with alarming regularity. (Originally published as a comic book series beginning in 1997.)

Superheroes

This is the category that is the most well known in the United States. It began with the first publication of *Superman* in 1938. Many others followed, including *Batman* and *Spiderman*. In addition to inspiring both movies and television shows, they've also influenced the creation of contemporary superheroes that are listed in the next section.

Traditional

Batman. Various authors. New York: DC Comics. *MJS*

The Fantastic Four. Various authors. New York: Marvel. *MJS*

The Justice League. Various authors. New York: DC Comics. *MJS*

Spiderman. Various authors. New York: Marvel. *MJS*

Superman. Various authors. New York: DC Comics. *MJS*

Wonder Woman. Various authors. New York: DC Comics. *MJS*

X-Men. Various authors. New York: Marvel. *MJS*

Contemporary

Avery, Fiona

Arana. New York: Marvel. *MJS*
Anya Corazon, a teen who lives in Brooklyn, New York, with her dad, is talked into becoming the Hunter for the Spider Society. The other members endow her with spider-like qualities that come in handy as she works to maintain world peace.

> *Volume 1*. 2005. 144p. ISBN: 0785115064pa.

> *Volume 2*. 2005. ISBN: 0785117199pa.

> *Volume 3*. 2006. ISBN: 0785118535pa.

Busiek, Kurt

Astro City. New York: DC Comics. *MJS*
Brian Kinney leaves life in the country, moves to Astro City, and works his way up from bus boy to superhero.

Robinson, James

Starman. New York: DC Comics. *MJ*
Jack Knight continues his family's superhero tradition. Determined to protect the Opal City, he takes up the cosmic rod invented by his father that harnesses energy and wields it in defense of the city.

Vaughan, Brian K.

<u>Ex Machina</u>**. La Jolla, CA: WildStorm.** <u>*S*</u>
Mitchell Hundred is an ordinary civil engineer, until working with a glowing light under the Brooklyn Bridge gives him the power to talk to machines. Now, after 300 years of being a superhero, he has been elected mayor of New York City. (Originally a twenty volume comic book series.)

*Volume 1: The First Hundred Days***. 2005. 136p. ISBN: 1401206123pa.**

*Volume 2: Tag***. 2005. 128p. ISBN: 1401206263pa.**

*Volume 3: Fact v. Fiction***. 2006. ISBN: 1401209882**

<u>Runaways</u>**. New York: Marvel Comics.** <u>*MJ*</u>
Six teens, aged eleven to sixteen, witness a secret ritual conducted by their parents involving human sacrifice. In this way, they discover that their parents are supervillians and that, as their children, they have superpowers, too. The teens, however, choose to use their powers for good and so come into direct conflict with their parents. (First issue released in 2004.)

Media-Related Graphic Novels

Nicieza, Fabian

<u>Buffy the Vampire Slayer</u>**. Milwaukie, OR: Dark Horse Comics.** <u>*JS*</u>

<u>Star Trek</u>**. Various authors. New York: DC Comics.** <u>*MJS*</u>

<u>Star Wars</u>**. Various authors. Milwaukie, OR: Dark Horse Comics.** <u>*MJS*</u>

Finest in the Realm

The Sandman by Neil Gaiman

The Hedge Knight by George R. R. Martin

Elfquest by Wendy Pini

Programming with Speculative Fiction

Speculative fiction plays in the realm of imagination, so it lends itself exceedingly well to a variety of programs from traditional book clubs to creative dramatics and theatrical productions. Here are some of the ways you, as a librarian, can use speculative fiction in programs.

Book Clubs

Using speculative fiction for book discussion groups is like using any other kind of fiction, except that using books in a trilogy, quartet, or series may prove cumbersome unless the group wants to read all of the books. Selecting a stand-alone title may be the best option. These books are marked in the preceding chapters.

Things to consider when constructing a book discussion program: First, think about dividing the group by age and have a middle school group and a high school group, or a junior high group and a high school group, depending on the school system in town. There can be a large interest gap between what a twelve year old and a sixteen year old would like to read and talk about. Second, serve snacks and include that information when advertising the program. Not only do teens like to have goodies, it helps to set a relaxed tone, giving teens the feeling that it's more like a social gathering than a school project.

Consider starting the discussion with an icebreaker activity that will help the teens get to know each other. This can be any kind of quick party game and does not have to be related to the subject of the discussion group.

Consider letting the teens choose which books they would like to read and discuss. One way that I have found works well is to provide teens with a variety of choices. Let them examine the possible candidates and choose the next book or books for the forthcoming meetings. Rereading the possible selections ahead of time will help you make recommendations to the teens. An alternative to having everyone reading the same book is to have the teens read whatever books they choose in the selected genre. Then the meetings would involve sharing the books they are reading instead of discussing a particular title. This opens up the opportunity for exploring the different subgenres of speculative fiction.

If discussing the same book, ask leading questions, not questions with yes-or-no answers. Stay away from simply detail-oriented questions. Encourage participants to share what they think and feel in response to the book. Don't be afraid to let the discussion veer off topic, but be prepared to steer it back. It may be that something in a book resonates with readers and they need to talk about it. Don't shy away from letting teens express negative opinions. Not all readers will enjoy the same thing. Encourage them to express why they didn't like it.

Consider suggesting that the group members jot down their thoughts about the books. These can be kept in a notebook or posted on a bulletin board where other teens can peruse the opinions of their peers. Word-of-mouth often works wonders in getting a book to circulate.

If there are only a few teens attending your book club, remember that small is not necessarily a bad thing. It can facilitate more in-depth discussions. Consider cosponsoring the group with a neighboring library or with the local middle or high school.

Select books that are personally interesting and that will generate discussion from the group leader as well as the participants. Remember, a book can be interesting without being a favorite. The important thing is to be engaged with the teens in the process of discussing the book.

Fantasy Fairs

The Harry Potter series, The Lord of the Rings, and The Chronicles of Narnia, all provide ample material from which to create a fair. They're well known, especially after the recent movie releases, and their fans often retain a thorough knowledge of the content. A fair combines a number of program elements into a single event. There are two basic ways to involve teens in a fair: have them plan, create, and run a fair for younger children, or run a fair for the teens themselves.

If your teens are creating a fair for younger children, they will need to meet several times to plan, create games and decorations, and finally set up and run the fair. The more the teens can generate and execute their ideas, the better. A fair can be done inside or outdoors; it involves setting up several activity stations related in some way the chosen fantasy. At least one teen should be present at each station to supervise the game or activity, since the participants will move freely from station to station. If the group of teen volunteers is too small for a full-fledged fair, select two or three activities from the following list and do them sequentially. Have the teens create signs for each station and decorate the program room if it will be held indoors. Some stations for a Harry Potter fair could include the following.

Face Painting

It helps to have an artistic volunteer to do this. Face painting supplies are readily available around Halloween, but can generally be found at art-supply stores or on Web sites such as www.dickblick.com. If no one feels confident about doing this, use rubber stamps that relate to the theme, with washable, nontoxic inkpads.

Wizard Hat Ring Toss

Purchase a ring-toss game (toy stores carry them in the summer, and general suppliers like *www.orientaltrade.com* often sell them as well). Purchase Styrofoam cones. Hollow out space in the center so that they easily slide each over the ring toss rods. Cover the cones with starry wrapping paper. Cut a hole in the center for the rods and mount the cones on the plates. Slide one cone onto each of the four rods. Use the plastic rings that come with the game (with thanks to children's librarian, Nancy O'Grady, who created this game for the Woodbridge Public Library in Woodbridge, New Jersey).

Triwizard Trivia

Teens who know the books will be able to generate lots of trivia questions. If they get stuck, *www.hp-lexicon.com* has every detail you ever wanted to know about Harry Potter, and teens can create questions with that information.

Divination with Professor Trelawny

Fold square paper into fortune-tellers (also know as cootie catchers) and have the attendees write theme-related fortunes. For example: Beware, a Hungarian Horntail dragon is all fired-up about you; Dumbledore's Army wants you; you will have a romantic relationship with someone in your seventh year at Hogwarts.

Potions with Professor Snape

From *The Book Wizard Parties* by Janice Eaton Kilby, this participatory demonstration involves taking a tumbler-sized cup made of glass and pouring in one-eighth cup of white vinegar. Have attendees select and add a few drops of food coloring and then let them sprinkle in a small amount of baking soda.

O.W.L.s

Create multiple choice quizzes about each book and print on parchment paper with calligraphic script. Create an answer key. Ten questions are the easiest number to grade. Grade using the grading system in *Harry Potter and the Order of the Phoenix*:

O = Outstanding

E = Exceeds Expectation

A = Acceptable

P = Poor

D = Dreadful

T = Troll

The participants will want their grades right away, so several teen volunteers may be needed for this station. Create an answer key by punching a hole over the correct answer to each question, so that when the key is on top of the quiz it is immediately apparent if the correct answer has been given. This will reduce turnaround time.

The Three Broomsticks

Children's librarian Linda Simpendorfer of the Livingston Public Library in Livingston, New Jersey, shared this great idea with me. Participants can make witch-hat cookies by cementing a Hershey's Kiss to the center of a plain round cookie (sugar cookies or Keebler Fudge Stripes both work) with frosting. They can also make edible magic wands by dipping rod pretzels in frosting and rolling the frosted end in sprinkles. Cream soda makes a nice "butterbear" and Jelly Belly jelly beans, which come in extraordinary flavors (although not "vomit" flavor!) and can be purchased at wholesale stores, serve well as "Bertie Bott's Every Flavor Beans," if the official Bertie Bott's are unavailable or too expensive.

Wizard Hats and Wands

Wizard hats can be made like princess hats. Select the appropriate size of construction paper, cut out a circle large enough to make a hat, cut a straight line to the center of the circle, and then slide one end under the other until you have a cone shape. Adjust to size and tape or staple. Decorate to taste. Wands can be made with dowels or unsharpened pencils. Glue one star on each side at one end of the dowel and decorate to taste.

Word Searches and Crossword Puzzles

Teens can create their own word searches and crosswords puzzles at *www.puzzlemaker.com.*

If the fair is for teens, replace the activities that appeal to younger fans, like the baking soda potion activity, with something more geared to appeal to older teens, such as a more complicated science experiment. Replace the fortune-teller activity by having the participants create their own dream interpretation handbook.

The <u>Harry Potter</u> books are probably the easiest ones to create a fair around because they are so widely known and have such a broad audience; but the above suggestions can be adapted for other works fantasy, such as <u>The Lord of the Rings</u> and <u>The Chronicles of Narnia</u>, by changing the names and decorations and tailoring the activity to the theme. In fact, the activities can be adapted to science fiction and horror as well, although the audience is smaller, and none of the books are as well known by teens as the above fantasies.

Trivia Contests

Trivia contests can focus on one series of books or books from a variety of genres, depending on the interest of the audience. Again, because Harry Potter is so well known, it's sure to be a popular program.

Team Contests

Create three sets of questions, one set for each round of play. Each set should be harder than the previous one. Create a set of especially difficult questions to be used as tiebreakers. Divide the attendees into teams (self-selected or random). For <u>Harry Potter</u>, the teams could be the names of the shops in Diagon Alley (Madam Malkin's, Flourish and Blotts, etc.). For

The Lord of the Rings, they could be Middle Earth place names (Lothlorien, Hobbiton, etc.). For The Chronicles of Narnia, they could be fantasy creature names (centaurs, unicorns, etc.) It works better to steer clear of gender-specific names, so that the teams are not divided along gender lines, and it is also recommended that specifically evil names, like Slytherin or Mordor, be avoided to reduce the distress of participants who do not want to be on teams with those names.

Ask each team a question and give the members a specified amount of time to confer and then answer. If the answer is right, the team gets one point. If wrong, the next team has a chance to answer and earn a point. At the end of the first round (for an hour-long program, it would be about fifteen minutes), eliminate the team with the lowest point total (or the two teams, depending on how many teams you have. By the last fifteen minutes, two teams should remain). Proceed with the next level of questions. These should be harder. At the end of the second round, the two teams with the highest points continue. Proceed with the next level of questions for the amount of time allotted. If the points are tied at the end, use the tiebreaker questions. Prizes and snacks make it extra entertaining.

Another team contest format is known as Battle of the Books, which started in the 1930s as a radio program broadcast in Chicago. It has developed into a reading-incentive program popular in schools. Participants all read the same set of books and are separated into teams. The number of participants on each team depends on how many are registered for the program. If this is a multisession program, schedule time for the teams to practice quizzing each other at the library. Have the participants write the questions, or you may provide them. Traditionally, questions begin with "In which book…" and answers contain the author and title, but that format can be modified, as long as the questions and answers are book-centered. Program length will dictate the number of teens who can participate, how many questions will be asked of each team, and how many rounds the battle will continue. The battle ensues in a quiz-show format, where the team members have a limited time for consulting with each other on the answers. The teams with the most points advance to the next round until you have a winning team (how many teams you eliminate depends on the length of your program and the number of participants). More information can be found at *www.battleofthebooks.com.*

Individual Contests

Create a *Jeopardy*-style answer board with categories related to the chosen set of books or to the genre. Answers are given and the participants must come up with the questions. The answers at the top of the category should be the easiest and at the bottom the hardest. The questions can be worth a monetary amount, and a teen or assistant can keep score. This program works best with a small group actually playing.

The single-book team contest can also be modified to an individual participant format, if the number of players is small enough. In this case, instead of forming teams, simply ask each participant the same number of questions each round, eliminating those with the lowest point total each time.

Dramatics: Theatrical and Creative

Scenes from speculative fiction can be adapted into a play or readers' theater format or can be used as a springboard for teens to create their own plays. This event entails blocking out time for a series of meetings, and the teens involved need to be able to make the commitment to attend each meeting. Once the teens have adapted or written their play, which should be brief enough to be performed during the scheduled program time, roles can be cast and tasks assigned. This can be done by the teens themselves, or by the librarian. Teens can create costumes, whether they're simple or elaborate, and sets, as well as to take parts in the play. While the teens must memorize their lines at home (if performing as a play), blocking and rehearsal will take place at the library or school. After a series of rehearsals, the culmination will be the performance. A readers' theater performance is simply a scaled-down version of a play where teens use only minimal props and costuming, and simply read from the script. These types of programs are ideal for the summer, when teens may have fewer commitments and has been held annually at the Piscataway Public Library in New Jersey, run first by Anne Lemay and then by Sharon Rawlins, who both shared their ideas with me.

Speculative fiction also provides ample material for creative dramatics, from games like charades to creative dramatic experiences. For charades, choose titles of well-known works of the genres and write them out on slips of paper. Divide the group into teams and play charades with your chosen titles.

For a creative dramatic experience that emphasizes enjoying character portrayal and storytelling as opposed to performance, select the scene to portray from a familiar story. Read that selection aloud to refresh everyone's memory. Have the attendees retell the story and then ask for volunteers to play the parts. More than one person can play each part. If a lot of teens are involved, inanimate objects can be roles (trees, cauldrons, etc.). Not everyone has to have a part. Being an audience member can be considered a role as well. When the scene is cast, walk through what the characters will do and say, then let them act it out. Encourage them to use their own words for dialogue and to make up things that they would like to add to the scene. When it's finished, have the audience members give feedback, beginning with what they liked about the way the scene was played. If there is interest, change parts and play the scene again.

References

Kilby, Janice Eaton, and Terry Taylor. *The Book of Wizard Parties*. New York: Lark Books, 2002.

Rowling, J. K. *Harry Potter and the Order of the Phoenix*. New York: Arthur A. Levine Books, 2003.

Resources

Battle of the Books: www.battleofthebooks.com

Dick Blick Art Supplies: www.dickblick.com

The Harry Potter Lexicon: www.hp-lexicon.com

Puzzle Making: www.puzzlemaker.com

Appendix B

Fantasy Lists

Sometimes, it's helpful to have specialized lists ready to copy, so what follows are two fantasy lists. The first one recommends other fantasies for Harry Potter fans. Many of the books involve the workings of wizards, featuring their education and/or escapades. Others revolve around magical adventures that would appeal to those entranced with the world of Hogwarts and its denizens.

The books on the second list, "Girl Power," all star strong female protagonists. It took quite awhile for modern fantasy to feature girls as the primary doers of daring deeds. Tamora Pierce, Patricia McKillip, and Robin McKinley are just three of the writers who have made a point of creating female heroes for their fantasies.

Fine Fantasy for Fans of Harry Potter

Alexander, Lloyd. The Chronicles of Prydain.
When the Horned King, warlord for Arawn Death-Lord, thunders through the forest outside of the Caer Dallben, home of Taran and his guardian Dallben the Enchanter, Taran the Assistant Pig-Keeper is catapulted into adventure. (*The Book of Three, The Black Cauldron, The Castle of Llyr, Taran Wanderer,* and *The High King*)

Alexander, Lloyd. *The Wizard in the Tree.*
As a trapped wizard emerges from the stump of Mallory's favorite tree, she attempts to convince him to save her village, although all he wants is to find his fellow wizards.

Bell, Hilari. *The Wizard Test.*
Dayven, a Watcherlad, is training to be a warrior and dreads the day he must take the wizard test. The last thing he wants to be is a lowdown wizard.

Chabon, Michael. *Summerland.*
Ethan is not very good at baseball, but when a group of fantastical creatures from another realm need him to win a game to save their world, he agrees to pitch in.

Colfer, Eoin. The Artemis Fowl Series.
When twelve-year-old Artemis Fowl, a criminal mastermind, schemes to capture a fairy for the gold needed to replenish the family fortunes, he embarks on a long association with the denizens of the underworld realm. (*Artemis Fowl, Artemis Fowl: The Arctic Incident, Artemis Fowl: The Eternity Code,* and *Artemis Fowl: The Opal Deception*)

Collins, Suzanne. The Underland Chronicles.
Gregor follows his baby sister down the laundry chute and arrives in an underground world populated by giant cockroaches, spiders, bats, and pale-haired humans who believe Gregor is the hero mentioned in their prophecies. (*Gregor the Overlander, Gregor and the Prophecy of Bane, Gregor and the Curse of the Warmbloods,* and *Gregor and the Marks of Secret*)

Cooper, Susan. The Dark Is Rising Sequence.
On his eleventh birthday, Will Stanton, a seventh son of a seventh son, discovers that he is the last of the Old Ones and must gather the six magical Signs that will help the Light defeat the forces of the Dark. (*Over Sea, Under Stone, The Dark Is Rising, Greenwitch, The Grey King,* and *The Silver on the Tree*)

Duane, Diane. So You Want to Be a Wizard Series.
Kit and Nita have each found a book in the library that teaches them how to be wizards. They join forces as they struggle to learn what's needed to combat the Lone Power. (*So You Want to Be a Wizard, Deep Wizardry, High Wizardry, Wizard Abroad, The Wizard's Dilemma, A Wizard Alone, Wizard's Holiday,* and *Wizards at War*)

Jones, Diana Wynne. <u>The Chrestomanci Chronicles</u>.
In a reality where many alternate worlds coexist, a nine-lived enchanter—the Chrestomanci—can enter them all. (*Charmed Life, The Magicians of Caprona, The Lives of Christopher Chant, Witch Week, Mixed Magics,* and *Conrad's Fate*)

Le Guin, Ursula K. <u>The Earthsea Cycle</u>.
Ged sails to the Isle of Roke to receive the training in wizardry he needs to control his power and unwittingly unleashes a great evil on Earthsea. (*A Wizard of Earthsea, The Tombs of Atuan, The Farthest Shore, Tehanu, Tales from Earthsea,* and *The Other Wind*)

Lewis, C. S. <u>The Chronicles of Narnia</u>.
Peter, Susan, Lucy, and Edmund walk through a magical wardrobe into the land of Narnia, where the animals can talk and it's always winter and never Christmas. (In publication order: *The Lion, the Witch and the Wardrobe*; *Prince Caspian*; *The Voyage of the Dawntreader*; *The Silver Chair*; *The Horse and His Boy*; *The Magician's Nephew*; and *The Last Battle*)

McKillip, Patricia A. <u>Riddle-Master: The Complete Trilogy</u>.
When the wizards disappeared from Hed, they left only riddles in their wake. Prince Morgon thought he had mastered them until a great evil threatens his kingdom. He must seek the High One for the answer that will save his people. (*The Riddle-Master of Hed, The Heir of Sea and Fire,* and *Harpist in the Wind.*)

Nimmo, Jenny. <u>The Children of the Red King</u>.
Charlie Bone thinks he's just an ordinary boy, until he starts hearing the conversations of people in photographs. Then Grandma Bone informs him that he is one of the Endowed and must attend Bloors Academy, where the Endowed engage in a generations-old struggle between good and evil. (*Midnight for Charlie Bone, Charlie Bone and the Time Twister, Charlie Bone and the Invisible Boy, Charlie Bone and the Castle of Mirrors,* and *Charlie Bone and the Hidden King*)

Nix, Garth. <u>The Keys to the Kingdom</u>.
When Arthur Penhaligon innocently accepts the first key, he wanders from his own world into that of the House, where he must duel the rulers of each Day to save his family and himself. (*Mister Monday, Grim Tuesday, Drowned Wednesday,* and *Sir Thursday*)

Pierce, Tamora. <u>The Magic Circle Chronicles</u>.
At Winding Circle Temple, four young people discover their magical abilities and learn to use them before they venture out into the world. (*Sandry's Book, Tris's Book, Daja's Book, Briar's Book, Magic Steps, Street Magic, Cold Fire, Shatterglass,* and *The Will of the Empress*)

Pullman, Philip. <u>His Dark Materials Series</u>.
In Lyra's world, everyone has a daemon—an animal companion that embodies a person's spirit. Hers is named Pantalaimon, and together they grow-up at Jordan College, Oxford. When Lyra's best friend disappears, Lyra and Pan journey into the unknown to find him, with only a mysterious golden compass to guide them. (*The Golden Compass, The Subtle Knife, The Amber Spyglass,* and *Lyra's Oxford*)

Riordan, Rick. <u>Percy Jackson and the Olympians</u>.
The Greek gods are alive and well and living on Mt. Olympus which now hovers at floor 600 of the Empire State Building. Their mortal offspring attend Camp Half-Blood so they can learn to elude monsters and survive in the twenty-first century. Percy Jackson thinks he's just a dyslexic kid with attention-deficit/hyperactivity disorder until a battle with the Minotaur lands him in Camp Half Blood where he learns the truth. (*The Lightning Thief* and *The Sea of Monsters*)

Sage, Angie. <u>The Septimus Heap Series</u>.
In a realm where there are many ordinary wizards and one Extraordinary Wizard, ordinary wizard Silas Heap does his best to protect all of his children. When Extraordinary Wizard Marcia warns him that his fosterling, Jenna, is in danger from the evil Dom Daniel, he whisks them away to the marshes where he hopes all will be well. (*Magyk* and *Flyte*.)

Stewart, Paul, and Chris Riddell. <u>The Edge Chronicles</u>.
Past the Deepwoods lies Edge, where Undertown rests on the ground and the city of Sanctaphrax floats above. Twig grew up in the Deepwoods but never quite fit in with the other wood trolls. He ventures out on his own and begins a series of events that lead him to Edge and beyond. (*Beyond the Deepwoods, Stormchaser, Midnight over Sanctaphrax, The Curse of the Gloamglozer, The Last of the Sky Pirates, Vox,* and *Freeglader*)

Stroud, Jonathan. <u>The Bartimaeus Trilogy</u>.
In an England where magic-wielders control the government, Nathaniel studies to become a magician and calls up the powerful djinni Bartimaeus to assist him. (*The Amulet of Samarkand, The Golem's Eye,* and *Ptolemy's Gate*)

Yolen, Jane. *Wizard's Hall*.
When Henry's mother sends him to study magic at Wizard's Hall, he discovers that although his ability to work wonders is limited, as the 113th pupil, it is up to him to save the school.

GIRL POWER

Berry, Liz. *The China Garden.*
Seventeen-year-old Clare is waiting to hear the results of her school exams when she accompanies her mother to the Ravensmere estate, where mystery, romance, and danger lurk.

Billingsley, Franny. *The Folk Keeper.*
Corinna disguises herself as boy and teaches herself how to be a Folk Keeper so that she can escape life in the orphanage. She never suspects that her skills at keeping the gremlin-like folk at bay will take her to Cliffsend where far more than a new job awaits her.

Bray, Libba. *A Great and Terrible Beauty.*
After the mysterious death of her mother, Gemma moves from India to London's Spence School for girls, where she discovers a gateway into another realm. (Sequel: *Rebel Angels*)

Croggon, Alison. **The Pellinor Quartet.**
Sixteen-year-old Maerad's life of drudgery is transformed when Bard Cadvan senses the power lying dormant within her and convinces her to escape with him to receive training as a Bard. (*The Naming* and *The Riddle*)

Fforde, Jasper. **The Thursday Next Series.**
In an England where dodos have been recreated and literature is of paramount importance, literary detective Thursday Next must stop criminals who wish to destroy the world's literature. (*The Eyre Affair, Lost in a Good Book, The Well of Lost Plots,* and *Something Rotten*)

Fletcher, Susan. **The Dragon Chronicles.**
Kaeldra and her kin have the legendary ability to speak to dragons, which lands them in some dangerous situations. (*Dragon's Milk, Flight of the Dragon Kyn,* and *The Sign of Dove*)

Kindl, Patrice. *Owl in Love.*
Instead of hunting at night as she is supposed to, Owl Tycho, a shape-shifter who can transform from human to owl at will, spends her nights perched outside the window of her beloved science teacher.

Levine, Gail Carson. *Ella Enchanted.*
Because of a fairy's gift of obedience, Ella grows up always having to do whatever anyone commands. In an attempt to break the spell, she ventures out on her own and encounters dwarves, giants, wicked stepsisters, and her prince charming.

McKillip, Patricia A. *The Forgotten Beasts of Eld.*
Sybel, daughter of a wizard, cares for the legendary beasts of Eld and raises Tam who was abandoned as a baby. But, unbeknownst to Sybel, he is the son of an enemy.

McKinley, Robin. *The Blue Sword.*
When King Corlath kidnaps Harry Crewe, a young woman who is bored with a life of growing oranges in the isolated colony of Daria, he recognizes immediately that she has the power to wield the legendary Blue Sword.

McKinley, Robin. *The Hero and the Crown.*
In this prequel to *The Blue Sword,* Aerin, the only child of a witch-woman from the North and the king of the mythical Damar, teaches herself how to slay dragons.

McNaughton, Janet. *An Earthly Knight.*
In twelfth-century Scotland, Jenny gives her heart to Tam Lin. Her father has other plans, and Jenny must find the courage to pursue her love.

Melling, O. R. *Hunter's Moon.*
When cousins Findahair and Gwenhyvar backpack through Ireland, Findahair is stolen away by the King of the Fairies, and Gwen must match wits with him and win back her cousin. (Sequel: *The Summer King*)

Napoli, Donna Jo. *Sirena.*
Sirena, a mermaid, knows that her song means death for any sailor that hears it, and so she exiles herself to the Isle of Lemnos, never dreaming an entrancing sailor will be marooned there.

Nix, Garth. The Abhorsen Sequence.
Sabriel and Lireal, two different Charter Mages, use all of their powers to save the Old Kingdom and the world. (*Sabriel, Lirael: Daughter of the Clayr, Abhorsen,* and *Across the Wall*)

Pattou, Edith. *East.*
To save her sister, Rose agrees to journey with the huge white bear to his castle-in-a-cave. She becomes entangled in both enchantment and danger in her new home.

Pierce, Tamora. The Song of the Lioness Quartet.
In Tortall, only boys are allowed to become knights. When Alanna disguises herself as a boy and begins her knightly education, she sets into motion events that will alter everything in the realm. (*Alanna: The First Adventure, In the Hand of the Goddess, The Woman Who Rides Like a Man,* and *The Lioness Rampant*)

Pratchett, Terry. *The Wee Free Men.*
When the Queen of Fairyland kidnaps her brother, Tiffany sets off to rescue him, armed with a frying pan and the aid of six-inch-high blue pictsies. (Sequels: *A Hat Full of Sky* and *Wintersmith.*)

Snyder, Midori. *Hannah's Garden.*
Cassie's grandfather is in the hospital, and she and her mother rush to reach him. They find him on the brink of death and his house and garden in a ruinous state. As Cassie tries to restore order, she becomes caught in the plots of two rival fairy clans.

Springer, Nancy. The Rowan Hood Series.
Unbeknownst to Robin Hood, he has a thirteen-year-old daughter living in the forest. When her mother, the healer Celandine of the forest fair folk, is murdered, Rosemary

decides to search for her famous father. (***Rowan Hood, Lionclaw, Outlaw Princess of Sherwood, Wild Boy,*** and ***Rowan Hood Returns: The Final Chapter***)

Wooding, Chris. *Poison*.
When the phaeries steal her baby sister, Poison, a rebellious teen, braves the dangers of a gruesome phaerie realm to confront the Lord of Phaerie himself.

Wrede, Patricia. <u>The Enchanted Forest Chronicles</u>.
Princesses must be ladylike and concentrate on their embroidery, and dragons must be fought by brave knights who rescue fair maidens—until Princess Cimerone decides that she will do things differently. (***Dealing with Dragons, Searching for Dragons, Calling on Dragons,*** and ***Talking to Dragons***)

Appendix C

Speculative Fiction in Audio-Visual Formats

Audio Books

Adams, Douglas

<u>**The Hitchhiker's Guide to the Galaxy Series.**</u> (Science)

Adams, Richard

Watership Down. (Animal)

Tales from Watership Down. (Animal)

Alexander, Lloyd

<u>**The Chronicles of Prydain.**</u> (Epic)

The Iron Ring. (Epic)

Allende, Isabel

<u>**The Alexander Cold Trilogy.**</u> (Alternate)

Anderson, Kevin J.

<u>**The Saga of the Seven Suns.**</u> (Science)

Anderson, M. T.

Feed. (Science)

The Game of Sunken Places. (Alternate)

Asimov, Isaac

I, Robot. (Science)

Atwater-Rhodes, Amelia

Hawksong. (Romance)

Snakecharm. (Romance)

Falcondance. (Romance)

Atwood, Margaret

The Handmaid's Tale. (Science)

Avi

Bright Shadow. (Wizard)

Perloo the Bold. (Animal)

Barker, Clive

<u>**The Books of Abarat.**</u> (Alternate)

Barron, T. A.

<u>**The Lost Years of Merlin.**</u> (Myth)

Barry, Dave, and Ridley Pearson

Peter and the Star Catchers. (Alternate)

Peter and the Shadow Thieves.

Barry, Max

Jennifer Government. (Science)

Beagle, Peter S.

Tamsin. (Dark)

Berry, Liz

The China Garden. (Romance)

Black, Holly

Valiant. (Alternate)

Blackwell, Gary

The Year of the Hangman. (Alternate)

Bloor, Edward.

Story Time. (Mystery)

Bond, Nancy

A String in the Harp. (Time)

Bradbury, Ray

Fahrenheit 451. (Science)

Bradly, Marion Zimmer

Lady of Avalon. (Myth)

The Mists of Avalon. (Myth)

Bray, Libba

A Great and Terrible Beauty. (Alternate)

Rebel Angels. (Alternate)

Brennen, Herbie

The Faerie Wars. (Alternate)

The Purple Emperor. (Alternate)

Brooks, Terry

The Shannara Series. (Epic)

Brown, Rita Mae

Murder, She Meowed. (Mystery)

Murder on the Prowl. (Mystery)

Pawing Through the Past. (Mystery)

Claws and Effect. (Mystery)

Catch as Cat Can. (Mystery)

Tail of the Tip-off. (Mystery)

Whisker of Evil. (Mystery)

Cat's Eyewitness. (Mystery)

Sour Puss. (Mystery)

Bruchac, Joseph

The Dark Pond. (Dark)

Bujold, Lois McMaster

The Curse of Chalion. (Epic)

The Paladin of Souls. (Epic)

Bunting, Eve.

The Presence. (Dark)

Cabot, Meg

The Mediator Series. (Dark)

Card, Orson Scott

Enchantment. (Fairy)

The Ender Wiggin Series. (Science)

Magic Street. (Alternate)

The Tales of Alvin Maker.
(Alternate)

Chabon, Michael

Summerland. (Alternate)

Child, Lincoln

Utopia. (Science)

Clarke, Susanna

Jonathan Strange and Mr. Norell. (Wizard)

Clements, Andrew.

Things Not Seen. (Science)

Colfer, Eoin.

The Artemis Fowl Series. (Alternate)

The Supernaturalist. (Science)

The Wish List. (Dark)

Collins, Suzanne

> <u>The Underland Chronicles.</u>
> (Alternate)

Constable, Kate

> <u>The Chanters of Tremaris Trilogy.</u>
> (Epic)

Cooney, Caroline

> *Goddess of Yesterday.* (Myth)

Cooper, Susan

> <u>The Dark Is Rising Sequence.</u> (Epic)
>
> *The King of Shadows.* (Time)

Coville, Bruce

> *The Song of the Wanderer.* (Myth)

Crichton, Michael

> *Timeline.* (Science)

Crossley-Holland, Kevin

> <u>The Arthur Trilogy.</u> (Myth)

Dahl, Roald

> *James and the Giant Peach.*
> (Alternate)
>
> *The Witches.* (Dark)
>
> *Whispering to Witches.* (Dark)

Davidson, Mary Janice

> *Undead and Unwed.* (Dark)
>
> *Undead and Unappreciated.* (Dark)
>
> *Undead and Unreturnable.* (Dark)

Delaney, Joseph

> *Revenge of the Witch.* (Dark)

Dickinson, John

> *The Cup of the World.* (Epic)
>
> *The Widow and the King.* (Epic)

Dickinson, Peter

> *Eva.* (Science)

Donaldson, Stephen R.

> *The Runes of Earth.* (Epic)

Duane, Diane

> <u>The Young Wizard Series.</u> (Wizard)

Dunkle, Claire

> *The Hollow Kingdom.* (Alternate)
>
> *Close Kin.* (Alternate)

DuPrau, Jeanne

> *The City of Ember.* (Science)
>
> *The People of Sparks.*

Farmer, Nancy

> *The House of the Scorpion.* (Science)
>
> *The Sea of Trolls.* (Epic)

Fforde, Jasper

> <u>The Thursday Next Series.</u>
> (Mystery)
>
> <u>The Nursery Crime Series.</u>
> (Mystery)

Funke, Cornelia

> *Dragon Rider.* (Myth)
>
> *The Thief Lord.* (Alternate)

Gabaldon, Diana

> <u>The Outlander Series.</u> (Romance)

Gaiman, Neil

> *Coraline.* (Dark)

Haddix, Margaret Peterson

> *Among the Hidden.* (Science)
>
> *Just Ella.* (Fairy)

Halam, Ann

Dr. Franklin's Island. (Science)

Harris, Charlaine

Dead as a Doornail. (Dark)

Heinlein, Robert A.

The Door into Summer. (Science)

Have Space Suite, Will Travel. (Science)

Starship Troopers. (Science)

Heneghan, James

The Grave. (Time)

Herbert, Brian

Prelude to Dune. (Science)

The Legends of Dune. (Science)

Hinton, S. E.

Hawkes Harbor. (Dark)

Hoffman, Alice

Probable Future. (Dark)

Hoffman, Mary

The Stravaganza Trilogy. (Alternate)

Hooper, Kay

The "Bishop" Special Crime Unit Series. (Dark)

Horowitz, Anthony

Raven's Gate. (Dark)

Huxley, Aldus

Brave New World. (Science)

Jacques, Brian

The Redwall Series. (Animal)

Jarvis, Robin

The Dark Portal. (Animal)

Jones, Diana Wynne

The Chestomanci Chronicles. (Wizard)

Jordan, Robert

The Wheel of Time. (Epic)

Keyes, Daniel

Flowers for Algernon. (Science)

Kindl, Patrice

Owl in Love. (Alternate)

King, Stephen

Cell. (Dark)

Klause, Annette Curtis

Blood and Chocolate. (Dark)

Koontz, Dean

Odd Thomas. (Dark)

Forever Odd. (Dark)

Kostova, Elizabeth

The Historian. (Dark)

Kress, Nancy

Beggars in Spain. (Science)

LeGuin, Ursula K.

The Earthsea Cycle. (Epic)

Gifts. (Alternate)

The Lathe of Heaven. (Science)

Levine, Gail Carson

Ella Enchanted. (Fairy)

The Two Princesses of Bamarre. (Alternate)

The Wish. (Alternate)

Levinson, Paul

The Plot to Save Socrates. (Science)

Levitin, Sonia

The Cure. (Science)

Lowry, Lois

The Giver. (Science)

Gathering Blue. (Science)

Messenger. (Science)

McCaffrey, Anne

The Chronicles of Pern. (Science)

The Saga of the Talents. (Dark)

The Tower and the Hive. (Dark)

MacHale, D. J.

The Pendragon Series. (Series)

Meyer, Kai

The Water Mirror. (Epic)

McKinley, Robin

The Blue Sword. (Epic)

The Hero and the Crown. (Epic)

Meyer, Stephanie

Twilight. (Dark)

Moon, Elizabeth

The Speed of Dark.
(Science)

Mosely, Walter

47. (Science)

Naylor, Phyllis Reynolds

Sang Spell. (Alternate)

Nicholson, William

The Wind on Fire Trilogy.
(Alternate)

Niffenegger, Audrey

The Time Traveler's Wife. (Time)

Nimmo, Jenny

The Children of the Red King.
(Wizard)

Nix, Garth

The Abhorsen Sequence. (Epic)

O'Brien, Robert

Mrs. Frisby and the Rats of NIMH.
(Animal)

Z for Zachariah. (Science)

Oppel, Kenneth

The Silverwing Trilogy. (Animal)

Orwell, George

Nineteen Eighty-Four. (Science)

Paolini, Christopher

The Inheritance Trilogy. (Myth)

Patterson, James

Maximum Ride: The Angel Experiment. (Science)

Pattou, Edith

East. (Fairy)

Paver, Michelle

Wolf Brother. (Myth)

Peck, Dale

Drift House. (Time)

Philbrick, Rodman

The Last Book in the Universe.
(Science)

Pierce, Tamora

Daughter of the Lioness Duology. (Alternate)

The Magic Circle Quartet. (Wizard)

The Song of the Lioness Quartet. (Alternate)

Pope, Elizabeth Marie

The Perilous Gard. (Mystery)

Pratchett, Terry

Discworld. (Alternate)

The Wee Free Men. (Alternate)

Hat Full of Sky. (Alternate)

Only You Can Save Mankind. (Science)

Prue, Sally

Cold Tom. (Alternate)

Pullman, Philip

Clockwork or All Wound Up. (Mystery)

Count Karlstein. (Dark)

The His Dark Materials Series. (Epic)

Putney, Mary Jo

A Kiss of Fate. (Romance)

Reiche, Dietlof

Ghost Ship. (Dark)

Rice, Anne

Interview with the Vampire. (Dark)

The Vampire Lestat. (Dark)

The Queen of the Damned. (Dark)

The Tale of the Body Thief. (Dark)

The Vampire Armand. (Dark)

Merrick. (Dark)

Blood and Gold, or, The Story of Marius. (Dark)

Blackwood Farm. (Dark)

Blood Canticle. (Dark)

Riordan, Rick

The Lightning Thief. (Myth)

The Sea of Monsters. (Myth)

Robinson, Kim Stanley

The Martian Romance Trilogy. (Science)

Rosoff, Meg

how i live now. (Science)

Roth, Philip

The Plot against America. (Alternate)

Rowling, J. K.

The Harry Potter Series. (Wizard)

Sage, Angie

Magyk. (Wizard)

Soto, Gary

Afterlife. (Dark)

Springer, Nancy

The Rowan Hood Series. (Myth)

Stewart, Paul

Beyond the Deepwoods. (Alternate)

Stormchaser. (Alternate)

Midnight over Sanctaphrax. (Alternate)

Stoker, Bram

Dracula. (Dark)

Straub, Peter

lost boy, lost girl. (Dark)

Stroud, Jonathan

The Bartimaeus Trilogy. (Wizard)

Turner, Megan Whelan

The Theif. (Alternate)

Twelve Hawks, John

The Traveler. (Alternate)

Tolkien, J. R. R.

The Hobbit. (Epic)

The Lord of the Rings. (Epic)

The Silmarillion. (Epic)

Vizzini, Ned

Be More Chill. (Science)

Weber, David

War of Honor. (Science)

Wells, H. G.

The Island of Dr. Moreau. (Science)

The Time Machine. (Science)

The War of the Worlds. (Science)

Whitcomb, Laura

A Certain Slant of Light. (Dark)

Williams, Maiya

The Golden Hour. (Time)

Willis, Connie

Dooms Day Book. (Science)

To Say Nothing of the Dog. (Science)

Wrede, Patricia C.

The Enchanted Forest Chronicles. (Myth)

Yolen, Jane

Briar Rose. (Fairy)

The Devil's Arithmetic. (Time)

The Sword of the Rightful King. (Myth)

Zevin, Gabrielle

Elsewhere. (Dark)

Videos

Adams, Douglas

The Hitchhiker's Guide to the Galaxy. (Science)

Adams, Richard

Watership Down. (Animal)

Alexander, Lloyd

The Black Cauldron. (Epic)

Asimov, Isaac

I, Robot. (Science)

Atwood, Margaret

The Handmaid's Tale. (Science)

Beagle, Peter S

The Last Unicorn. (Myth)

Bradly, Marion Zimmer

The Mists of Avalon. (Myth)

Bradbury, Ray

Fahrenheit 451. (Science)

Crichton, Michael

Timeline. (Science)

Dahl, Roald

James and the Giant Peach. (Alternate)

The Witches. (Dark)

Ende, Michael

The Neverending Story. (Epic)

Goldman, William

The Princess Bride. (Fairy Tale)

Heinlein, Robert A.

Starship Troopers. (Science)

Herbert, Frank

Dune. (Science)

Jacques, Brian

Redwall. (Animal)

Jones, Diana Wynne

Howl's Moving Castle. (Alternate)

Le Guin, Ursula K.

A Wizard of Earthsea. (Epic)

The Tombs of Atuan. (Epic)

L'Engle, Madeleine

A Wrinkle in Time. (Science)

Lewis, C. S.

The Lion, the Witch and the Wardrobe. (Alternate)

O'Brien, Robert

Mrs. Frisby and the Rats of NIMH. (Animal)

Orwell, George

Nineteen Eighty-Four. (Science)

Paolini, Christopher

Eragon.

Rice, Anne

Interview with the Vampire. (Dark)

Rowling, J. K.

Harry Potter and the Sorcerer's Stone. (Wizard)

Harry Potter and the Chamber of Secrets. (Wizard)

Harry Potter and the Prisoner of Azkaban. (Wizard)

Harry Potter and the Goblet of Fire. (Wizard)

Stoker, Bram

Dracula. (Dark)

Tolkien, J. R. R.

The Hobbit. (Epic)

The Lord of the Rings. (Epic)

Wells, H. G.

The Island of Dr. Moreau. (Science)

The Time Machine. (Science)

The War of the Worlds. (Science)

Yolen, Jane

The Devil's Arithmetic. (Time)

Best Books for Book Clubs

Alexander, Lloyd

The Iron Ring. (Epic)

The Wizard in the Tree. (Wizard)

Almond, David

Skellig. (Alternate)

Anderson, M. T.

Feed. (Science)

The Game of Sunken Places. (Alternate)

Thirsty. (Dark)

Avi

Perloo the Bold. (Animal)

Beagle, Peter S.

The Last Unicorn. (Myth)

Bechard, Margaret

Spacer and Rat. (Science)

Bell, Hilari

The Wizard Test. (Wizard)

Berry, Liz

The China Garden. (Romance)

Bujold, Lois McMaster.

The Curse of Chalion. (Epic)

Card, Orson Scott

Ender's Game. (Science)

Clarke, Susanna

Jonathan Strange and Mr. Norrell. (Wizard)

Clements, Andrew

Things Not Seen. (Science)

Colfer, Eoin

The Wish List. (Dark)

Cooper, Susan

King of Shadows. (Time)

Curry, Jane Louise

The Black Canary. (Time)

Dickinson, Peter

The Ropemaker. (Alternate)

Emshwiller, Carol

The Mount. (Science)

Farmer, Nancy

The House of the Scorpion. (Science)

The Sea of Trolls. (Alternate)

Ferris, Jean

Once upon a Marigold. (Fairy)

Fforde, Jasper

The Eyre Affair. (Mystery)

Gaiman, Neil

Coraline. (Dark)

Stardust. (Alternate)

Geras, Adele.

Troy. (Myth)

Goodman, Alison

Singing the Dogstar Blues. (Science)

Hale, Shannon

The Goose Girl. (Fairy)

Jones, Diana Wynne

Howl's Moving Castle. (Alternate)

Jordan, Sherryl

The Hunting of the Last Dragon. (Myth)

Kindl, Patrice

Lost in the Labyrinth. (Myth)

Owl in Love. (Alternate)

Klause, Annette Curtis

Blood and Chocolate. (Dark)

Silver Kiss. (Dark)

Kushner, Ellen

Thomas the Rhymer. (Romance)

L'Engle, Madeleine

A Wrinkle in Time. (Science)

Levine, Gail Carson

Ella Enchanted. (Fairy)

The Wish. (Alternate)

Lowry, Lois

The Giver. (Science)

McKillip, Patricia A.

The Alphabet of Thorn. (Alternate)

Winter Rose. (Fairy)

McKinley, Robin

Beauty: A Retelling of the Story of Beauty and the Beast. (Fairy)

The Hero and the Crown. (Epic)

Rose Daughter. (Fairy)

Mosely, Walter

47. (Science)

Napoli, Donna Jo

Beast. (Fairy)

Sirena. (Myth)

Naylor, Phyllis Reynolds

Jade Green: A Ghost Story. (Dark)

O'Brien, Robert

Mrs. Frisby and the Rats of NIMH. (Animal)

Oppel, Kenneth

Airborn. (Alternate)

Pattou, Edith

East. (Fairy)

Pullman, Philip

Clockwork or All Wound Up. (Mystery)

Rees, Douglas

Vampire High. (Dark)

Vande Velde, Vivian

Never Trust a Dead Man. (Mystery)

Westerfeld, Scott

Peeps. (Dark)

Willis, Connie

Doomsday Book. (Science)

Wooding, Chris

The Haunting of Alaizabel Cray. (Dark)

Poison. (Alternate)

Yolen, Jane

The Devil's Arithmetic. (Time)

The Sword of the Rightful King. (Myth)

Zevin, Gabrielle

Elsewhere. (Dark)

Resources

Books

Allen, Judy. *Fantasy Encyclopedia*. Boston: Kingfisher, 2005.

Ansell, Janice, and Pam Spencer Holley. *What Do Children and Young Adults Read Next?* Farmington Hills, MI: Gale, 2004.

Barron, Neil, editor. *Anatomy of Wonder: A Critical Guide to Science Fiction*. 5th edition. Westport, CT: Libraries Unlimited, 2004.

Card, Orson Scott. *How to Write Science Fiction and Fantasy*. Cincinnati, OH: Writer's Digest Books, 1990.

Clute, John, and John Grant, editors. *The Encyclopedia of Fantasy*. New York: St. Martin's Press, 1997.

Clute, John, and Peter Nichols, editors. *The Encyclopedia of Science Fiction*. New York: St. Martin's Griffin, 1995.

D'Ammassa, Don. *Encyclopedia of Science Fiction*. New York: Facts On File, 2004.

Fonseca, Anthony J., and June Michele Pulliam. *Hooked on Horror*. 2nd edition. Westport, CT: Libraries Unlimited, 2002.

Gates, Pamela. *Fantasy Literature for Children and Young Adults*. Lanham, MD: Scarecrow, 2003.

Gillespie, John T., and Catherine Barr. *Best Books for Middle School and Junior High Readers: Grades 6–9*. Westport, CT: Libraries Unlimited, 2004.

Best Books for High School: Grades 9–12. Westport, CT: Libraries Unlimited, 2004.

Hartwell, David G. *Age of Wonders: Exploring the World of Science Fiction*. New York: Tor, 1996.

Herald, Diana Tixier. *Fluent in Fantasy: A Guide to Reading Interests*. Englewood, CO: Libraries Unlimited, 1999.

Herald, Diana Tixier. *Teen Genreflecting: A Guide to Reading Interests*. 2nd edition. Westport, CT: Libraries Unlimited, 2003.

Herald, Diana, Tixier, and Bonnie Kunzel. *Strictly Science Fiction: A Guide to Reading Interests*. Englewood, CO: Libraries Unlimited, 2002.

Jones, Patrick. *A Core Collection for Young Adults*. New York: Neal-Schuman, 2003.

Jones, Stephen, and Kim Newman, editors. *Horror: 100 Best Books*. New York: Carroll & Graf, 1990.

Jones, Stephen, and Kim Newman, editors. *Horror: Another 100 Best Books*. New York: Carroll & Graf Publishers, 2005.

Joshi, S. T., and Stefan Dziemianowicz. *Supernatural Literature of the World: An Encyclopedia*. Westport, CT: Greenwood Press, 2005.

Kunzel, Bonnie, and Suzanne Manczuk. *First Contact: A Reader's Selection of Science Fiction and Fantasy*. Lanham, MD: Scarecrow Press, 2001.

Lynn, Ruth Nadelman. *Fantasy Literature for Children and Young Adults: A Comprehensive Guide*. 5th ed. Westport, CT: Libraries Unlimited, 2005.

Marcus, Leonard S. *The Wand in the Word: Conversations with Writers of Fantasy*. Cambridge, MA: Candlewick, 2006.

McCarty, Michael. *Giants of the Genre: Interviews with Science Fiction, Fantasy and Horror's Greatest Talents*. Rockville, MD: Wildside Press, 2003.

Stableford, Brian. *Historical Dictionary of Science Fiction*. Lanham, MD: Scarecrow Press, 2004.

Historical Dictionary of Fantasy Literature. Lanham, MD: Scarecrow Press, 2005.

Tolkien, J. R. R. *The Tolkien Reader*. New York: Ballantine Books, 1966.

Westfahl, Gary, editor. *The Greenwood Encyclopedia of Fantasy and Science Fiction: Themes, Works, and Wonders*. Westport, CT: Greenwood Press, 2005.

Wintle, Justin, and Emma Fisher. *The Pied Pipers: Interviews with the Influential Creators of Children's Literature*. New York: Paddington Press, 1975.

Web Sites

Science Fiction, Fantasy, and Horror

Database of Award-Winning Children's Literature: http://www.dawcl.com/search.asp

Fantastic Fiction: http://www.fantasticfiction.co.uk/

Genrefluent: http://www.genrefluent.com/

Horror Writer's Association Reading List: http://www.horror.org/

The Internet Movie Database: http://www.imdb.com/

The Internet Speculative Fiction Database: http://www.isfdb.org/cgi-bin/index.cg

The Kent District Library's "What's Next?" Database: http://www.kdl.org/libcat/whatsnext.asp

New York Public Library's Books for the Teen Age: http://teenlink.nypl.org/bta1.cfm

Romantic Science Fiction and Fantasy: http://www.romanticsf.com/

Science Fiction and Fantasy: http://www.sfsite.com/

Science Fiction and Fantasy: http://www.sfsite.com/

Science Fiction and Fantasy Net Home: http://www.sff.net/

Science Fiction and Fantasy Related Sites: http://robertsullivan.org/sf/index.html

Science Fiction and Fantasy Research Database: http://lib-edit.tamu.edu/cushing/sffrd//

Science Fiction and Fantasy World: http://www.sffworld.com/

Sci/Fan: Books and Links for the Science Fiction Fan: http://www.scifan.com/

Teen Reads: http://www.teenreads.com/

The TV SciFi Network: http://www.scifi.com/scifiction/

The Urchronia Alternate History Database: http://www.uchronia.net/intro.html

Young Adult Science Fiction and Fantasy Editor Sharyn November: http://www.sharyn.org/children.html

Harry Potter

Bloomsbury's Harry Potter: http://www.bloomsburymagazine.com/harrypotter/

Harry Potter Lexicon: http://www.hp-lexicon.org/index-2.html

Harry Potter Movies: http://harrypotter.warnerbros.com/

Harry Potter Parties: http://www.potterparties.com/

Mugglenet: http://www.mugglenet.com/

Scholastic's Harry Potter: http://www.scholastic.com/harrypotter/home.asp

The Lord of the Rings

The Lord of the Rings Movies: http://www.lordoftherings.net/

The One Ring: http://www.theonering.net/index.shtml

The Tolkien Society: http://www.tolkiensociety.org/

Graphic Novels

Graphic Novels for Public Libraries: http://my.voyager.net/~sraiteri/graphicnovels.htm

The Lair: The Website Reviewing Graphic Novels: http://lair.noflyingnotights.com/

No Flying Tights for Teens: http://www.noflyingnotights.com/

Authors

Douglas Adams: http://www.douglasadams.com/

David Almond: http://www.randomhouse.com/features/davidalmond/

Kevin J. Anderson: http://www.wordfire.com/

Piers Anthony: http://www.hipiers.com

Sarah Ash: http://www.sarah-ash.com/

Amelia Atwater-Rhodes: http://www.randomhouse.com/features/atwaterrhodes/home.htm

Avi: http://www.avi-writer.com/

Kage Baker: http://www.kagebaker.com/

T. A. Barron: http://www.tabarron.com/tabarron/

Hilari Bell: http://www.sfwa.org/members/bell/

Liz Berry: http://www.lizberrybooks.com/

Joanne Bertin: http://www.futurefiction.com/joanne_bertin.htm

Franny Billingsley: http://www.frannybillingsley.com/

Anne Bishop: http://www.annebishop.com/

Holly Black: http://www.blackholly.com/

Gary Blackwood: http://mowrites4kids.drury.edu/authors/blackwood/

N. E. Bode: http://www.theanybodies.com/

Ray Bradbury: http://www.raybradbury.com/

Marion Zimmer Bradley: http://mzbworks.home.att.net/

Libba Bray: http://www.libbabray.com/

Herbie Brennan: http://www.herbiebrennan.com/

Terry Brooks: http://www.terrybrooks.net/

Rita Mae Brown: http://www.ritamaebrown.com/

M. N. Browne: http://www.nmbrowne.com/

Joseph Bruchac: http://www.josephbruchac.com/

Lois McMaster Bujold: http://www.dendarii.com/

Jim Butcher: http://www.jim-butcher.com/

Meg Cabot: http://www.megcabot.com/index.cfm

Dia Calhoun: http://www.diacalhoun.com/

Orson Scott Card: http://www.hatrack.com/

Suzy McKee Charnas: http://www.suzymckeecharnas.com/

C. J. Cherryh: http://www.cherryh.com/

Arthur C. Clarke: http://www.clarkefoundation.org/

Susanna Clarke: http://www.jonathanstrange.com/

David Clement-Davies: http://www.davidclementdavies.com/

Eoin Colfer: http://www.eoincolfer.com/

Suzanne Collins: http://www.suzannecollinsbooks.com/

Louise Cooper: http://www.louisecooper.com/

Susan Cooper: http://www.thelostland.com/welcome.htm

Kate Constable: http://www.kateconstable.com/

Bruce Coville: http://www.thelostland.com/welcome.htm

Roald Dahl: http://www.roalddahl.com/

Mary Janice Davidson: http://www.maryjanicedavidson.net/

Charles de Lint: http://www.sfsite.com/charlesdelint/

Philip K. Dick: http://www.philipkdick.com/

Peter Dickinson: http://www.peterdickinson.com/

Stephen R. Donaldson: http://www.stephenrdonaldson.com/

Diane Duane: http://www.dianeduane.com/

David Duncan: http://www.daveduncan.com/

Clare Dunkle: http://www.claredunkle.com/

Jeanne DuPrau: http://www.jeanneduprau.com/index.shtml

David Farland: http://www.runelords.com/

Raymond Feist: http://www.raymondfeistbooks.com/

Jasper Fforde: http://www.jasperfforde.com/

Eric Flint: http://www.ericflint.net/

Diana Gabaldon: http://www.cco.caltech.edu/~gatti/gabaldon/gabaldon.html

Neil Gaiman: http://www.neilgaiman.com/

Adele Geras: http://www.adelegeras.com/

Mary Downing Hahn: http://www.childrensbookguild.org/hahn.htm

Shannon Hale: http://www.childrensbookguild.org/hahn.htm

Barbara Hambly: http://www.barbarahambly.com/

Victoria Hanley: http://www.victoriahanley.com/

Charlaine Harris: http://www.charlaineharris.com/

Lian Hearn: http://www.theotori.com/BookGeneral/author.asp

Robert A. Heinlein: http://www.heinleinsociety.org/

Frank Herbert: http://www.dunenovels.com/

Robin Hobb: http://www.robinhobb.com/

Mary Hoffman: http://www.maryhoffman.co.uk/

Kay Hooper: http://www.kayhooper.com/

Anthony Horowitz: http://www.anthonyhorowitz.com/

Erin Hunter: http://home.earthlink.net/~lupuscatella/id96.html

Brian Jacques: http://www.redwall.org/

Robin Jarvis: http://www.robinjarvis.com/

Diana Wynne Jones: http://www.dianawynnejones.com/

Robert Jordan: http://www.tor.com/jordan/

Lene Kaaberbol: http://www.kaaberboel.dk/uk-index.htm

Guy Gavriel Kay: http://www.brightweavings.com/

Elizabeth Kerner: http://elizabethkerner.com/

Patrice Kindl: http://www.patricekindl.com/

Stephen King: http://www.stephenking.com/

Dean Koontz: http://www.randomhouse.com/bantamdell/koontz/

Annette Curtis Klaus: http://www.childrensbookguild.org/klause.htm

Nancy Kress: http://www.sff.net/people/nankress/

Mercedes Lackey: http://www.mercedeslackey.com/

Justine Larbelstier: http://www.justinelarbalestier.com/

Ursula K. Le Guin: http://www.ursulakleguin.com/

C. S. Lewis: http://www.cslewis.org/

Lois Lowry: http://www.loislowry.com/

J. D. MacHale: http://www.thependragonadventure.com/

Ian R. MacLeod: http://www.ianrmacleod.com/

Gregory Maguire: http://www.gregorymaguire.com/

Juliet Marillier: http://www.julietmarillier.com/

George R. R. Martin: http://www.georgerrmartin.com/

Anne McCaffrey: http://www.annemccaffrey.net/

Robin McKinley: http://www.robinmckinley.com/

Rosalind Miles: http://www.rosalind.net/

Donna Jo Napoli: http://www.donnajonapoli.com/

William Nicholson: http://www.williamnicholson.co.uk/05/index.asp

Garth Nix: http://www.garthnix.co.uk/

Andre Norton: http://www.andre-norton.org/

Kenneth Oppel: http://www.kennethoppel.ca/

Christopher Paolini: http://www.alagaesia.com/

Michelle Paver: http://www.michellepaver.com/

Meredith Ann Pierce: http://www.moonandunicorn.com/

Tamora Pierce: http://www.tamora-pierce.com/

Terry Pratchett: http://www.terrypratchettbooks.com/

Philip Pullman: http://www.philip-pullman.com/

Melanie Rawn: http://www.melanierawn.com/

Laura Resnick: http://www.sff.net/people/laresnick/

Anne Rice: http://www.annerice.com/

Rick Riordan: http://www.rickriordan.com/

J. K. Rowling: http://www.jkrowling.com/

Rose E. Sabin: http://www.erosesabin.com/

Angie Sage: http://www.septimusheap.com/

Darren Shan: http://www.darrenshan.com/

Neal Shusterman: http://www.storyman.com/

Dan Simmons: http://www.dansimmons.com/

Paul Stewart: http://www.randomhouse.com/kids/edgechronicles/

R. L. Stine: http://www.rlstine.com/

Peter Straub: http://www.peterstraub.net/

Jonathan Stroud: http://www.bartimaeustrilogy.com/home.html

Judith Tarr: http://www.sff.net/people/judith%2Dtarr/

J. R. R. Tolkien: http://www.tolkien.co.uk/frame.asp

Harry Turtledove: http://www.sfsite.com/~silverag/turtledove.html

John Twelve Hawks: http://www.randomhouse.com/features/traveler/

Megan Whalen Turner: http://home.att.net/~mwturner/

Vivian Vande Velde: http://www.vivianvandevelde.com/

Lawrence Watt-Evans: http://www.watt-evans.com/

David Weber: http://www.davidweber.net/

Elizabeth Wein: http://www.elizabethwein.com/

H. G. Wells: http://www.hgwellsusa.50megs.com/

Scott Westerfeld: http://www.scottwesterfeld.com/

Tad Williams: http://www.tadwilliams.com/

Chris Wooding: http://www.chriswooding.com/

Patricia C. Wrede: http://www.dendarii.force9.co.uk/Wrede/

Jane Yolen: http://www.janeyolen.com/

Timothy Zahn: http://www.futurefiction.com/timothy_zahn.htm

Awards

ABBY: American Booksellers Book of the Year Award given annually by the American Booksellers Association in both the adult and children's categories. Renamed the Book Sense Book of the Year Award in 2000. (http://www.bookweb.org/news/awards/370.html)

ALAN: An American Library Association (ALA) Notable Book, determined annually by the Association for Library Service to Children (ALSC) Notable Children's Book Committee. (http://www.ala.org/ala/alsc/alsc.htm)

Alex: An American Library Association Award given annually by the Young Adult Library Services Association (YALSA) to ten books written for adults with special appeal to young adults grades six through twelve, determined by committee.

Andre Norton Award: First given in 2006, to be awarded annually by the Science Fiction and Fantasy Writers of America, Inc., for a science fiction or fantasy novel for young adults. Winner determined by a vote of active members. (http://www.sfwa.org/awards/nortonguide.htm)

Arthur C. Clarke Award: Given annually to a work of science fiction published in the United Kingdom, by a panel whose members are appointed by the British Science Fiction Association, the Science Fiction Foundation, and the Science Museum. (http://www.appomattox.demon.co.uk/acca/)

BBYA: An ALA Best Book for Young Adults, determined annually by the Young Adult Library Services Association (YALSA) Best Books for Young Adults Committee. (http://www.ala.org/ala/yalsa/yalsa.htm)

Boston Globe Award and Honors: Given annually by *Horn Book* and *The Boston Globe*, determined by an independent panel of three judges, new each year, selected by Horn Book editors in consultation with a *Boston Globe* representative. (http://www.hbook.com/awards/bghb/)

Bram Stoker Award: Given annually by the Horror Writer's Association. Includes a category "Work for Young Readers." (http://www.horror.org/stokers.htm)

CLABY: The Canadian Library Association's Young Adult Book Award, given annually to a Canadian author by the Young Adult Canadian Book Award Committee. (http://www.cla.ca/awards/yac.htm)

Carnegie Medal: The British Library Association children's book award given annually by the Chartered Institute of Library and Information Professionals' Youth Library Group. (http://www.carnegiegreenaway.org.uk/)

Edgar Allen Poe Award: Given annually for best mystery of the preceding year by the Mystery Writers of America's panel of judges, includes categories for adult works and young adult, and juvenile fiction. (http://www.mysterywriters.org/pages/awards/winners05.htm)

Eleanor Cameron Award: Given annually by the Golden Duck committee for excellence in Middle Grade science fiction. (http://www.goldenduck.org/winners.php)

Governor General's Literary Award: Given annually to a Canadian citizen by the Canada Council for the Arts. Includes a category for children's books. (www.canadacouncil.ca/prizes/ggla)

Hal Clement Award: Given annually by a Golden Duck committee for excellence in young adult science fiction. (http://www.goldenduck.org/winners.php)

Hugo Award: Given annually by the World Science Fiction Society, voted on by conference members. (http://worldcon.org/hugos.html)

Locus Award: Given annually by Locus Magazine in categories that include best science fiction novel, best fantasy novel, and best young adult novel, voted on by subscribers. (www.locusmag.com)

Muse Medallion: Given annually by the Cat Writers' Association. Winner determined by three independent association judges. (http://www.catwriters.org/)

Mythopoeic Awards: Given annually by the Mythopoeic Society with a category for adult literature and a category for children's literature which "honors books for younger readers (from 'Young Adults' to picture books for beginning readers), in the tradition of *The Hobbit* or *The Chronicles of Narnia*," voted on by the members. (http://www.mythsoc.org/awards.html)

National Book Award: Given annually to a work by an author from the United States, selected by a five-member, independent judging panel, includes a category for "Young People's Literature." http://www.nationalbook.org/nba.html)

Nebula Award: Given annually by the Science Fiction and Fantasy Writers of America, Inc., winner determined by a vote of active members. (http://www.sfwa.org/awards/)

Newbery Medal and Honor: Given annually to the author of the most distinguished contribution to American literature for children published in the U.S. during the preceding year. Authors must be citizens or residents of the U.S., selected by the ALSC Newbery Committee. (http://www.ala.org/ala/alsc/awardsscholarships/literaryawds/newberymedal/newberymedal.htm)

Philip K. Dick Award: Given annually by the Philadelpha Science Fiction Society for a work of distinguished science fiction published as an original paperback in the United States Judge by a five-member panel. (http://www.philipkdickaward.org/)

Printz Award and Honors: Given annually by the YALSA Michael L. Printz Committee. (http://www.ala.org/ala/yalsa/booklistsawards/printzaward/Printz,_Michael_L__Award.htm)

Prix Aurora Awards: The Canadian Science Fiction and Fantasy Association award, voted on by conference members. (http://www.sentex.net/~dmullin/aurora/)

Smarties Award: Given by the British Book Trust annually to a citizen or resident of the United Kingdom. Nominees selected by a panel of judges, and the winners are voted on by children. Now called the Nestle Children's Book Prize. (http://www.booktrusted.com/nestle/prize.html)

Sydney Taylor Award: Given annually by the Sydney Taylor Book Award Committee of the Association of Jewish Libraries, recognizing the best in Jewish children's literature. (http://www.jewishlibraries.org/ajlweb/awards/st_books.htm)

TBYA: Top Ten Best Books for Young Adults, selected by the YALSA Best Books Committee from the complete Best Books for Young Adults list.

Whitbread Award: Given annually in five categories, one of which is children's. Three judges select the winners in each category. A nine-judge panel determines the overall winner from the winners of the five original categories. (http://www.whitbread-bookawards.co.uk/)

World Fantasy Awards: Given annually by World Fantasy Award Committee, voted on by conference members. (http://www.worldfantasy.org/awards/)

Author Index

Title Index

Duology, trilogy, quartet, and series titles are underlined.
Individual book titles are in italics.

Subject Index

Abenaki, 49. *See also* Native Americans
adventures, 1, 19, 22, 25, 36-7, 40, 46, 49,
    53-54, 77, 82, 86-87, 90, 92, 100, 106,
    115, 128, 136, 146, 151, 156, 168,
    173-180, 203, 250
Africa, 62-63, 156
African-Americans, 120, 171
afterlife, 178, 216, 217, 220-221
airships, 114, 209
Aksum (Africa), 62-63
Alaska, 163
Alexander, Lloyd
   interview with, 20-21
   profile of, 20
   quote from, xii
aliens, 168, 171, 174, 177, 182, 185-190, 198,
    252, 253
alternate and parallel worlds. *See* worlds,
    alternate and parallel
alternate history. *See* history, alternate
Amazon (River), 93
Amazons, 46
American Revolution, 110
Anansi, 49
Anchorage, 209
anorexia, 208, 210
animals, talking, 104, 107, 134, 136, 146-157
apprentices, 2-3, 5, 16, 25, 31, 46, 68-69, 81,
    84, 90, 92, 97, 100, 170, 237
Arabia, 64
Arawn, Death-Lord, 22-23. *See also*
    characters, personifying evil.
Ariadne, 44
Arnold, Benedict, 110
Arthur, King, 38, 43, 50-63, 103, 168
Arthurian Fantasy, 50-63
artificial intelligence, 178, 208
assassination, 29, 130, 204
assassins, 6, 31, 78, 80, 152, 190
asthma, 108
Athens, 44
Australia, 98, 239
autism, 5, 192
Avalon, 51, 52, 55. *See also* Arthur, King

Baba Yaga, 68
bards, 22, 27, 30, 36, 159
Bartimaeus, 16
baseball, 103
bastards, 31, 45, 78, 79, 84
bats, 104, 155, 156
battles, 4, 19, 23, 27-28, 38, 46, 51-52, 54, 78,
    86, 105, 108, 136, 140, 142, 174, 222,
    226-227, 242
Beauty and the Beast, 73, 75. *See also*
    novelization of fairy tales
Berlin, 242
Beverly Hills, 137
Black Death, 185, 206
Black, Holly
   interview with, 118-119
   profile of, 117
blindness, 25, 64, 190, 211
boggarts, 216, 238
books, entering the world of, 39, 105, 135, 252
Britain. *See* England
brothers, 12, 16, 33, 44, 49, 52, 63, 88, 123,
    124, 128, 206, 220, 221, 235
bullies, 4, 31, 86, 107, 109, 208, 221, 225

Caesar, 232
California, 48, 192, 206, 216, 219, 241, 242,
    244, 245, 247
Camelot, 52, 53, 54, 55, 56, 63. *See also*
    Arthur, King
Canada, 95, 106, 120, 162, 188, 224
cancer, 5, 106, 161, 224
castles, 7, 12-13, 22-24, 27, 31-32, 54-55, 73,
    75, 81, 97, 101, 105, 130, 137, 143,
    150, 168, 228, 251
cats, 12, 82, 146, 151-152, 155-157, 169
centaurs, 46, 86, 101
changelings, 122-123, 135
characters
   biracial, 161
   from nursery rhymes, 135, 251
   inspired by Chinese legends, 144
   of Jamaican descent, 168
   Jewish, 159, 162, 164, 206
   Muslim, 75

Index of Award-Winning Titles

Boston Globe Award

Boston Globe Honor

Bram Stoker Award

**Bram Stoker Work for Young Readers
    Award**

**Canada's Governor's General Award for
    Children's Literature**

About the Author

Born in Manhattan and a long-time resident of New Jersey, Susan Fichtelberg has been a lover of fantasy fiction since first encountering Tolkien's *Lord of the Rings* at age twelve. In her nineteen years as a children's librarian, Susan has served as the president of the Children's Services Section of the New Jersey Library Association and has presented fantasy booktalks and programs for the New Jersey Library Association, the New Jersey Association of School Libraries, the New Jersey Education Association, The Witching Hour: A Harry Potter Symposium, and the World Science Fiction Convention. She is also a contributor to the *Continuum Encyclopedia of Young Adult Literature*.

Susan is an avid traveler and enjoys photography, writing fiction, and (of course!) reading. She currently resides in Woodbridge, New Jersey.